PhotoImpact 6 Wizardry

Stephanie Baker-Thomas

**Copyright © 2001
East of the Sun Publishing
PO Box 110063
Naples, Florida 34108-0102**

PhotoImpact 6 Wizardry

Copyright © 2001 by Stephanie Baker-Thomas

All rights reserved. Printed in the United States of America. No part of this book may be reproduced in any form or by any means, or stored in a database or retrieval system, without prior written permission of the author except in the case of brief quotations embodied in critical articles and reviews. Making copies of any part of this book for any purpose other than your own personal use is a violation of United States copyright laws. For information, write to East of the Sun Publishing, P.O. Box 110063, Naples, Florida, 34108-0102.

Library of Congress Catalog No.: 2001116946

ISBN: 0-9668559-2-2

This book is sold as is, without warranty of any kind, either express or implied, respecting the contents of this book, including but not limited to implied warranties for the book's quality, performance, merchantability, or fitness for any particular purpose. Neither East of the Sun Publishing nor its dealers or distributors shall be liable to the purchaser or any other person or entity with respect to any liability, loss or damage caused or alleged to have been caused directly or indirectly by this book.

Printed in the United States of America

First Edition

Published by
East of the Sun Publishing
P.O. Box 110063
Naples, Florida 34108-0102

Acknowledgments

This book is dedicated to my husband, Lowell, and to our children, Victoria and Geoffrey. You all are the best!

Thanks also to all my online "PI Headbanger" friends who hang out with me via email and on my bulletin board and mailing lists. I've made friends with hundreds of PhotoImpact enthusiasts over the past couple of years and look forward to making many more. It's impossible to name everyone who has helped and inspired me, but I send my most special thanks to Kelly, Tracy, Dawn, Margaret, Skippy, Irishmiss, Cedge, Shirley, Elenyte, Wynne, Johanna, Fr. Michael, Chatty Cathy, Jimshay, Carol UK and Ron. It is an honor to hang out with you all.

As always, thanks to Ulead Systems, Inc. for making such a fantastic product.

Finally, I'd like to thank Phil Cooke of PhilC Designs Ltd, http://www.philc.net, for his most gracious and invaluable assistance with the cover artwork. His beautiful Poser sorceress was a natural for enhancement in PhotoImpact, and helped this cover to come alive.

About the Author

Stephanie Baker-Thomas, PhD, is a licensed clinical psychologist and writer. For four years she has written weekly tutorials on her web site, "Stephanie's PhotoImpact Tutorials." She is also the author of "Fun With PhotoImpact 4.2" and "Skating Through PhotoImpact 5.0." Married and the mother of two children, she lives with her family in Naples, Florida.

Table of Contents

Foreword xiii

Section 1: The Big Picture 17

    Chapter 1: Introduction to the Work Space 19
        Menu Commands 20
        Standard Toolbar 20
        Attributes Toolbar 23
        Tool Panel 23
        Color Palette 24
        Status Bar 24
        The EasyPalette 26
        Quick Command Panel 26
        Brush Panel 31
        Keyboard Shortcuts 33

    Chapter 2: Working With Files 37
        New 37
        Open 42
        Visual Open 44
        Open From Web 46
        Restore 48
        Close 48
        Save 48
        Save As 48
        Save for Web 48
        Preview in Browser 49
        Batch Convert 50
        Place 51
        Scanner 51
        Digital Camera 55
        Import 56
        Export 57
        Capture 70
        Print Preview 71
        Print 72

Preferences	75
Recent Files	85
Exit	85

Chapter 3: Viewing and Displaying Files 87

Add a View	87
Actual View	87
Maximize at Actual View	88
Zoom	88
Fit in Window	88
Full Screen	88
Remove Menu Bar	88
Show Base Image	89
Show Marquee	89
Show Box Around Objects	89
Photo Properties	89
System Properties	90
Toolbars & Panels	90
Ruler	91
Guidelines & Grid	91

Active Learning Exercises for Section 1 93

Create a New File Preset	93
Opening a File	95
Visual Open	97
Send an Image	99
Send a Web Page	100
Create and Send a Web Album	101
Create and Send a Web Slide Show	108
Print Preview and Printing	112
Customizing Preferences	115
Controlling Image View and Customizing the Work Space	117

Section 2: Working With Selections 121

Chapter 4: Making and Cropping Selections 123

Standard Selection Tool	124
Lasso Selection Tool	126
Magic Wand Selection Tool	128
Bezier Curve Selection Tool	130
Moving and Transforming Selections	132

Table of Contents

    Cropping Selections 133
Chapter 5: The Selection Menu **137**
    Select Base Image 137
    Select Previous Selection 138
    None 138
    All 138
    Invert 138
    Border 138
    Expand/Shrink 139
    Similar 140
    Soften 141
    Convert to Object 141
    Preserve Base Image 141
    Import Selection 142
    Export Selection 142
    Copy Selection to Object Library 143
Active Learning Exercises for Section 2 .... **145**

Section 3: Working With Objects 167

Chapter 6: The Path Tools **169**
    Path Drawing Tools 169
    Outline Drawing Tool 175
    Line and Arrow Tool 180
    Path Edit Tool 184
    Send a Web Page 100
Chapter 7: The Text Tool **189**
    Editing Text With the Attributes Toolbar 189
    Editing Text With the Object Properties Box 196
    Editing Text With the Material Dialog Box 197
    Editing Text With the Object Menu 197
    Edting Text With the EasyPalette 197
    Adding or Removing a Text Object Shadow 197
    Splitting a Text Object Shadow 199
    A Few Words About Sharing Text Objects 199
Chapter 8: The Stamp Tool **201**
    Select a Stamp 202
    Add a Stamp 202

vii

Delete a Stamp 203
Import Picture Tube 203
Stamp Attributes Toolbar 204
Editing Stamps With the Brush Panel 206

Chapter 9: The Object Menu **209**
New 209
Duplicate 210
Merge 210
Merge All 210
Merge as Single Object 210
Delete 211
Select All Objects 211
Edit Path 211
Web Attributes 211
Wrap 212
Convert Object Type 216
Group 217
Ungroup 217
Align 218
Arrange 219
Shadow 220
Split Shadow 221
Import Object 221
Export Object 222
Copy to Object Library 223
Properties 224

Chapter 10: The Transform Tool **227**
Resize 227
Slant 227
Distort 228
Perspective 228
Rotate Using a Horizontal Line 228
Rotate Using a Vertical Line 228
Rotate Freely 229
Virtual Trackball 229
Rotate by Degree 231
Reset Center 231
Rotate & Flip 231

Chapter 11: The Object Eraser Tools 233
Converting a Selection to an Object for Erasing 233
Object Paint Eraser Tool 234
Object Magic Eraser Tool 236

Active Learning Exercises for Section 3 239

Section 4: Image Editing: Lights, Camera, Action! 281

Chapter 12: The Edit Menu 283
Undo Before 283
Redo to 284
Clear Undo/Redo History 284
Repeat 284
Cut 284
Copy 284
Paste 285
Clear 285
Clipboard 285
Crop 286
Duplicate 286
Fill 286
Fadeout 291
Expand Canvas 292
Rotate & Flip 293
Stitch 293
Trace 294
Mask Mode 296

Chapter 13: The Format Menu 297
Auto Process 297
Style 298
Brightness & Contrast 299
Color Balance 300
Hue & Saturation 302
Focus 303
Tone Map 304
Invert 306
Level 306
Histogram 307

Equalize 308
Calculation 308
Post-processing Wizard 309
Dimensions 310
Resolution 311
Frame & Shadow 312
Data Type 316
Color Table 317
Windows Wallpaper 318

Chapter 14: The Effect Menu 319

Blur & Sharpen 320
Noise 321
Camera Lens 321
2D 323
3D 323
Natural Painting 323
Special 323
Video 326
Warping 326
Custom Filter 326
Custom Effect 328
Paint on Edges 329
Animation Studio 330
Artist Texture 333
Creative Warp 336
Creative Lighting 337
Creative Painting 340
Creative Particle 342
CreativeTransform 344
Creative Type 345
Magic Kaleidoscope 347
Magic Light 349
Magic Gradient 351
Magic Turnpage 353
Digimarc 354
Other Effect Menu Commands 356

Chapter 15: The Retouch, Clone and Paint Tools 359

Constants in the Attributes Toolbar 360
Retouch Tools 361

Paint Tools 363
Clone Tools 365
Brush Panel 367
Painting With Textures 369
Active Learning Exercises for Section 4 .... **371**

Section 5: Adding Sparkle and Color 421

Chapter 16: The Fill Tools and Palette Ramp Editor 423
Bucket/Solid Fill Tool 423
Gradient Fill Tools 427
Palette Ramp Editor 429

Chapter 17: The Material Dialog Box 433
Common Elements in the Material Dialog Box 433
Color/Texture Tab 434
Bevel Tab 437
Border/Depth Tab 438
Bump Tab 439
Reflection Tab 440
Transparency Tab 441
Shadow Tab 441
Light Tab 443
Shading Tab 444

Chapter 18: The EasyPalette 447
Accessing the EasyPalette 447
Resizing and Moving the EasyPalette 447
Galleries 449
Libraries 458
Layer Manager 465

Active Learning Exercises for Section 5 .... **469**

Section 6: Web Magic 489

Chapter 19: The Web Menu 491
Component Designer 491
Background Designer 501
Button Designer (Any Shape) 503

xi

Button Designer (Rectangular)	505
Add HTML Text Object	507
Grid & Partition	510
Shift Image	511
Create Seamless Tile	512
HTML Properties	513
Image Map	513
Rollover	514
Slicer	517
Helper Program	519
Trim Object	520
Image Optimizer	520

Chapter 20: The Image Optimizer 521
Image Optimizer Similarities 522
Similarity #1: Previewing Effects of Settings 522
Similarity #2: Previewing Effects of Batch Testing 525
Similarity #3: Saving and Deleting Presets 525
Similarity #4: Creating Transparency 526
The JPG Image Optimizer 530
The GIF Image Optimizer 532
The PNG Image Optimizer 535

Active Learning Exercises for Section 6 539

Glossary 575

Index 579

Foreword

Why I Wrote This Book

I have been writing PhotoImpact tutorials for four years on my web site, Stephanie's PhotoImpact Tutorials. In 1999, I wrote and published the first book written in English about Ulead's PhotoImpact. "Fun With PhotoImpact 4.2" was my response to many requests that I write such a book.

My email pointed clearly to the conclusion that web page builders and graphics artists were hungry for more information about this awesome and powerful image editing program. Within a month of my first book's release, PhotoImpact 5.0 debuted. There were so many significant improvements, changes and additions that I wrote "Skating Through PhotoImpact 5.0," which was published in July, 2000.

"PhotoImpact 6 Wizardry" is about the best version of PhotoImpact ever. It will teach you about new and enhanced web features of the program, including the ability to build HTML web pages right in the work space. This book will help you to find and use the tools and commands that you need to create a particular image effect, to make great looking web graphics and to build unique web pages, albums and slide shows.

Congruent with my professional training as a clinical psychologist and my tutorials writing experience, this book contains many exercises to help you master PhotoImpact 6. These "Active Learning Exercises" are the heart of the book. They can help turn you into a PhotoImpact 6 wizard.

I hope that you enjoy using this book!

Stephanie Baker-Thomas
March, 2001

Who Should Read This Book

"PhotoImpact 6 Wizardry" is aimed at beginning to intermediate level users of PhotoImpact 6. I've tried to write a book that will help you to find easily and use efficiently all of PhotoImpact's terrific, time-saving features. This book wasn't designed to offer an exhaustive "Bible" approach to using this extraordinary program. Rather, it is intended to be a practical, hands-on guide to PhotoImpact's menu commands, toolbars and incredible built-in filters, plug-ins and other special effects. Many screen shots were included to help you to access the customizability built into the program via dialog boxes. In brief, this book will help you to find what you need to do the vital image editing tasks you want to perform.

How This Book is Organized

The chapters in "PhotoImpact 6 Wizardry" are grouped together in six different sections, based on the types of imaging tasks being discussed.

> Section 1: The Big Picture
> Section 2: Working With Selections
> Section 3: Working With Objects
> Section 4: Image Editing: Lights, Camera, Action
> Section 5: Adding Sparkle and Color
> Section 6: Web Magic

Each section starts with an overview page outlining its chapters and their contents, followed by a series of exercises to reinforce learning concepts within the section. At the end of the book is a Glossary and a comprehensive Index.

How to Get the Most from This Book

At the end of each section of the book are a series of mini-tutorials called "Active Learning Exercises." These exercises show how (and why) to use menu commands and tools, often in combination, to perform common imaging tasks. They will also introduce you to some of PhotoImpact's most dazzling features.

Of course, you don't have to do the Active Learning Exercises. However, they were specially designed to make learning how to use the program easier and more fun by leading you, step-by-step, through the creation of specific image effects. Care was taken to create exercises which reinforce the information presented in each section. For example, Section 1 contains exercises that show you, in detail, how to build a web album and a web slide show.

To benefit optimally from the exercises at the end of the sections, it's necessary to use the same images that I used, or your results will not look like mine do in the book. You can get all of the images, .UFO objects, tone maps and other files needed to complete the exercises from http://www.eastofsun.com/wizard/index.htm. These files are in

ZIP file format to save download time. You will need to unzip these files to your hard drive. I'd suggest that you create a folder on your hard drive for the images and objects, naming the folder "pi6book_exercises" or something similar. Within this folder, make three subfolders and name them "images," "album" and "slideshow" to organize the images you will use for the exercises in this book.

Finally, at the end of the exercises I don't tell you to "Close out the image." I am confident that you'll know that at the end of an exercise you should close out the image, or save it to your hard drive if you want to keep it. However, some exercises do ask you to keep an image open for the next exercise.

Important Patch Information

Just before this book went to the printer, Ulead issued a PhotoImpact 6 patch. The 11 MB patch can be downloaded from Ulead's web site, at http://www.ulead.com/tech/pi_ftp.htm.

This patch resolves a number of bugs noted during the first few months of the program's release. Primary among them were duplicate font names for various languages in the Font list, as well as other problems which are detailed on Ulead's patch download page. An undocumented benefit of the patch is the addition of 6 great new Merge methods, which are accessible through the Merge dropdown list in the Attributes toolbar, Object Properties dialog box and Fill dialog box.

Unfortunately, installation of the patch will delete the "jewel" Preset thumbnails from the Button Designer, Any Shape dialog box. However, if you wish to get them back, you can download UAnyBtn.pst from Ulead's site, or from my web site at http://www.eastofsun.com/wizard/jewelbtn.zip.

PhotoImpact 6 Wizardry

Section 1: The Big Picture

When you find yourself exploring a new town, not knowing where major streets and landmarks are can make it difficult to find what you are looking for. Finding your way around PhotoImpact 6 can be challenging, too, if you have never "visited" PhotoImpact before. This is a large and powerful program with many tools and menu commands. Without a "map" to guide you, it could take quite a while to find what you need on your own. This is particularly likely to be true if you are switching over from another image editor. The first section of this book shows you how to find what you need to begin exploring and harnessing the wizardry of PhotoImpact 6.

In the **Introduction to the Work Space**, you will see how menus, toolbars and panels are laid out elegantly and intuitively to maximize ease of use, and how innovative additions to the interface make it easier than ever to customize the work space to suit your own personal work style. There are nearly always at least two (and often three or four) ways to access commands and tools in PhotoImpact, and this section discusses them in detail. If you are someone who prefers keyboard shortcuts, a complete listing of shortcuts is included. How to display or hide toolbars and images, magnification of images, and using the ruler, guidelines and grids round out this section.

Working With Files outlines what you need to know about opening, acquiring, sharing, saving and printing your files. Whether you are opening a file, creating a new one, or acquiring a file from your scanner or digital camera, you should know how to do so in a way that yields the optimal results for your purpose. For example, the number of colors and resolution of the image must be correct in order to yield the best image for web or print, and there are important differences between opening or saving a new HTML web page file versus opening or saving an image file.

Once you know how, it is easy to share web albums and slide shows with your friends online, to email images, and to upload images and web pages directly to your web site. You will also learn how to set important preferences for PhotoImpact in general, for customizing toolbars and panels, and how to utilize color management technology to increase congruence between what you see on your monitor and printed output.

Viewing and Displaying Files shows how to control the way in which images and objects are displayed in PhotoImpact, as well as the visibility and accessibility of toolbars, panels and other image editing helpers.

Active Learning Exercises Create a New file preset; Opening a File; Visual Open; Send an Image; Send a Web Page; Create and Send a Web Album; Create and Send a Web Slide Show; Print Preview and Printing; Customizing Preferences; Customizing Preferences; Controlling Image Viewing and Customizing the Work Space.

Chapter 1: Introduction to the Work Space

The information in this book will be easier to learn if you invest some time going over the layout of the PhotoImpact work space. Once you have a good idea where everything is, the sections on specific menu commands, toolbars and their associated options will be easier to understand and put to use.

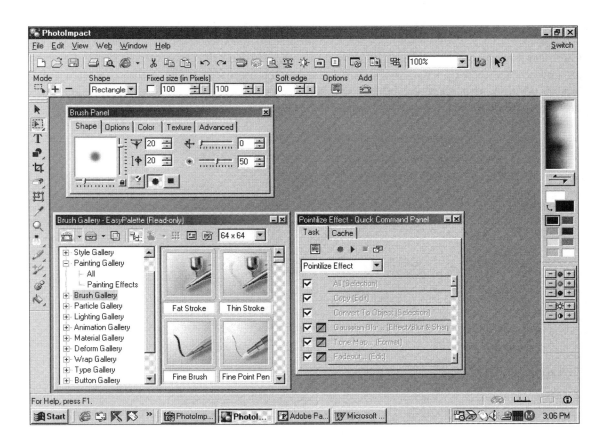

One thing you will notice right away is that PhotoImpact makes it easy to find and use its many image editing tools and commands. If you are unsure about a tool icon, hold your cursor over it without clicking. In a moment a little popup box will tell you the name of the tool and its keyboard shortcut, if one is available.

Many tools and commands have secondary flyout menus, or dropdown menus offering a range of choices. Similarly, many of the dialog boxes have an Options button that you can click to tweak effects. There is almost always more than one way to perform a specific task. For example, to Undo an edit, choose Edit, Undo Before, *or* click the Undo button, *or* right click and Undo.

Menu Commands

Click on a menu item to access its dropdown menu, then drag the cursor down to select an option. Some dropdown menus offer secondary menus that fly out to the right (or left, depending the space available). Just slide the mouse across and down to select the desired option.

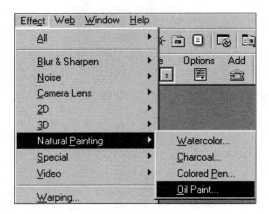

Standard Toolbar

1. **New** Creates a new file. You may also choose File, New from the menu or hit Ctrl+N.

2. **Open** Opens a previously created and saved image file in the work space. You may also choose File, Open from the menu or hit Ctrl+O.

Chapter 1: Introduction to the Work Space

3. **Save** Saves the active image. When selected for a new image, the Save As box opens. When selected for a previously saved image presently open in the work space, the image is automatically saved to its existing folder under its existing name and file format. You may also choose Save or Save As from the File menu, or hit Ctrl+S.

4. **Print** Opens the Print box (with various options) so that the image can be printed. You may also choose File, Print from the menu or hit Ctrl+P.

5. **Print Preview** Opens a separate Print Preview screen (with various options) so that you can view how the image will look on a printed page. You may also choose File, Print Preview from the menu.

6. **Browser Preview** Previews the active image in Internet Explorer or Netscape.

7. **Cut** Cuts an active selection or object and places it into the Clipboard. You may also choose Edit, Cut from the menu, or hit Ctrl+X.

8. **Copy** Copies an active selection or object and places it into the Clipboard. You may also choose Edit, Copy from the menu, or hit Ctrl+C.

9. **Paste** Inserts Clipboard contents as an object into the active image. You may also choose Edit, Paste to access a variety of pasting options from the menu, or hit Ctrl+V.

10. **Undo** Undo the last image edit. You may also choose Edit, Undo Before from the menu, click the Undo button or hit Ctrl+Z.

11. **Redo** Redo the last image edit. You may also choose Edit, Redo To from the menu, click the Redo button or hit Ctrl+Y.

12. **Scanner** Click to begin acquiring an image from a scanner.

13. **Digital Camera** Click to download images from a digital camera.

14. **Post-processing Wizard** Accesses the Post-processing Wizard, a series of dialog boxes that permit you to quickly fix problems commonly found in scanned images.

15. **Color Balance** Opens the Color Balance box, which allows you to adjust the color

of an image, selection or object.

16. **Brightness & Contrast** Opens the Brightness & Contrast box, from which you may adjust image, selection or object brightness and contrast.

17. **EasyPalette** Opens the EasyPalette. By default, the EasyPalette opens with the Gallery last used. Click on the Galleries button to select a different Gallery.

18. **Frame & Shadow** Instantly accesses the Frame & Shadow box, which allows you to add a frame and shadow to an image.

19. **Start/Stop Capture** Toggles on or off the Screen Capture utility, which allows you take a screen shot of whatever is currently on your monitor.

20. **Tile EasyPalette with an image** When selected, a dropdown menu of tiling methods appears. Choose one to tile the EasyPalette with the active image.

21. **Layout** When selected, choose from a dropdown list of Basic, Intermediate or Advanced toolbars and panels, or select toolbars and panels individually. If the Attributes toolbar disappears, click the Layout button and select Intermediate to make it visible. New to PhotoImpact 6, choose to display tool panels for selected tools, including the Selection, Path, Eraser, Retouch, Paint, Clone and Fill tools. These are the tool panels which ordinarily slide out to the right of the main toolbar. These tool panels can be docked or float anywhere in the work space.

22. **Zoom** Adjust the zoom level of the active image. You may view images at 100% (actual size), zoom out in increments up to $1/16^{th}$ actual size, or zoom in up to 16X actual size. New to PhotoImpact 6 are Fit In Window and Last Ratio. You may also choose the Zoom Tool from the Tool Panel, or View, Zoom, Zoom In/Zoom Out from the menu to adjust the magnification of an image.

23. **Help** Opens the Help Topics: Ulead PhotoImpact Help box. Get help from the Contents, Index and Find tabs. Help can also be accessed from Help in the menu bar, or by pressing F1. In addition, most dialog boxes also offer a Help button for context-specific Help. First click the Help button, then click on the toolbar or command about which you need more information.

Attributes Toolbar

The Attributes toolbar offers the quickest and easiest way to edit the attributes of a tool. Of course, the contents of the Attributes toolbar will vary by the image editing tool being used. For example, the Attributes toolbar shown below is for the Text tool.

If you look at the screen shot below, however, you will see that the Attributes toolbar for the Paintbrush tool is quite different.

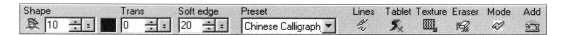

A constant in the Attributes toolbar is the Add button, which allows you to save custom attributes for a selected tool. For example, if you have a favorite brush size, color, transparency and texture for painting flower petals, you can save those attributes without having to recreate them every time you want to paint a flower petal. Simply click the Add button. Doing so opens the Add to EasyPalette dialog box. Name the preset and save it to My Gallery. Once a preset has been saved in this way, it can be used again easily by dragging and dropping (or double clicking) on its thumbnail.

Tool Panel

The Tool panel runs vertically along the left side of the work space. From top to bottom, it contains the Pick, Selection, Text, Path, Crop, Object Paint Eraser, Transform, Eyedropper, Zoom, Retouch, Paint, Clone, Stamp (replaces Object Clone from prior versions) and Bucket Fill tools. All except the Pick, Crop, Eyedropper and Stamp tools have associated tool trays that slide out to the right.

To access the tools in the toolbar, press and hold down on the mouse button until the tool tray slides out, or click on the tiny blue triangle in the button's lower right corner. Choose a tool by clicking on it. The tool tray slides back in and an icon representing the selected tool appears in the tool panel. Remember that you can also select a tool from the toolbar by clicking on the Layout button in the Menu Bar.

Color Palette

The Color Palette consists of three parts:

Current Palette Shows all available colors in the active image's palette. Click on a color to make it the foreground color, or right click to make it the background color. When working with a True Color image, click on the double-headed arrow under the "rainbow" to toggle color mode from True Color to a reduced-color palette.

Quick Palette Shows a palette of currently assigned brush colors. The color square with the outline around it is the current foreground color. Position the cursor briefly (do not click) over any color square to display its Red, Green and Blue values, Hex code, and Hue, Saturation and Brightness values in the Status Bar. To change brush color, click on a different color square. This makes it easy to paint with a preset palette of colors. Right click in a color square to change the color.

Quick Color Controls Allow you to edit quickly the level of Red, Green or Blue, or to edit lightness/darkness and contrast. Quick Color Controls are useful for minor image editing. For more sophisticated editing, you will likely want to use the Format menu commands.

Status Bar

The status bar runs along the lower edge of the work space. The contents of the status bar vary according to where the cursor is placed in the work space. For example, if you want to make a rectangular selection from the extreme top left of an image, position the cursor so that the X,Y coordinates in the status bar display 0, 0. That way you will be sure you are starting in the upper left corner. To create a selection exactly 200 X 200 pixels, drag the mouse until the status bar shows the desired coordinates (200, 200).

Information about image color is also available in the status bar. Click on a color with the Eyedropper to display in the status bar its Red, Green and Blue values, Hex code and Hue, Saturation and Brightness values.

Chapter 1: Introduction to the Work Space

On the far right of the status bar are four icons for Mask Mode, Units, Data Type and Display Photo/System Property.

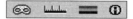

Mask Click on the Mask icon to enter Mask mode. You can also enter Mask mode by choosing Edit, Mask Mode. The Mask command is discussed in detail in the section on image editing.

Units Click on the Units icon to choose from pixels, inches or centimeters as the unit of measure. The Units icon also provides a quick way to turn on or off the Ruler, Guidelines and Grid, and their associated options. These commands can also be accessed from the View menu.

Data Type Click on the Data Type icon to convert data type. It is a good idea to leave "Create a New Image" selected, as this results in a new image of the selected data type opening in the work space. This reduces the likelihood of unwanted permanent edits to the original image. The data type for the active image will be grayed out in the list.

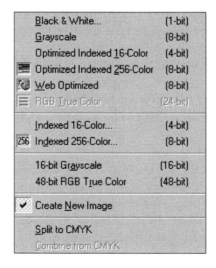

You can also split a True Color image to CMYK (cyan, magenta, yellow, black). Split to CMYK generates four grayscale images representing each of the color channels. Combine to CMYK combines these four images into a True Color image. Split to CMYK is a

25

process you are unlikely to use very much unless you take your work to a professional printer. However, some unexpectedly lovely effects can be achieved by splitting to CMYK and combining the images in different ways.

Display Photo/System Property Provides a handy way to determine the active image's data type, height and width, name, file format and file size. If no image is open in the work space, clicking on this icon opens a System Properties box with four tabs containing information about your computer system's Memory, Disk, Display and Plug-ins. The View menu also permits access to Photo Properties and System Properties information.

The EasyPalette

The EasyPalette is the brightest star in PhotoImpact's constellation of fabulous features. It allows you to find and apply brilliant Gallery effects quickly and easily from thumbnails. These thumbnails, called "Quick Samples," show how Gallery effects will look when applied to an image, selection or object. You may apply a Gallery effect by double clicking on its thumbnail, or by dragging and dropping the thumbnail right onto the image. For many Gallery presets, you can right click on a thumbnail and choose from a dropdown list of options that permit you to tweak these effects. Although many of the Gallery effects accessed from the EasyPalette can also be accessed via the Format and Web menus and submenus, the EasyPalette is a faster and more intuitive way to work.

In addition to its preset Galleries, the EasyPalette houses Libraries which contain Path and Image objects which ship with the program. You may also add your own objects to My Library or a custom Library. To use an object from a Library, just drag from its thumbnail into an empty area in the work space, where it will open in its own window, or drag onto a pre-existing image.

The EasyPalette can take up a lot of room. Click on the Minimize icon on the EasyPalette's blue title bar to minimize it and make room in the work space. It will roll itself up so that only the blue title bar shows. Click on the Maximize icon to open it fully again. You can also drag on its sides to resize it. Because it is a central feature of PhotoImpact, the chapter on the EasyPalette discusses its features in detail.

Quick Command Panel

The Quick Command Panel is a handy way to automate frequently performed tasks. These tasks are similar to word processing macros, in that a sequence of commands has been recorded and saved to the Quick Command Panel. The Task tab, shown below, offers 10 preset tasks. Simply select a task and click Play to apply.

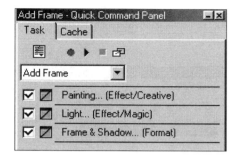

You may deselect steps in any task by unchecking them. Similarly, you may custom edit the steps in the task, which are selected by default, by clearing the diagonal line in the task's box. ▨ When the task is played, it will stop at the deselected step in the task so that you can enter your own values for that particular dialog box.

The preset tasks range from the practical to the fantastic. With one click, the image below was matted and framed, hung on a wood paneled wall and spotlighted.

27

PhotoImpact 6 Wizardry

Icons running along the top of the Task tab permit you to create and edit tasks.

Task Menu

Click on the Task Menu icon to view available options.

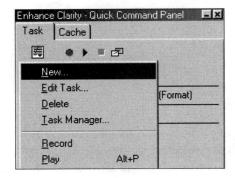

New Save time and mouse clicks by automating frequently performed sequences of commands. One such task might be copying a selection, pasting it as a new image and merging the pasted object with the base image.

To create a new task that does all of this automatically, open an image in the work space. Click the Task Menu icon and select New. Doing so opens the New Task box.

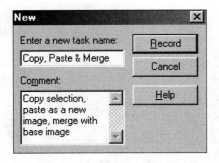

Enter a name for the new task, in this case, "Copy, Paste & Merge," and add a brief description of what the task does in the Comment box. Click the Record icon to begin recording the task. From now until you click the Stop icon, each command or tool that

28

you select will be included in the recorded task. Copy the image in the work space, choose Edit, Paste, As A New Image, then right click and Merge the pasted object with its base image. Click the Stop button to stop recording.

Close out the image you just pasted and merged, leaving only the original open in the work space. To test the task you recorded, select the "Copy, Paste & Merge" task from the "Show All Existing Tasks" dropdown list. Click the Play button and instantly a new copy of the image opens in its own window, merged with the base image.

The benefits of being able to record frequently performed tasks will become apparent readily as you gain experience with PhotoImpact. For example, to save a web button object as an object independent of the base image, you might record a task that selects Web, Image Optimizer, chooses the "Save selected objects" only option, then saves the button as a 256 color optimized GIF. If you make many web graphics sets, this one task alone could save you literally hours of mouse clicks.

Edit Task Opens the Edit Task box from which you may edit tasks from the Task tab by adding or removing options from PhotoImpact's predetermined Menu commands. For example, select the Make Button preset task and choose Edit Task to add a save with the Image Optimizer to the task. When the Edit Task box opens, the two steps of the task, Any Shape (Button Designer) and Shadow (Object) appear in the right window of the dialog box. To add to the Task, choose Web from the Menu dropdown list and select Image Optimizer. Click Add to add Image Optimizer to the task. Click OK to finish editing the task.

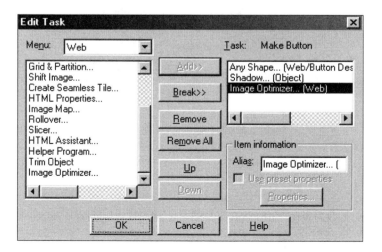

Now when you play the Make Button task, it will include opening the Image Optimizer so you can save the button to the desired web image file format. The Quick Command Panel's Make Button task will show that Image Optimizer has been added to the task.

You can also delete a part of task. Select it in the right window of the Edit Task box and click Remove. Replace a deleted command by selecting another predetermined command from the left window and clicking Add. Rearrange the command sequence by clicking the Up and Down buttons until you are satisfied with it, then click OK.

Delete Select a task in the Quick Command Panel, then click on the Task Menu icon. Choose Delete to remove the selected task. A dialog box opens advising that "This command cannot be undone. Are you sure you want to continue?" If you are sure you want to delete the task, choose Yes.

Task Manager The Task Manager provides another way to create new tasks, or to edit, delete, rename, import or export preset tasks.

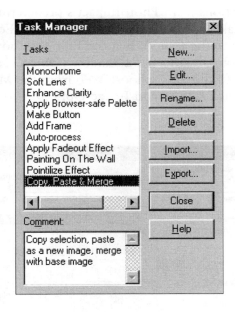

For example, if you devise a helpful task, you might want to share it with others by exporting it. From the Task Manager, select the desired task and click the Export button. The Save As dialog box opens, and the task will be saved with the .TSK file extension. The recipient of the task can then Import it into their own Quick Command

Panel by choosing Import.

Cache Tab

The Quick Command Panel's Cache tab provides shortcuts to your most recently used and frequently performed tasks. Tasks not used recently are rotated out, and newer ones replace them. Cache tab tasks are not customizable.

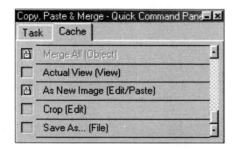

Click on any command in the cache to perform a task or open its related dialog box. Lock a task to keep it in the cache permanently. Click on a lock to unlock the task.

Brush Panel

The Brush Panel offers the highest level of control over the attributes of the Retouch, Paint and Clone tools. The number of tabs available for each tool, and their associated options, will vary by the tool selected.

Paint Tools

The Brush Panel for the Paint tools has five tabs. From the Color tab, choose to paint with one or multiple colors. Edit the selected color's Delta Hue, Delta Saturation and Delta Brightness from the Color tab. From the Shape tab, edit brush size and shape, brush angle and soft edge, as well as Apply method, transparency and line style. Edit brush spacing or fade in and fadeout from the Advanced tab, or drawing tablet users can edit pressure options (size and transparency). From the Textures tab, select one of the Texture options to paint with texture, or use your own texture. The Particle Pen and Drop Water Paint tools have only four tabs each.

The Brush Panel for the Paintbrush tool is shown below.

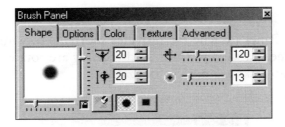

Clone Tools

The Brush Panel for each of the Clone tools has four tabs: Shape, Options, Texture and Advanced. The Brush Panel for the Clone-Paintbrush, Options tab, is shown below.

Note that the Options tab offers choices regarding Apply method, line style, transparency and the point from which cloning begins in the source image.

Retouch Tools

The Brush Panel for the Retouch tools offers three tabs: Shape, Options and Advanced. The Brush Panel for the Smudge Retouch tool, Options tab, is shown below.

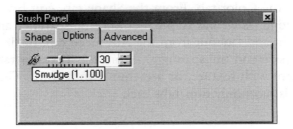

Chapter 1: Introduction to the Work Space

For some Retouch, Paint and Clone tools, options will be grayed out because they are inapplicable for a particular tool. For example, although the Color tab appears for the Drop Water Paint tool, no color choices are available for water. From the Options tab, the Apply method offers the Always Merge method only. However, the type of line (freehand, straight, connected), as well as transparency, may still be edited from the Options tab.

Any time you create a custom brush effect that you might want to use again, simply save it to the EasyPalette's My Gallery. Custom edit the brush attributes from the Brush Panel, then click on the Attributes toolbar's Add button to open the Add to EasyPalette dialog box.

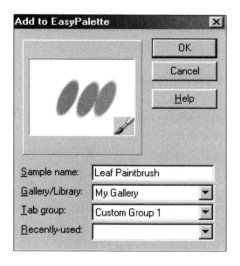

Give the custom brush a name in the Sample name box and save it to My Gallery and a Tab group. From now on, whenever you want to use this custom brush, just double click on its thumbnail in the EasyPalette's My Gallery. Immediately, the selected custom Retouch, Paint or Clone tool, with the appropriate color, brush size and shape, angle, transparency, etc. will be selected.

Keyboard Shortcuts

Throughout this book, keyboard shortcuts appear as alternatives to menu and toolbar commands. The following is a complete list of PhotoImpact 6 keyboard shortcuts.

File Menu

Ctrl + N	Creates a new image file
Ctrl + O	Opens a folder where you last saved an image file
Ctrl + Shift + O	Opens the Visual Open dialog box
Ctrl + W	Closes the current image file. If you have not saved the file, you are prompted to do so
Ctrl + S	Saves the current image file
Ctrl + P	Prints the current image file
F11	Start capturing
F6	Displays the Preferences dialog box
Ctrl + Q	Quits PhotoImpact. If you have any image files open that have not been saved, you are prompted to do so

Edit Menu

Ctrl + Z	Undoes the last menu command
Ctrl + Y	Redoes the last menu command
Ctrl + T	Repeats the last menu command
Ctrl + X	Cuts the current selection
Ctrl + C	Copies the current selection to the clipboard
Ctrl + V	Pastes image data from the clipboard as an object
Del	Deletes the current selection and fills the space with the specified background color. Deletes the active object. Also deletes a path or a control point when in Path Edit Tool.
Ctrl + R	Crops the image to the current selection
Ctrl + D	Duplicates the base image and any objects, creating a new image file
Ctrl + F	Opens the Fill dialog box, where you can select to fill the selection with a solid color, gradient or texture
Ctrl + H	Opens the Fadeout dialog box
Ctrl + K	Enables/Disables Mask mode by placing a tinted mask over your image except where a selection exists

View Menu

Ctrl + 1	Creates another copy of the image file
Ctrl + 0 (#)	Displays the image at its actual size

Ctrl + M	Maximizes the window and displays the image at 1:1 ratio
+	Zooms in progressively on the image
-	Zooms out progressively on the image
Ctrl+Shift+0	Resizes the current image to the largest magnification that will completely fit in a window
Ctrl + U	Hides all toolbars and panels and displays the image at full screen
Alt + Enter	Displays the Photo Properties dialog box
Ctrl + (#)	Magnifies or reduces the image view in different sizes. The image will be scaled to fit in the window at all times
Ctrl+Shift+G	Displays or hides Guidelines
Ctrl+Shift+S	Snaps to Guidelines
Ctrl+Shift+R	Displays or hides Grid lines
Ctrl+Shift+N	Snaps to Grid lines

Format Menu

F9	Automatically adjusts the brightness of the image
Ctrl + B	Opens the Brightness & Contrast dialog box
Ctrl + L	Opens the Color Balance dialog box
F7	Opens the Focus dialog box
F8	Opens the Tone Map dialog box
Ctrl + G	Opens the Dimensions dialog box, where you can adjust the size of the image

Selection Menu

Space	Selects the Base Image
Ctrl+A	Selects the entire contents of the image
Ctrl+Shift+A	Selects all objects in an image
F5	Preserve Base Image

Object Menu

Q	Show/Hide marquee
Ctrl+Shift+Enter	Opens the Object Properties dialog box when there is an active object

Window Menu

Shift + F5	Arranges all open windows diagonally in the workspace from left to right and top to bottom
Shift + F4	Evenly distributes all open windows vertically in the workspace

Help Menu

F1	Starts the Ulead PhotoImpact online help
Shift + F1	Activates the Context Sensitive Help. Just click an item in question

Miscellaneous

G	Show Global Viewer (if available)
Z	Switch to the Zoom Tool
'	Display Tools submenu
F3	Find next – EasyPalette
Alt + P	Play – Quick Command Panel
Tab	Show/Hide Toolbars and Panels
E	Toggles between Painting and Erase mode when in Painting Tool
Ctrl + F1	Show/Hide EasyPalette
Ctrl + F2	Show/Hide Quick Command Panel
Ctrl + F3	Show/Hide Brush Panel
C	Switch to the Eyedropper Tool
X	Switch Foreground and Background color
W	Switch to the Pick Tool
Arrow keys	Moves the object up/down one pixel or to the left/right. This works on all tools except for Painting/Retouch/Clone/Fill tool
Ctrl+Shift+Del	Deletes the selected thumbnail from the EasyPalette
Page Up/Down	Scroll image vertically
Home/End	Scroll image horizontally

Chapter 2: Working With Files

One of the most exciting new features of PhotoImpact 6 is that you may now create web images and entire web pages right in PhotoImpact. You can then upload them directly to your web site from the work space via the File menu commands. The addition of a simple HTML editor to PhotoImpact signals this powerful image editing program's emergence as the leader in a new age of web imaging tools and raises the bar for competition.

Another major and welcome addition to PhotoImpact 6 is the ability to open and edit file formats associated with other popular image editing programs. You may now open and edit .PSD and .PSP image files.

If you are a PhotoImpact veteran, familiar File menu commands will help you to open new images, previously saved images, and images acquired from a scanner or digital camera. In addition, the File menu provides the means to Save, Place and Print images. You can also use these commands to Send images as email attachments. A terrific new feature is the ability to export web albums (collections of thumbnails linked to their source images) and HTML slide shows, right from the work space.

A variety of commands accessed from the File menu's Preferences allow you to specify general program preferences and customize the appearance of the Standard Toolbar. Users of Windows 98, NT 5.0 and Windows 2000 may take advantage of Color Management technology available from the File menu commands.

New (Ctrl+N)

Choosing the right options for a new image will save you time and trouble down the road. Take care to select the right resolution, data type and canvas color for your purpose when creating a new file. For example, if you want to print out a photo of your new baby to send to your friends, you will want to choose a higher resolution than you would choose for a navigation button on your web page. Similarly, speedy download is important for web images, which means using fewer colors than you would choose to print out a photo on glossy photo paper.

Choose File, New, click on the New button, or hit Ctrl+N to access the New dialog box. As you can see in the dialog box at the top of the next page, a number of new file options are available in PhotoImpact 6.

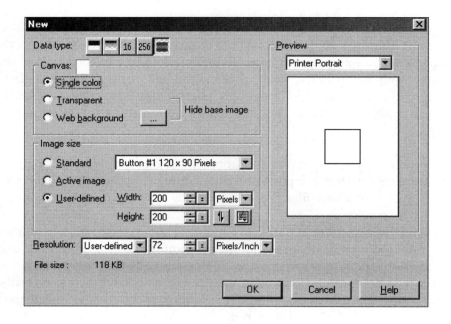

Data Type

Select a data type: Black & White, Grayscale, 16 Color, 256 Color or True Color (looks like a rainbow). Be aware that some of PhotoImpact's most spectacular effects, as well as 3D Text and Path objects, can only be created in True Color images.

Canvas

By default, the new file's canvas color is Single Color, white. Click in the canvas color box to select a different color.

Single Color The default for new images is a single color background.

Transparent This much-requested option is new to PhotoImpact 6. If selected, a gray checkerboard background, as specified in Preferences, will be seen in the base image.

Web Background Select this option and click the Browse button to open the

HTML Properties dialog box, from which you may select a preset background or one that you create yourself. The HTML Properties box has four tabs, and opens at the Background tab.

General tab Fill in the blanks to set HTML attributes for the web page. These include a web page title, the name of the author, key words describing the content of your web page (indexed by search engines), the file to which images associated with the web page will be saved (by default, images, or specify a different folder) and the encoding character set you wish to use.

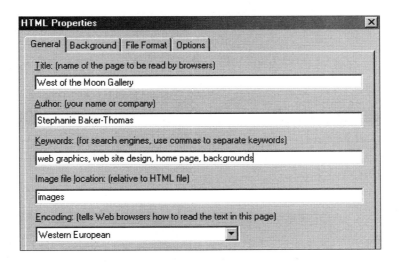

Background tab Select a background property for the page: None (browser default), a color, a texture (choose from a Preset or Designer to create a tile in the Background Designer), or one of your own image files. You may also choose to offset a tiling background by a specific number of pixels.

Be sure to check out the preset backgrounds, which harmonize nicely with many of the buttons, banners and other web graphics in the Component Designer and the Template Library. These web images are a good starting point for newbie web page builders.

File Format tab Select a web image file format for the background, simple text and shape images and object images. By default, simple text and shape images are saved as 256 Indexed Color GIF's and object images are saved as 75% Progressive JPG's. You can override these settings, if you wish, when you save the web page.

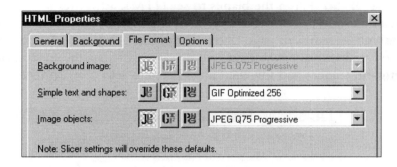

Options tab By default, all options are selected: Generate HTML background (creates HTML background tag for the web page), Slice as separate images (for faster download), General relative URL for local references and Copy referenced images to subfolder (by default images are saved to the images folder). Deselect options as desired.

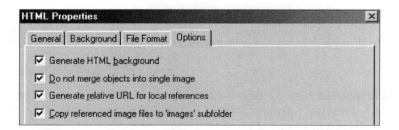

Image Size

There are three different sections from which you may choose an image size. New to PhotoImpact 6 is the ability to create User-defined presets for new files. For example, if you often start with a 300 X 300 pixel True Color image with a black canvas, you may now create a custom preset with these attributes and access it from the Image Size section of the New dialog box. Even better, if you use this preset once, the next time you choose File, New, the preset will "stick," and you will not have to reset its attributes.

Standard Choose from preset standard web image sizes ranging from a 750 X 550 pixel web page, to a standard 468 X 60 pixel banner, to an 88 X 31 pixel "micro button." These new standard sizes are another welcome time saver for web graphics designers. You may also choose from a range of convenient image and paper, card, photo and envelope sizes.

Active Image Creates a new image the same size as the current active image.

User-defined Custom define width and height in pixels, inches or centimeters. Click the toggle switch to reverse the width and height attributes easily. To create your own custom preset for new images, first enter width and height attributes, select a canvas color and resolution, then click on the button with the red check mark. Choose Add User-defined Size to open the associated dialog box.

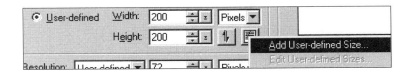

Enter a descriptive name (e.g., "200 X 200 White") for the custom preset and click OK. From now on, the preset will appear in the User-defined section.

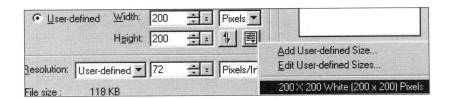

Note that once a User-defined preset has been added, it can be edited or deleted.

Resolution Select a resolution for the new image: Display, Inches or User Defined; a numerical value; and choose whether to have dots per inch/dots per centimeter.

File Size Displays the current file size. The final size of the image will likely be different, depending on its final content.

Preview

Choose a Preview size from the dropdown list. Preview sizes include Printer Portrait, Printer Landscape, and a variety of monitor screen sizes, The Preview window shows how the image looks relative to the method selected.

Open (Ctrl+O)

Choose File, Open, click on the Open button, or hit Ctrl+O to access the Open dialog box.

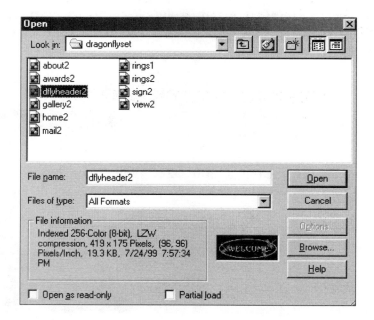

Look in Select a drive from the Look in dropdown list, then click the Browse button to browse to the folder and file you wish to open.

File name The selected file appears in the File name box.

Files of type The default setting of All Formats lists every image file type PhotoImpact recognizes, per your Preferences. If you are browsing a folder and you know the image you want to open is a .JPG, select JPG to browse only JPG files.

Open as read-only It is a good idea to leave this option selected to protect images from unwanted changes made to originals. For example, if you try out a Creative Painting template on a treasured photo and inadvertently save it with the edit when prompted to do so while closing it out, the original image will be lost. If you select Open as read-only you must give an edited image a different file name in order to save it. From the File menu, the Save option will be grayed out. You will be prompted with the Save As dialog box to save the edited image.

Partial Load Your computer's resources can be taxed by redrawing edits made to a larger image, particularly if you have set the Undo/Redo number to a higher value in Preferences. Partial load is useful for editing larger images, as it only opens a selected portion of the image.

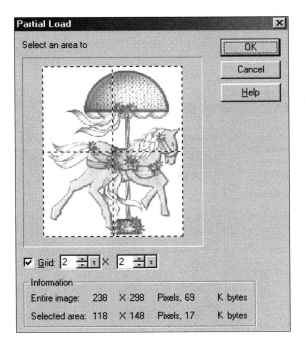

When Partial Load is selected, a default 2 X 2 grid of the image appears in the Preview window. The grid can be modified by changing the number of rows and columns. Click on the grid cell you wish to open. The information at the bottom of the dialog box shows the size of the total image and of the selected cell. Click OK to open the selected cell.

Alternatively, you can open a custom-defined area of the image. Deselect the box next to Grid. The grid will disappear and a selection area with control points will replace it. Drag on a control point to resize the selection area or move it to a different location in the image. Click OK to open only that part of the image.

When you are finished editing the partially loaded image, the entire image (not just the part you opened) will be saved with the changes made to it, unless you changed the data type or made the selected area larger or smaller than it was originally. In those cases, the Save option will be grayed out. You will be prompted with the Save As dialog box to give the image a new name prior to saving it.

Visual Open (Shift+O)

Visual Open lets you open files visually, from thumbnails rather than from file names. So even if you cannot remember the name of the file you wish to open, you can find and open it from its thumbnail.

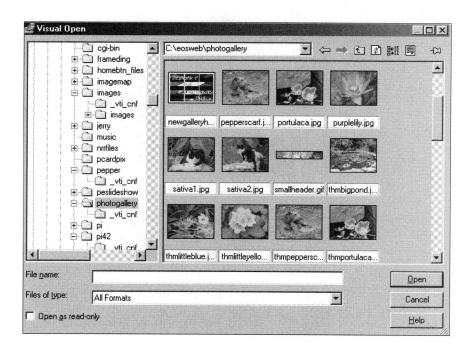

The left pane shows all of the folders on your computer's drives. Click on a folder to select it. The right preview window displays thumbnails of image files in the folder. To open an image, select it and click Open, or double click on its thumbnail.

Much-requested new features were added to Visual Open, including the ability to keep Visual Open open and minimized while you are working, and to sort thumbnails by size or other selected criteria. At the very top of the Visual Open dialog box you may access these useful new options.

Go to last folder visited Navigates back to the previous folder.

Forward Navigates to the next folder in your history. This is only available if you have clicked "Go to last folder visited" before.

Up one level Goes up one level in your folder heirarchy.

Refresh If you have added images since opening Visual Open, their thumbnails will be added with the Refresh command.

Switch view mode Toggles between thumbnail and list view.

View Menu Presents submenus of display, sorting and thumbnail options.

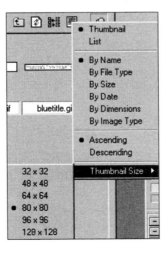

The bottom of the Visual Open dialog box contains file information and options.

File Name Name of the selected file.

Files of Type Select all file types, or choose to browse only certain image file types.

Open as read-only Edits to the image will not be saved under the file name. This prevents you from accidentally saving unwanted edits to an original image. You must choose File, Save As and give the file a new name in order to save it.

Open From Web

Open from Web permits you to load an image or web page from your hard drive, from an intranet or directly from the Internet. You must be connected to the Internet if you wish to open an image or web page from the Internet.

Image Accesses Open Image From Web Page, which acts as a browser window.

Address Enter the URL on which the web image you wish to open resides, or select a URL from a recently visited web page. If you are opening a page from your own computer or intranet, click the open file icon to access the Open dialog box and browse for the desired HTML page. When the page opens, click on an image to select it for opening in the work space.

Selected file name The name of the selected image file appears in this box.

Original file name Used only when an original image file format is different (e.g., .BMP) than the selected web image.

Locate PhotoImpact tries to locate on your local computer the most likely original version of the selected image, by similarity of file format.

Open web page as image Accesses Open Web Page as Image, which functions like a browser. From here you may open an entire web page and edit it as an image. Crop the web page image from the upper left corner by entering values for width and height.

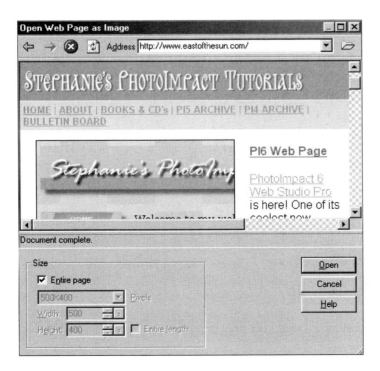

> **Address** Enter the URL of the web page you wish to open as an image, or select a URL from recently visited web pages. If you are opening a page from your own computer or intranet, click the open file icon to access the Open dialog box and browse for the desired HTML page.
>
> **Size** Deselect to open the entire web page in the work space as an image.
>
>> **Entire page** The entire web page opens as an image in the work space.
>>
>> **Width** Specify a width for the web page in pixels.
>>
>> **Height** Specify a height for the web page in pixels.
>>
>> **Entire length** The entire length of the web page opens as an image in the work space. The height will reflect the Height in pixels that you have selected.
>
> **Open** Opens the web page as an image in the work space.

Restore

Be cautious about choosing Restore, since this command cannot be undone. Restore returns the image to its state at the time of the last save. Edits will be lost.

Close (Ctrl+W)

Closes out the active image. If it has been edited, you will be prompted to save before closing.

Save (Ctrl+S)

Saves the active image.

Save As (Shift+Ctrl+S)

Opens the Save As dialog box. You may rename a previously saved image using Save As.

Save for Web

New to PhotoImpact 6, Save for Web creates an HTML web page document and/or optimizes web images. Select an option from the secondary menu.

Entire Image (Shift+Ctrl+W) Opens the Image Optimizer to save the entire image.

As Single Object Opens the Image Optimizer to save all of the objects in the base image as a single object.

As Individual Object Opens the Image Optimizer to save selected objects one at a time, individually.

As HTML (Ctrl+Alt+W) Opens the Save As dialog box to save the file as an HTML web document (.HTM file extension). All web images on the page will be saved to an images folder, automatically. If PhotoImpact encounters another web image with the same name in the images folder, a warning message appears asking if you want to overwrite the image file, rename it or cancel the save.

Update Image in HTML Opens the Update Image in Web Page window to save new or edited images directly to an HTML web page file.

Preview in Browser

Select Internet Explorer (Ctrl+Alt+0) or Netscape (Ctrl+Alt+1) to view the image as well as its file size, dimensions and the HTML code generated to create a web page containing the image(s).

You may also view the image tiled on a web page in your browser of choice.

Batch Convert

Batch Convert converts all of the files in a folder (and its subfolders, if desired) to a specified image type or file type. In the example shown below, all of the .BMP images in the Source folder will be converted to JPG images at 80% compression, then saved to a different destination folder in order to preserve the originals.

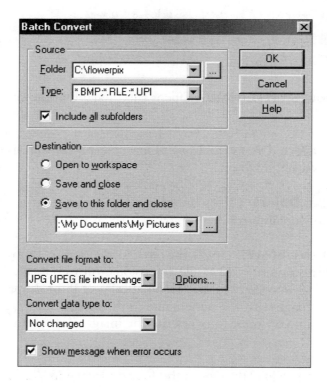

To perform a Batch Convert, first determine which folders and files will make up the Source file:

Source Folder Click to browse for the folder you wish to convert.

Source Type By default all file types in the specified folder will be converted. To convert only a selected file type, choose one from the Type dropdown list.

Include all subfolders Select to include images in subfolders also.

Next, select a destination for the converted images:

Open to work space Converted images will all open in the work space.

Save and close Be careful with this option, which overwrites the original files. Save to another folder to preserve your original images.

Save to this folder and close Converted images will be saved to a specific destination folder, preserving the originals. Browse to the desired folder.

Convert file format to Select an image file format for the converted images.

Options Click to select Save options. For image files to be converted to JPG, GIF or PNG format, Image Optimizer choices will appear in the "Convert data type to" dropdown list. For images converted to non-web image format, you must select a Save option from the "Convert data type to" dropdown list.

After selecting all of the attributes for the Batch Convert, click OK. Depending on how many images must be converted, the process can take from a few seconds to a minute or two. Once the conversion has been completed, a Task Report dialog box shows the results of the conversion. If any problems were encountered during the Batch Convert, they will be noted. To save the Task Report, click Save. To close out the Task Report, click Close.

Place

Accesses the Open dialog box. Browse to the file you wish to place in the active image as an object or base image.

Scanner

If you have never opened an image from your scanner directly into the work space before, the Scanner button will be grayed out. Choose File, Scanner, Select Source. Browse the hard drive to select your scanner. Once you have identified your scanner, PhotoImpact will recognize it in the future. The Scanner button will become available and your scanner will appear among the File, Scanner submenu choices (F7), along with the option to select your scanner with Post-processing.

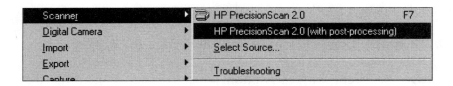

Choosing the option to select your scanner with Post-processing is recommended. Doing so opens the Acquire dialog box, which allows you to access a number of helpful image correction features. The Acquire dialog box has four tabs: Slicing, Calibration, Destination and Post-processing.

Slicing Tab

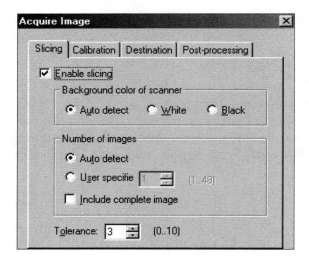

Enable slicing A useful choice if you are scanning several images at a time, slicing lets you "slice" the separate images from a page full of images.

Background color of scanner Choose from white, black or Auto-detect.

Number of images Choose from Auto-detect, User-specified or Include complete image.

Chapter 2: Working With Files

Tolerance Specify a value, with lower values yielding higher quality images.

Calibration Tab

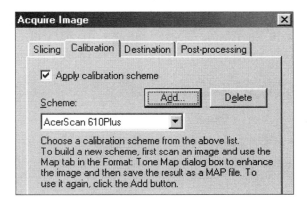

Apply calibration scheme Check to see if your scanner is listed among the schemes in the Scheme dropdown list. If it is, select it and check Apply calibration scheme. PhotoImpact's corrective tone map for your scanner will be applied to the scanned image automatically, yielding optimal results.

If your scanner is not among the Schemes listed but you have previously created and saved a Tone Map (.MAP file extension) you wish to use, click on the Add button to open the Load Tone Map dialog box. Browse your hard drive for the desired tone map and click OK. Select Apply calibration scheme and click Acquire to begin scanning. The tone map you loaded will be applied to the scanned images automatically. From now on, the corrective tone map will appear among the choices in the Scheme dropdown list, unless you delete it.

What should you do if your scanner is not among those in the Scheme dropdown list, and you have never saved a tone map before? One option is to do without a Scheme or tone map. Simply click Acquire to begin scanning with default settings and use the Post-processing Wizard to tweak image correction later. If you seldom scan images, you may be satisfied with this method.

If you scan often, however, you might want to take a long, critical look at your images. Do your scanned images often need edits such as Brightness & Contrast, Focus and other image correction processes to look their best? If so, it is worth investing a little time to create and save a tone map to enhance your scanned images. Tone maps are discussed in detail in the Format Menu chapter.

Destination Tab

From the Destination tab, determine where scanned images will go.

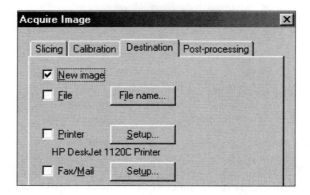

New image Opens the scanned image in its own window in the work space.

File Saves the scanned image as a file. Click on File name to name the file and browse to the folder to which you will save it.

Printer Immediately sends the scanned image to your default printer. Click Setup to change your printer's settings.

Fax/Mail Sends the scanned image via fax or, for users of Microsoft Outlook Express only, as an email attachment. Click Setup to configure Fax/Mail for your email program.

Post-processing Tab

The availability of Processing options will vary by the Type of processing selected.

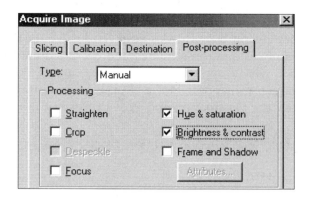

Digital Camera

If you have never opened an image from your digital camera directly into the work space before, the Digital Camera button will be grayed out. Choose File, Digital Camera, Select Source. Browse the hard drive to select your digital camera. Once you have identified your digital camera, PhotoImpact will recognize it in the future. The Digital Camera button will become available and your digital camera will appear among the File, Digital Camera submenu choices, along with the option to select your digital camera with Post-processing.

Choosing the option to select your digital camera with Post-processing is recommended. Doing so opens the Acquire dialog box, which allows you to access a number of helpful image correction features. The Acquire dialog box has four tabs: Slicing, Calibration, Destination and Post-processing.

Note that the Acquire Image dialog box for digital cameras is exactly the same as it is for scanners, except the Slicing tab options are grayed out. Refer to the options available from these tabs in the Scanner section preceding this one.

Just as you would to optimize images acquired from your scanner, click on the Calibration tab and review the digital camera schemes in the Scheme dropdown list. If your digital camera is listed, select it, choose "Apply calibration scheme" and click Acquire to import the image. PhotoImpact's corrective tone map for your digital camera will be applied to the image automatically.

If your digital camera is not among the Schemes listed but you have previously created and saved a tone map (.MAP file extension) you wish to use, click on the Add button to open the Load Tone Map dialog box. Browse your hard drive for the desired tone map and click OK. Select "Apply calibration scheme" and click Acquire to import the image. The tone map you loaded will be applied to your digital camera images automatically. From now on, the tone map will appear in the choices offered in the Scheme dropdown list. Make selections from the Destination and Post-processing tabs, just as you would for a scanner.

Import

Displays the Open dialog box as a means of opening .RAW or other unrecognized plug-in file types. Browse to the file that you wish to open and click OK. Doing so opens the Import RAW File dialog box, which has three sections.

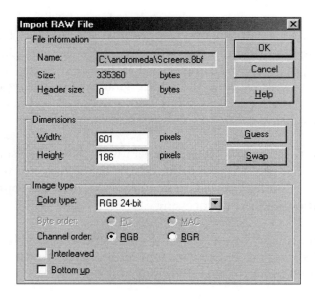

File Information The name of the selected file and its file size are displayed. Specify a value in the Header size box for the reserved data space at the beginning of the file.

Dimensions Displays the width and height of the file in pixels. Guess estimates width and height based on image size. Click Swap to reverse width and height values.

Image Type

Color type Select one from the dropdown list.

Byte order Choose PC or MAC to regulate how data is stored in each pixel. Use this option when files will be shared between PC and MAC computers (available for Grayscale 16-bit and RGB 48-bit images only).

Channel order Specify the order of color channels in each pixel. Interleave allows you to export pixel values by sets of color channels, by selected channel order. The default is to export selected color channels one after the other. When selected, Bottom up lets you store image data from bottom to top or the other way around.

Export

Several handy new features cluster under the Export command, which allows you to post an image or a web page directly to the Internet, to send the image or web page as an email attachment, to export RAW files, or export a Web Album or Web Slide Show.

Post to Web

When the Post to Web dialog box opens, choose whether to export an image or an entire HTML web page directly to the Internet.

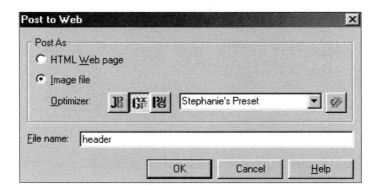

HTML Web Page If you want to export a web page, select Post as, HTML Web Page. Give the web page document a name. Note that the default of .HTM is added to the file name. If your server requires an .HTML file extension, type .HTML after the file name. Click OK to open the Web Publishing Wizard. Enter the information requested as the Wizard steps you through the process of uploading the web page to your site. Remember that any images included in the web page will be uploaded to your images directory.

Image File If you choose to post an image, select a web image file format (JPG, GIF or PNG) and associated options from the Optimizer dropdown list. These options are limited, but you may click on the Image Optimizer button to open its dialog box to tweak the optimization attributes. Give the file a name and click OK to open the Web Publishing Wizard. Enter the information requested as the Wizard steps you through the process of uploading the image to your web site. The image will be posted to your web site's images directory.

Send

Invoke Send to send a web page or an image as an email attachment. When the Send dialog box opens, choose whether to send a Web Page or Image File.

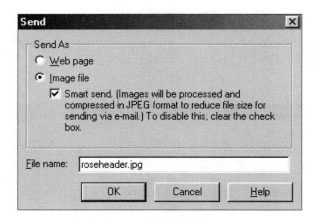

Web Page Web site and graphics designers will be delighted with this new option, which permits you to send an entire web page file as an email attachment in your default email client. The web page is sent as an .EXE file, which is a self-extracting compressed file. The recipient can choose to open the file or save it to a folder, then open it.

Be aware that for security reasons, many people will no longer accept or open email attachments, particularly .EXE files. If you plan to email a web page file to someone, it is common sense, as well as courtesy, to advise them of your plan to do so *prior* to emailing the .EXE file to make sure that they want to receive it.

Image File Use the Send command to send JPG image files only. If the image is a new one, give it a name. By default, a newly created image will be saved to your Windows Temp folder. Select "Smart sending" for automatic file compression in the Image Optimizer, or deselect for no compression.

Regardless of whether you send as a Web Page or Image File, the Send command works the same way. Click OK to close the Send box. A new email message window for your default email client opens in the work space. The web page or image file will be sent as an attachment to the email.

Only one image at a time can be sent with Send. However, you may send other images previously saved to your hard drive as additional attachments. If you wish to send the web page or image immediately, choose the Send option for your email client. Otherwise, choose your mail program's option for sending email later.

RAW Export

Exports .RAW files to a folder via the Save As dialog box. Name the file and browse to the folder to which you wish to save it. Click OK to close the Save As dialog box, which is followed by the Export RAW File dialog box.

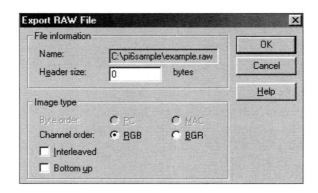

File Information The name of the selected file is listed. Specify a value in the Header size box for the reserved data space at the beginning of the file.

Image Type

Color type Select one from the dropdown list.

Byte order Choose PC or MAC to regulate how data is stored in each pixel. Use this option when files will be shared between PC and MAC computers (available for Grayscale 16-bit and RGB 48-bit images only).

Channel order Specify the order of color channels in each pixel. Interleave allows you to export pixel values by sets of color channels and by selected channel order. The default is to export selected color channels one after the other. When selected, Bottom up lets you store image data from bottom to top or the other way around.

Web Album

To create an album right in the PhotoImpact work space, select Web Album. This will open the Select Image dialog box.

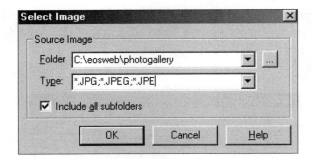

In the Source image section, click the Browse button. Doing so opens the Browse for Folder dialog box so you can select the folder containing the images from which you wish to create an album. Click OK to return to the Select Image dialog box. From the Type dropdown list, select the file type(s) you wish to include in the album. Include all subfolders is selected by default. Click OK to open the Export Web Album dialog box.

Output tab

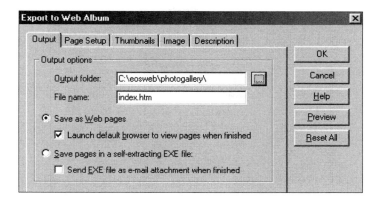

Output Options By default, the Output folder is the \Windows\TEMP\Ulead\Web folder. Click the Browse button to select a different folder. The default file name is index.htm. If your home page is already index.htm, it is a good idea to give the file a different name (e.g., album.htm), so it does not overwrite your existing home page.

Save as Web pages This option is selected by default, and launches your browser so you can view the album after you click OK.

Save pages in a self-extracting EXE file Selecting this option allows you to save an album as an .EXE file. Select "Send EXE file as an email attachment when finished" to send the album to someone as an email attachment. This means that the recipient of the album will be able to view it in a browser, without having to install a special viewer.

Once again, you should know that for security reasons, many people will no longer accept or open email attachments, particularly .EXE files. If you plan to email a web album to someone, it would be wise to inform them of your plan to do so *prior* to emailing the .EXE file. That way you can be sure that they want to receive and open the file.

Page Setup tab

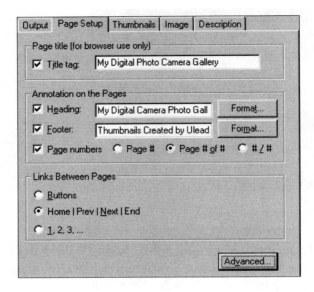

Page Title Select Title tag and enter a page name to include a page title. The page title is viewable only in a web browser.

Annotation on the Pages Select or deselect a heading and footer for the album page(s), and a page numbering style. For headings and footers, click Format to edit the font, font size, style, alignment and color.

Links between pages Choose from button, text or numbers.

Advanced Click Advanced to access more editing options, such as Background color or image, text and link colors. You can also select a sound file that will play while viewing the album.

The Advanced Page Settings dialog box is shown at the top of the next page.

Chapter 2: Working With Files

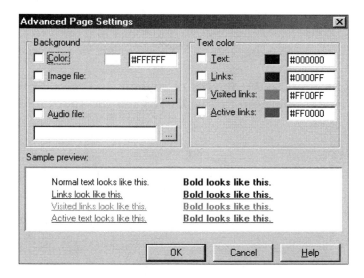

Thumbnails tab

Edit the thumbnail arrangement relative to the displayed full size image.

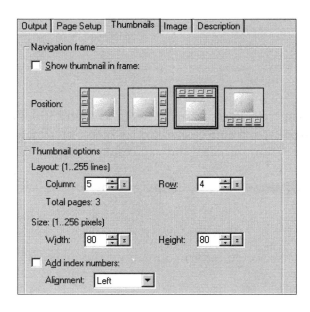

PhotoImpact 6 Wizardry

Navigation frame By default, "Show thumbnail in frame" is deselected. This creates a web page with thumbnails. Click on a thumbnail to view its corresponding full size image on a separate web page. Select "Show thumbnail in frame" to create a framed web page with thumbnails in one frame and the full size image in another frame.

Thumbnail options Choose the number of columns and rows for the thumbnail layout, thumbnail size in pixels (up to 256 X 256) and add Index numbers if desired.

Image tab

Specify how large the displayed image will appear and edit image compression values.

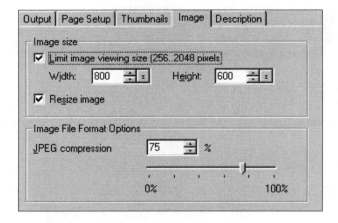

Image size Limit image viewing size is selected and set to 800 X 600 pixels by default, as this is a popular browser resolution size. Resize image automatically enlarges the image to the maximum allowable size, but can result in distortion.

Image File Format Options Choose an image compression value.

Description tab

You may elect to display selected information about the images in the album.

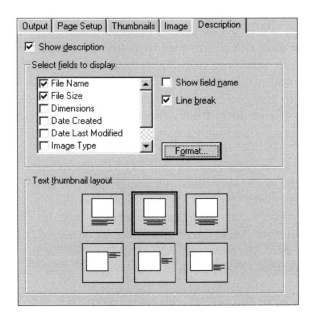

Show description Show description, including file name and file size, is selected by default, together with Line break (inserts line break after each displayed field, or deselect to have all displayed fields on one line). Select other fields for display as desired, or deselect Show description to show none. Select Show field name to display the name of the field as well as the description.

Format Click the Format button to edit font, font size, style and color.

Text thumbnail layout Select a layout for the text description relative to the thumbnail from the graphical examples.

Uploading and Viewing the Web Album Online When you have finished selecting all attributes of the album, click Preview to view it in your default browser. Click OK to save the album. The main page will be saved as index.htm. Several subfolders are created automatically: Images, Page and Thumbs. Copies of the source images for the slide show will be placed in the Images folder, however, the GIF navigation images for index.htm will be saved to the main directory. The Page folder contains a web page document for each image in the album, and their GIF navigation images. The pages are named image1.htm, image2.htm, and so on. The Thumbs folder contains the album's thumbnails. They are named tn_image1.jpg, tn_image2.jpg, etc.

Remember when uploading the album files to your server that the file structure on your remote server and the file structure of the album as saved to your computer must match exactly or your album will not work online. You must upload the images and web pages making up the album to the correct main directory, images directory, page directory and thumbs directory. If you do not have these directories on your server, make them first, then upload the images and web pages for the album to the appropriate directory.

You may know that some servers require the .HTML file extension, rather than the .HTM used in PhotoImpact's web album pages. If that is the case, you must rename all of your album pages to reflect the .HTML file extension, and edit all of the links in the source code for every page. One way to do this after saving the album is to display each page in your default browser, view the source code in Notepad, make the necessary changes, then save the file. Alternatively, you can open the file in your HTML editor to make the necessary changes.

Finally, the HTML code for the web album refers to the directories in which images and web pages can be found in this manner:

<a href= "page\image1.htm">

The backward slash (\) after page will be read OK by the Internet Explorer browser, but may not be read by other browsers, resulting in some visitors not being able to see your album. To be sure that all visitors to your web album can see it, the backward slashes should be replaced with forward slashes (/), so they look like this:

<a href="page/image1.htm">

Again, you can make these changes by displaying the source code in a browser, changing and saving it, or by opening the files in your HTML editor to make and save the changes.

Web Slide Show

Web Slide Show creates an HTML slide show that can be viewed by visitors to your web page, or compressed into a self-extracting .EXE file. The slide show is set up in frames. All of the images for the slide show will be saved to an images folder.

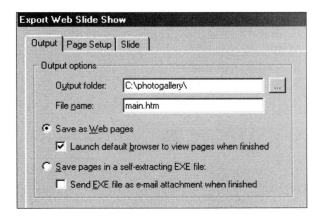

Output tab

Output Options Click the Browse button to select a different folder. The slide show is presented in a framed web page. Do not change the default file name, main.htm, or the slide show will not work.

Save as Web pages This option is selected by default, and launches your browser to view the slide show after you click OK.

Save pages in a self-extracting EXE file Selecting this option allows you to save a slide show as an .EXE file. Select "Send EXE file as an email attachment when finished" to send the slide show to someone as an email attachment. This means that the recipient of the slide show will be able to view it in a browser without having to have a special viewer.

Once again, because of computer viruses and security issues, be careful about sending .EXE files. Some people may not want or accept email attachments. Be a good netizen and notify the proposed slide show recipient in advance if you plan to send the slide show as an email attachment.

Page Setup tab

Page Title Select Page title tag and enter a page name to include a page title, viewable only in a web browser.

Annotations Select or deselect a heading and footer for the slide show page(s), and a page numbering style. For headings and footers, click Format to edit the font, font size, style, alignment and color.

Links between pages Choose from button, text or numbers.

Advanced Click Advanced to access more editing options, such as Background color or image, text and link colors, or a sound file to play while viewing the slide show.

Slide tab

Image size Limit image viewing size is selected and set to 800 X 600 pixels by default. Edit this size as desired. Resize image automatically enlarges the image to the maximum allowable size, but can result in distortion.

Image File Format Options Choose an image compression value.

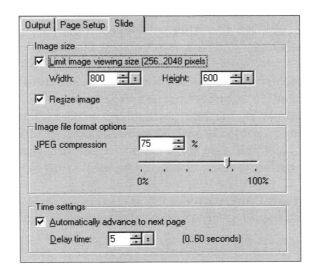

Time settings By default, Automatically advance to next page is selected, with a delay of 5 seconds. Change the delay time as desired, or deselect Automatically advance to next page to control progression of the slide show manually.

Uploading and Viewing the Web Slide Show Online When you have finished selecting all attributes of the slide show, click Preview to view it in your default browser. Click OK to save the slide show. The frames page will be saved as main.htm, while the pages with the images for the slide show will be saved as main1.htm, main2.htm, and so on. Several subfolders are created automatically: Images, Page and Thumbs. Copies of the source images for the slide show will be placed in the Images folder, however, the GIF images for the manual slide show will be saved to the main directory.

Remember when uploading the slide show files to your server that the file structure on your remote server and the file structure of the slide show must match exactly or your slide show will not work. You must upload the images making up the slide show to an images directory. If you do not have an images folder on your server, make one and upload the images to that directory.

Finally, remember that some servers require the .HTML file extension, rather than the .HTM used in PhotoImpact's slide show. If that is the case, you must rename all of your slide show pages to reflect the .HTML file extension, and edit all of the links in the source code for every page. An easy way to do this after saving the slide show is to display each page in your default browser, view the source code in Notepad, make the necessary changes, then save the file. Alternatively, open the files in your HTML editor to make and save the changes.

Finally, the HTML code for the web slide show refers to the directories in which images can be found in this manner: <a href="images\image1.jpg"> The backward slash (\) after images will be read OK by the Internet Explorer browser, but may not be read by other browsers, resulting in some visitors not being able to see your slide show. To be sure that all visitors to your web slide show can see it, the backward slashes should be replaced with forward slashes (/), so they look like this: <a href="images/image1.jpg">

Again, you can make these changes by viewing the source code in a browser, changing and saving it, or by editing and saving the files in your HTML editor.

Capture

Capture allows you to "take a picture" or screen shot of what you see on your monitor.

Setup

Choose Setup to specify the attributes for the behavior of the screen capture.

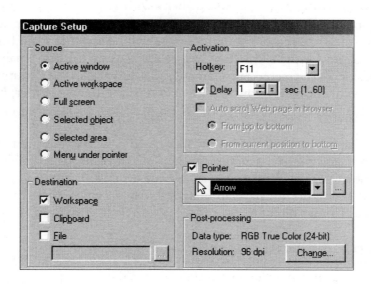

Source Indicate which area of the screen will be captured. You can choose to capture only the active window, the active work space, full screen, a selected object, a selected area or the menu under the pointer.

Destination Choose whether the capture will go to the work space, the Clipboard, or to a file. If File is selected, click the Browse button and select the folder to which the capture will be saved.

Activation Select a hotkey from the dropdown list. Enter a value for Delay to delay the capture for a number of seconds (up to 60). Select Multiple Capture if you want a series of captures.

Pointer The default pointer is an arrow. Select a different pointer from the dropdown list.

Post-processing The current data type and resolution is listed. Click Change to edit.

Print Preview (Ctrl+Alt+P)

Select Print Preview, click on the Print Preview button or hit Ctrl+Alt+P to position, resize and preview an image, to modify your printer's settings or to print an image.

Print Click the Print button to open the Print dialog box. Click OK to print the image just as it appears in the preview window.

Setup Accesses the Print Setup dialog box for your default printer. You may change the printer's Properties or Paper Size and Orientation from here.

Resize When selected, the image is surrounded by a bounding box with control handles. Drag one of the control handles to make the image larger or smaller. Hold down on the Shift key while dragging to preserve the height to width proportion.

Copies Indicate the number of copies to be printed.

Start From Specify (in inches) the distance from the top and left edges of the paper for printing the image, or accept the default values.

T Title Opens the Title dialog box. Enter a title for the image if desired, then click OK. Titles appear centered over the printed image.

Options Click Options for a dropdown list including: Fit to Page, Center Horizontally or Center Vertically.

View Click View to access the dropdown list including: Actual View, Zoom In or Zoom Out. Select Ruler to view a ruler along the top and left edges of the paper.

Close Click to close Print Preview and return to the work space.

Print (Ctrl+P)

Choose Print, click the Print button or hit Ctrl+P to open the Print dialog box.

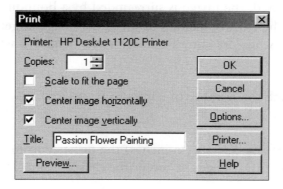

Printer Displays your default printer.

Copies Indicates the number of copies to be printed.

Scale to fit the page Automatically resizes the image to fit the printed page.

Center image horizontally Centers the image in the middle of the page, horizontally.

Center image vertically Centers the image in the middle of the page, vertically.

Title Give the image a title, which will be printed, centered, over the image.

Options The options available will vary depending upon the type of printer. If you have a non-PostScript printer, you will see two tabs, Calibration and Halftone. If you have a PostScript printer, the two tabs will be Calibration and PostScript.

> **Calibration tab** Regardless of whether your printer is PostScript or non-PostScript, from this tab select or deselect the application of corrective measures for the printed output.

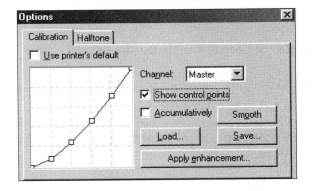

> **Channel** Apply to the Master, Red, Green or Blue channel.
>
> **Show control points** Displays control points on the graph. Choose Smooth to smooth out the mapping curve, for a more natural look.
>
> **Accumulatively** Corrective measures accumulate in aggregate.

Load Opens the Load Tone Map dialog box so that a previously saved tone map can be applied to the printed image.

Apply Enhancement Choose from pre-determined mapping curves and functions, including: Darken, Lighten, Highlight, Midtone, Darken Midtone, Lighten Midtone, Highlight & Shadow and Reset.

Save Opens the Save Tone Map dialog box.

Halftone tab The Halftone tab appears for printers that do not support PostScript printing. Deselect Printer's Default to configure the printing of halftone images.

Shape Select a shape (Diffused, Round, Elliptical, Diamond, Line, Square, Cross) for the pixels in the image.

Optimized Screen The best range of colors for optimal printed output.

Frequency Specify the distance between the centers of each halftone dot.

Angle Specify the angle for the printed dots.

PostScript tab The PostScript tab only appears if you have a PostScript printer installed.

Use PostScript Level 2 features Accesses PostScript 2 quality and compression options.

Best quality Prints at the best possible quality.

Compress bitmap Compresses the image data being printed.

Default Returns to default settings.

Compress Specify a type and level of compression.

Type Choose a compression type from the dropdown list.

Level Select a level of compression, with lower values resulting in lower quality printing.

Printer Accesses the Print Setup dialog box for your printer.

Preferences

Select General, Customize Standard Toolbar or Color Management.

General (F6)

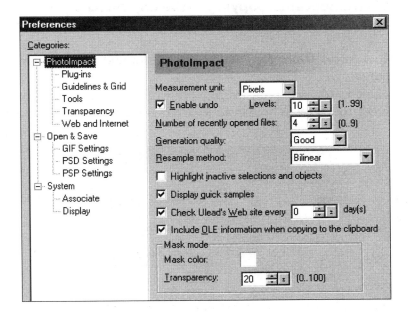

PhotoImpact

Measurement unit Select pixels, inches or centimeters from the dropdown list.

Enable undo Specify a value for the number of Undos.

Generation quality Select Fair, Good or Best.

Resample method Select Nearest Neighbor (most compact, poorest quality), Bilinear or Bicubic (least compact, highest quality). Bilinear is selected by default.

Highlight inactive objects or selections Select to show inactive objects.

Display quick samples Select to show the Quick Samples thumbnails in dialog boxes. If deselected, these options in many Effect dialog boxes will be bypassed.

Check Ulead's web site every (#) days Selected by default. Deselect to stop PhotoImpact from dialing up Ulead at the specified interval.

Include OLE information when copying to the Clipboard Allows embedding of Clipboard contents as an OLE object, so it can be pasted into another program.

Mask Mode Click in the Color Box to edit Mask color and transparency.

Plug-ins To enable third party plug-ins to work with PhotoImpact, select a blank checkbox, then click the Browse button to locate the folder and file of the plug-in.

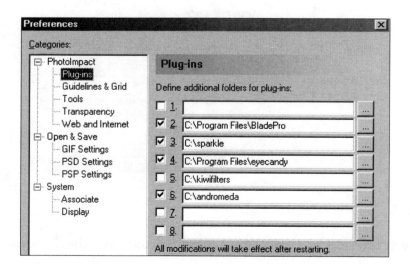

You do not need to install third party plug-ins to a PhotoImpact folder in order to use them. However, it is important to specify the correct path to the plug-in. Note that you must close PhotoImpact and open it again before the plug-in will be available at the bottom of the Effect menu commands. Although many plug-ins and filters work with PhotoImpact, not all of them do. Before you invest money in a plug-in or filter, consult its manufacturer to make sure that it will work with PhotoImpact.

Guidelines & Grid

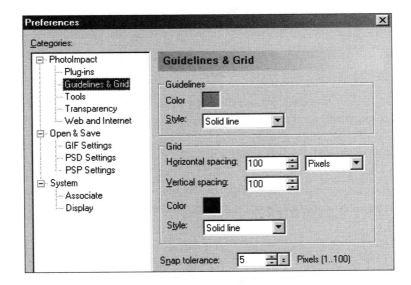

Guidelines Click in the Color box to select a Color, and select a line style (solid, dashed, dotted) from the Style dropdown list.

Grid Enter values for horizontal and vertical spacing of Grid lines, choosing pixels, inches or centimeters from the dropdown list. Click in the Color box to change Grid line color. Select a line style (solid, dashed, dotted) from the Style dropdown list.

Snap tolerance Choose a value for how close to the Grid line the cursor must be to "snap" to it.

Tools

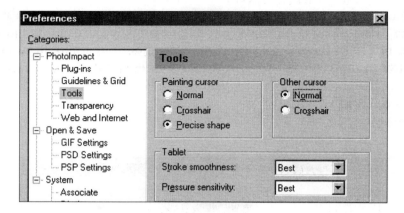

Painting cursor Select normal, crosshair or precise shape. Precise shape is a wonderful option for digital painters, as the cursor is shown at exact size and shape.

Other cursor Select normal or crosshair.

Tablet Customize drawing pen functions by choosing Fair, Good or Best from the Stroke Smoothness and Pressure Sensitivity dropdown lists.

Transparency

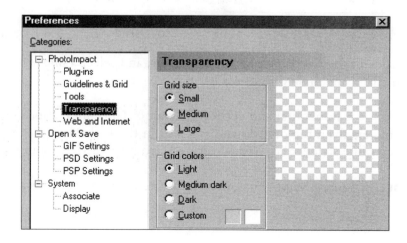

Grid size Select a Small (the default), Medium or Large gray-toned checkerboard pattern for the transparent background.

Grid colors Choose from Light (light gray and white, the default), Medium Dark (medium gray and light gray) or Dark (black and dark gray). Select Custom to select your own colors for the transparent background checkerboard. Click in each Color box to select a color.

Web & Internet

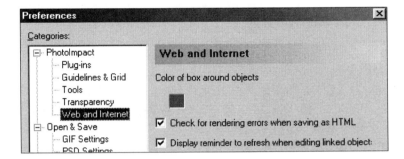

Color of box around objects The default is red. Click in the Color box to select another color.

Check for rendering errors when saving as HTML Selected by default.

Display reminder to refresh when editing linked objects Selected by default.

Open & Save

Use Visual Open When deselected (the default), you retain the choice of using both File, Open and File, Visual Open to open images. When selected, both File, Open *and* File, Visual Open will access the Visual Open dialog box. Visual Open can tie up system resources as it generates thumbnails, so leave this option deselected if your RAM is limited.

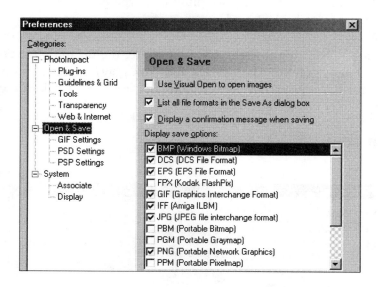

List all file formats in the Save As dialog box Selected by default, or select file formats individually from the list. For the selected file formats, click Options when the Save dialog box opens to access the Save Options dialog box. The Save Options dialog box allows you to configure and tweak further the attributes of the save, like the choices shown below in the UFO Save Options dialog box.

Display a confirmation message when saving Deselect to avoid the confirmation message.

>**GIF Settings** Determines which frames in a GIF animation will open, and where. Choose from: Open each frame as an object, Open each frame as a new document, Open the first frame only or Use Ulead GIF Animator to open.

PSD Settings Determines how PSD files will be opened and saved.

> **PSD Open Options** Select from "Open each layer as an object" or "Open the composited image or first layer only." Be careful with the latter option. If it is selected, all layers in the object will be merged with the base image prior to opening and you will not be able to edit and save it again in PSD format. "Ask when opening" is selected by default, so that you can make a choice regarding opening PSD files every time. Deselect if desired.
>
> **PSD Save Options** Select from "Save each object as a layer" (preserves objects for later editing) or "Save the merged image" (merges with the base image and precludes further editing of layers).

PSP Settings Determines how PSP (Paint Shop Pro) files will be opened. Choose from: "Open each layer as an object" or "Open the composited image or first layer only." "Ask when opening" is selected by default, so that you can make a choice regarding opening PSP files every time. Deselect if desired.

System

From System, specify how Windows manages memory when you are running PhotoImpact.

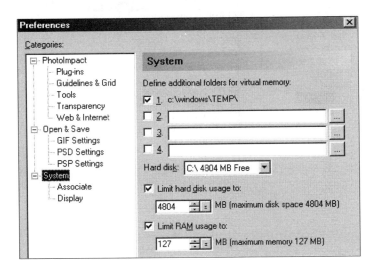

Define folders for additional memory By default, Windows assigns temporary files to the \TEMP folder. To select additional folders for memory management, select a box then click the Browse button to designate another folder.

Hard disk Select the drive to which temporary files are assigned.

Limit hard disk usage to Specify a value for PhotoImpact to manage disk use when the program is running.

Limit RAM usage to Specify for PhotoImpact to manage RAM usage when the program is running.

Associate Select the file formats that you wish to associate with PhotoImpact. If you click on an image file format associated with PhotoImpact from Windows Explorer, the file will open automatically in PhotoImpact. You can choose "Select All" to associate all available image types with PhotoImpact, or click Customize to associate only certain file formats.

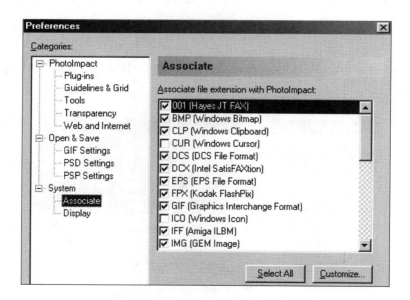

Display Adjusts how PhotoImpact displays images when the selected Display method is HiColor (16 bit) or 256 Color mode.

HiColor dithering Select if your Display is set to High Color and you want to display True Color images optimally.

View images with a common palette Select when you are in 256 color mode to open 256 color and grayscale images at the same time, or to compare 256 color images.

Ignore background color Devotes system resources to the active image only. The color in inactive images may appear wrong in this mode.

Monitor gamma Optimizes monitor display by editing the color squares so that they both appear to be the same color.

Customize Standard Toolbar

Custom edit the Standard Toolbar to make your work easier.

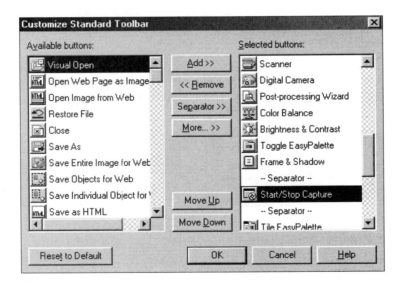

Available buttons Select a button to add it to the toolbar. Click the Add or Separator buttons to reorganize the toolbar. Click the More button to open the Customize Buttons dialog box, to choose from a selection of colorful BMP buttons.

Selected buttons Select a button in the toolbar, then click the Remove, Move Up or Move Down buttons to reorganize the toolbar. Click the More button to replace the standard button with a different one from the Customize Buttons dialog box.

Reset to Default Reverts back to the standard toolbar.

Color Management

Select Color Management to take advantage of new color management technology, which embeds color profiles for specific devices in your image files. Color Management is available for Windows 98, NT 5.0 and Windows 2000 users only. When the Color Management dialog box opens, select Enable Color Management and choose either Basic Color Management or Proofing.

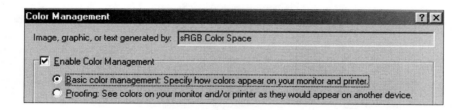

Basic Color Management Select this option to match the color produced by your output device (e.g., your printer) to the color viewed on your monitor.

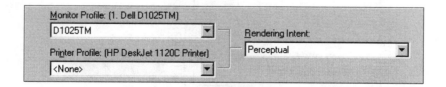

Monitor Profile Select your monitor from the dropdown list.

Printer Profile Select a printer from the dropdown list. If no printer other than the default has been installed, the dropdown list will display "None."

Rendering Intent Choose from Perceptual, Relative Colorimetric, Saturation or Absolute Colorimetric.

Proofing Select Proofing to view on your own monitor and printer how image colors would look if printed by a different output device. For example, you may do the prepress work for a book on your home computer, then take the files to a professional print shop. Proofing lets you see how the colors in the images will look when printed by the printer at the print shop.

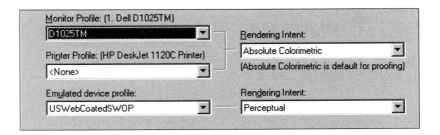

Monitor Profile Select your monitor from the dropdown list.

Printer Profile Select your printer from the dropdown list. If no printer other than the default has been installed, the dropdown list will display "None."

Rendering Intent Choose from Perceptual, Relative Colorimetric, Saturation or Absolute Colorimetric, as it applies to *your* output device (e.g., printer).

Emulated Device Profile Select a profile for the device you wish to emulate from the choices in the dropdown list

Rendering Intent Choose from Perceptual, Relative Colorimetric, Saturation or Absolute Colorimetric, for the emulated device.

Recent Files

Displays the files most recently opened in the work space. The number of files listed reflects the number selected in Preferences, General.

Exit (Ctrl+Q)

Exits PhotoImpact.

PhotoImpact 6 Wizardry

Chapter 3: Viewing and Displaying Files

View menu commands control how images are displayed in the PhotoImpact work space. In addition, they control the visibility and/or accessibility of toolbars and panels, the ruler, base image transparency, marquees around objects, guidelines and grids, and the display of image or system properties.

Zooming in or out gives greater control over image editing. To select a small area within an image, Zooming in at up to 1600% magnification will help you to pinpoint an area for accurate selection. If an image is too large to fit into the work space at actual size, Zooming lets you see the entire image as small as 5% of actual size. Alternatively, you may want to superimpose a grid of fine lines over an image for precision placement of objects, deselect the default red broken line which appears around objects in PhotoImpact 6, or display only the transparent base image.

View menu commands are among the ones you will use most often. They are easy to use but a few have idiosyncracies worth learning about.

Add a View (Ctrl+I)

Add a View opens a copy of the active image in the work space. When you edit the original image, the exact same changes will be made to the added view. Adding a view is really helpful when you have Zoomed in on an image and want to see how edits will look at actual size. The added view saves you from having to switch back and forth from Actual Size to a magnified view of the image. You can have up to eight views of an image open at the same time.

If you want a duplicate of an image (and all its objects) that will not change as the original image is edited, do not select Add a View. Instead, choose Edit, Duplicate, Base Image Only, or hit Ctrl+D.

Actual View (Ctrl+O)

The active image is shown at its actual size. Depending on the size of the image, all of it may not be visible at one time. Scrollbars can be used to bring hidden parts of the image into view. The image window can be resized by dragging on its borders.

Maximize at Actual View (Ctrl+M)

The active image is shown at actual size with regard to detail. The gray area surrounding the image expands to fill the entire work space. If other images are open in the work space, they will remain open but will not be visible. To return to normal viewing, click on the Restore button.

Zoom

Zoom in to magnify an image at up to 1600% of its actual size, or Zoom out to show the image in increments of 5%, 10% 25%, 33%, 50%, 67% or 75% of actual size. You can also Zoom in by clicking on the + (plus) key, and Zoom out by clicking on the − (minus) key. Use scrollbars to view parts of the image that are not in immediate view, or resize the image window by dragging on its borders. You can also Zoom in or Zoom out by using the Zoom dropdown list in the menu bar.

Fit In Window (Shift+Ctrl+O)

Displays the image at the largest magnification possible which will still fit in a window.

Full Screen (Ctrl+U)

Displays a full screen preview of the active image at its current magnification. To get out of full screen mode, click Escape.

Remove Menu Bar

As the name indicates, this command hides the top menu bar and the task bar at the bottom of the screen, but their functions will still be accessible via keyboard shortcuts.

All toolbars currently in use will remain visible. Removing the menu bar allows more space for image editing. Accidentally selecting Remove Menu Bar can be a disconcerting experience, however, as you may wonder where everything went. Just hit the Escape key to return to normal viewing.

Show Base Image (Ctrl+F5)

Toggles between showing and hiding the base image. When deselected, the base image is hidden and you will see either a transparent checkerboard pattern or a web page background tile (if one has been chosen).

Show Marquee (Ctrl+F8)

Toggles between showing and hiding the selection marquee around active objects.

Show Box Around Objects (Ctrl+F7)

Toggles between showing and hiding the broken line bounding box around objects (red for web objects, green for other objects).

Photo Properties (Alt+Enter)

Displays the attributes of the active image (data type, width, height, resolution and size) and specifics of the file (name, format, saved file size and other information).

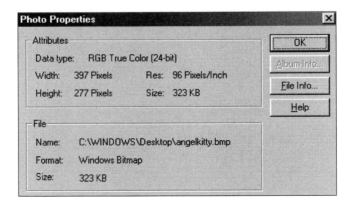

System Properties

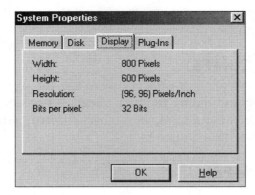

There are four tabs: Memory (Version, Physical Memory, Processor Type); Disk (drive information); Display (Width, Height and Resolution of the active image, and bits per pixel); Plug-ins (path to plug-ins folder and total number of image filters).

Toolbars & Panels

Select to display or deselect to hide toolbars and panels. Click Options to select which toolbars and panels will appear by default. Doing so opens a secondary Options dialog box, from which you may customize the appearance of buttons and tool tips.

Note that you can turn Tooltips on and off, select Large buttons if you have trouble seeing the small ones, and deselect color buttons.

Ruler

Displays a Ruler along the left and top edges of the active image. A broken line moves along the ruler as you move the cursor. The Ruler is useful when you want to draw horizontal lines every 10 pixels or so, or place objects within the base image a certain distance apart.

Units of measure for the Ruler can be pixels, inches or centimeters. Change the unit of measure by clicking on the Unit button in the status bar.

Guidelines & Grid

Toggle between displaying and hiding Guidelines (Shift+Ctrl+G), or to lock, clear or snap to guidelines (Ctrl+Shift+S). Also toggles between displaying and hiding the Grid (Shift+Ctrl+R), and invoking Snap to Grid (Shift+Ctrl+N).

Choose File, Preferences, General, and select Guidelines & Grid to change the color, unit of measurement and appearance (solid line, dotted line, dashed line) of guidelines and grids.

The Big Picture: Active Learning Exercises

Some of these exercises require you to open images associated with this book. Open the images from the file on your hard drive to which you have saved them.

Create a New File Preset

1. Often you will find yourself starting with a new file that is the same size and color. In this exercise you will create a preset for a 400 X 400 pixel white canvas, edit the preset, and delete it.

2. Choose File, New to open the New dialog box. Click the data type "rainbow" icon to make an RGB True Color file. If the Canvas color is not white, click in the Canvas color box and select white. In the "Image size" section, select "User-defined," and enter 400 for the Width and Height in Pixels. Click the Options button (it has a little checkmark on it) and select "Add User-defined Size."

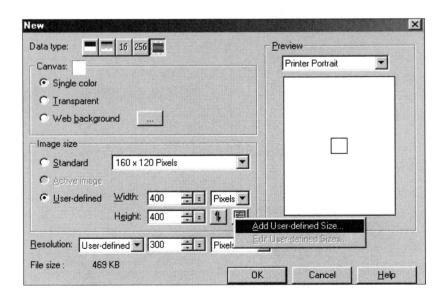

3. When the Add User-defined Size dialog box opens, give the preset a name, e.g., My 400X400 Preset, and click OK.

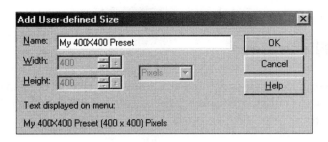

4. Back at the New dialog box, click Options again to see that your new preset has been added. Select it and click OK to open a new, 400 X 400 pixel image with a white canvas.

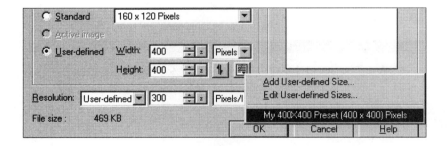

5. Close out the new image and choose File, New again. Click Options and select "Edit User-defined Size."

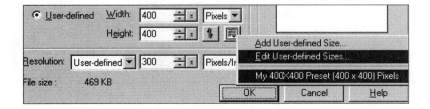

6. When the Edit User-defined Size dialog box opens, click Change. Doing so opens

the Change User-defined Size dialog box. Change the preset name to "My 300X300 Preset" and change the Width and Height to 300 pixels.

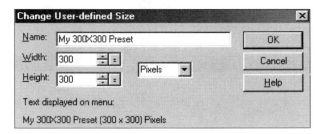

7. Click OK, then click OK again to return to the New dialog box. Click Options and note that the name of the preset has been edited, as well as the Width and Height.

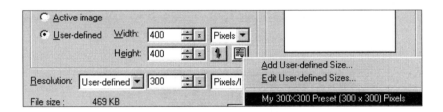

8. Select the preset and click OK to open a new 300 X 300 pixel file with a white canvas. Close out the new image.

9. Now you will delete the preset. Choose File, New. When the New dialog box opens, make sure "My 300X300 Preset" is selected, then choose Edit User-defined Size. When its dialog box opens, click Delete.

10. Click Options and you will see that the preset is no longer available.

Opening a File

1. The purpose of this exercise is to show how to open files in a variety of ways.

2. Choose File, Open to access the Open dialog box. Browse to pelican.bmp. When the file opens in the work space, close out the file.

3. Choose File and place your cursor over Recent Files. You will see that pelican.bmp is at the top of the list.

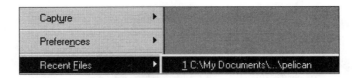

4. Select pelican.bmp and it will open in the work space. Close it out again.

5. Hit Ctrl+O. When the Open dialog box appears, select pelican.bmp again. Before doing anything else, select "Partial load." Now click Open.

6. When the Partial Load dialog box opens, a 2 row X 2 column grid is superimposed over the image by default. Edit the grid to 3 rows X 3 columns. Click on the center cell in the grid, which contains the pelican. This cell will be active, surrounded by an animated broken line.

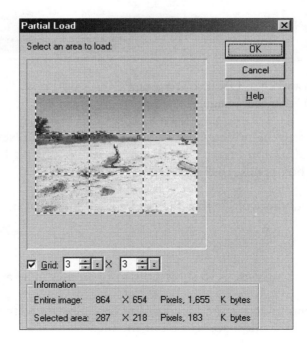

7. Click OK to open only the center cell in the grid. Close out the image.

Visual Open

1. Choose File, Visual Open to open the Visual Open dialog box. Browse to portulaca.jpg and select its thumbnail.

2. ![pushpin] Click on the push pin icon in the upper right corner to keep Visual Open open even when minimized.

3. Next click on the Switch View Mode button.

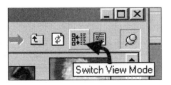

PhotoImpact 6 Wizardry

4. In this mode, thumbnails are replaced by list mode, which includes detailed image information like file name, file type, size, date last modified, dimension and data type.

5. Click Switch View Mode again to return to thumbnail mode. Click the Options button and hold the cursor over Thumbnail Size to display a submenu. From here you can select a different size for the thumbnails. Select the largest size, 128 X 128.

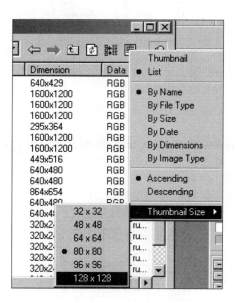

98

The Big Picture: Active Learning Exercises

6. Now when you view the thumbnails, they are much larger and take up a lot of room. Click Options, Thumbnail Size and select 80 X 80 again.

7. While the portulaca.jpg thumbnail is selected, select "Open as Read-only," then click Open. The image opens in the work space.

8. Choose File and note that the "Save" option is grayed out. By opening in "Read-only" mode, the original image is preserved from unwanted edits. Only the "Save As" option is available under the File menu commands.

9. Close out the image.

10. If you want to open another image via Visual Open, you do not have to choose File, Visual Open (or Shift+O) to access Visual Open again. Look at the task bar at the bottom of the work space, where you will see its icon.

11. Click on Visual Open in the task bar to open it again. Click on the X button to close it now.

Send an Image

1. Hit Ctrl+O to access the Open dialog box. Deselect Partial load. Browse to countrygal.jpg, select it and click Open.

3. When the image opens in the work space, choose File, Export, Send. Doing so opens the Send dialog box.

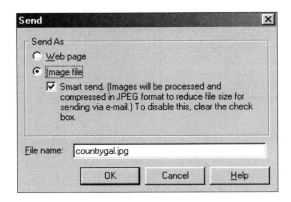

PhotoImpact 6 Wizardry

4. Note that Send As, Image file is selected by default, as is "Smart send." If you do not want the image to be compressed, deselect "Smart send."

5. Click OK and a new email message window will open in the work space. Address the email to your own email address and make a note in the Subject line that you are testing the PI6 Send feature. You will see that the attachment is included in the email attachment line automatically.

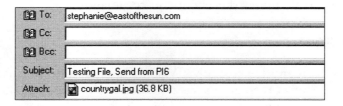

6. If you are not currently online, choose your default email client's option to send the email later. If you are online, send the email now. You should receive the email with the image attached the next time you check your email.

Send a Web Page

1. Open the EasyPalette's Template Library. Double click on the Web Page 1 thumbnail to select it. Alternatively, drag from the thumbnail to an empty area in the work space. The template will open in its own window.

2. A web page filled with objects will open in the work space. Right click and Merge All.

3. Choose File, Export, Send. When the Send dialog box opens, select Web Page.

Doing so will gray out all of the other options.

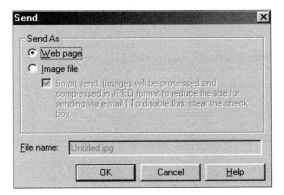

4. Click OK and a new email message window will open in the work space. Address the email to your own email address and make a note in the Subject line that you are testing the PI6 Send a Web Page feature. You will see that the attachment (Untitled.exe, 112 kb) is included in the email automatically.

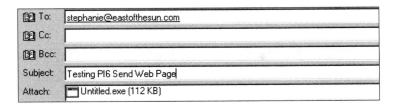

5. If you are not currently online, choose your default email client's option to send the email later. If you are online, send the email now. You should receive the email with the web page attached the next time you check your email.

Create and Send a Web Album

1. The purpose of the following exercise is to use a group of four images to make a web album. When the album is created, the very large images will be converted to 640 X 480 compressed .JPG images.

2. Choose File, Export, Web Album to open the Select Image dialog box. Click the Browse button to browse to the folder with the images for the web album. Use the Browse button to navigate to and select the album folder that contains album1.bmp, album2.bmp, album3.bmp and album4.bmp.

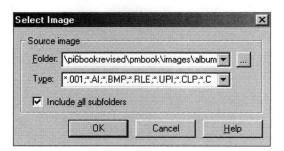

3. Click OK to open the Export to Web Album dialog box. You will need to make choices from each of the five tabs. These choices will affect the appearance of the album. Start with the Output tab. For the Output folder, select the same folder, e.g., album, that contains the four images. By default, this page will be named index.html. Leave the defaults of "Save as web pages" and "Launch default browser to view pages when finished" selected.

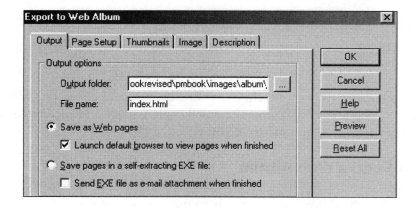

4. Click on the Page Setup tab next. From here you may change the default heading and footer text for the web album. Select a page numbering method. For "Links Between Pages," select any option except buttons.

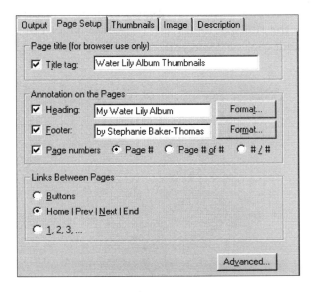

5. To edit the web page background color or image, click Advanced in the Page Setup tab. Doing so opens the Advanced Page Settings dialog box. Edit the web page background, as well as text and link colors. Click OK to close the dialog box.

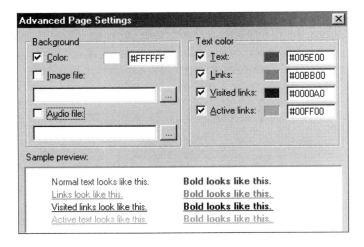

6. Click on the Thumbnails tab. If "Show thumbnail in frame" is selected, the album will be set up in frames. If "Show thumbnail in frame" is not selected, clicking on a thumbnail displays the full size image on a separate page. For this exercise, do not select a framed layout. Select "Add index numbers" and a page alignment option.

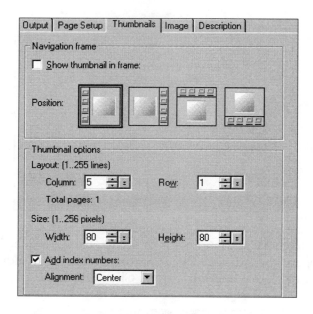

7. Click the Image tab. In the Image size section, limit the viewing size of the images to 640 X 480 pixels. Make sure that "Resize images" is selected to prevent the need to scroll. Edit the .JPEG compression to 85% for better quality.

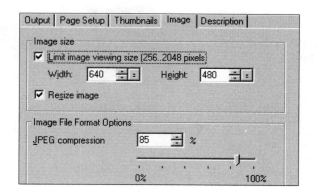

8. Finally, click the Description tab. In this section, select the information about the images that you wish to display. Select File name only to save space around the thumbnails. Choose a "Text thumbnail layout" from the graphical choices.

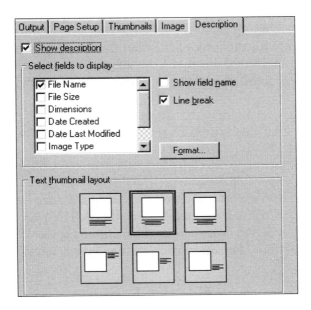

9. Click the Format tab to edit the text describing the thumbnails. Doing so opens the Text Format dialog box. Edit the font, size or color as desired and click OK to close the box.

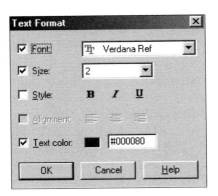

10. Now that all of the attributes for the web album have been selected, click Preview to check out the album before saving it. Your default browser will be launched to display the album. Click on the links to view the images, then close the browser. If you are not happy with the album the way it is, go back to the individual tabs and edit as desired.

11. When you are happy with the look of the album, click OK. It might take a moment or two for the album to be saved, then your default browser will open to show the album. When you are finished looking at it, close the browser.

12. Go to Windows Explorer to view the album file to which you have saved the web album. You will see that in addition to the original images, PhotoImpact 6 has created a number of HTML pages (including one for the background sound if you have included one), as well as three folders called Images, page and thumbs.

13. Click on each folder to view its contents. The Images folder contains the .JPG versions of the four .BMP images used in the album. The page folder contains an HTML page for each of the four images. The thumbs folder contains thumbnails generated for the album. The thumbnails are named tn_slide1.jpg, tn_slide2.jpg, etc.

14. When you upload the web album to your server so you can view it online, you will need to be careful to preserve the file structure created on your hard drive by PhotoImpact 6. Specifically, all of the files in the album main directory must be uploaded to the main directory on your server. You must create three subdirectories called Images, page and thumbs on your server, and upload the files in your local computer folders to the same folders on your server. If you do not do so, your web album will not work.

15. Because the attributes of the album you have just created are "sticky," in the sense that they are still there until you create another album, now it is time to send yourself the album as a self-extracting .EXE file. Choose File, Export, Web Album.

16. Doing so opens the Select Image dialog box. The next part is very important. From the Type dropdown list, select .BMP, .RLE and .UPI file types only. If you do not, every image added to the folder when the album was created will appear in the new .EXE album. You want this new .EXE file to be based only on the original .BMP images. Click OK.

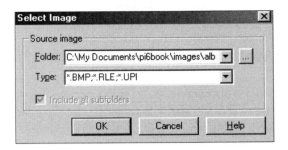

17. When the Export to Web Album dialog box opens, from the Output tab, change the Output folder to album. Change the Output options to "Save pages in a self-extracting EXE file," and "Send EXE file as an email attachment when finished."

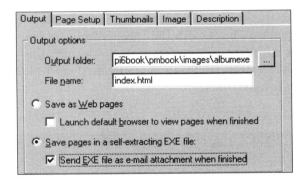

18. Click OK to save the album as a self-extracting .EXE file. PhotoImpact 6 will launch a new email message window for your default email client automatically. Address the email to your own email address and type in a subject line. Note that the .EXE file has been included as an attachment (UleadWeb.EXE), and that it is 213 kb.

PhotoImpact 6 Wizardry

19. Send the email to yourself now if you are online, or use your email client's option to send the email next time you go online.

Create and Send a Web Slide Show

1. The purpose of the following exercise is to use a series of four .BMP images to make a web slide show. When the slide show is created, the very large .BMP images will be converted to 640 X 480 compressed .JPG images.

2. Choose File, Export, Web Slide Show to open the Select Image dialog box. Click the Browse button to browse to the folder with the images for the slide show. Use the Browse button to navigate to and select the slideshow folder that contains slide1.bmp, slide2.bmp, slide3.bmp and slide4.bmp.

3. Click OK to open the Export to Web Slide Show dialog box. You will need to make choices from each of the three tabs. These choices will affect the appearance of the slide show. Start with the Output tab. For the Output folder, select the same folder, e.g., slideshow, that contains the four images. By default, this page will be named main.html. Leave the defaults of "Save as web pages" and "Launch default browser to view pages when finished" selected.

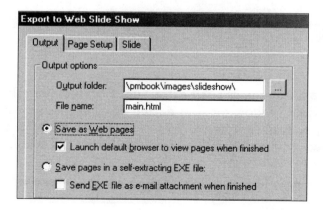

4. Click on the Page Setup tab next. Change the default heading and footer for the web slide show to My Bug Slide Show. Font, font size and color can be edited by clicking on the Format button next to heading or footer. Doing so will open the

Text Format dialog box. Change the heading and footer text color to white, then click OK to close the Text Format box.

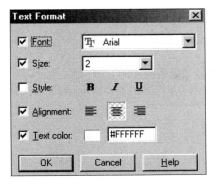

5. When returned to the Page Setup tab, select a page numbering method. For "Links Between Pages" select Buttons. These buttons will be created for you automatically.

6. To edit the web page background color or image, click Advanced. From the Advanced Page Settings dialog box. Edit the Background color to black, and choose harmonizing text and link colors. The Preview window shows how they will look. If you want to include a music file, browse to the one you wish to use. Click OK.

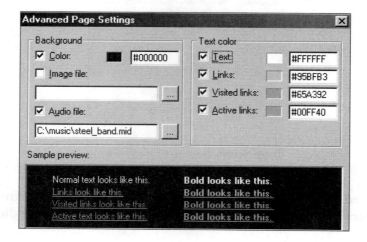

7. Click the Image tab. In the Image size section, limit the viewing size of the images to 640 X 480 pixels. Make sure that "Resize images" is selected. These .BMP images will be compressed as .JPG images for the web. Set the .JPG compression to 75%. Under "Time settings," deselect "Automatically advance to next page."

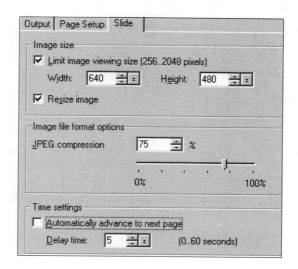

8. Now that all of the attributes for the web slide show have been selected, click Preview to check out the slide show before saving it. Your default browser will be launched to display the slide show. Click on the appropriate buttons to view the images, then close the browser. If you are not happy with the slide show the way it is, go back to the individual tabs and edit as desired.

9. When you are happy with the look of the slide show, click OK. It might take a moment or two for the slide show to be saved, then your default browser will open to run the slide show. When you are finished looking at it, close the browser.

10. Go to Windows Explorer to view the slideshow file to which you have saved the web slide show. You will see that in addition to the original images, PhotoImpact 6 has created a number of HTML pages (including one for the background sound if you have included one), and images for the slide show navigation buttons. An Images folder has been automatically created, as well. Click on the Images folder to view its contents, which include the .JPG versions of the four .BMP images used in the slide show.

11. When you upload the web slide show to your server so you can view it online, you will need to be careful to preserve the file structure created on your hard drive by PhotoImpact 6. Specifically, all of the files in the slide show main directory must be uploaded to the main directory on your server. You must create an Images directory on your server, if you do not already have one, and upload the Images files to this folder on your server. If you do not do so, your web slide show will not work.

12. Because the attributes of the slide show you have just created are "sticky," in the sense that they are still there until you create another slide show, now it is time to send yourself the slide show as a self-extracting .EXE file. Choose File, Export, Web Slide Show.

13. Doing so opens the Select Image dialog box. The next part is very important. From the Type dropdown list, select .BMP, .RLE and .UPI file types only. If you do not, every image added to the folder when the slide show was created, including the navigation buttons, will appear as images in the new .EXE slide show. Click OK.

14. When the Export to Web Slide Show dialog box opens, from the Output tab, change the Output folder to slideshow. Change the Output options to "Save pages in a self-extracting EXE file," and "Send EXE file as an email attachment when finished."

15. Click OK to save the slide show as a self-extracting .EXE file. PhotoImpact 6 will launch a new email message window for your default email client automatically. Address the email to your own email address and type in a subject line. Note that the .EXE file has been included as an attachment (UleadWeb.EXE), and that it is 197 kb.

```
To:      stephanie@eastofthesun.com
Cc:
Bcc:
Subject: My Bug Slide Show
Attach:  UleadWeb.exe (197 KB)
```

16. Send the email to yourself now if you are online, or use your email client's option to send the email next time you go online.

Print Preview and Printing

1. Often photos, particularly digital photos, need a little work to help them look their best for printing. The purpose of this exercise is to open a large digital photo, color correct it with a preset tone map, then increase its resolution so that it can be printed successfully on a single page.

2. Hit Ctrl+O to access the Open dialog box. Browse to caterpillar.bmp and select it. Choose "Open as Read-only" and click Open.

3. As you can see, this is a very large photo, 1600 X 1200 pixels. It has good detail and is well focused, but it is a bit too dark. It is not a good candidate for printing in its current state, as it is too big to be printed on a single sheet of paper. To prove it to yourself, choose File, Print Preview. Only the top left corner of the image will show in the Preview window. If you were to print it as it is now, you would print out only the portion of the photo visible in Print Preview. Click Close to return to the work space.

4. First you will change the resolution so that the printed image will fit on the page. Choose Format, Resolution to open the Resolution dialog box. Note that the current resolution is 72 dpi. In the "New resolution" section, select "User defined," changing the pixels per inch to 300. From the Preview dropdown list, choose

Printer Portrait. Note by looking at the Printer Portrait preview that the image at its new resolution will fit entirely on a printed page. Click OK to close the box.

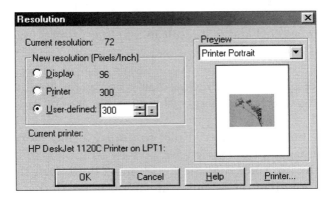

5. Because you have not yet reached the part of this book showing how to create tone maps, this exercise shows how to load one already created especially to correct this photo. Choose File, Print to open the Print dialog box.

6. Click the Options button to open the Options dialog box. Click the Calibration tab. All of the options will be grayed out at first. Deselect "Use printer's default" to access advanced options.

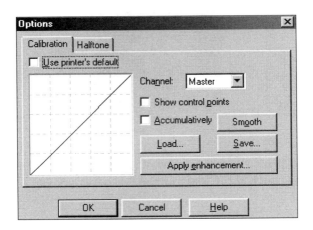

7. Click Load to open the Load Tone Map dialog box. Browse to tonemap1.MAP. Select it and click Open. Click OK to close the Load Tone Map box.

8. When you are returned to the Calibration tab in the Options dialog box, you will not notice any significant changes in the appearance of the photo. However, the tone map has been applied and will result in a lighter printed image with a more complete range of colors.

9. Click Preview to open the Print Preview dialog box again. By default, the image is aligned with the top and left corners of the printable area of the page.

10. Click on the View button and select Ruler to display a ruler along the left and top edges. Drag the image in the Preview window to position it so that it is at the 4 inch mark along the top ruler, and the 2 inch mark on the left side ruler. If you watch carefully as you drag the image, you will see a fine dotted line on the top and left side rulers which indicates the image's current horizontal and vertical position.

11. If you would like to print the image now, click the Print button. When the image has finished printing, click the Close button.

Customizing Preferences

1. Hit Ctrl+N to access the New dialog box. Create a new 300 X 300 RGB True Color image, single color, with a black canvas. Click OK.

2. Choose View, Guidelines & Grid, Grid or hit Ctrl+Shift+R to display gridlines. If your Preferences are currently set to the default of black gridlines, you will not see anything on your new black image.

3. Choose File, Preferences, General (or hit F6) to open the Preferences dialog box. Choose Guidelines & Grid. In the Grid section, edit the Horizontal and Vertical spacing to 25 pixels each. Click in the Color box and choose white. Select Dotted line from the Style dropdown list. Leave the Snap tolerance at the default value.

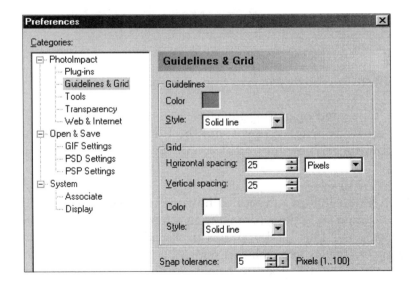

4. Click OK. A dotted white gridline should appear on the black image now. Now that you have changed the gridline color it will not show up well on a white or light color base image, so hit F6 to return to the Preferences box. Select Guidelines & Grid. Click in the Grid Color box again and select black.

5. While the Preferences dialog box is still open, click on PhotoImpact. Change the level of Undo to 4. You will get a warning box telling you how this will affect your ability to recapture edits. Just click OK.

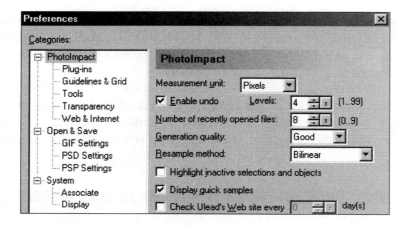

6. Hit Ctrl+Shift+R to remove the grid from the image.

7. Choose File, Open and open dragonfly.ufo. Use the Pick tool to drag the dragonfly object onto the black image. Copy it into the Clipboard, then paste it back into the base image four times. Now hit Ctrl+X to cut the active the object out of the base image.

8. Choose Edit, Undo Before and look at how many actions you can Undo. Although you have performed six actions (dragging in a new object, pasting it four times, cutting it once), only four Undo options are listed, because that is how you have set your Preferences. This is important to remember when you are performing extensive image editing. It does little good to be able to Undo if your Undo level is set too low. Similarly, a too-high Undo level will tax your system resources, particularly if you are working with resource-intensive .UFO objects.

9. To return to a reasonable Undo level, hit F6 to reopen the Preferences dialog box. Click PhotoImpact. Edit the Undo level to 10 (or higher, depending on resources).

Controlling Image Viewing and Customizing the Work Space

1. Choose File, Open to access the Open dialog box. Select catonroof.bmp and click Open.

2. Look at the image's blue title bar. The name of the image is displayed, as well as its current magnification and size in pixels (1600 X 1200 pixels). Only limited information is displayed. For example, if you wanted to apply a Creative Effect menu command to this image, you might want to make sure that it is an RGB True Color first.

3. To find out more about the image, choose View, Photo Properties to open its dialog box. Note that the Attributes section reveals that this is an RGB True Color image, its height and width in pixels, resolution and file size. In the File section, the file name, complete with the full path to the image, is displayed. Also revealed is the file type and file size.

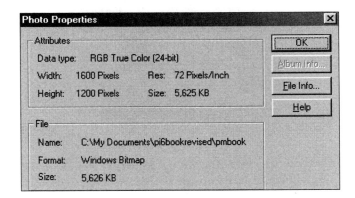

4. Click on the File information button to open a secondary dialog box that reveals additional information, namely that this is an uncompressed image. Click OK to close the box, then click OK again to close the Photo Properties box.

5. Since this image is displayed at a magnification which permits it all to fit into the work space, you are viewing it at less than actual size. Choose View, Actual Size, or hit Ctrl+0, to display the image at actual size within its window. The window will expand to fill the entire work space. You can no longer see the entire image at once.

6. Press and hold down on the Global Viewer icon in the lower right corner of the image window. This icon only appears when the image at its current magnification cannot fit completely in the window.

7. A small Global Viewer window opens when you press and hold down on its icon. If you just click it, nothing will happen. Inside the Global Viewer is a bounding box. Without releasing the mouse, drag on the bounding box to move the area contained within the bounding box into view in the image window.

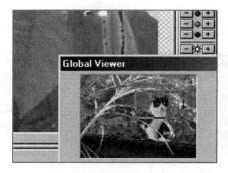

8. Choose View, Full Screen to view the image at actual size, displayed on an empty screen. Do not panic because you cannot see the work space. Click Escape to return to the work space and normal viewing.

9. Choose View, Zoom, 25% to view the image at a much smaller magnification. Note that you can also Zoom In and Zoom Out by using the Zoom tool in the tool panel, or by selecting an option from the Zoom dropdown list in the upper right corner of the menu bar.

10. Choose View, Toolbars & Panels, Options to open the Options dialog box. Select the following options: EasyPalette, Quick Command Panel and the Selection Tools toolbar. The latter will appear in the area at the top of the work space. This makes it possible for you to choose a Selection tool without having to use the slide out tool

panel to select one.

11. This Selection Tool panel does not have to stay where it is. Move it by dragging it to just below the Bucket fill tool on the lower left side of the work space.

12. Close out the catonroof.bmp image. Hit Ctrl+O to access the Open dialog box. Browse to skateboy.jpg, select it and click Open.

13. In the Quick Command Panel, which you just accessed, click on the "Show all existing tasks" down arrow and select Painting On The Wall. This task creates an amazingly lifelike framed picture hung on a wood paneled wall, complete with a spotlight. As dramatic as its effect is, however, the task adds 300 pixels on all sides of the frame, creating a very large image.

14. This can be edited, however. Deselect the preset from "Expand canvas." Doing so will stop the task at that point, so you can edit the amount of space around the framed picture.

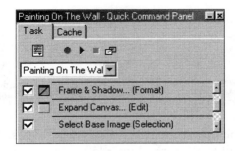

15. Click Play. The task will begin playing. When it reaches the point at which extra canvas is added, the task will stop playing and the Expand Canvas dialog box will open. Select "Expand sides equally" and change the value to 100. Click OK to continue playing the task.

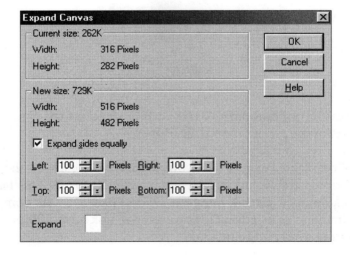

16. Note the rich look of the framed image. Want to give it a pop art look? Select the Pointilize Effect task from the dropdown list and click Play. The framed picture will look quite different when the task has played completely.

Section 2: Working With Selections

PhotoImpact 6 offers an efficient array of selection tools and menu commands that permit you to isolate, or select, a portion of an image for editing. As you gain experience in working with photos and web images, you will likely appreciate the idea of making and editing selections more and more. For example, you might want to select an uninteresting outdoor background in a photo and fill it with an exciting gradient fill, add a lens flare or lightning effect, or replace it with a Parisian street scene image. Similarly, you might want to select a person from one image and paste him or her into another image.

To take advantage of this kind of image editing magic, you must learn how to use the Selection tools to make and crop selections, and to work with menu commands specific to selections.

Making and Cropping Selections discusses in detail the four basic selection tools available in PhotoImpact 6: The Standard, Lasso, Magic Wand and Bezier Curve. You will learn how to use each one of the Selection tools to make selections from different kinds of images. This section also discusses how to specify a Selection tool's characteristics via the Attributes toolbar, including how to create lovely, softened edges. This chapter also explores the new Crop tool, which lets you select, resize and crop a selection with one handy tool. Selections made with the Crop tool can include the base image, objects only, or both base image and objects.

The Selection Menu details how these commands are used to manipulate selections in a variety of useful ways. Once a selection has been made, you can fill it, add a border, soften its edge, invert it, import and export it, convert the selection to an object, and perform other useful tasks specific to editing selections.

Active Learning Exercises Standard Selection tool; Lasso Selection tool; Magic Wand Selection tool, Bezier Curve Selection tool; Cropping with the Crop Tool; Import a Selection.

Chapter 4: Making and Cropping Selections

Make a selection when you wish to edit part of an image or crop it. A static broken line appears around a selection area. Only one selection area can be active at a time. Although a selection can be edited without affecting the rest of the image, it remains part of the original image. Selections can be moved and they can be reshaped with the Transform tool.

There are four Selection tools: the Standard (arrow), the Lasso, the Magic Wand and the Bezier curve. The icon for the chosen Selection tool appears on the button in the tool bar. To access the Selection tools, position the cursor over the button, then press and hold down on the mouse button until the tool tray slides out. Alternatively, click on the tiny blue triangle in the lower right corner of the button.

If you use Selection tools often, and most people do, consider taking advantage of the new toolbar customization capabilities. No longer do you have to keep clicking the Selection tool button and switching from one Selection tool to the other. Simple choose View, Toolbars & Panels, Selection Tool and they can be accessed at the bottom of the Toolbar, just under the Bucket fill tool button. Other tools from the Toolbar can be displayed in this manner as well, via "floating," dockable tool button panels.

Keyboard shortcuts provide a way to add to or subtract from an existing selection. Press down on the letter A as you select, and the latest selection will be added. To subtract part of a selection, press down on the letter S to remove the selected area. You can modify selections with the appropriate Mode options in the Attributes toolbar, too.

Standard

The easiest and quickest way to make a selection. Edit from the Attributes toolbar.

Mode

Choose from "Make a new selection," "Change an existing selection by addition," or "Change an existing selection by subtracting."

Shape

Choose a shape for the selection (Rectangle, Square, Ellipse, Circle) from the dropdown list. To make a freehand selection of a specific size, position the cursor in the extreme upper left corner of the base image until the coordinates in the status bar at the bottom left of the screen are 0,0. Press and hold down on the mouse button while dragging down and to the right. When the coordinates change to the size of the selection desired, release the mouse button.

Fixed size (in pixels)

Select to make a selection of a specific width and height in pixels. Click in the base image and the fixed size selection will appear.

Soft edge

Specify a Soft edge of 1-150 pixels. Be careful not to soften an edge by more pixels than there are left over between the edge of the selection and the edge of the image. If there are only 5 pixels between the edge of the selection and the edge of the image, and you soften by 20 pixels, you will get a hard, ugly line along the softened edge.

Chapter 4: Making and Cropping Selections

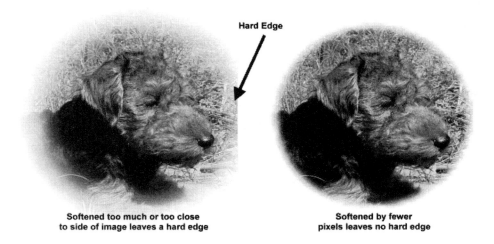

Softened too much or too close to side of image leaves a hard edge

Softened by fewer pixels leaves no hard edge

If you forget to select a soft edge in the Attributes toolbar before making the selection, right click on the selection and choose Soften. Doing so opens the Soften dialog box.

Enter a value for the Soft edge, from 1 to 150 pixels, then click OK.

Options

Click on the Options button to access. It is a good idea to leave Preserve Base Image and Move Selection Marquee selected.

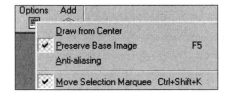

125

Draw From Center Available only for the Standard Selection tool, creates a Selection starting at the center and moving outward.

Preserve Base Image (F5) Allows you to move a Selection without affecting the underlying base image.

Anti-aliasing Smoothes the edges of a selection.

Move Selection Marquee (Ctrl+Shift+K) Preserves the base image when a selection is moved. If a selection is moved when deselected, the base image is filled with the current background color, leaving a "hole" in the image. You may wish to leave Preserve Background Image selected unless you want a hole in your base image.

Lasso

The Lasso Selection tool is useful for selecting an irregularly shaped object from a background, like the flower selected from the image below.

There are two ways to use the Lasso selection tool. The first method is to press and hold down on the mouse button while dragging continuously along the edges of an object. This method works best when you are selecting from an image with strong contrast. The second method is to click the mouse button, drag a short distance and click, drag again and click, etc. until you have a series of lines that are all connected to each other. Regardless of which method you use, you must double click the mouse button to finish the selection.

Specify characteristics of the Lasso Selection tool in the Attributes toolbar.

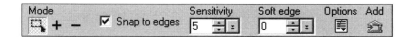

Mode

Choose from "Make a new selection," "Change an existing selection by addition," or "Change an existing selection by subtracting."

Snap to Edges

Snap to Edges can help you obtain a more accurate selection when there is a great deal of contrast between the background and the part of the image you wish to select. Sensitivity of the "snap" can be set from 1-10. Experimentation may be necessary to find the best Sensitivity for a particular selection.

Soft edge

Specify a Soft edge of 1-150 pixels.

Options

Click on the Options button to access. It is a good idea to leave Preserve Base Image (F5) and Move Selection Marquee selected.

> **Preserve Base Image** Allows you to move a Selection without affecting the underlying base image.
>
> **Anti-aliasing** Smoothes the edges of a selection.
>
> **Move Selection Marquee (Ctrl+Shift+K)** Preserves the base image when a Selection is moved. If a Selection is moved when deselected, the base image is filled with the current background color, leaving a "hole" in the image. Leave Preserve Background Image selected unless you have a specific reason not to do so.

Magic Wand

The Magic Wand selects pixels by Similarity in color. It it most useful for selecting part of an image containing few or strongly contrasting colors. Sometimes it is easiest to use the Magic Wand Selection tool to select a simple background, then Invert the selection to select a more complex object of central focus, as shown below.

Set the basic characteristics for the Magic Wand Selection in the Attributes toolbar.

Mode

Choose from "Make a new selection," "Change an existing selection by addition," or "Change an existing selection by subtracting."

Similarity

Enter a Similarity value to determine the range of colors to be included in the Selection. If Similarity is set to 99%, nearly every color pixel in an image will be selected. If Similarity is set at 10%, you may not get enough of a selection. Often you will have to experiment with Similarity to get the best result.

Select by Line/Area

Choose Line to select while dragging the mouse over an area in the base image. Choose Area to select only color pixels in the area where you click the mouse.

Search Connected Pixels

Selects similar color pixels adjacent to the selection area only. Pixels falling within the range that are not immediately adjacent to the selection area will not be selected.

Options

Click on the Options button to access. It is a good idea to leave Preserve Base Image and Move Selection Marquee selected.

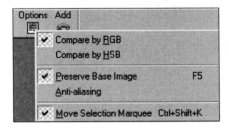

Compare by RGB Selects colors based on Similarity of their RGB values.

Compare by HSB Selects colors based on Similarity of the HSB domain.

Preserve Base Image (F5) Allows you to move a Selection without affecting the underlying base image.

Anti-aliasing Smoothes the edges of a selection.

Move Selection Marquee (Ctrl+Shift+K) Preserves the base image when a Selection is moved. If a Selection is moved when deselected, the base image is filled with the current background color, leaving a "hole" in the image. Leave Preserve Background Image selected unless you have a specific reason not to do so.

Bezier Curve

The Bezier Curve Selection tool creates both an editable path (surrounded by square control points) *and* a selection, depending on how the "Toggle" switch is set in the Attributes toolbar. The selection can be of a preset shape or done freehand. A freehand Bezier Curve selection was made to select this irregularly shaped dog from the background. Note that in Path mode the selected object is surrounded by square control points, while when in Selection mode the familiar broken line appears around the selection.

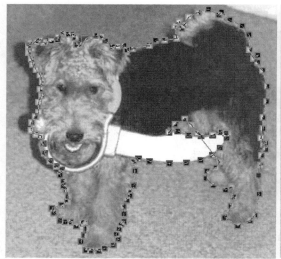
Bezier Curve Selection in Path Mode

Bezier Curve Selection in Selection Mode

Specify characteristics of the Bezier Curve Selection tool in the Attributes toolbar. Make note that some of the attributes shown in the attribute bar below will be grayed out, depending on Toggle and Mode status.

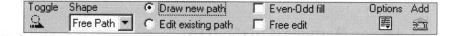

Toggle

Select or deselect to toggle from Path to Selection mode. To edit a Bezier Curve-created selection area, make sure that you have toggled into Path mode. To edit an existing path, select "Edit existing path" in the Attributes toolbar and drag on a control point to edit the path. To add to the selection, choose "Draw a new path" and continue selecting.

If you try to copy a Bezier Curve-created path into the Clipboard, or try to fill it with the Fill tool, nothing will happen until you click on the Toggle button to move into Selection mode. In Selection mode, you can copy and paste the selection into another image, fill it, or apply Creative, Magic and other effects.

Shape

Choose a shape (Rectangle, Square, Ellipse, Circle, Free Path) from the dropdown list. Free Path can be used to "cut out" an irregularly shaped object from a background. To use the Freehand option, click in the base image and drag, click and drag again, repeating until the desired shape has been created. Double click to close the path.

Draw a New Path

By default, Draw a New Path is selected. Choose Draw a New Path if you are in Edit exiting path mode and you wish to add another path.

Edit Existing Path

To edit a path of a preset shape, make sure the Toggle button is in Path (not Selection) mode and that Edit existing path is selected. Position the cursor over a control point along the path until it turns into an arrow with a small black box to the right. Click on a control point to display smaller squares at the ends of "handles" that you can drag to reshape the curve of a path, or simply drag on a control point to move it.

Even-Odd Fill

When there are two or more overlapping paths/selections, this option fills every other part of their combined areas with a selected color or texture fill.

Free edit

Free edit is only available when the Toggle switch is in Path mode. When Free edit is selected, the angle at which two lines meet in a control point can be changed. Deselecting Free edit preserves the angle and smooth edges of the path.

Options

Options are available only when the Bezier Curve Selection tool is in Path mode *and* Edit Existing Path has been selected. Some options are available only when there are multiple paths in the base image.

> **Group Path** Groups paths so that edits are applied to all groups at one time.
>
> **Ungroup Path** Ungroups grouped paths.
>
> **Delete** Deletes a path or segment of a path from the base image.
>
> **Duplicate** Creates a copy of the selected path.
>
> **Align left** Aligns selected paths on the left.
>
> **Align center** Aligns selected paths along the center of a vertical axis.
>
> **Align right** Aligns selected paths on the right.
>
> **Distribute horizontally** Distributes paths evenly along the horizontal axis.
>
> **Distribute vertically** Distributes paths evenly along the vertical axis.

Moving and Transforming Selections

Selections can be moved from one location in an image to another by dragging, provided "Move Selection Marquee" is selected from the Options choices in the Attributes toolbar and you are in "Make a new selection" mode.

Selections can be transformed too. After making a selection, choose the Transform tool, then select a Freely transform option from those available in the Attributes toolbar. Being able to resize a selection is very handy. If your first attempt at a selection is not accurate, you can make it larger or smaller, distort the selection's shape and even rotate the selection, if necessary, to select exactly the area in which you are interested.

Cropping Selections

No longer is it necessary to use one tool to make a selection and another to crop. The new Crop tool in PhotoImpact 6 makes it a snap to make and resize rectangular selections with the same tool. Selections can include objects within the base image as well.

To crop an image, select the Crop tool. Drag a selection within the image. When you release the mouse button, a selection marquee (broken line) with control handles surrounds the selection. Note that in the screen shot below, there are three round object "thought bubbles," the largest of which contains a text object question mark. The selection marquee will include these independent objects.

The Attributes toolbar, shown below, reveals information about the selection, including its X,Y coordinates within the base image and selection crop box size.

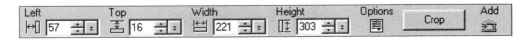

Left Displays in pixels the amount of space from the left side of the image.

Top Displays in pixels the amount of space from the top of the image.

Width Shows the width of the crop box, in pixels.

Height Shows the height of the crop box, in pixels.

Enter different values for Left, Top, Width or Height, or use the up and down arrows.

To crop the selection area and any objects within it, double click, hit Enter or click the Crop button. The objects within the selection will be retained, independent of the base image. However, if you wish to resize the selection before cropping it, drag on the control handles as desired, then hit Enter or click the Crop button. If you wish to otherwise tweak the selection, choose additional options from the Attributes toolbar.

Options Displays a menu of cropping options.

Selection and all objects The crop includes all of the base image and all of the objects within the selection area.

Active selection object(s) The crop includes all of the base image and the currently selected object(s) within the selection area. This option will be grayed out if there are no active objects selected when the crop is made. In this screen shot, the question mark was the active object and the "Active selection object(s)" option was chosen. Note that hitting Crop results in the crop including only the question mark object.

Entire image The crop includes the entire image.

Clear Removes the cropping selection marquee.

Remember that the Crop tool only works for rectangular selections. If you make an elliptical selection, then choose the Crop tool and hit Enter or Crop, you will still end up with a rectangular selection.

PhotoImpact 6 Wizardry

Chapter 5: The Selection Menu

Often only part of an image is selected for editing. Selection menu commands include an array of manipulations specific to the editing of these selections. With Selection commands you can Invert a selection, deactivate a selection (or object) and select the base image, Expand or Shrink a selection, add a Border, Soften a selection to create a vignette effect, Convert to Object, Import and Export a selection, or add it to the EasyPalette. Many of these commands are also available by right clicking on a selection.

Select Base Image (Space Bar)

Deactivates an active selection or object, making the base image active. When the base image is selected, it can be filled in any number of ways, without affecting the object(s) in the base image. In the example shown below, an image object is shown while it is active, then shown after Select Base Image was invoked and the background filled with a texture from the Fill Gallery.

Object selected **Base image selected and filled**

Select Previous Selection

Reselects a previous selection area after you have made another selection in the base image.

None

Deactivates all selections.

All (Ctrl+A)

Selects the entire image.

Invert

Inverts or reverses a selection area. This is helpful when you are trying to select a part of an image from the background.

Sunflower Selected   Selection Inverted, Background Selected

As you can see in the example above, it can be easier to select similarly colored parts of an image first, then Invert the selection to select an area of interest.

Border

Adds a border around a selection. The border can be filled with a texture, a color or effect.

Chapter 5: The Selection Menu

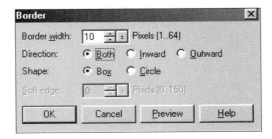

Border width From 1-64 pixels.

Direction Choose to have the border include area Inside the selection, Outside the selection or Both inside and outside.

Shape Select a Box shape (retains a hard edge) or a Circle shape (rounds the edges of the selection area).

Soft edge Create a soft edge from 1-150 pixels, if desired.

In the example shown below, a border was added to the selection, then the border was filled with a contrasting texture from the Fill Gallery.

Expand/Shrink

Enlarge or reduce the size of a selection area.

139

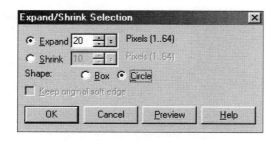

Expand/Shrink Choose to make the selection larger or smaller.

Pixels Enter a value from 1-64 pixels.

Shape Select a Box shape (retains a hard edge) or a Circle shape (rounds the edges of the selection).

Keep original soft edge If the selection already had a soft edge, select to keep it soft. If the selection did not have a soft edge, this option will be grayed out.

Similar

Expands a selection area by a value specified in the Color Similarity box.

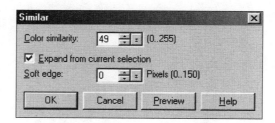

Color similarity Enter a value from 1-255, with higher values selecting increasingly more outside of the current selection area.

Expand from current selection Includes all pixels in the image falling into the Similarity range. Deselection limits the expansion of the selection to only those pixels in the appropriate range that are in contact with currently selected pixels.

Soft edge Softens the edge of the selection from 0-150 pixels.

Soften

Softens the perimeter of a selection, from 1-150 pixels, creating a soft, feathered edge.

Softened edges on elliptical selections can result in a lovely, vignette effect, or help a selection to blend in better with a textured background. Shown below is a selection, and the same selection with a softened edge.

Selection   Softened Selection

Convert to Object (Ctrl+Shift+O)

Converts a selection to an object.

Preserve Base Image (F5)

Leaves the base image unchanged when a selection is moved. If deselected, the base

141

image will be filled with the current background color when the selection is moved. Unless you want to create a "hole" in the image, it is best to leave Preserve Base Image selected. Note that for early copies of PhotoImpact 6, Preserve Base Image is "on" even if this option is deselected.

Import Selection

Permits you to use a grayscale or black and white image as a mask. Lighter areas of the Imported selection are more transparent, and darker areas are less transparent.

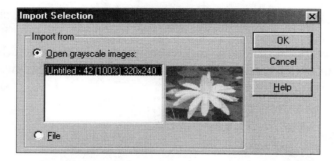

Open image Select a grayscale or black and white image currently open in the work space. For example, you might create a new grayscale copy of a True Color image, then Import the grayscale copy as a mask to selectively apply a gradient fill.

File Choose to Import a grayscale or black and white image from your hard drive. Select File and click OK to access the Open dialog box. Browse your hard drive for the file you wish to Import and click OK.

Export Selection

Creates a grayscale version of the selection area.

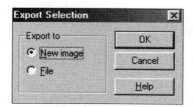

New image Generates a new grayscale image from the selection area in the work space.

File Opens the Save As dialog box, so that the new grayscale image can be saved to a folder on your hard drive.

Copy Selection to Object Library

When selected, opens the Add to EasyPalette dialog box.

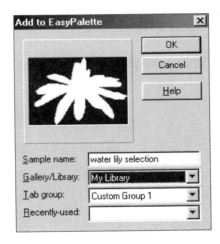

Give the selection a name and save it to My Library. The next time you want to use the selection, just drag and drop it from the EasyPalette onto the image, or double click the thumbnail. You will see the broken line indicating an active selection on the image after doing so.

143

Working With Selections: Active Learning Exercises

Standard Selection Tool

1. The purpose of this exercise is to demonstrate how to make and modify selections with the Standard selection tool.

2. Choose File, Open. Browse to the swingset.bmp file and select "Open as Read-only." Click Open.

3. Choose the Standard selection tool. In the Attributes toolbar, choose "Make a new selection" from the Mode options. Select Rectangle from the Shape dropdown list. Make sure that "Fixed size" is deselected and that Soft edge=0.

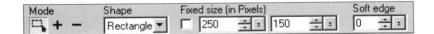

4. Draw a selection that encompasses both girls on the swing.

5. Choose Selection, Border (or right click, Border) to open the Border dialog box. Add a 10 pixel border to the selection, Direction=Both, Shape=Box, Soft edge=0.

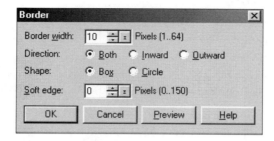

6. You will see a border around the selection. Use the Quick Color Controls on the right side of the work space to lighten the border. Click the "sun" key's plus (+) sign 8 times to lighten the border selection. It will be much lighter.

7. Hit Ctrl+R to crop the image down to the lightened border. Click in the base image to deactivate the border. The broken line signifying an active selection will disappear.

8. To add a little extra polish, choose Edit, Expand Canvas. When the Expand Canvas dialog box opens, select "Expand sides equally" to expand by 3 pixels on all sides. Do not click OK yet. Right click in the Expand color box and choose Eyedropper.

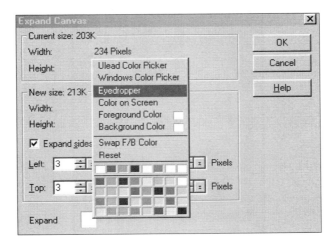

9. When the Eyedropper dialog box opens, move the cursor into the Preview window. Click on the dark red rope holding up the swing with the Eyedropper, selecting a color directly from the image.

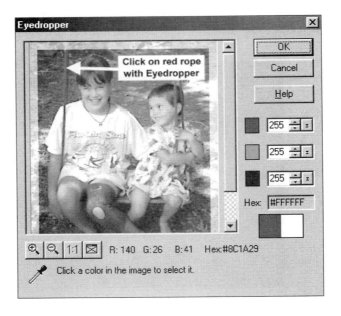

10. Click OK to close the Eyedropper box. Click OK again. Now the image has a faded border and a bright band of harmonizing dark red, creating an instant "frame."

11. Choose Edit, Undo Before, Create New Selection (seven prior edits). If your Undo level is not high enough to go back that far, close the image out and re-open it.

12. In the Attributes toolbar, select Ellipse from the Shape dropdown list. Make a rounded selection to include most of the girls sitting on the swing.

13. Right click on the selection and choose Soften. In the Soften dialog box, soften the edge by 10 pixels and click OK.

14. You will not see much difference if you look at the image, but a softened edge has been created. To view it, right click on the selection and choose Convert to Object. Drag the selection into an empty area in the work space, where it will open in its own window. Right click and Merge. The selection has a lovely, vignette soft edge.

Lasso Selection Tool

1. The purpose of this exercise is to learn how to use the Lasso to select around the edges of an irregularly shaped flower. Because the contrast between the flower and the water in the background is fairly good, the flower is a good candidate for a Lasso selection.

2. Hit Ctrl+O to access the Open dialog box. Browse to purplelily.jpg and select "Open as Read-only." Click Open.

3. This large image cannot be shown at actual size in its window. Choose View, Actual View, or hit Ctrl+0. Now you can navigate around in the image by dragging on the vertical and horizontal scroll bars, or by pressing and holding down on the Global Viewer icon to access the Global Viewer. Whichever method you use, you will want the top of the flower to show. The bottom petal, which extends downward and is cut off at the bottom of the picture, will not show in its entirety.

4. Choose the Lasso selection tool. In the Attributes toolbar, choose "Make a new selection" for the Mode. Select "Snap to edges" and set the Sensitivity to 10, which is the highest level. The Soft edge should be 0.

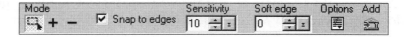

5. Make a selection by dragging slowly and carefully along the edges of the flower. You can do this either of two ways: by clicking, dragging and clicking to make connecting lines, or by dragging around the entire top of the flower without releasing the mouse button. With either method you must double click to close the selection. Try both methods to see which one works best for you. Do not worry if you make a mistake, you can correct it later. When you are finished, the top of the flower will be selected.

6. In the Attributes toolbar, change the Mode to "Change an existing selection by addition." This will allow you to add the bottom petal to the selection. Scroll down so that the bottom petal is showing. Start at the bottom of the previous selection

and drag around the bottom petal. Double click to finish the selection. You should have the entire flower selected now.

7. Take a good look at your selection. If you need to add to the selection anywhere, while still in "Change an existing selection by addition" Mode, add to the selection. If you have included some of the background by mistake in the selection, change the Mode to "Change an existing selection by subtraction" and deselect the portion that does not belong there. Fine tune the selection until you are satisfied with it. Change the Mode back to "Make a new selection."

8. It is almost impossible to get every scrap of the background out of a selection. To doctor the selection a bit, choose Selection, Expand/Shrink (or right click, Expand/Shrink). When the Expand Shrink dialog box opens, Shrink the selection by 2 pixels, Shape=Circle (because this is a rounded flower). Since you did not create a soft edge while making the selection, "Keep original soft edge" will be grayed out. Click OK to shrink the selection.

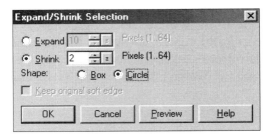

9. Right click on the selection and choose Convert to Object. To make the background invisible while further refining the selection, choose View, and deselect "Show Base Image" (or hit F5). The background will be replaced by a checkerboard pattern indicating a transparent background.

10. Select the ![icon] Object Paint Eraser tool. In the Attributes toolbar, set the size to 10, Transparency=0 and Soft edge=10. Zoom in if you need to, to see what you are doing. Go around the edges of the flower with the Eraser to clean up the edges. You may need to make the size smaller (e.g., 5 or so) to get into the corners. If you make a mistake, right click and Undo or click the Recover button to return an erased area to the selection.

11. Refine the edges of the flower with the Eraser. Switch back to the Standard selection tool and drag the flower object to an empty area in the work space, where it will open in its own window. It should look clean and smooth-edged. If it does not, work on it some more with the Object Paint Eraser tool until it looks good.

12. Now that you have done all the work of selecting it, save it to your EasyPalette so that you can use it again in the future. Switch to the Standard selection tool and drag the flower object to the EasyPalette. Doing so will open the Add to EasyPalette dialog box. Name the object Water Lily and save it to My Library. Click OK to close the box.

13. Take a look at My Library in your EasyPalette. You will see a thumbnail for Water Lily.

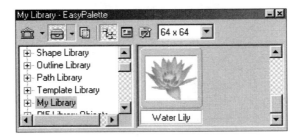

14. Drag from the thumbnail into an empty area in the work space. A fresh copy of the object will open in its own window. Close it out without saving it. If you do not want to keep the object in the EasyPalette, right click on its thumbnail and choose Delete. You will be asked if you really want to delete the object. Choose "Yes" and the thumbnail will be removed from the EasyPalette.

Magic Wand Selection

1. The purpose of this exercise is to learn several different ways to make a Magic Wand selection. You will select the sky in a photo taken at a sunny beach and fill it with wispy fog to create a slightly different mood.

2. Choose File, Open and browse to pilings.bmp. Select "Open as Read-only" and click Open.

3. Choose the Magic Wand selection tool. In the Attributes toolbar, select "Change an existing selection by addition." For "Select by" choose Line. Set the Similarity to 10. This is a relatively low Similarity value, but since the sky appears to be solid blue a higher value may not be needed. Make sure "Search connected pixels" is selected, so that pixels adjacent to where you click will be selected too.

4. Click in the upper left corner of the image to begin selecting the sky. You will notice right away that the Similarity of 10 is not high enough to select the entire sky *if you just click in the background*.

5. Click in the area immediately to the right of the previously selected area. More of the sky will be selected, but there will still be places that are not included in the selection. Continue clicking in non-selected areas to include them. It is unlikely that you will get all of the sky selected in this manner. It is just too imprecise a method for selecting all of this sky. Right click and choose None to get rid of the selection, or hit the space bar.

6. Now try another method that *will* work at a Similarity value of 10. Starting in the upper left corner, drag a line across the sky and down to the lower right corner. You can see the line as you draw it in the image (see top of facing page).

Working With Selections: Active Learning Exercises

7. When you release the mouse button, the entire sky should be selected.

8. Choose Selection, None to get rid of the selection. In the Attributes toolbar, for "Select by" choose Area. Drag across from the upper left to the upper right corner.

PhotoImpact 6 Wizardry

9. When you release the mouse button, most of the sky will have been selected. You are likely to see small areas that were not selected. Right click and choose None.

10. Finally, there is a way to select the entire sky with one click by increasing the Similarity value. In the Attributes toolbar, set the Similarity to 49. Position the cursor in the center of the sky at the top of the image and click to select the sky.

11. Now that the sky has been selected, have some fun with it. Open the EasyPalette's Particle Library. Double click on Fog 2.

12. The sky will be filled with wispy white fog. Click the space bar to deactivate the selection and view the image with the fog added.

Bezier Curve Selection

1. The purpose of this exercise is to practice making Bezier Curve selections of an irregularly shaped object. You will learn to edit a preset shape and to make a selec-

156

tion freehand, as well as how to toggle in and out of path and selection mode.

2. Hit Ctrl+O to access the Open dialog box. Browse to pelican.bmp. Choose "Open as Read-only" and click Open.

3. Choose the Bezier Curve selection tool. In the Attributes toolbar, select Ellipse from the Shape dropdown list. Note that most of the options in the Attributes toolbar are grayed out at this point.

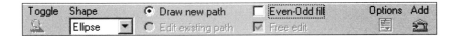

4. Draw an elliptical selection around the pelican. There are four, square red control points on the perimeter of the shape. Just as you can edit Path objects in PhotoImpact 6, you can edit Bezier Curve selection control points.

5. You will see that when you release the mouse button after making the selection, additional options appear in the Attributes toolbar. Select "Edit existing path" and "Free edit."

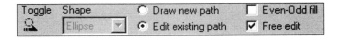

6. Click on the control point on the right side of the selection. Doing so displays two smaller squares which, when dragged, serve as a kind of "fulcrum" to reshape the curve of the path on either side of the control point. Simultaneously smaller squares for reshaping the curve to the right of the top and bottom control points appear.

7. Edit the upper small square just above the right side control point by dragging it toward the pelican's neck. You will see that the curve of the selection is reshaped.

8. Drag the lower small square down and to the right a bit to includes the tailfeathers. You may need to drag on the large control point itself to get a smooth curve.

9. Click on the top control point to select it. Now you have the little square fulcrums on both side of the selected control point. Drag the small right square on the right side of this control point toward the large control point and dip down slightly, to reshape the curve of the selection as shown.

10. Click on the left control point to select it and display the two small squares. Drag the large control point to the right, close to the pelican's bill. Drag the top small square above the control point upward and slightly to the right, to reshape the selection. Drag the bottom small square down and slightly to the right to mirror the curve on top.

11. Choose Edit and you will see that Cut and Copy are grayed out. You cannot perform these tasks when the Bezier Curve is in Path mode. The buttons in the menu bar for these commands is grayed out too. To get into Selection mode, click the

Toggle button in the Attributes toolbar. Choose Edit again and the Cut and Copy functions will be displayed now.

12. In the image, the Path boundaries will be replaced by the familiar broken line denoting a selection. Switch to the Standard selection tool. Right click on the selection and choose Soften. When the Soften dialog box opens, soften the edge of the selection by 15 pixels.

13. Right click on the selection and choose Convert to Object. Drag the newly created object to an empty area of the work space, where it will open in its own window. Right click and Merge. You have just created an irregularly shaped, softened selection which follows the contours of the pelican's shape.

14. Return to the original pelican image by clicking on the blue title bar. Click in the base image to make sure no active selections will interfere with the next selection exercise.

15. Choose the Bezier Curve selection tool again. In the Attributes toolbar, select Free Path from the Shape dropdown list. Click and drag around the basic shape of the pelican, leave space around it. Each click produces an editable control point. Double click to close the selection.

16. Choose View, Zoom, 200%. If you take a close look at the selection, you will see that all of the lines between the control points are perfectly straight. This can be OK along the pelican's bill, but not so good along the top of the head or around the front and back, or other curved areas. In the Attributes toolbar, click the Toggle button. Select "Edit existing path" and "Free edit."

17. When a selection is drawn freehand with the Bezier Curve, the Attributes toolbar options are different. The available options are the same ones you would see if you had drawn a path with the Path Drawing tool. In the "Edit point" section, make sure "Pick point" is selected, and that you are in "Free edit mode."

18. Find a straight line that should be curved. Click on the line to select it. Under "Convert line" in the Attributes toolbar, select the curved line option, "Convert path to curve segment." Doing so will turn the straight line into a curve. Edit the shape of this curve by clicking on a control point adjacent to it and dragging on the small squares at the ends of the "fulcrums," just as you did in the first Bezier Curve selection exercise.

19. Note that among the options in the Attributes toolbar in the "Edit point" section are "Add point" and "Delete point." You may use these to add or delete control points along the path. If you do use them, be careful to return to "Pick point" before attempting to edit a control point. Continue around your selection, selecting lines to turn them into lines or curves as needed, then editing them from their control points, until you have a selection which is a reasonable outline of the pelican's shape.

20. When you are satisfied with the Bezier Curve selection, click the Toggle button in the Attributes toolbar. Do not be alarmed when the selection is filled with a solid color. You have created a path object and PhotoImpact is treating it as such. It is no longer a selection.

21. Note that the Path Edit tool is selected, and you are in Path Edit mode. Click the Path Edit button in the Attributes toolbar to select the Path Drawing tool automatically. In the Attributes toolbar, choose Selection from the Mode dropdown list.

22. Now that you have your selection back, right click and choose "Convert to Object." Choose the Standard selection tool or the Pick tool to drag the object into an empty area of the work space, where it will open in its own window. Right click and Merge.

Cropping With the Crop Tool

1. The purpose of this exercise is to use the Crop tool to make and crop a rectangular selection in a very large photo of an egret surrounded by water at the beach.

2. Choose File, Open and browse to egret.bmp. Select it, choose "Open as Read-only" and click Open. This is a large image, too big to put online. While you could just resize it, doing so would lose a lot of detail. Cropping offers a better solution.

3. Select the Crop tool. Drag a large rectangular selection around the egret. The selection you make with the Crop tool will be surrounded by a Crop box with control handles.

4. The selection is a little large in proportion to the bird. Position your cursor over a control point until it turns into a double-headed arrow, then drag on the control point to resize the Crop box so it is better proportioned.

5. Take a look at the Attributes toolbar. The Left, Top, Width and Height values indicate the coordinates of the selection. While it is not important for this exercise, you could make a selection with these coordinates by simply entering the desired values into these boxes, without even having to drag a selection.

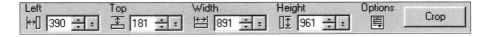

6. To crop the image, you have several options. Either click the Crop button in the Attributes toolbar, hit Ctrl+R or double click on any control handle. The area outside of the Crop box will be deleted, leaving only the egret selection. Hit Ctrl+0 to view the egret at actual size. Since the cropped image is still quite large and too big to fit into the image window at actual size, use the Global Viewer to move around in the image window to view the egret at full size.

Import a Selection

1. The purpose of this exercise is to Import a Grayscale mask based on a True Color image, in order to create a fantasy effect.

2. Hit Ctrl+O to access the Open dialog box. Navigate to the PhotoImpact 6 Samples folder. Select bridge.jpg and select "Open as Read-only."

3. In the task bar, click on the Image Type icon, which looks like a rainbow (arrow).

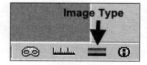

4. Make sure "Create a new image" is selected. Choose Grayscale (8 bit) from the data type choices. A new Grayscale version of the True Color image will open in the work space.

5. Click on the blue title bar of the True Color image to make it active. Choose Selection, Import Selection. Select Import from "Open grayscale images." The Grayscale version of the image will be selected.

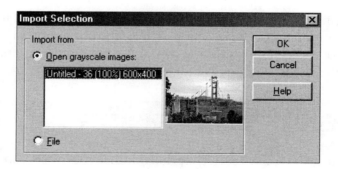

6. Click OK to close the Import Selection dialog box. Immediately you will see a selection appear on the True Color image. This selection represents the Grayscale mask you have just Imported onto the True Color image. If color is applied to the image now, the mask will affect how the color is applied to the image. Darker areas

in the Grayscale mask will block the color, and lighter areas, which represent greater transparency, will show the color.

7. To test this Grayscale mask, open the EasyPalette's Fill Gallery, Gradient. Double click on Rays 16 to apply this gradient to the masked image.

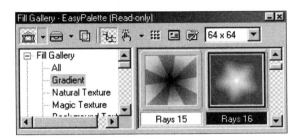

8. Click the space bar to deselect the selection. The gradient has created a dramatically different look for this image. Note how the dark areas such as the trees and the body of the bridge itself remain relatively untouched by the gradient fill, but the lighter areas such as the sky and water take on deeper tones of the gradient.

Section 3: Working With Objects

Simply put, an object is anything you add to an image without merging with the base image. There are three kinds of objects: Path, Text and Image objects. Creating and editing them is the focus of this section of the book.

The Path Tools focuses on the four Path tools: the Path Drawing tool, the Outline Drawing tool, the Line and Arrow tool and the Path Edit tool. It is very helpful to find out how to create Even-Odd fills, how to add and delete control points from paths, turn curved lines into straight lines (and vice versa), deform paths, create complex objects from multiple paths, change bevels, group paths and more.

The Text Tools will get you up to speed on adding text, including impressive 3D text with drop shadows. Explore new features like editing text spacing, kerning and shifting the text baseline. An improved Text Entry Box permits direct editing of font, color, font size and more. Critical distinctions between creating text for images versus creating HTML text for web pages are discussed too.

The Stamp Tool introduces playful Image object stamps, a fun new addition to PhotoImpact 6. Use the colorful stamps that ship with the program, or learn to make your own stamps by saving them as .UFO objects and importing them into your "stamp collection."

The Object Menu commands, in conjunction with the Pick tool, let you control the appearance, visibility and attributes of Path, Text and Image objects. Improved organization of the Object menu commands streamlines your workload by letting you add objects directly from your own files, Libraries or the Component Designer. You can even add HTML text to web page files. Once Path or Text objects have been created, you can bend, distort and wrap them in countless ways, or edit objects from the Object Properties Box, including assigning HTML properties to them.

The Transform Tool shows how to create interest by resizing, rotating, flipping and distorting objects with the Transform tool.

Object Eraser Tools discusses these great new tools: the Object Paint Eraser and the Object Magic Eraser, which make it easy to get rid of parts of objects that you do not need. The erasers only work on Image objects, so you must convert Path and Text objects to Image objects to be able to use them.

PhotoImpact 6 Wizardry

Active Learning Exercises Using the Pick Tool and Object Menu commands; Making Navigation Buttons; Making Complex Path Objects; Wrapping a Path Object Around a Path; Wrapping Text Along a Freehand Path; Bending a Path Object; Working with Image Objects; Making 3D Text; Making Your Own Stamps; Adding a Stamp.

Chapter 6: The Path Tools

PhotoImpact 6 features four unique Path tools: (1) the Path Drawing tool; (2) the Outline Drawing tool; (3) the Line and Arrow tool; and (4) the Path Edit tool. To access the Path tools, press and hold down on the Path tool button, or click on the tiny blue triangle in its lower right corner. Select a tool and its icon will appear on the button.

PhotoImpact 6 makes it is easier than ever before to edit path objects. Save time and mouse clicks by clicking on the Path Edit tool right in the Attributes toolbar. Remember, too, that you can customize the toolbar to display all four Path tools at the same time. Simply choose View, Toolbars & Panels, Path Tool Panel to display a floating toolbar which, as shown below (arrow), can be dragged to and docked in any convenient spot in the work space.

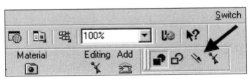

Path Drawing Tool

Set the basic characteristics for the path object from the Attributes toolbar.

Shape

Click on Shape to choose a preset shape (Rectangle, Square, Ellipse, Circle, Rounded Rectangle, Diamond), or select the new Spline tool, the Bezier/Polygon or a Custom Shape from the Custom Shape dialog box.

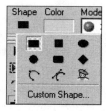

Preset Select a preset shape, then drag the shape in the base image.

Spline This fantastic new Path Drawing tool allows you the freedom to create path objects, including very complex ones, in literally any shape. Click to start a path then drag, then click and drag again. Each time you click, an editable path control point appears. As you drag from the control point, the path curves, depending on how far you drag the cursor. Double click to close a Spline path.

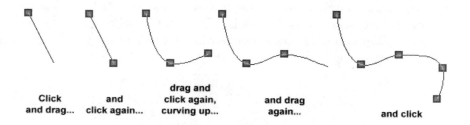

Click and drag... and click again... drag and click again, curving up... and drag again... and click

Bezier/Polygon Similar to the Spline tool, the Bezier/Polygon tool lets you draw freehand shapes, but all of the lines between the control points are straight. Click and drag to create editable control points. Double click to close a Bezier/Polygon path.

Custom Shape Select to open the Custom Shape dialog box. PhotoImpact 6 features some fantastic new shapes that look very much like dingbat fonts. These shapes lend themselves well to web graphics such as border backgrounds and buttons.

When Custom Shape is selected, the Custom Shape dialog box opens. Select a Custom Shape and click OK to draw a path with the shape.

> **Importing Custom Shapes** You can add your own Custom Shapes, but they must be of the .AI file type. However, you cannot create .AI files in

PhotoImpact. Fortunately, there are a number of inexpensive programs that will create .AI files. For example, Creature House Expression, Micrografx Windows Draw, and Mayura Draw are all popular among PhotoImpact users who make and share their .AI shapes with others online.

To Import new .AI shape files, from the Custom Shape dialog box click on the Import button. Doing so opens the Input AI File dialog box.

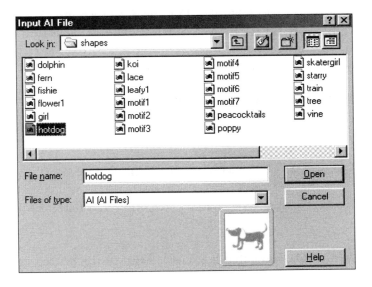

Browse to the .AI file you wish to Import. Select the file and click Open. The .AI file will be Imported. Its thumbnail will appear in the Custom Shapes dialog box (as well as the EasyPalette's Shape Library). Now select the newly Imported Custom Shape's thumbnail, click OK and draw the desired path shape. You will be able to edit this path shape just as you would any other path object.

Draw with the new Custom Shape

Color

Click in the Color box to select a color from among the Ulead Color Picker, the Windows Color Picker, the Eyedropper, Color on Screen, Foreground Color, Background Color, Swap Foreground/Background Color, Reset, a selection of the most recently used colors, standard colors, a Gradient Fill, Natural Texture or Magic Texture. From the Color box you can also select Fadeout.

Mode

For True Color images these include: 2D Object, 3D Round, 3D Chisel, 3D Trim, 3D Pipe, 3D Custom, Horizontal Deform, Vertical Deform, Selection and Continue Draw. Modes for 256 Indexed Color include: 2D Object, Horizontal Deform, Vertical Deform, Selection and Continue Draw.

2D Object The object is flat and two dimensional.

3D Round Creates a 3D object with a rounded bevel.

3D Chisel Creates a 3D object with a sharply chiseled bevel.

3D Trim Creates a 3D object via shading, resulting in a flatter look than other 3D modes.

3D Pipe Creates a 3D object that is hollowed out in the center, creating a rounded "donut" shape.

3D Custom Creates a 3D object with a variety of edge bevels. To select a custom 3D bevel, click on the Material button in the Attributes toolbar, then click on the Bevel tab to select one of five custom bevels.

Horizontal Deform Displays the object's horizontal path, including editable control points. Drag on the large square control points to deform the object. Drag on small squares at the end of "fulcrums" to reshape the curve of the path associated with a control point. When you are through editing the object's path, choose a 2D or 3D mode from the Mode dropdown list.

Vertical Deform Displays the object's vertical path, including editable control points. Drag on the large square control points to deform the object. Drag on small squares at the end of "fulcrums" to reshape the curve of the path associated with a control point.

When you are through editing the object's path, choose a 2D or 3D mode from the Mode dropdown list.

Selection Converts a path object into a selection area. This means that you can create Custom Shape or freehand objects, place them over an area of interest in an image, then turn the path object into a uniquely shaped selection by switching to Selection mode.

Continue Draw If you wish to draw two or more paths, select Continue Draw. Control points will appear around the path being drawn. If the path objects overlap, be sure to select or deselect Odd-Even Fill from Options to insure the desired result.

Options

Select or deselect options for the path object(s).

Galleries Select to display a submenu accessing the EasyPalette's Material, Deform and Wrap Galleries.

Even-Odd Fill Available only when in Continue Draw Mode, select to fill every other part of overlapping objects, or deselect to fill all objects uniformly. The complex object shown below was created with Even-Odd Fill selected.

Even-Odd Fill Selected

Shadow Opens the Shadow dialog box so you can add a shadow.

Split Shadow Available only after a shadow has been added, select to detach the shadow from its associated object.

Anti-aliasing Select to smooth the edges of a path object.

Border

The Border slider is somewhat different in PhotoImpact 6. Press and hold on the down arrow to display the Border slider, sliding the cursor to the little arrow and dragging it to increase or decrease the size of the border. Alternatively, enter a value directly into the Border box.

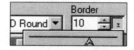

If you have selected a Radial Gradient Fill, editing the border size allows you to fit the entire gradient into the text. An interesting "outline" effect, can be achieved using this technique.

Depth

The Depth slider works like the Border slider. Press and hold on the down arrow to display the Depth slider, sliding the cursor to the little arrow and dragging it to increase or decrease its value. Positive values create a convex border, while negative values create a concave border. A depth of zero results in flat text with no border. Alternatively, enter a value directly into the Depth box.

Light

Repositions the focus of currently selected light attributes in the Material box. Move the cursor around, then click when you are satisfied with a light effect.

Material

Click on the Material button to open the Material dialog box, from which you may edit object attributes. The Material dialog box is discussed in detail in its own chapter.

Editing

Selects the Path Edit tool and toggles the object into Path Edit mode, making it faster and easier to edit Path objects.

Add

Opens the Add to EasyPalette dialog box, from which you may save object attributes. Give the preset a name and save it to to a Gallery and Tab group.

Outline Drawing Tool

Set the basic characteristics for the path object in the Attributes toolbar.

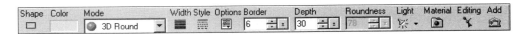

Shape

Click on Shape to choose a preset shape (Rectangle, Square, Ellipse, Circle, Rounded Rectangle, Diamond), or select the new Spline tool, the Bezier/Polygon or a Custom Shape from the Custom Shape dialog box.

Preset Select a preset shape, then drag the shape in the base image.

Spline This new Path Drawing tool gives you the freedom to create unique path objects, including very complex ones, to suit any need. Click to start a path then drag, then click and drag again. Each time you click, an editable path control point appears. As you drag from the control point, the path curves, depending on how far you drag the cursor. Hold down on the Ctrl key to make a straight line between control points. Double click to close a Spline path.

Bezier/Polygon Similar to the Spline tool, the Bezier/Polygon tool lets you draw freehand shapes, but all of the lines between the control points are straight. Click and drag to create editable control points. Double click to close a Bezier/Polygon path.

Custom Shape Select to open the Custom Shape dialog box.

PhotoImpact 6 Wizardry

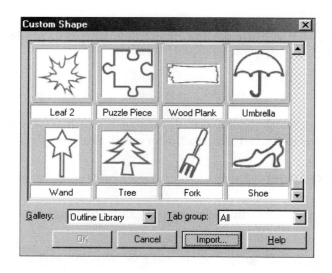

Although you may Import new Custom Shapes (.AI files) for use with the Outline Drawing tool, you can only Import solid filled objects. You cannot Import shapes which consist of multiple path objects (one with separate petals on a flower, for example).

Color

Click in the Color box to select a color from among the Ulead Color Picker, the Windows Color Picker, the Eyedropper, Color on Screen, Foreground Color, Background Color, Swap Foreground/Background Color, Reset, a selection of the most recently used colors, standard colors, a Gradient Fill, Natural Texture or Magic Texture. From the Color box you can also select Fadeout.

Mode

For True Color images these include: 2D Object, 3D Round, 3D Chisel, 3D Custom, Horizontal Deform, Vertical Deform, and Selection. Modes for 256 Indexed Color include: 2D, Horizontal Deform, Vertical Deform, Selection and Continue Draw.

2D Object The object is flat and two dimensional.

3D Round Creates a 3D object with a rounded bevel.

3D Chisel Creates a 3D object with a sharply chiseled bevel.

3D Custom Creates a 3D object with a variety of edge bevels. To select a custom 3D bevel, click on the Material button in the Attributes toolbar, then click on the Bevel tab to select one of five custom bevels.

Horizontal Deform Displays the outline object's horizontal path, including editable control points. Drag on the large square control points to deform the object. Drag on the smaller squares to reshape the curve of the path associated with a control point. When you are through editing the object's path, choose a 2D or 3D mode from the Mode dropdown list.

Vertical Deform Displays the outline object's vertical path, including editable control points. Drag on the large square control points to deform the object. Drag on the smaller squares to reshape the curve of the path associated with a control point. When you are through editing the object's path, choose a 2D or 3D mode from the Mode dropdown list.

Selection Converts an outline path object into a selection area.

Width

Select a line width in pixels (1-9) from the dropdown list.

Alternatively, click on More to access the Color and Line dialog box.

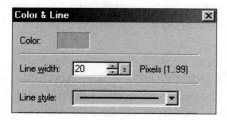

Style

Select a line style from the graphical representations in the dropdown list.

Options

Select or deselect options for the outline object.

Galleries Select to display the EasyPalette.

Shadow Opens the Shadow dialog box so you can add a shadow.

Split Shadow Available only after a shadow has been added, select to ungroup the shadow from its associated object.

Anti-aliasing Select to smooth the edges of an outline path object.

Border

The Border slider is somewhat different in PhotoImpact 6. Press and hold on the down arrow to display the Border slider, sliding the cursor to the little arrow and dragging it to increase or decrease the size of the border. Alternatively, enter a value directly into the Border box.

Depth

The Depth slider works like the Border slider. Press and hold on the down arrow to display the Depth slider, sliding the cursor to the little arrow and dragging it to increase or decrease its value. Positive values create a convex border, while negative values create a concave border. A depth of zero results in flat text with no border. Alternatively, enter a value directly into the Depth box.

Light

Repositions the focus of currently selected light attributes in the Material dialog box. Move the cursor around, then click when you are satisfied with a light effect.

Material

Click on the Material button to open the Material dialog box, from which you may edit object attributes. The Material dialog box is discussed in detail in its own chapter.

Editing

Selects the Path Edit tool and toggles the object into Path Edit mode, making it faster and easier to edit Path objects.

Add

Opens the Add to EasyPalette dialog box, from which you may save object attributes. Give the preset a name and save it to to a Gallery and Tab group.

Line and Arrow Tool

Set the basic characteristics for the line or arrow object in the Attributes toolbar.

Shape

Click in the Shape box to choose an arrow shape: Straight, Spline or Bezier/Polygon.

An example of each arrow shape is shown below.

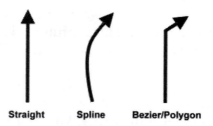

Straight Creates straight lines or arrows. Click to start and click to finish.

Spline Creates curved lines or arrows, similar to the Spline Path Drawing tool. Click to start, drag, then click. Drag again and curve the line or arrow in the desired direction while dragging. Editable control points appears as you click. Double click to finish the curved line or arrow.

Bezier/Polygon Click to start, then drag and click to create angled arrows consisting of joined straight lines. Double click to finish the angled line or arrow.

Color

Click in the Color box to select a color from among the Ulead Color Picker, the Windows Color Picker, the Eyedropper, Color on Screen, Foreground Color, Background Color, Swap Foreground/Background Color, Reset, a selection of the most recently used colors, standard colors, a Gradient Fill, Natural Texture or Magic Texture. From the Color box you can also select Fadeout.

Mode

For True Color images these include: 2D Object, 3D Round, 3D Chisel, 3D Custom, Horizontal Deform, Vertical Deform, and Selection. The Line and Arrow tool is not available for 256 Indexed Color images.

2D Object The line or arrow object is flat and two dimensional.

3D Round Creates a 3D object with a rounded bevel.

3D Chisel Creates a 3D object with a sharply chiseled bevel.

3D Custom Creates a 3D object with a variety of edge bevels. To select a custom 3D bevel, click on the Material button in the Attributes toolbar, then click on the Bevel tab to select one of five custom bevels.

Horizontal Deform Displays the line or arrow object's horizontal path, including editable control points. Drag on the large square control points to deform the object. Drag on the smaller squares to reshape the curve of the path associated with a control point. When you are through editing the object's path, choose a 2D or 3D mode from the Mode dropdown list.

Vertical Deform Displays the line or arrow object's vertical path, including editable control points. Drag on the large square control points to deform the object. Drag on the smaller squares to reshape the curve of the path associated with a control point. When you are through editing the object's path, choose a 2D or 3D mode from the Mode dropdown list.

Selection Converts a line or arrow path object into a selection area.

Width

Select a line width in pixels (1-9) from the dropdown list. Click More to access the Color & Line dialog box to edit other line or arrow attributes.

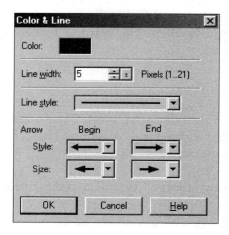

Style

Select a line style from the graphical representations in the dropdown list.

Arrow

Select an arrow style.

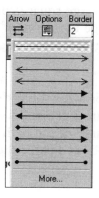

182

Options

Select or deselect options for the line or arrow object.

Galleries Select to display a submenu accessing the EasyPalette's Galleries.

Shadow Opens the Shadow dialog box so you can add a shadow.

Split Shadow Available only after a shadow has been added, select to ungroup the shadow from its associated object.

Anti-aliasing Select to smooth the edges of a line or arrow path object.

Border

The Border slider is somewhat different in PhotoImpact 6. Press and hold on the down arrow to display the Border slider, sliding the cursor to the little arrow and dragging it to increase or decrease the size of the border. Alternatively, enter a value directly into the Border box.

Depth

The Depth slider works like the Border slider. Press and hold on the down arrow to display the Depth slider, sliding the cursor to the little arrow and dragging it to increase or decrease its value. Positive values create a convex border, while negative values create a concave border. A depth of zero results in flat text with no border. Alternatively, enter a value directly into the Depth box.

Light

Repositions the focus of currently selected light attributes in the Material box. Move the cursor around, then click when you are satisfied with a light effect.

Material

Click on the Material button to open the Material dialog box, from which you may edit object attributes. The Material dialog box is discussed in detail in its own chapter.

Editing

Selects the Path Edit tool and toggles the object into Path Edit mode, making it faster and easier to edit Path objects.

Add

Opens the Add to EasyPalette dialog box, from which you may save line or arrow object attributes. Give the preset a name and save it to a Gallery and Tab group.

Path Edit Tool

Use the Path Edit tool to reshape any previously created path object, outline path object, or line or arrow object. Remember that you can access the Path Edit tool from the Attributes toolbar when any Path tool is selected by choosing Path Editing. Make sure that there is an active object in the base image, click the Toggle button to get into Path Edit mode, then set the basic characteristics for the Path Edit tool in the Attributes toolbar.

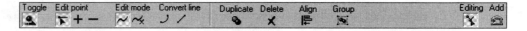

Toggle

Click the Toggle button to enter and exit path edit mode. Until the toggle button is selected, the Path Edit tool's Attributes toolbar options will be grayed out.

Toggle Off   Toggle On Shows Path   Click Path Shows Control Points

When Toggle is selected, the active object will be replaced by its path. Click anywhere on the path to display control points. Clicking on the path also makes available the Attributes toolbar's Edit point and Edit mode options.

Edit Point

Choose whether to edit an existing control point, add a control point or delete a control point.

Pick point Choose this option, then click on a large square control point to select it for editing. Doing so displays smaller squares that you can drag to edit the shape of the path associated with that control point. Alternatively, drag on a large control point to reposition it.

Add point Select this option, then click anywhere on the path to add an editable control point.

Delete point Select this option, then click on a control point to delete it.

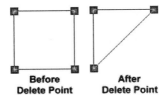

Edit mode

Non-free edit mode Choose to retain angle settings and control points when editing.

Free edit mode Choose to freely edit angle settings.

Convert Line

You must be in Pick point mode (not Add point mode or Subtract point mode) to be able to use Convert line.

Convert path to curve segment Click on the segment of the path that you wish to edit. Doing so turns that segment a different color, indicating that it has been selected. Select Convert path to curve segment, then click on its control point to display smaller squares that can be dragged to reshape the path into a curve.

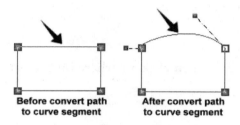

Before convert path to curve segment   After convert path to curve segment

Convert path to line segment Click on the segment of the path that you wish to edit. Doing so turns that segment a different color, indicating that it has been selected. Select Convert path to line segment and the curve converts to a straight line.

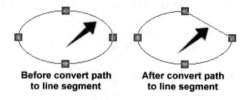

Before convert path to line segment   After convert path to line segment

Duplicate

Adds a duplicate of the path. By default the duplicate is the active path. This is a handy feature when you want to make several objects, all exactly the same size.

Delete

Deletes the active path.

Alignment

When there are two or more paths in the base image, hold down on the Shift key while clicking on other paths to select them.

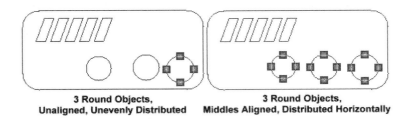

3 Round Objects, Unaligned, Unevenly Distributed   3 Round Objects, Middles Aligned, Distributed Horizontally

The Alignment button will then become available. Click to choose an alignment method: Align Left, Align Center, Align Right, Align Top, Align Middle, Align Bottom, Distribute Horizontally and Distribute Vertically.

Here are the objects aligned and distributed horizontally, after toggling back into 3D Mode.

Grouping

Available only when two or more paths are selected at the same time, click Grouping to Group or Ungroup.

Editing

Click to Toggle to the Path Edit Tool, or back to another Path tool.

Add

Click the Add button to add the Path Edit tool's attributes to the EasyPalette. Doing so opens the Add to EasyPalette dialog box. Give the attributes a name and save to a Gallery and Tab group.

Chapter 7: The Text Tool

PhotoImpact 6 heralds the inclusion of a significantly improved Text tool. New features in the Text Entry Box permit you to edit the spacing between lines of text, change the baseline of specific characters, fine tune character spacing and adjust kerning between individual letters. Attributes such as font, size, color, style and alignment can be edited directly in the Text Entry box, too.

Innovative Bend and Wrap features, discussed in detail in the chapter on Object menu commands, make it easy to perform complex custom distortions. For simple distortions of text objects, however, the Text tool's Horizontal Deform and Vertical Deform options are available from the Mode dropdown list in the Attributes toolbar. In addition, the chapters on the Effect and Creative menu commands, and the EasyPalette's Deform and Wrap Galleries discuss ways to make text really stand out.

Because of these wonderful new text features, creating eye-catching text with drop or perspective shadows is easier than ever. Be sure to start with a True Color image, or you will not be able to make 3D text, nor will you be able to apply the program's many special filters, plug-ins and effects to text. Make sure that if you want to add text to a web page file that you use the Web, Add HTML Text Object command, instead of using the Text tool. If you add text to a web page file with the Text tool, it will be treated as an image rather than HTML text.

There are five primary ways to edit text: (1) Using the choices available in the Attributes toolbar; (2) Right clicking on text to access the Object Properties dialog box; (3) Clicking on the Material button in the Attributes toolbar to access the Material dialog box; (4) Choosing Object, Wrap; and (5) Dragging and dropping textures, gradients and other special effects from the EasyPalette.

Editing Text With the Attributes Toolbar

Click on the Text tool, then make basic choices about how the text will appear from the Attributes toolbar's options.

Font

Click the down arrow to scroll through the fonts in the dropdown list. If you already know which font you want to use, you can type the first few letters of the font name. Doing so will save time by jumping closer to the name of the font you wish to use.

Size

Click the down arrow to choose a point size for the text. Lower values result in smaller text, while higher values create larger text.

Style

Click on the Style button to view choices from the dropdown list. Selecting Galleries opens a submenu from which you may choose to open the EasyPalette's Material, Deform and Wrap Galleries.

Color Box

Click in the Color box to access fill options: Ulead Color Picker, Windows Color Picker, Eyedropper, Color on Screen, Foreground Color, Background Color, Swap Foreground/Background Color, Reset, Gradient Fill, Magic Texture Fill, Natural Texture Fill or Fadeout (accesses the Edit menu's Fadeout dialog box).

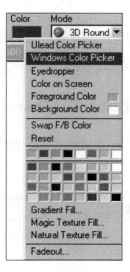

Ulead Color Picker Opens the Ulead Color Picker.

Windows Color Picker Opens the Windows Color Picker.

Eyedropper Pick a color in the image by clicking on it with the Eyedropper.

Color on Screen Click on any color on screen to select it.

Foreground Color Fills with the Foreground color.

Background Color Fills with the Background color.

Swap F/B Color Swaps the Foreground and Background colors.

Reset Resets the Foreground color to black and the Background color to white.

Gradient Fill Opens the Gradient Fill dialog box. For a Two-Color Gradient fill click in the color boxes to select the beginning and ending colors for the gradient from the Ulead Color Picker and select a Ramp (RGB, HSB clockwise/counterclockwise). Alternatively, right click in the color boxes to choose from a wider range of color options. For a Multiple-Color Gradient fill, click in its color box to open the Palette Ramp Editor. The Palette Ramp Editor is discussed in detail in the Fill Tools chapter.

Magic/Natural Texture Fill If Natural Texture Fill or Magic Texture Fill is selected, the Texture Library box opens. Scroll through the choices and select one for the fill. You can edit a Magic (but *not* a Natural) Texture's appearance, by clicking on the Options button in the Texture Library box. Doing so opens a secondary Magic Textures dialog box which permits editing of the Magic Texture. The use of Magic and Natural Textures as fills is discussed in detail in the chapter on Edit menu commands.

Fadeout Opens the Fadeout dialog box, which applies a grayscale mask to the text. The Fadeout feature is discussed in the chapter on Edit menu commands.

Mode Click on the down arrow to choose from the Mode dropdown list. For True Color images these include: 2D Object, 3D Round, 3D Chisel, 3D Trim, 3D Pipe, 3D

Custom, Horizontal Deform, Vertical Deform and Selection. For 256 Indexed Colors or less, the Mode dropdown list offers only 2D Object, Horizontal Deform, Vertical Deform and Selection.

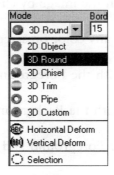

2D Object Text is flat and two dimensional.

3D Round Creates 3D text with a rounded bevel.

3D Chisel Creates 3D text with a sharply chiseled bevel.

3D Trim Creates 3D text via shading, resulting in a flatter look than other 3D modes.

3D Pipe 3D text that is hollowed out in the center, creating a rounded pipe effect.

3D Custom Creates 3D text with a variety of edge bevels. To select a custom 3D bevel, click on the Material button in the Attributes toolbar, then click on the Bevel tab to select from one of five custom bevels.

Horizontal Deform Displays the text's horizontal path, including editable control points. Drag on the large square control points to deform text. Drag on small squares to reshape the curve of the path associated with a control point. When you are through editing the text path, choose a 2D or 3D mode from the Mode dropdown list.

Vertical Deform Displays the text's vertical path, including editable control points. Drag on the large square control points to deform text. Drag on small squares to reshape the curve of the path associated with a control point. When you are through editing the text path, choose a 2D or 3D mode from the Mode dropdown list.

Selection Converts a text object into a selection area.

Border The Border slider is somewhat different in PhotoImpact 6. Press and hold on the down arrow to display the Border slider, sliding the cursor to the little arrow and dragging it to increase or decrease the size of the border. Alternatively, enter a value directly into the Border box.

If you have selected a Radial Gradient Fill, editing the border size allows you to fit the entire gradient into the text. An interesting "outline" effect, can be achieved using this technique.

Depth The Depth slider works like the Border slider. Press and hold on the down arrow to display the Depth slider, sliding the cursor to the little arrow and dragging it to increase or decrease its value. Positive values create a convex border, while negative values create a concave border. A depth of zero results in flat text with no border. Alternatively, enter a value directly into the Depth box.

Light Repositions the focus of currently selected light attributes. Move the cursor around, then click when you are satisfied with a light effect.

Material Click on the Material button to open the Material dialog box, from which you may edit text attributes. The Material dialog box is discussed in detail in its own chapter.

Add Opens the Add to EasyPalette dialog box, from which you may save text attributes. Give the preset a name and save it to to a Gallery and Tab group.

Text Entry Box

Click anywhere in the base image to open the Text Entry box.

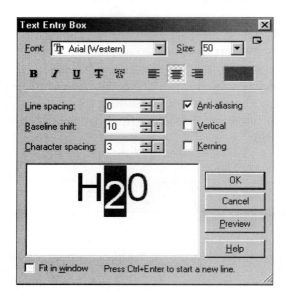

Font Select a font from the dropdown list.

Size Select a font size from the dropdown list.

Show Hide Options Click to display a smaller Text Entry Box without the advanced formatting options.

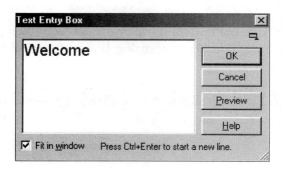

Style/Alignment/Color Select an option from those available. Click in the Color box to select a different text color.

Line spacing Change the amount of space between lines of text, with higher values resulting in more room between lines.

Baseline shift Changes the vertical position of text, raising or lowering the text above the baseline. Positive values drop the text below the baseline and negative values raise the text. In the example shown below, the 2 was formatted to a different size and the baseline shifted to 10.

$$H_2 0$$

Character spacing Edits the amount of space between the characters, with higher values increasing the space and lower values reducing the space between characters.

Turn   Turn

Default character spacing   Edited character spacing spreads letters out

Anti-aliasing Smooths out the rough edges of text.

Vertical When selected, rotates text 90 degrees clockwise.

Kerning Edits the space between selected characters. For example, often when an "A" and a "V" are close together there is too much space between them. Kerning lets you to adjust the spacing between such characters to improve their appearance.

RAVE   RAVE

Without Kerning, excess space between A and V   With Kerning, space between A and V is reduced

195

Fit in window Select to force all text to appear in the preview window. Choosing this option can make a long line of text look very small and hard to edit.

In the Text Entry Box, type in the text using Shift for capital letters, just as you would in a word processor. If you have several lines of text to type, hit Ctrl+Enter for a "carriage return." If you just hit Enter, the Text Entry Box will close. Veteran users of PhotoImpact will be happy to learn that now they can type an unlimited number of characters per line. Click OK to close the Text Entry Box. Right click on text and choose Edit Text to edit.

Editing Text With the Object Properties Box

Continue to edit transparency and other features by right clicking and choosing Properties to access the Object Properties dialog box, which contains three tabs: General, Position & Size and Hyperlink.

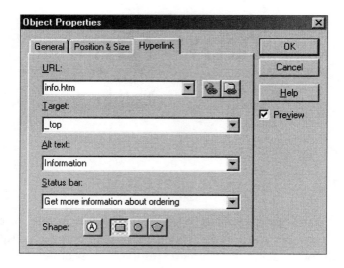

New to the PhotoImpact 6 Object Properties dialog box is a Hyperlink tab for attaching URL, target frame, Alt text and Status bar web attributes to an object. These web attributes can be added to text objects as well. In addition, you may name a text object, show or hide it, change its Merge method, edit transparency, and set a transparent color from the General tab. You may also lock or unlock text location within the base image or resize the text object from the Position & Size tab. The Object Properties dialog box is discussed in detail in the Object menu chapter.

The Object Properties dialog box can also be accessed by right clicking on a text object's thumbnail in the EasyPalette's Layer Manager and choosing Properties.

Editing Text With the Material Dialog Box

After setting the basic characteristics of text from the Attributes toolbar, you can edit further by clicking on the Material button. Doing so accesses the Material dialog box, which offers great flexibility in filling text and controlling its final appearance. From there you can fine tune the shadow, change the angle of light reflection or the number of lights reflecting from the text, apply a bump map to the fill, or fill with an image or texture from your hard drive. The Material dialog box is discussed in detail in its own chapter.

Editing Text With the Object Menu

While text is active, choose Object, Wrap and select a command from the flyout submenu. These commands are discussed in detail in the Object menu chapter.

Editing Text With the EasyPalette

Select the basic features of your text in the Attributes toolbar, then edit further from the EasyPalette. Access the EasyPalette's Material, Deform and Wrap Galleries by clicking on the Style button and choosing Galleries, or by opening the EasyPalette and selecting a Gallery directly. Drag and drop effects from thumbnails in the EasyPalette Galleries onto text (or double click a thumbnail). The EasyPalette chapter provides detailed information about applying Gallery effects.

Adding or Removing a Text Object Shadow

Add or remove a drop or perspective shadow in any of these five ways: (1) Click the Style button in the Attributes toolbar and select Shadow; (2) Right click on active text and choose Shadow; (3) Choose Object, Shadow; (4) Click on the Material button to open the Material dialog box and select the Shadow tab; and (5) In the Layer Manager, select the text object's thumbnail, right click and choose Shadow. When the Shadow dialog box opens, select Shadow to add a shadow, or deselect to remove a shadow.

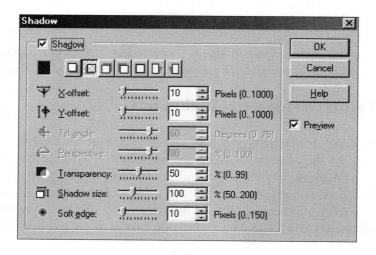

Color Click in the Color box to choose a color for the shadow from the Ulead Color Picker. Alternatively, right click to choose from a wider range of color options.

Direction Choose a direction in which the shadow will fall.

X and Y Offset Enter values (up to 1,000 pixels) for the shadow offset.

Tilt angle Edit the angle of the shadow.

Transparency Enter Transparency values for the shadow, with higher values resulting in more transparency, and lower values yielding less transparency.

Shadow size Specify the shadow size (from 50% to 200%), with 100% resulting in a shadow the same size as the object, 50% yielding a shadow half as large as the object, and so on.

Soft edge Specify the number of pixels (1-150) for the Soft edge. The higher the value, the closer to the center of the object the shadow starts and the less definition it has around its edges.

Splitting a Text Object Shadow

A shadow can be split from its corresponding active text object so that it can be edited independently. Split a shadow from text using either of these two methods: (1) Click the Style button in the Attributes toolbar and select Split Shadow; (2) Choose Object, Split Shadow. Curiously, the ability to right click and Split Shadow is not present in PhotoImpact 6, nor can a shadow be split from the Layer Manager thumbnails.

A Few Words About Sharing Text Objects

Border backgrounds and buttons are often created with dingbat fonts. Instead of displaying letters of the alphabet, dingbats are special pictorial fonts used for decoration. For example, a horizontal line of dingbats might be used as a web page divider.

If you are one of the many people who like to make and share objects with other PhotoImpact users, be aware that objects made in PhotoImpact 6 cannot be used in prior versions of PhotoImpact. Also, you should be aware that text objects are a little trickier to share than are path or image objects. Sharing an object requires you to save it in Ulead's proprietary .UFO (Ulead File for Objects) file type. When saved as a .UFO, the object is saved independent of the base image. That means that you, or someone you share it with, can open the object in PhotoImpact and edit it later.

However, if you create a text object, including one made from a dingbat font, the person you share the object with will not be able to edit it unless he or she has the exact same font installed on their computer. There is a way around this problem, though. After creating a text object, and before saving it, choose Object, Convert Object Type, From Text to Path. Then save the object as a .UFO file. Changing it to a path object frees a text object from the constraints placed upon it by virtue of being created with the Text tool. Now if you share these objects with other PhotoImpact users, they will be able to edit them even if they do not have the same font used to make the object.

Creating text objects from fonts for your own use is unlikely to cause problems as long as you honor the font designer's terms or you have outright purchased the font. However, think twice about copyright before creating objects from any font and sharing them with others. While you may have purchased a font for your own use, or been given permission to use a linkware or shareware font on your own web page, most font designers will not give permission for you to give away their property as objects to any PhotoImpact user who wants them.

Like all intellectual property, fonts are copyrighted. That means that the right to distribute and sell them are the property of the people who designed them. It is illegal to redistribute and/or sell someone else's copyrighted work without their permission. As tempting as it may be to turn a dingbat font into an object, then make it available for download from your web site, you should not do so without the font designer's permission. Some font designers will agree to let you make these objects available to others, either freely or with some restrictions. However, others may not allow you to do so, and you must abide by their assertion of their rights or risk legal consequences. Similarly, image objects made from copyrighted photos or other artwork should not be shared with others without obtaining permission from the holder of copyright.

Chapter 8: The Stamp Tool

The Stamp Tool is new to PhotoImpact 6. It replaces and greatly improves upon what used to be the Object Clone Tool. The Stamp tool includes a library of bright, playful stamps which are actually .UFO objects. These stamps can be used to decorate borders or buttons or just to add some colorful zip anywhere on a web page. Here are a small sampling of the preset stamps.

You can make your own stamps from .UFO objects too, and add them to your "stamp collection" easily. Add a single object as a stamp, or add a stack of variations on a stamp, like these original teddy bear stamps.

Users of both PhotoImpact and Paint Shop Pro will be delighted to find that they can now import Paint Shop Pro picture tubes as stamps. No more convoluted saving to .PSD format and converting to an object. Now you can import tubes quickly and easily in one brief operation.

Access stamps by clicking on the Stamp Tool button. Set stamping characteristics from the Attributes toolbar.

Click thumbnail to select stamp Click to select a stamp from those already installed, or click the down arrow to select an option from the dropdown list.

Select stamp Displays thumbnails of existing stamps.

Add stamp Accesses the Open dialog box. Browse to the folder and .UFO object file you wish to import as a stamp. If you want to have variations of the stamp, put all of the objects into the same base image and save them as a single .UFO file.

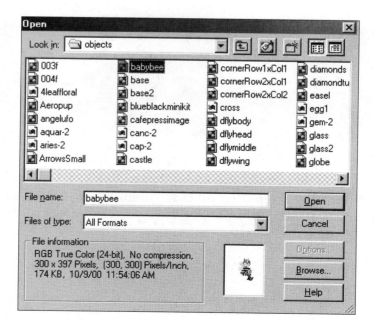

Click Open. A thumbnail for the stamp appears in the "Select stamp" box, and its thumbnail will be added to the other stamp thumbnails.

Now you can use and edit the added stamp, just like any other stamp.

Delete stamp Opens the Delete custom stamp dialog box. Select the thumbnail of the stamp you want to delete and click Delete. You can only delete stamps that you have added yourself.

Import picture tube Accesses the Open dialog box. Browse to the folder and .TUB picture tube file you wish to import as a stamp. Click Open. A thumbnail for the stamp will be added to the rest of the stamp thumbnails.

203

View Displays thumbnails of the variations of the selected stamp. For example, if the penguin stamp is selected, 8 thumbnail variations will be displayed.

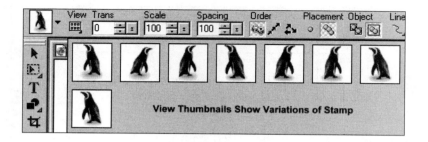

Transparency Edit the transparency of the stamp. Higher values result in greater transparency.

Scale Edits the size of the stamp, up to 500%. The default is 100. Enter a value directly into the box, or press and hold down on the down arrow, then drag the slider to edit.

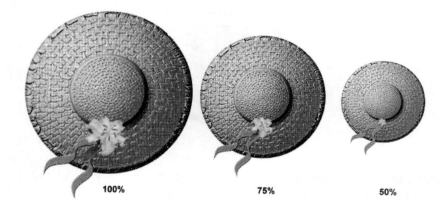

Spacing Edits the amount of space between the stamps when you drag a string of them, up to 200. The default is 100. Enter a value directly into the box, or press and hold down on the down arrow, then drag the slider to edit.

Order Specify the order in which stamps are added to the base image. This is only important if you have a preferred stacking order.

>**Random** Some stamps are at the top of the stack of the objects, some are applied behind others. Random is selected by default.
>
>**Sequential** The latest stamp is at the top of the stack of objects.
>
>**Angular** When a line of stamps is dragged in the base image, the objects appear in a straight line.

Placement Specifies how the stamps are applied.

Stamp   Trail

>**Stamp** You must click to add each stamp. You cannot drag a trail of stamps when Stamp is selected.
>
>**Trail** Click to add one stamp, or drag to add a string or trail of stamps. Trail is selected by default.

Object Determines if the stamps are treated as individual stamps, or clustered together as a group. In reality, it does not matter much which option you choose. All you have to do is click in the base image with the Pick or Selection tool to deactivate the objects, which can then be selected and edited individually.

>**Separate objects** Each stamp is a separate object.
>
>**Single object** All the stamps are grouped together.

Lines Choose whether to stamp Freehand, Straight lines or Connected lines. You must double click to finish up if you choose Connected lines. Straight lines is a good way to make a fun frame or border for another image.

Tablet By default None is selected, which means that the drawing pen will be treated the same as a mouse. The only drawing tablet option available for stamps is Transparency.

Add Choose to save custom Stamp Tool attributes. Click Add to open the Add to EasyPalette dialog box. Give the custom Stamp effect a name and save it to My Gallery.

Editing Stamps With the Brush Panel

The Brush Panel contains four tabs for editing stamps: Shape, Options, Color and Advanced.

As can be seen in the screen shot above, these tabs contain the same options available in the Attributes toolbar, except for the Color tab. The Color tab permits you to perform Hue (color) shifts that result in unique artistic effects.

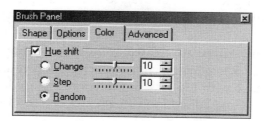

Experiment with the Hue shift options: Change, Step and Random. Change and Step result in variations of predominant tones, or shifting the stamp colors around the color wheel.

Random Hue Shift

One of the most interesting effects results from Random, which changes the major color scheme of the stamp. If you want to make a series of the same stamp with different colors, the Random option provides an easy way to do so.

Chapter 9: The Object Menu

Object menu commands allow you to control the appearance, visibility and attributes of objects within the base image. From the Object menu, you can merge objects with the base image, group/ungroup or combine objects, duplicate objects, convert object type, align and space objects within the base image, add or split a shadow from its corresponding object, import and export objects, add objects to an EasyPalette Library, or edit them via the Object Properties dialog box. Many of the Object menu commands can also be accessed by right clicking and selecting an option from a dropdown list.

Improved organization of the Object menu in PhotoImpact 6 means that its tasks cluster more logically. A truly welcome addition are a collection of New object commands which allow you to add objects from a file, a Library or the Component Designer, to add a Rollover button with two or three states or to add an HTML Text object. Other innovative new Object menu commands allow you to edit the web attributes of objects such as rollovers and components, to Wrap or Bend objects into different shapes and along a path, and to edit objects without having to select the Path Edit tool.

New

The New object commands make it easier than ever before to add new objects to a base image. Select a new object option from the dropdown list.

Image Object via Copy Copies an active selection and turns it into an object in the base image. If there is no active selection, this command is grayed out. It is similar to the Convert to Object command with "Preserve Base Image" selected. No image data goes into the Clipboard.

Image Object via Cut Cuts an active selection from the base image and turns it into an object. If there is no active selection, this command is grayed out. It is similar to the Convert to Object command with "Preserve Base Image" deselected, so a "hole" appears in the base image. No image data goes into the Clipboard.

Image Object from File Access the Open dialog box, from which you can open an image that will be placed as an object in the base image. This is essentially the same as choosing File, Place, As Object.

Image Object from Library Opens the EasyPalette's Image Library, from which you can drag and drop an object into the base image.

Link Object from File (Shift+L) For web images (JPG, GIF, PNG) only, accesses the Open dialog box so that a web image can be linked to the current image and output to a web page.

Component Object Opens the Component Designer so you can add a web image component to the image.

Rollover Object (Shift+R) Opens the Rollover dialog box so you can create the code for a rollover button. You must have two or three objects selected at the same time, or this command will be grayed out.

HTML Text Object (Shift+T) Opens the HTML Text Entry Box so that you can add text to your web image. Text can be formatted with HTML for inclusion in a web page.

Duplicate

Creates a duplicate of the selected object(s), without placing image information into the Clipboard. You can also right click and Duplicate.

Merge (Shift+M)

Merges the selected object(s) with the base image. You can also right click and select Merge.

Merge All (Ctrl+Shift+M)

Merges all objects with the base image. You can also right click and select Merge All.

Merge as Single Object Merges all selected objects into one object. In prior versions of PhotoImpact, this command was "Combine as Single Object." This is a permanent process. Once Path or Text objects have been merged as a single object, their attributes can no longer be edited.

There are two ways to select multiple objects for the Merge as Single Object command.

1. Click on the first object with either the Pick or Standard Selection tool, then hold down on the Shift key while clicking on other objects. When all of the desired objects have been selected, choose Object, Merge as Single Object, or right click and choose Merge as Single Object.

2. Open the EasyPalette's Layer Manager. Click on an object thumbnail to select it, then hold down on the Shift key while clicking on the thumbnails for other objects you wish to select. Right click on one of the thumbnails and choose Merge as Single Object. Using the Layer Manager makes it easier to select objects when there are many objects within the base image.

Delete

Deletes an active object from the base image. You can also right click and choose Delete, or hit the Del key.

Select All Objects (Ctrl+Shift+A)

A terrific new feature in PhotoImpact 6, you can now select all of the objects in the base image at one time.

Edit Path (Shift+E)

Another newcomer to PhotoImpact 6, this command immediately switches to the Path Edit tool, selects the Toggle button in the Attributes toolbar, and displays the path control points. It makes editing path objects a whole lot easier than before. When you are finished editing the Path object, click the Toggle button. The Path Edit tool will still be selected, so remember to select the Path Drawing tool again to edit the object's attributes.

Web Attributes

Web Attributes permit you to edit the attributes of web objects (link object, component or rollover).

Refresh Link Updates edits made to a link object file.

Break Link Converts the link object to a regular Image object.

Split Component Removes the web attributes of component objects, converting the component into separate Path objects.

Split Rollover Takes away the web attributes of rollover objects, converting them to separate objects.

Wrap

New to PhotoImpact 6, the Wrap commands permit you to distort Text or Path objects in exciting new ways.

Bend Bends and/or repeats Text (or Path) objects.

Repeat Specify how the duplicated objects will appear.

> **Count** The number of repeats.

Spacing The amount of space, in pixels, between duplicates.

Stretch to fit Select to force the objects to conform to the baseline.

Bending Specify bending attributes.

> **Amount** Specify the direction and power of the bend. A value of 100 or -100 results in a complete circle. A value of 50 results in curving half circle, with positive values creating a "frown" shape and negative values creating a "smile" shape.

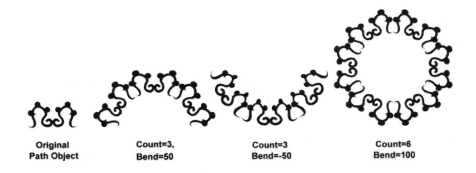

Original Path Object | Count=3, Bend=50 | Count=3 Bend=-50 | Count=6 Bend=100

> **Position/Size** Specify where the Bend starts along the baseline, and the size of the Path or Text object.
>
> **Start height** The starting size of the object, which will gradually expand to the End Height. A negative value will flip the object upside down.

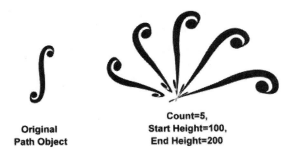

Original Path Object | Count=5, Start Height=100, End Height=200

End height The ending size of the object. A negative value will flip the object upside down.

Start position Determines where along the baseline the Bend starts. A value of 0 begins at the beginning of the baseline, and a value of 100 represents the end of the baseline.

Advanced Enables you to perform additional manipulations of the objects.

Fit text position to path Fits objects to the baseline, with the object's vertical features perpendicular to the baseline.

Distort text to fit path Forces the object to distort to follow the baseline.

Vertical Fits the left side of the object to the baseline, positioning the object sideways, creating a slightly different look to the bend.

Add Text to Active Path Replaces a *solid* active path with text forced into its shape. If the Path object has an opening in it, this command will not work. You can even add text to unique Path objects you make yourself with the Spline or Bezier/Polygon tools. First create a Path object, then choose Add Text to Active Path. Doing so opens the Text Entry Box. Type in the desired text and click OK.

As shown below, the text replaces the Path object.

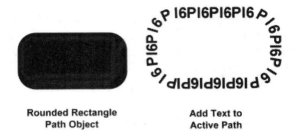

Rounded Rectangle
Path Object

Add Text to
Active Path

Select From Wrap Gallery Wraps or Bends Path or Text objects from presets in the EasyPalette's Wrap Gallery. Double click on an effect thumbnail to apply.

The Wrap Gallery's Path Wrap 14

Fit Together Create a solid Path object and another Path object or a Text object. While one object is active, hold down the Shift key while clicking on the other object so that both of them are selected at the same time. Now choose Fit Together. The solid Path object will be replace by the other object.

PhotoImpact 6 Wizardry

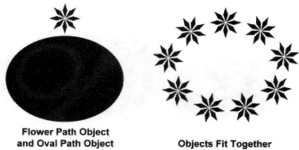

Flower Path Object
and Oval Path Object

Objects Fit Together

Get Wrap Path When an object has been wrapped to another object, Get Wrap Path restores a path shape to the wrapped object.

Get Wrap Path

Remove Wrap Unwraps the wrapped object, returning to two separate objects.

Edit Wrap Properties Quickly edit the wrapped object's Path shape by selecting Edit Wrap Properties. Immediately the Path Edit tool is selected and the object is toggled into Path Edit mode.

Properties (Shift+W) Opens the Wrap dialog box, from which you may change the number of repeats of the object, its beginning and ending height, etc.

Convert Object Type

Changes the object type: From Text to Image, From Path to Image, From Text to Path, From Image to Path, Reset Text/Path Object and Reset Image Transform. At times you may need to convert an object type in order to perform a particular type of edit. For example, to use the Object Eraser tool, you must first convert a Path or Text object to an Image object.

If you make objects out of dingbat fonts, it is a good idea to convert these Text objects to Path objects if you plan to share them with others. If you do not convert them to Path objects, the people you share them with will not be able to use them unless they have the same dingbat font installed on their computers. Converting to a Path object frees the object from the constraints placed upon it as a Text object.

Group (Ctrl+Alt+G)

Two or more selected objects are grouped together with this command. When Grouped, objects are *temporarily* connected together as one unit, but they can be disconnected from one another with the Ungroup command. There are two ways to select multiple objects to Group them.

1. Click on the first object with the Pick or the Standard Selection tool, then hold down on the Shift key while clicking on other objects. Select Object, Group or right click and select Group.

2. Open the EasyPalette's Layer Manager. Click on an object thumbnail to select it, then hold down on the Shift key while clicking on thumbnails for other objects. Right click on a thumbnail and select Group. When all of the objects in a base image are Grouped, you will only see one thumbnail in the Layer Manager. When the objects are Ungrouped, the individual thumbnails will reappear.

Since Grouped objects are only temporarily connected to one another, you will not be able to add a shadow to them as a unit. Use the Merge as Single Object command instead, then choose Object, Shadow (or right click, Shadow) to add a shadow to two or more objects.

Ungroup

Ungroups Grouped objects, restoring them to independent object status. Grouped objects must be active for the Ungroup command to be available. Alternatively, you can right click on an active Group of objects and choose Ungroup, or right click on the Grouped objects thumbnail in the Layer Manager and choose Ungroup. Click in the base image to deactivate objects to complete the Ungroup command.

Align

A handy way to align two or more selected objects on the same plane or to center them within the base image. Align commands can also be accessed by right clicking.

Top The tops of the selected objects are aligned.

Bottom The bottoms of the selected objects are aligned.

Align, Top   Align, Bottom

Left The left sides of the selected objects are aligned.

Right The right sides of the selected objects are aligned.

Center Horizontally The centers of the selected objects are aligned horizontally.

Center Vertically The centers of the selected objects are aligned vertically.

Center Both The centers of the selected objects are aligned on top of one another.

Space Evenly Regulates the spacing of three or more selected objects.

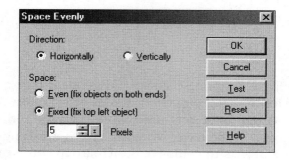

Direction Specify if the spacing should be distributed Horizontally or Vertically.

Space Select Even to distribute existing space between the first and last object evenly. Choose Fixed to specify a number of pixels between the objects, beginning with the top left object.

Test Click the Test button to preview the selected spacing values.

Reset Cancel out previously selected spacing values and try again.

Arrange

The Pick tool must be selected in order to access this command, which changes the stacking order of overlapping objects. The Arrange Order options, as well as more advanced Arrange commands, are also available in the Attributes toolbar.

Bring Forward Moves the selected object forward one layer in the stack.

Send Backward Moves the selected object back one layer in the stack.

Bring to Front Moves the selected object to the top of the stack.

Send to Back Moves the selected object to the bottom of the stack.

Bring Ball Forward   Send Ball Backward   Send Heart to Back

Shadow

Adds a shadow to the active object. You can also right click and choose Shadow.

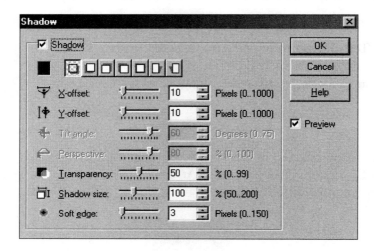

Color Click in the Color box to select a shadow color.

Direction Choose a direction in which the shadow will fall.

X and Y Offset Enter values (up to 1,000 pixels) for the shadow offset.

Tilt angle Edits the angle of the shadow.

Transparency Edits shadow transparency, with higher values resulting in more transparency, and lower values yielding less transparency.

Shadow size Specify a shadow size (from 50% to 200%), with 100% resulting in a shadow the same size as the object, 50% yielding a shadow half as large as the object, and so on.

Soft edge Specify the number of pixels for the soft edge, which helps the shadow to blend with the background. The higher the value, the closer to the center of the object the shadow begins and the less definition it will have around its edges.

Split Shadow

Splits the shadow from its corresponding active object. The shadow may be edited independently. In the example shown below, the original drop shadow was split from its object, moved to the left slightly, then distorted with the Transform tool.

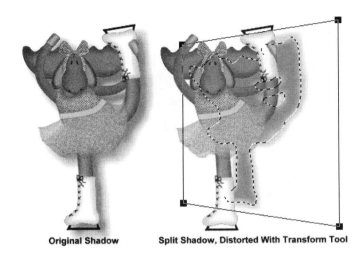

Original Shadow　　Split Shadow, Distorted With Transform Tool

Split Shadow is grayed out if there are no active objects, or if multiple objects are selected.

Import Object

Replaces an active object with an imported one. It is important to note that you cannot Import a truly independent object that has not been merged with the base image. The active object is actually replaced by an image file (or a selection within it), either one that is open in the work space or from a folder on your hard drive. The Import Object label derives from the fact that anything added to a base image is considered an object.

Import from　Choose to Import an image, or selection within an image currently open in the work space, or an image file from your hard drive.

Replace　Choose whether to replace the active object in the destination image with the Imported image and selection, the image only or selection only.

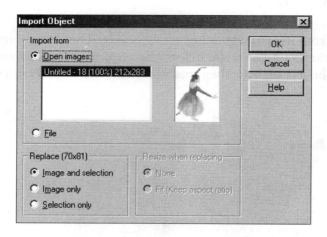

Resize when replacing Select None to Import the object at its actual size, or Fit to resize the object (maintaining height to width proportion).

Export Object

Exports an active object as a new image in the work space, as a file, or as a mask.

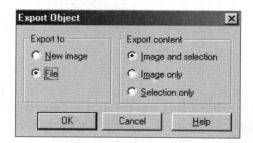

Export to Choose New to Export as a new, untitled image in the work space, or File to access the Save As dialog box so you can save to a folder on your hard drive.

Export content Export Image and selection (the image object and its mask as a selection), Image only (Exports the object as a selection) or Selection only (Exports a grayscale mask as a new grayscale image).

Copy to Object Library

Saves an active object or group of objects to the EasyPalette. Selecting Copy to Object Library opens the Add to EasyPalette dialog box. You may also drag an object or selected objects onto the EasyPalette to open the Add to EasyPalette dialog box.

Sample name Give the object a name.

Gallery/Library Select a Library to save to from the dropdown list.

Tab group Choose a Tab group to save to from the dropdown list.

Recently used Select a Library and Tab group from the dropdown list of those recently used.

If multiple selected objects are copied to a Library, a dialog box appears asking if you want to "Save multiple objects as a single thumbnail in the Object Library?" Click Yes to save the Grouped objects as one thumbnail. Any time you wish to use the grouped objects again, just drag from the thumbnail into the work space. This is a clever way to save an object or a Group of objects so that they can be edited over and over again.

Properties (Ctrl+Shift+Enter)

Opens the Object Properties dialog box, from which a number of an object's attributes may be edited. You can also right click on an active object and choose Properties to access this dialog box. There are three tabs in the Object Properties dialog box.

General Tab

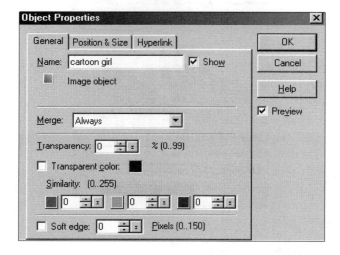

Name Give the object a name, if desired. Naming objects can be helpful for identification and sorting purposes when there are multiple objects in the base image. The type of object (Path, Text or Image) will appear directly under the name. The name of the object will also appear under its thumbnail in the Layer Manager, making it easier to keep track of objects and to select the right one for editing.

Show Shows the object in the base image. If deselected, the object is hidden.

Merge Select a Merge method from the dropdown list to specify how the color characteristics of the object will Merge with the base image. Interesting and sophisticated effects can be achieved by varying Merge method.

Transparency Enter a value for object transparency, with higher values resulting in greater transparency.

Transparent color Select to assign transparency to a color. Click in the associated Color box to select a color.

Similarity Specify Red, Green and Blue Similarity values of the transparent color.

Soft edge Creates a soft edge from 1-150 pixels.

Position & Size Tab

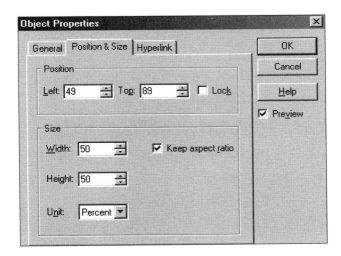

Position The left and top coordinates of the active object within the base image.

Lock Locks the position of the active object within the base image.

Size Select a width and height for the object by choosing pixels or percent from the dropdown list.

Keep aspect ratio When selected, maintains height to width ratio when resizing.

Hyperlink Tab

If the object will be used as a button or navigation image on a web page, you may enter a number of attributes for it from the Hyperlink tab.

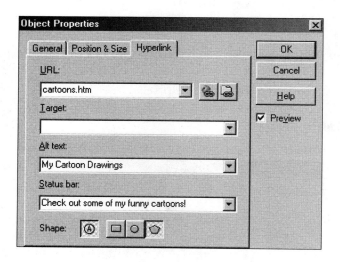

URL Enter the URL for the link. Click on the Remote URL icon to browse the Internet for the link, or click on the Local URL icon to link to a file on your local computer.

Target Select a target frame from the dropdown list to make the linked URL open in a specific frame.

Alt Text Enter alternate text to be seen if the image fails to load properly.

Status bar Enter text to be displayed in the browser's status bar when the mouse is over the object on a web page. Status bar text gives you the opportunity to tell a little about the linked page.

Shape Defines the linked object's shape that will be sensitive to a mouse moving over it. Choose from Auto detect, Rectangular, Circle or Polygon.

Chapter 10: The Transform Tool

The Transform tool can be used to create interesting distortions and other image effects. It comes in handy when you want to add a perspective slant, flip horizontally or vertically, redefine horizontal or vertical alignment, slant, or otherwise tweak images, selections and objects.

Select a Transform method from the Attributes toolbar.

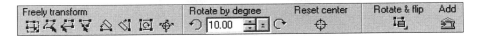

The Attributes toolbar's "Freely transform" options control the type of transformation applied to the image. Position the cursor over a control point until it turns into a double-headed arrow, then press and hold down on the mouse button while dragging on a control point.

Resize

Freely resizes an image, selection or object. To preserve the object's height to width ratio, hold down on the Shift key while dragging on control points.

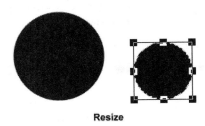

Resize

Slant

Horizontal or vertical alignment is slanted, but the lines remain parallel to one another.

Distort

Freely distorts the shape of an image, selection or object from any control point.

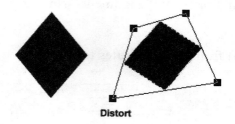
Distort

Perspective

Distorts an image, selection or object to give it the appearance of having depth or distance.

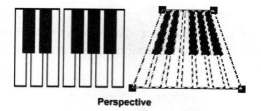
Perspective

Rotate Using a Horizontal Line

Instead of a bounding box, a horizontal line with a control point on each end appears on the image, selection or object. Position the cursor over a control point until it turns into a double-headed arrow. Press and hold down on the mouse button while dragging. Double click to rotate.

Rotate Using a Vertical Line

Instead of a bounding box, a vertical line with a control point on each end appears. Position the cursor over a control point until it turns into a double-headed arrow. Press and hold down on the mouse button while dragging. Double click to rotate.

Rotate Freely

Freely rotate by positioning the cursor over a control handle until it turns into a curved, double-headed arrow. Press and hold down on the mouse button while dragging. When you release the mouse button, the object will rotate.

Virtual Trackball

Creates perspective and depth, as if an object has been placed inside a ball and rotated. The Virtual Trackball can be applied to path objects only. To apply to an image object, select Object, Convert Object Type, From Image to Path. To apply to a selection, right click and Convert to Object, then choose Object, Convert Object Type, From Image to Path.

When the Virtual Trackball is selected, a circle with a square in the middle surrounds the object. The square represents the object and projection centers.

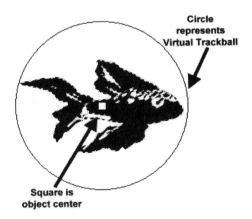

Double click on the square in the middle of the circle to adjust the object and projection centers. Doing so reveals two bounding boxes with control points. Position the cursor over a control point until it turns into a double-headed arrow. Press and hold down on the mouse button while dragging.

229

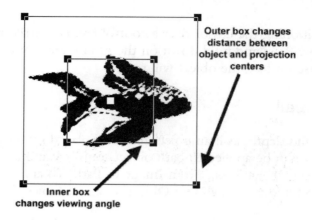
Outer box changes distance between object and projection centers

Inner box changes viewing angle

Make the inner box smaller or larger to change the viewing angle, and make the outer box smaller or larger to modify the distance between the object center and the projection center.

After changing the viewing angle and/or projection center(s), double click on the small square again. The trackball circle outline will reappear. Press and hold down on the mouse button while dragging along the left or right sides of the circle to rotate along the x axis, or horizontal plane. Similarly, press and hold down on the mouse button while dragging along the top or bottom of the circle to rotate along the y axis, or vertical plane. Press and hold down on the mouse button while dragging anywhere outside the circle to rotate along the z axis.

After Trackball Distortion

⟲ 10.00 ⟳ Rotate by degree

Enter a value for degree of rotation directly into the box, or use the up and down arrows to change values. Click on the curved arrows to rotate counterclockwise or clockwise.

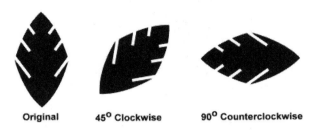

Original   45° Clockwise   90° Counterclockwise

⊕ Reset center

When the Freely Rotate option is selected you can move the center, around which rotation occurs. Reset center returns the center to the middle of the object.

Rotate & flip

Click for a submenu offering a quick way to Rotate Left 90 Degrees, Rotate Right 90 degrees, Rotate 180 degrees, Flip Horizontally and Flip Vertically.

Chapter 11: The Object Eraser Tools

Two indispensible new Object Eraser tools grace the PhotoImpact 6 Tool Panel, the Object Paint Eraser tool and the Object Magic Eraser tool. Both are intended for use with Image objects only. In order to use them with Path or Text objects, it is necessary to convert them to Image objects first. Make sure that you are finished editing Path or Text object attributes before converting them to Image objects.

Converting a Selection to an Object for Erasing

First make a selection from the image. The selection will be surrounded by a static broken line.

Right click on the selection and choose Convert to Object, or hit Ctrl+Shift+O. You will notice that the broken line around the selection is animated, indicating that it is an object.

To make it easier to work with the object, deselect View Base Image (Ctrl+F5) from the View menu. You will get a "Show/Hide Base Image Confirmation" box stating that you are about to hide everything in the image except the object. Click OK. Everything but the object will disappear and the base image will show only the gray checkerboard signifying a transparent background.

PhotoImpact 6 Wizardry

Now you can use either of the Eraser Tools on the object. You may notice than even when part of an object has been erased, the bounding box around it continues to encompass the erased areas, which can be restored by clicking on the Recover button in the Attributes toolbar.

When you are done editing, the excess space around objects can be eliminated by clicking Trim, or choosing Web, Trim Object. You cannot recover after trimming.

Object Paint Eraser Tool

The Object Paint Eraser lets you vary the transparency of the erasure by varying pressure as the eraser passes over the object. Drawing tablet users, in particular, will surely appreciate the relationship between pressure and transparency of the erasure. The Object Paint Eraser can be used to create unique masks, especially fancy edge masks.

Set the characteristics of the Object Paint Eraser from the Attributes toolbar.

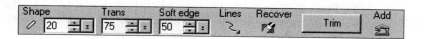

Shape Select a shape from the dropdown list. To make it easier to predict how the eraser will behave, be sure to set the Painting cursor to "Precise Shape" via the File,

Preferences, General, PhotoImpact, Tools menu command. Brush shape can be edited from the Brush Panel.

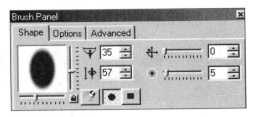

Size/Transparency/Soft edge Enter values in the appropriate boxes, or use the up and down arrows to edit.

Lines Click to choose Freehand, Straight lines or Connected lines.

Recover Toggles into Paint mode, so you can paint back an erasure. Deselect to return to Eraser mode.

Trim Gets rid of the extra space around an object. Once Trim is selected, you will no longer be able to recover erased areas of the object.

Add Opens the Add to EasyPalette dialog box so you can save to the EasyPalette.

Using the Object Paint Eraser, you can create unique edge effects like these.

PhotoImpact 6 Wizardry

The Object Paint Eraser can be useful for combining combining two or more objects, both of different colors, to create a new composite object.

Two different color flowers   Erase half of each flower   Combine

You can also erase away all of the unwanted part of an object to refine the selection, then use the object in another setting or as part of a collage. Here is the cat shown earlier in this chapter, cut out via selection and playing with a "mouse."

Object Magic Eraser

The Object Magic Eraser makes it extremely easy to eliminate parts of objects by color Similarity. Set the Object Magic Eraser's characteristics in the Attributes toolbar. Remember that the object to be erased must be an image object.

The first thing you will notice about the Attributes toolbar is that there is no brush size or shape associated with the Object Magic Eraser tool. Instead, what is actually erased will depend upon the Similarity of color, whether you select by line or area and whether or not you choose the "Search connected pixels" option.

Select by Choose whether to select by Area or Line. If you choose to select by Line and drag over the object, you may drag in any direction and lines may curve.

Similarity Choose a Similarity value (0-255), with higher Similarity values selecting a broader range of color pixels.

Transparency Transparency level ranges from 0-99, with higher values resulting in greater transparency.

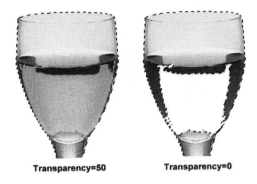

Transparency=50   Transparency=0

Search connected pixels Selects only pixels connected to the selection area. Deselect to search for similar pixels in the entire image.

Anti-aliasing Select to smooth the edges of the erased area.

PhotoImpact 6 Wizardry

Working With Objects: Active Learning Exercises

Using the Pick Tool and Object Menu Commands

1. The purpose of this exercise is to learn how to manipulate and arrange objects.

2. Choose File, Open. Browse to and select 4hearts.ufo. Click Open.

3. When the image opens in the work space, you will see four heart shaped objects. The leftmost object only will be selected, with an animated broken line around it. A static green broken line box will appear around all of the objects, however. To get rid of the object boxes, choose View and deselect "Show Box Around Objects."

4. Choose the Pick tool.

5. Select Object, Select All Objects. Note that all of the objects are selected now.

6. Choose Object, Align, Top. Doing so will line up the tops of all four objects.

7. To distribute the hearts evenly choose Object, Align, Space Evenly. When the Space Evenly dialog box opens, for Direction choose "Horizontally," and for "Space" select Even.

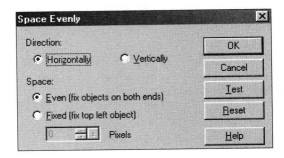

8. Click OK to close the Space Evenly box. Now the hearts are distributed evenly across the base image.

9. Choose Object, Group to temporarily group the objects together. Drag them around in the base image, and you will see that they all move together, preserving the alignment and spacing.

10. Choose Object and you will see that Shadow is grayed out. This is because you cannot add a shadow to Grouped objects.

11. Right click and choose Ungroup to disconnect the hearts. Hit the space bar to deselect the objects. The animated broken line around them will disappear because they are no longer grouped together. Drag each object a little so that they are no longer perfectly aligned and spaced.

12. Click on any heart object to make it active. Hit Ctrl+Shift+A to select all objects again.

13. Look in the Attributes toolbar's "Align" options. If you hold your cursor briefly over each icon, a pop-up box will display the button's function. Click on the Align Bottom button. The objects will line up so that the bottoms are all on the same horizontal plane.

14. Click on the Align Left button. All of the hearts will be stacked under the red heart, which is the only one that will still be visible.

15. Click in the base image to deactivate all active images. Drag the objects so that they all overlap, but you can still see them individually. Click on the red heart, which will still be at the top of the stack, to make it active.

Working With Objects: Active Learning Exercises

16. In the Attributes toolbar, click the Send to Back option.

17. Now the red object is at the bottom of the stack of hearts.

18. Click the green heart to make it active. In the Attributes toolbar's Order options, choose Bring to Front. Now the green heart object is at the top of the stack.

19. Click the yellow-gold heart object to make it active. In the Attributes toolbar's Order options, click Send Backward. Doing so sends the object back one layer only.

20. Drag the heart objects so that they are in a roughly horizontal line.

21. Click on the pink heart object. Right click and choose Properties to open the Object Properties dialog box. From the Size & Position tab, in the Size section, choose Percent from the Unit dropdown list. Make sure "Keep aspect ratio" is selected and change the size to 75%.

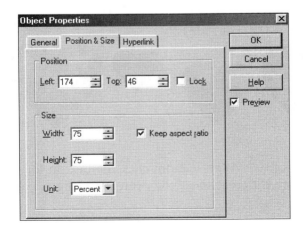

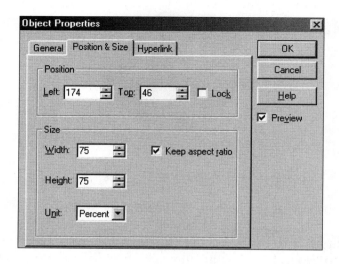

22. Click OK to close the Object Properties box. The pink heart object is now 75% of its original size.

23. Click on the red heart to select it. Choose Object, Properties to open the Object Properties dialog box. As you did for the pink heart, edit the size of the red heart object to 50% of its original size. Click OK to close the Object Properties box.

24. Right click on the newly edited red heart object and choose Duplicate. Drag this duplicate red heart object to the left, placing it in the center of the line of hearts, between the pink and gold heart objects. Hit Ctrl+Shift+A to select all objects.

25. In the Attributes toolbar's Align section, click the button for Center Vertically. Even though the hearts are different sizes, the centers are aligned along the same horizontal plane now.

26. Right click and choose Align, Space Evenly. When the Space Evenly dialog box opens, choose to align Horizontally. In the "Space" section, choose Fixed and enter a value of 5 for the spacing.

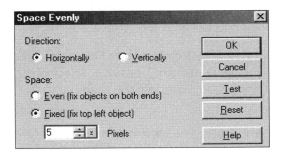

27. Click OK to close the Space Evenly box. The heart objects will be spaced 5 pixels apart.

28. While all of the objects are still selected, choose Object, Merge As Single Object. The objects are no longer individual objects. They are all part of the same object, even though there are spaces between them.

29. Right click and choose Shadow. When the Shadow dialog box opens, create a black shadow with the values shown in the screen shot below.

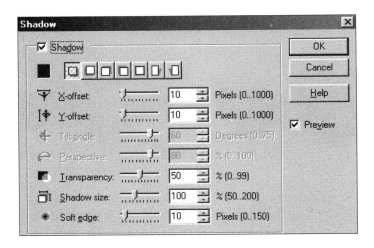

30. Drag the object around in the base image, noting that the shadow is "hooked" to it. Now choose Object, Split Shadow.

31. Click in the base image to deactivate all objects. Click on the shadow and you will see that you can drag it around the base image, but the heart object remains where it was.

32. Click on the shadow if it is not already active. Select the Transform tool. In the Attributes toolbar's "Freely Transform" options, select Slant. Drag the top right control point slightly to the left, slanting the shadow.

33. Select the Pick tool again. Right click on the shadow and choose Properties. When the Object Properties dialog box opens, from the General tab, edit the Transparency to 65%.

34. The shadow has been edited by distorting its shape and changing its transparency. Drag the shadow back up to the heart object and position it so that it falls to the right of the object.

35. Hit Ctrl+Shift+A to select all objects. Right click and select Merge As Single Object. You will see an alert box that says "Some objects have a non-default attribute. The attributes of such objects will be lost after this action. Do you want to continue?"

This is a caution that once the shadow and the object are merged together, the objects can no longer be edited independently. Click Yes to close the alert box.

Making Navigation Buttons

1. The purpose of this exercise is to make and edit simple web site navigation buttons using the Path Drawing and Text tools. If you have trouble making the button and text, you can open practicebutton.ufo to take a look at how the button is constructed.

2. Hit Ctrl+N to access the New box. Choose to make a new True Color file with a white canvas. Under "Image size," select User-defined and make the file 300 pixels wide X 300 pixels high. Click OK.

3. ![icon] Select the Path Drawing tool.

4. In the Attributes toolbar, click Shape and select Rounded rectangle.

5. Click in the Attributes toolbar's Color box and select light gray. Make sure 3D Round is selected from the Mode dropdown list.

6. Draw a rounded rectangle path object about the size of a large web button.

7. Press and hold down on the Roundness down arrow in the Attributes toolbar to edit the shape of the button. Drag the slider until the value is 70 and then release the mouse button.

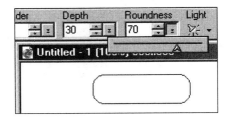

245

8. By editing the Roundness of the button, it looks slightly different, less round and more square around the corners.

9. In the Attributes toolbar, select 3D Custom from the Mode dropdown list. You will see a different kind of bevel around the edges of the button.

10. The default 3D Custom bevel is a bit too large for the button. To edit it, press and hold down on the Border slider in the Attributes toolbar. Drag the slider to the left to make the border a smaller size of 7.

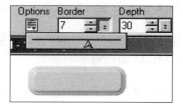

11. Editing the Border of the bevel on the button leaves a lot more room for text by flattening out the surface.

12. In the Attributes toolbar, click the Options button. Choose Galleries, Material.

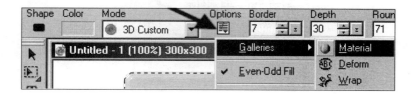

13. Doing so opens the EasyPalette's Material Gallery. Select Plastic, then double click on the Blue 5 thumbnail to apply the effect to the button.

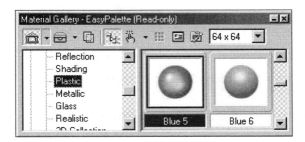

14. Instantly the button takes on the blue color and shading of the thumbnail.

15. Right click and choose Shadow to open the Shadow dialog box. Select Shadow. You will see that the default shadow is much too large for this small button. Leave the shadow color black, but edit the X and Y offset, Transparency and Soft edge to the values shown in the screen shot below. Click OK to apply the shadow.

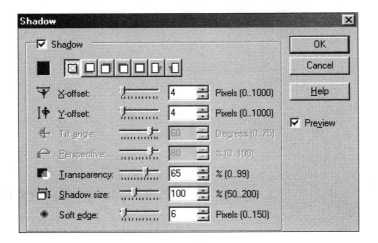

247

16. A small, soft shadow has been added. It is just enough to help the button "pop out" of the background.

17. Click in the base image to deactivate the button.

18.  Select the Text tool. In the Attributes toolbar, select 2D Round from the Mode dropdown list.

19. Click in the base image to open the Text Entry Box. By default, the Arial font at size 100 is selected. This is much too large for the button. From the size dropdown list, select 20, or just select the 100 and replace it with 20. Click in the Color box and change the black default to navy blue. Click the Bold icon. Type HOME and click OK to close the box.

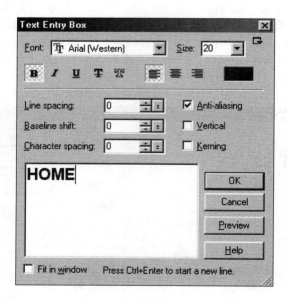

20. Drag the text to the button and center it. Note that the Attributes toolbar has changed to reflect the new font size and color.

Working With Objects: Active Learning Exercises

21. Right click on the active text and choose Edit Text to re-open the Text Entry Box. Select the HOME text. To spread the text characters out a bit, edit the Character spacing to 5. Click in the Color box and select green to replace the navy blue. Click OK to close the box.

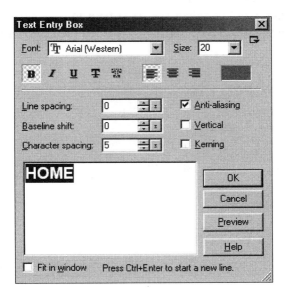

22. Select the Pick tool. While the text is still active, hold down on the Shift key and select the button too, so both are selected at the same time. In the Attributes toolbar's "Align" section, click Center Horizontally. Now the text is perfectly centered on the button.

23. While both objects are selected, right click and choose Merge As Single Object. Once objects are merged, their properties can no longer be edited separately.

24. For the purposes of this exercise, assume that this button would be used on a white web page background. Right click on it and choose Duplicate. Drag the duplicate button into an empty area in the work space, where it will open in its own window. Right click and Merge.

249

25. Click on the original button's blue title bar to make it active. Reverse the process of merging both the Path and Text objects by choosing Edit, Undo Before, Combine Objects.

26. Click on the HOME text to make it active, then right click and choose Edit Text. Note that you do not have to select the Text tool in order to edit text. When the Text Entry Box opens, select HOME and replace it with AWARDS. Click OK to close the box.

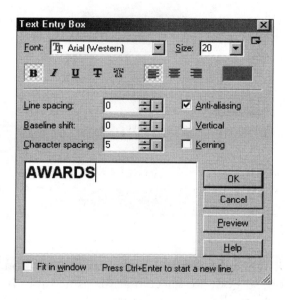

27. Follow steps 22 through 24 above to center the text on the button, merge the text and button as a single object, duplicate and drag the button to open in its own window.

28. Continue making buttons in this manner, making one each for GRAPHICS, LINKS and CONTACT. This is an easy way to make a set of matching web page buttons.

Making Complex Path Objects

1. The purpose of this exercise is to learn how to combine multiple paths, applying an Even-Odd Fill, to create a complex object which could serve as a remote control.

2. Choose File, New and create a new True Color file with a white canvas. Under "Image size," select User-defined and make the file 300 pixels wide X 300 pixels high. Click OK.

3. Select the Path Drawing tool. In the Attributes toolbar, click Options and select Even-Odd Fill.

4. In the Attributes toolbar, choose 3D Round from the Mode dropdown list. Click in the Color box and select gray. Click Shape and select Custom Shape. When the Custom Shape dialog box opens, select Rounded Rectangle 2 and click OK.

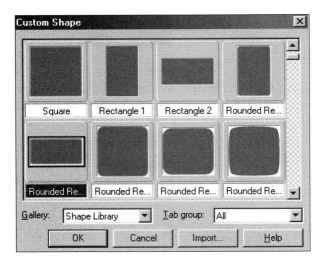

5. Draw a large rounded rectangle that stretches across, but still fits in the base image.

6. From the Mode dropdown list, select Continue Draw. As soon as you do so, the 3D object will change to a black and white path outline.

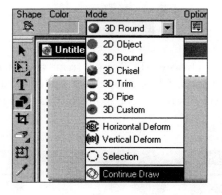

7. Click Shape and select Custom Shape. When the Custom Shape dialog box opens, select Vertical Waves and click OK. Draw a path starting in the lower left corner of the rounded rectangle. Do not get too close to the left or bottom edge.

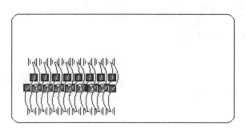

8. Click Shape again and choose Circle. Draw a large circle on the right side of the rounded rectangle.

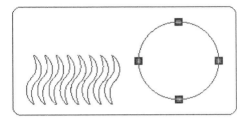

9. Draw a small circle in the upper left side of the rounded rectangle, just above the vertical wave path.

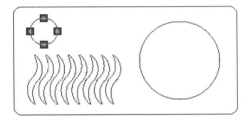

10. From the Mode dropdown list, choose 3D Round. The object will "plump up" but the additional paths added to the object will not be filled in because Even-Odd Fill was selected.

11. Now you will add two more small circle path objects to this complex object. In the Attributes toolbar, click on the ![Edit] Edit button.

253

PhotoImpact 6 Wizardry

12. In path outline view, each path is shown with red control points around it. Click in the base image so that all paths are deselected, then click on the small circle path. Right click on it and choose Duplicate Path. Right click on the duplicate and choose Duplicate Path again, so there are 3 of the small circle paths altogether.

13. Drag the last duplicate circle path over toward the large circle path, so it is on roughly the same horizontal plane as the first circle path. Drag the other duplicate circle path in the middle of the two of them.

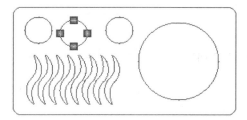

14. While one of the duplicates is selected, hold down on the Shift key and click on the other two circle paths, so that all three are selected at the same time.

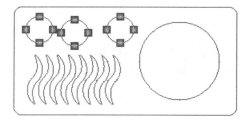

15. In the Attributes toolbar, click Align and select Align Top.

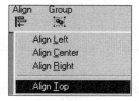

16. By aligning the tops of the objects, they are now all exactly on the same horizontal plane. To distribute them evenly, while all three circle paths are still selected, click Align again, but this time choose Distribute Horizontally. The three paths will be distributed evenly with the left and right anchoring paths staying where they are.

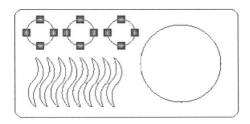

17. In the Attributes toolbar, click the Toggle button to toggle back into 3D Round Mode. This complex object would make a nice remote control.

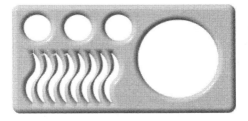

18. Select the Path Drawing tool. In the Attributes toolbar, click the Options button and choose Galleries, Material to open the EasyPalette's Materal Gallery. Select 3D Collection and double click on Shiny Rim to apply a metallic finish to the object.

19. Click in the base image to deactivate the object. Draw a large circle path just big enough to fill in the circular "hole" on the right side of the object. Position the circle object over the opening. In the EasyPalette's Material Gallery, 3D Collection, double click on Neon Red.

20. Right click on the red circle object and choose Arrange, Send to Back. This will send the red circle object to the bottom of the stack. In the Attributes toolbar, drag the Depth slider to the right until its value is 20. This will "plump up" the red circle object.

21. Draw a small circle object just large enough to fill in one of the small circular "holes" along the top of the object. Position the circle over the left opening. In the EasyPalette's Material Gallery, select 3D Collection and double click on Blue. Right click on the small blue circle object and Duplicate. Repeat, so you have three small blue circle objects. Position each one over an opening. Right click on each object and choose Arrange, Send to Back.

22. Select the Pick tool. Right click on an object to select it, then hit Ctrl+Shift+A to select all of the objects. Right click and Merge As Single Object.

Wrap a Path Object Around a Path

1. The purpose of this exercise is to gain practice at Wrapping a path object around another path.

2. Choose File, New and create a new True Color file with a white canvas. Under "Image size," select User-defined and make the file 300 pixels wide X 300 pixels high. Click OK.

3. Select the Path Drawing tool. The Color and Mode do not matter for this exercise. In the Attributes toolbar, click Shape, Custom Shape. When the Custom Shape dialog box opens, select the Heart thumbnail and click OK.

4. Draw a large heart object in the center of the base image. Draw a very small heart (about 1/4 inch) next to the large one. The small heart object will have an animated broken line around it, indicating that it is the active object in the base image.

5. Right click and choose Select All Objects. The small heart object and the large one are both selected at the same time.

6. Choose Objects, Wrap, Fit Together. The large heart object will disappear, and the small heart object will be wrapped around its path.

Wrapping Text Along a Freehand Path

1. The purpose of this exercise is to learn about Wrapping text along a freehand path.

2. Choose File, New and create a new True Color file with a white canvas. Under "Image size," select User-defined and make the file 300 pixels wide X 300 pixels high. Click OK.

3. Select the Line and Arrow tool. In the Attributes toolbar, click Shape and choose Spline.

4. Select 2D from the Mode dropdown list. Color does not matter. Click Width and select a line width of 5. Click Style and select a solid line. Click Arrow and select a line without an arrow, the first option.

5. Starting on the left side, click to start the line, drag a short distance and click again, across the base image. You will notice that after you click, you can curve the line you created prior to clicking. Continue across the base image, making a gently curving line. Double click to end the path.

6. When you release the mouse, a solid, curved line object appears in the base image.

7. Right click on the curved line object and choose Wrap, Add Text to Active Path. Doing so opens the Text Entry Box, which will have a default text of "Enter text here" selected. Replace the default text with Gently Curving Line. Select this new text and change the font to Arial, Size 16, Bold. Edit the Character spacing to 5, to spread the characters out a bit.

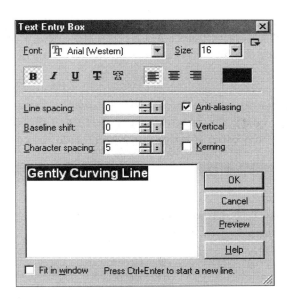

8. Click OK to close the Text Entry box. The Gently Curving Line text will replace and take the shape of the line path you created.

Bending a Path Object

1. The purpose of this exercise is to Bend a Path object, turning it into a kind of faux dingbat. Then you will save the attributes of the command to My Gallery for future use.

PhotoImpact 6 Wizardry

2. Choose File, New and create a new True Color file with a white canvas. Under "Image size," select User-defined and make the file 300 pixels wide X 300 pixels high. Click OK.

3. Select the Path Drawing tool. In the Attributes toolbar, click Shape and select Custom Shape. When the Custom Shape dialog box opens, choose Decoration 8. Click OK to close the box.

4. Back in the Attributes toolbar, select 3D Round from the Mode dropdown list. Color does not matter. Draw a Path object about one-half (1/2) inch tall.

5. While the object is active, choose Object, Wrap, Bend to open the Bend dialog box. Because you want this object to repeat enough times to create a fairly solid shape, edit the Count to 6. Leave the Spacing at the default of 0 to keep the repeated shapes right next to each other. In the "Bending" section, edit the Amount to 100 (values of 100 or –100 will both result in a complete circle).

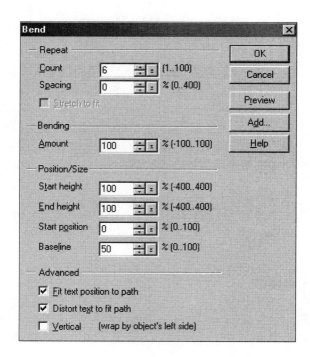

Working With Objects: Active Learning Exercises

6. Since the attributes create faux dingbats easily, save them to the EasyPalette by clicking on the Add button. Doing so opens the Add to EasyPalette dialog box. Give the Bend attributes a name (e.g., Ding Maker) and save it to My Gallery.

7. Click OK to close the dialog box. Look at My Gallery in the EasyPalette, and you will see that a thumbnail for these Bend attributes has been added.

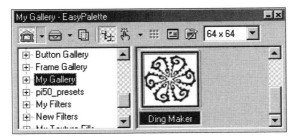

8. When returned to the Bend dialog box, click OK to apply the Bend command to the Path object. The object will be repeated six times and form a complete circle.

261

9. In the Attributes toolbar, click Options and choose Galleries, Material. Doing so opens the EasyPalette's Material Gallery. Select Metallic and double click Copper 6.

10. Because the surface area of the object is rather small, the default bevel overwhelms it and makes the surface look like a dull mustard color. To add shine, increase the surface area. In the Attributes toolbar, press and hold down on the Border slider, dragging it to the left to about 7. The object will brighten up considerably.

11. If you add a round Path object to the center of the object and a slight drop shadow, it would make a great faux dingbat for a web page border background.

12. Click Delete to get rid of the object. You should have an empty base image.

13. Select the Text tool and click in the base image to open the Text Entry box. Choose a font and size that will yield a fairly large, fancy capital S.

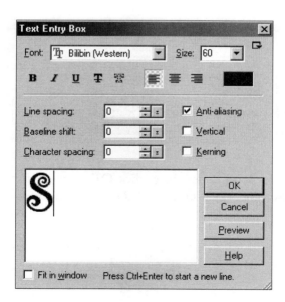

14. In the EasyPalette's My Gallery, double click on the Ding Maker preset created earlier. It will automatically Bend the Text object into a faux dingbat.

15. If you do not want to keep the Ding Maker preset in My Gallery, right click on its thumbnail and choose Delete. You will see an alert box asking if you really want to delete the preset. If you want to get rid of it, choose Yes.

Working With Image Objects

1. The purpose of this exercise is to show how the same Image object can be used in several images to create different, fun effects.

2. Hit Ctrl+O to access the Open dialog box. Browse to boyobject.ufo. This Image object has already been "cut out" for you. Right click on it and Duplicate it.

3. Hit Ctrl+O to access the Open dialog box. Browse to the PhotoImpact 6 Samples folder. Select Waterfall and click Open.

4. Using the Pick tool, drag the duplicate object into the image and position it in the lower left corner. Right click and Merge. It really does look like this photo was taken with the boy in front of the waterfall.

5. Close out the waterfall image. Choose File, Open to access the Open dialog box. Browse to and select benched.bmp. Click Open.

6. Return to the object, right click and Duplicate. Drag the duplicate boy object into the benched image, just to the left of the girl. You will see right away that the object is disproportionately larger than the girl.

7. Right click on the object and choose Properties. When the Object Properties dialog box opens, click the Position and Size tab. In the Size section, resize the object to 75%. Make sure "Keep aspect ratio" is selected. Click OK.

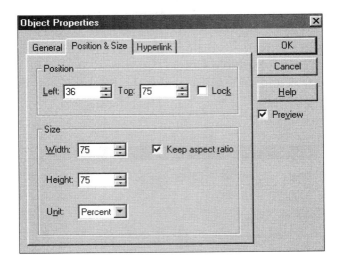

8. Because the object has been made smaller, some sharpness has been lost. To restore detail, choose Format, Focus. Select the thumbnail on the right in the top row to sharpen up detail in the object. Click OK.

9. Right click and Merge. If you did not know better, it would be difficult to tell that the boy had been added to this photo. Close out the benched image.

10. Finally, hit Ctrl+O to access the Open dialog box. Browse to the PhotoImpact 6 Textures folder. Select Water 4 and click Open.

11. Choose the Standard Selection tool. In the Attributes toolbar, select Ellipse from

the Shape dropdown list. Draw a slightly flattened ellipse in the center of the water. Right click and choose Soften. When the Soften box opens, Soften by 20 pixels.

12. Hit Ctrl+H to open the Fadeout dialog box. Select the Radial Fill Type and Multiple Colors. Click in the Multiple Colors Color box. When the Palette Ramp Editor opens, select Palette 8 and click OK to close the Palette Ramp Editor and return to the Fadeout dialog box.

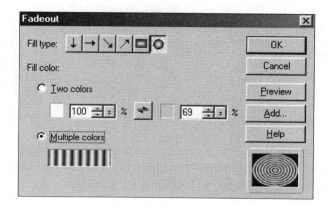

13. Click OK to apply the Fadeout. From the Quick Color Controls on the right side of the work space, click the Lighten (Sun) key's plus (+) sign three times to lighten the area inside the fadeout selection. It looks similar to ripples on water.

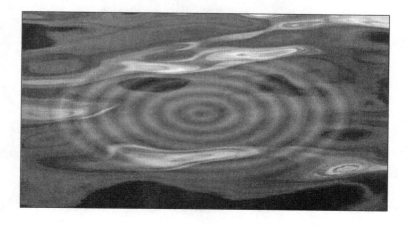

14. Drag the boy object into the new image, over the ripples you just created. He is too big to fit into the center of the ripples, so select the Object Paint Eraser tool. Erase the bottom half of the object, so that just his head and shoulders are sticking out of the water. Round off any sharp angles at the botton of the object. Click Trim.

15. Right click on the object and Duplicate. Choose Edit, Rotate & Flip, Flip Vertically. Drag the flipped duplicate object so that it is exactly underneath the top one.

16. Right click on the upside-down object and choose Properties. When the Object Properties box opens, click the General tab and edit the Transparency to 75%. Click OK to close the Object Properties box.

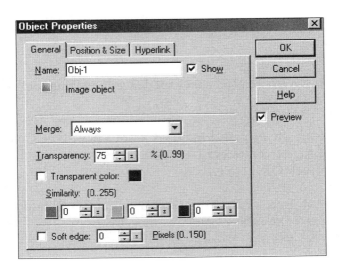

PhotoImpact 6 Wizardry

17. Note that editing Transparency has created a reflection. Right click and choose Arrange, Send Backward, so the reflection is behind the original object. Drag it, if necessary, so that it lines up perfectly underneath the boy emerging from the water.

18. Right click and Merge All. Without using any special filters, you have mimicked the look of ripples on the surface of water, complete with reflection.

Making 3D Text

1. The purpose of this exercise is to gain experience in making and editing 3D Text objects.

2. Hit Ctrl+N to access the New dialog box. Create a new True Color file with a white canvas. Under "Image size," select User-defined and make the file 500 pixels wide X 200 pixels high. Click OK.

3. Select the Text tool. In the Attributes toolbar, select 3D Round from the Mode dropdown list. Leave the other settings as they are.

4. Click in the base image to open the Text Entry Box. Select any font you like from the Font list, and a fairly large font size (e.g., 60 or more). Click in the Color box and select bright blue. Select Bold text, and "Fit in Window" so you can see all of the text. Type "PhotoImpact 6." Click OK to close the box.

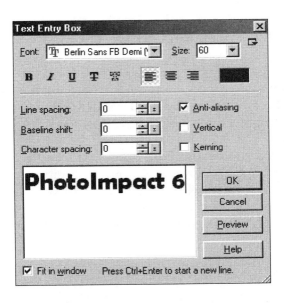

5. In the Attributes toolbar, click on the Material button to open the Material dialog box. Click the Color/Texture tab and select Gradient Color. Doing so opens the Gradient Fill dialog box. For Fill type, select the left to right arrow option. Select Multiple Colors.

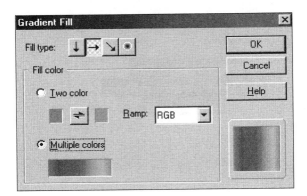

6. Click in the Multiple Colors Color box to open the Palette Ramp Editor. Select Palette 29 and click OK to close the Palette Ramp Editor. When you are returned to the Gradient Fill dialog box, click OK again to apply the gradient fill.

7. The blue 3D text is now a rainbow of colors. Click the Material button again to re-open the Material dialog box. Click the Shading tab and select Metallic. From the Metallic dropdown list, select Gold. Click OK to close the box. Now your text has a metallic sheen.

8. To shine the text up a bit, expose more surface area and less bevel. In the Attributes toolbar, press and hold down on the Border slider and drag it to the left to 7. Notice how much brighter and shinier the text is now.

9. Right click on the text and choose Edit Text to re-open the Text Entry Box. Select the text and edit the font size down to 40 or less. Position the cursor at the end of the PhotoImpact 6 text, then hold down on the Ctrl key while hitting Enter. On this second line, type "The best image editor." Hold down on the Ctrl key and hit Enter again, then type "for the web." Select all three rows of text and Align Center. Click OK.

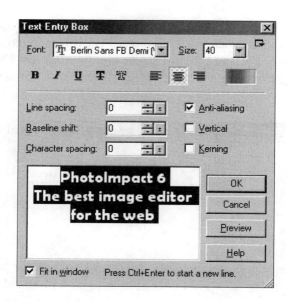

10. Now there are three lines of centered text.

11. In the Attributes toolbar, click the Style button and choose Shadow. When the Shadow box opens, add a black shadow with these attributes. Click OK to apply.

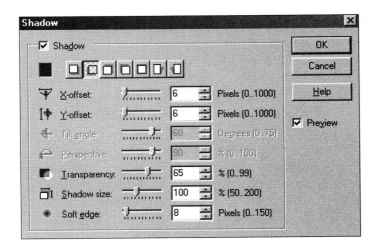

12. A nice, soft shadow which helps the text to stand out better has been added to the Text object.

Making Your Own Stamps

1. The purpose of this exercise is to make two .UFO objects for stamps, using simple, 2D Path objects: a ladybug and a bee. Later on, you will add them to your Stamps. If you have trouble making the stamps, you can use bugstamps.ufo.

2. Choose File, New to create a new True Color file with a white canvas. Under "Image size," select User-defined and make the file 300 pixels wide X 300 pixels high. Click OK.

3. First make the ladybug. Select the Path Drawing Tool. In the Attributes toolbar, click Shape and select Ellipse. Click in the Color box and select red. From the Mode dropdown list, choose 2D.

4. Draw a small, wide ellipse.

5. Choose Object, Convert Object Type, From Path to Image. Now select the Object Paint Eraser. In the Attributes toolbar, click Lines and select Straight Lines. Drag across the bottom of the ellipse, cutting off the bottom and making it flat. Click Trim to get rid of the excess space around the object.

6. Select the Path Drawing tool. In the Attributes toolbar, click Shape and select Circle. Click in the Color box and select black. Draw a small circle for the ladybug's head. Drag it onto the left side of the body. Right click, Arrange, Send Backward.

7. Draw a slightly smaller circle object. Right click and Duplicate two times. Position the new circle objects on the body.

8. Select the Line and Arrow tool. Click Shape in the Attributes toolbar and select Spline. Click in the Color box and select black. Select 2D from the Mode dropdown list. Click Width and select 1. Click Style and select a solid line. Click Arrow and

select the option with a small ball on each end.

9. Click and drag two slightly bent antennae. Drag them onto the front of the ladybug's head. Right click, Select All Objects. Right click, Merge As Single object.

10. Switch to the Paintbrush tool. In the Attributes toolbar, select Fine Brush from the Preset dropdown list. Change the Size to 1 and Soft edge to 1.

11. Select the Pick tool. Click on the ladybug object to make it active, then hit Shift+P to perform the Paint on Edges command. This will put a fine black line around the object to help it stand out better.

12. Next, make a bee. Click in the base image to deactivate the ladybug. Choose the Path Drawing tool. In the Attributes toolbar, click Shape and select Ellipse. Click in the Color box and select a bright orange-yellow color. From Mode, select 2D.

13. Draw a tall ellipse for the bee's body.

14. Select the Transform tool. In the Attributes toolbar, from the Freely Transform options, select Perspective. Drag the lower right control point toward the center of the body, making the bottom of the body narrower.

15. Choose Object, Convert Object Type, From Path to Image. Now you can paint stripes on the bee's body.

16. Select the Paintbrush tool. In the Attributes toolbar, select Wide Square Marker from the Preset dropdown list. Click Shape and select the vertical line shape.

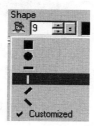

17. While the bee body is active, paint a series of curving black stripes.

18. Select the Path Drawing tool. In the Attributes toolbar, click Shape and select Circle. Click in the Color box and select black. Draw a small black circle for the bee's head. Position it on top of the body.

19. Click in the base image to deactivate the head. Click Shape in the Attributes toolbar and select Custom Shape. When the Custom Shape box opens, select Arrow 4. Click OK. Draw a small arrow shape for the stinger. ➤

20. Choose Edit, Rotate & Flip, Rotate 90 Degrees Right. Drag the stinger to the bottom of the bee's body. Right click, Arrange, Send to Back.

21. Select the Line and Arrow tool. You need to make two antennae for the bee, using the same settings used for the ladybug. Click and drag a slightly curved antenna. Right click, Duplicate. Then Edit, Rotate & Flip, Flip Horizontally. Place the antenna at the top of the head.

22. To make the wings, select the Path Drawing tool. In the Attributes toolbar, click Shape and select Ellipse. From the Mode dropdown list, select 3D Round. Draw a tall ellipse for the wing.

23. In the Attributes toolbar, click Options, Galleries, Material. From the EasyPalette's Material Gallery, 3D Collection, right click on Glass 2 and select Modify Properties and Apply. Doing so opens the Material dialog box. Click the Shadow tab and deselect Shadow. Click OK to close the box.

24. The wing is a semi-transparent ellipse with faint tracings to suggest the texture of insect wings. Choose Object, Convert Object Type, From Path to Image.

25. Select the Linear Gradient Fill tool.

26. In the Attributes toolbar, for Fill Method select Multiple Colors. Change the Transparency to 75. Click in the Color box to open the Palette Ramp Editor. Select Palette 30. Click OK to close the Palette Ramp Editor.

27. Drag diagonally from the top left of the wing to the bottom right of the wing. It will be filled with a pastel gradient.

28. Select the Transform tool. From the Attributes toolbar's Rotate options, rotate the wing 50 degrees counterclockwise. Right click and Duplicate. Rotate the duplicate 40 degrees counterclockwise.

29. While the wing is active, hold down on the Shift key and select the other wing, so both are selected at the same time. Right click and choose Group. Right click and choose Duplicate, which creates a duplicate of both wings.

30. In the Attributes toolbar's "Rotate & flip" section, choose Flip Horizontally. Drag the wings so that they are centered on both sides of the body.

31. While the duplicate pair of wings is active, right click, Send to Back. Click on the other pair of wings and right click, Send to back. The wings are now behind the body.

32. Select the Paintbrush tool. In the Attributes toolbar, select Fine Brush from the Preset dropdown list. Edit the Size to 1, and Soft edge to 1.

33. Select the Pick tool and tap in the base image, then click on the bee body to select it. Hit Shift+P to Paint on Edges, outlining the body. Shift+Click the other parts of the bee, including both antennae, the head, body, stinger and two pairs of wings. When all are selected, right click and choose Merge As Single Object.

Working With Objects: Active Learning Exercises

34. While the bee object is active, choose Web, Trim Object. Click on the ladybug and choose Web, Trim Object. Leave both objects in the same base image.

35. Choose File, Save As. When the Save As dialog box opens, navigate to a folder on your hard drive. Give the objects a name, e.g., bugstamps. Save as a .UFO file and click Save. If you have .UFO Save Options enabled, you will get a secondary dialog box for the save. In that case, select "None" and click OK, then click Save.

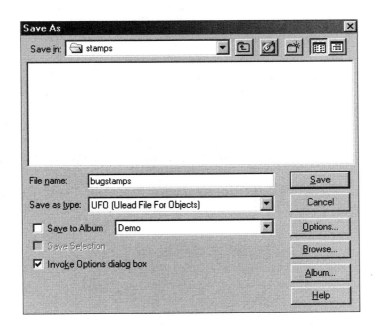

36. Now comes the moment of truth. Close out the file with the two bug stamps.

Adding a Stamp

1. The purpose of this exercise is to Add the two bug stamps you just made and saved as .UFO objects.

2. Choose File, New to create a new True Color file with a white canvas. Under "Image size," select User-defined and make the file 400 pixels wide X 400 pixels high. Click OK.

PhotoImpact 6 Wizardry

3. Select the Stamp tool.

4. In the Attributes toolbar, click the Stamp Menu down arrow and select Add Stamp.

5. When the Open dialog box appears, browse to the folder to which you saved the bugstamps.ufo file. Select it and click Open.

6. After a moment, a thumbnail for the newly added stamp will appear in the Attributes toolbar, indicating that the stamp has been added. To prove it to yourself, click View in the Attributes toolbar, and you will see a thumbnail for the ladybug and the bee.

7. Click in the base image to see your first stamp. Click again to see the next one. They should repeat, alternating. Click Delete to get rid of the stamps.

8. In the Attributes toolbar, change the Scale value to 50, to make the stamps 50% of actual size. Stamp a few stamps to see how they look when made smaller. Delete the stamps by clicking Delete. In the Attributes toolbar, change the Scale back to 100.

9. Choose View, Toolbars & Panels, Brush Panel. When the Brush Panel opens, click the Color tab and select "Hue Shift." There are three options, but choose Random.

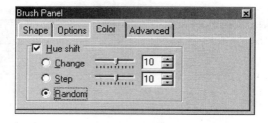

10. Click a few times in the base image to see the results of the Hue Shift. Delete the stamps when the base image is full.

Painting on Edges Necklace with Stamps

1. Hit Ctrl+N to open the New dialog box. Open a new 400 X 400 pixel white canvas.

2. In this exercise you will make a necklace by painting on the edges of a curved line with a pearl stamp. If you have difficulty making the shapes, download necklace.zip.

3. Select the Paintbrush tool. In the Attributes toolbar, select Round Stroke 1 from the Preset dropdown list. Click Mode to enter Paint as Object mode. Paint a wavy line that will serve as the shape of the necklace. When you are finished painting the line, click Mode again to exit Paint as Object mode.

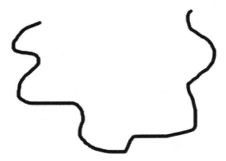

4. While the painted line is still active, select the Stamp tool. In the Attributes toolbar, click the Stamp down arrow and choose the settings shown below.

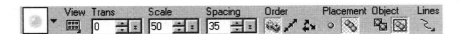

5. Hit Shift+P (or choose Effect, Paint on Edges) to invoke the Paint on Edges command. The line will be covered with pearls. Hit the space bar to deactivate objects.

6. Select the Pick tool. Click on the painted black line to make it active, then hit Delete to get rid of it. You will be left with just the string of pearls.

7. Select the Path Drawing tool. In the Attributes toolbar, select 3D Round from the Mode dropdown list. Color does not matter. Click Shape and select Custom Shape. When the Custom Shape dialog box opens, select Heart and click OK. Draw a heart shape to dangle from the center of the pearl necklace.

8. To dress up the heart, click Options in the Attributes toolbar and select Galleries, Material. Doing so opens the EasyPalette's Material Gallery. From the Metallic tab double click on a metallic gold or copper preset to add shine to the heart object.

9. Click Shape and select Rectangle. Make a small 3D rectangle to serve as the left side clasp. Switch to the Transform tool and rotate it 30 degrees or so counterclockwise to position it on the left side of the necklace.

10. Click Shape and select Ellipse. For Mode, select 3D Pipe. Make a small, narrow ellipse for the other side of the necklace. Drag the Border slider down to 1 or 2 to make it smaller and flatter. Position it on the right side of the necklace.

11. With the Pick tool, right click on the 3D Pipe ellipse and Duplicate to make a jump ring. Drag the duplicate down to the heart, rotating it as necessary.

12. Hit Ctrl+Shift+A to select all objects. Right click, Merge as Single Object. Right click, Shadow to open the Shadow dialog box. Add a shadow to the necklace.

13. Right click, Merge All. In just a few steps you have made a beautiful necklace.

Section 4: Image Editing: Lights, Camera, Action!

Here is where you will learn about the little work horses of image editing, Edit menu commands. Master these basics, then spread your wings and fly with the Format and Effect menu commands. Perform sophisticated color corrections almost effortlessly, or take advantage of PhotoImpact's most dazzling image effects. The Retouch, Paint and Clone tools let you enhance existing images, or create your own original works of art.

Edit Menu Commands explores in detail the grunt work of image editing, including undoing and redoing edits, duplicating, copying and pasting. Get a little fancier by applying fadeout masks, refine selections with Mask Mode, rotate and flip images, stitch multiple images together to create panoramas, or trace images and selections to create editable Path objects. Once you have worked the basic image to your satisfaction, you will be ready to take it to the next level of enhancement with Format menu commands.

Format Menu Commands provide powerful, effective fixes for image imperfections. Learn how to use these commands to tweak color balance, hue and saturation, focus and brightness and contrast, or to change image size, resolution and data type. Find out about tools which automate the correction of problems commonly found in scanned and digital images. For the greatest degree of control over color distribution, create and save tone maps to tweak light, dark and midtones to perfection. If you are looking for a show-stopping look, now is the time to move on to Effect menu commands.

Effect Menu Commands are, unquestionably, the brightest stars in PhotoImpact's constellation of image editing tools. This section will show how to use them to create subtle enhancements as well as awesome, jaw-dropping effects. Add a soft, Gaussian blur to an image or restore detail and sharpness. Or go straight over the top by adding lightning bolts, lens flares and particles like fireflies and stars. Add dramatic spotlights, deeply emboss text or cover it with flames, or create a delicate watercolor or oil painting from a photo. What is more, you will learn how to turn many of these magical effects into editable key frame animations.

The Retouch, Paint and Clone Tools explores the similarities and differences among these tools. You will learn how to paint in object mode, and to paint and clone with textures to add surface interest to 2D images. Use handy tools for colorizing, color replacement and cloning to create unique image effects, or remove red eye, scratches and noise with retouch tools. Bump up your control and fine tune by mastering the Brush Panel, which permits the greatest flexibility in tweaking brush settings.

Active Learning Exercises Painting and Editing Clipboard Clipboard Contents; Stitching and Cloning a Panorama; Editing a Photo With a Tone Map and Custom Framing; Editing a Photo With a Custom Tone Map; Editing Photo Color With Style Filters; Color Correcting a Photo With Color Balance; Editing With Hue & Saturation; Reducing Size and Editing Focus/Sharpness of a Photo; Removing Red Eye from a Digital Photo; Removing Green Eye from a Digital Photo; Making a Snowglobe with Creative Particle; Natural Painting Applied to a Photo; Creative Painting Applied to a Photo; Painting and Retouching Image Objects; Artistic Cloning Effects; Cloning to Remove Unwanted Objects; Creating an Animation Studio Animation; Animating Text With Creative Type; Creating a Lighting Animation.

Chapter 12: The Edit Menu

Edit menu commands perform much of the basic work of image editing, such as Undoing and Redoing edits, copying and pasting, filling selections, cropping and duplicating. From Edit you can expand the canvas around an image, apply a Fadeout effect, refine a selection with a mask, rotate and flip an image or object, stitch two images together or trace a selection or image and turn it into an editable 3D Path object. Laying the groundwork for more spectacular effects, Edit commands can whip your image into shape for more advanced editing with PhotoImpact's awesome built-in filters and plug-ins. The availability of Edit menu commands varies by Data Type. For example, the Trace command is available for True Color images only. If an Edit command is grayed out, it is unavailable for an image as it currently exists.

Because PhotoImpact offers more than one way to peform most tasks, a number of Edit options can be accessed by simply right clicking. To Undo the last edit, you can right click and choose Undo. However, to Undo the last 10 edits to an image, it is more efficient to choose Edit, Undo Before, and Undo up to the desired edit. Similarly, you can right click and Merge All to merge multiple objects with the base image, saving time and mouse clicks. As you become more familiar with PhotoImpact, you will learn which Edit commands are more quickly accessed by right clicking.

Undo Before

Undo Before accesses a list of edits to the image since it was last saved. The edits are listed in chronological order, with the most recent edit at the top of the list. Select the point to which you want to Undo from this list. Alternatively, click the Undo arrow.

The number of edits in the Undo Before list will reflect the Undo level set in Preferences, General under the File menu. Try to balance the Undo number against your computer's RAM. Image files can be quite large, particularly those containing many UFO objects. Setting too high an Undo level can tax your computer's resources by forcing it to hold huge amounts of information in memory. If you are operating with 64 MB of RAM, or have more than one program open at a time, you will want to set a lower number for Undo level (e.g., 5 or 10). If you have 128 MB or more of RAM, you may enable many more levels of Undo.

Redo To

Sometimes you may Undo an edit, then decide that you really want it back. Choose Redo To to select from a list of recent edits.

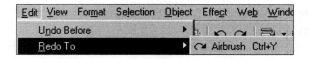

Alternatively, you can click on the Redo arrow.

Clear Undo/Redo History

When selected, a warning box appears that says "This command cannot be undone. Are you sure you want to continue?" Consider carefully before choosing Clear Undo/Redo History, which essentially eliminates all Undo and Redo opportunities.

Repeat (Last Command) (Ctrl+T)

Repeats the last Edit command. This is a fast way to duplicate an object repeatedly.

Cut (Ctrl+X)

Cuts an active selection or object from the base image. You can also click on the Cut button.

Cutting a selection area leaves an empty space in the base image, while cutting an object simply removes it from the base image. If no selection has been made or if there are no active objects in the base image, the entire base image will be cut. It can be alarming if you select Cut by mistake, instead of Copy. If that happens, just choose Edit, Undo Before, right click and choose Undo, or click the Undo button.

Copy (Ctrl+C)

Copies the image, or an active selection or objects within the base image, into the

Clipboard. Alternatively, click on the Copy button.

Paste

The Paste submenu specifies how Clipboard contents will be pasted into the base image.

As Object (Ctrl+V) Clipboard contents are pasted into the base image as an object. After it is pasted, you can right click on an object, select Properties, and edit from the Object Properties dialog box.

Into Selection Clipboard contents are pasted into an active selection. You will see a crosshair in the center of the pasted object, which is "hooked" to the crosshair. Move the cursor around without pressing down on the mouse button to position the object within the selection area. Click to fix the pasted object in place. This is a good way to paste a larger object into a smaller area. Position the pasted object so that only the part you want to show is visible within the selection area, then click.

Fit Into Selection Clipboard contents are pasted into a selection area and automatically resized to fit the selection.

Under Pointer Clipboard contents are pasted into the base image with a crosshair in the center. The pasted object is "hooked" to the crosshair. Move the cursor around without pressing down on the mouse button to position the object within the base image. Click to fix the pasted object in place.

As A New Image (Shift+Ctrl+V) Pastes Clipboard contents into its own window in the work space. The object will have an animated broken line running around it, indicating that it is an object independent of the base image.

Clear

Clear removes a selection or object from the base image. If the image contains no active selection or object, the entire base image will be replaced with the current background color.

Clipboard

Allows you to work directly with the Clipboard in several different ways.

Load Loads an image file directly into the Clipboard without even having to open it in the work space.

Save Opens the Save As dialog box, in which you may save the Clipboard contents as an image file.

Display Clipboard content opens in its own window in the work space. Handy if you are not sure what is in the Clipboard right now. When you click anywhere in the work space the image will close.

Crop (Ctrl+R)

Crop eliminates part of an image, while preserving the rest of it. First, make a selection. Then choose Edit, Crop, or hit Ctrl+R. More advanced crop options can be accessed by choosing the Crop tool in the Tool Panel.

Duplicate

Duplicates a base image and its objects in a variety of ways.

Base Image With Objects (Ctrl+D) Creates a duplicate of the base image and all objects. The objects in the duplicate remain editable, just as they are in the original image. This is a wonderful feature when you are concerned about editing past the point of no return in your original image, as you will have a "back up" open in case you edit past your Undo Before level and do not like the results of editing.

Base Image With Objects Merged Creates a duplicate with all of its objects merged with the base image. The objects can no longer be edited.

Base Image Only Creates a duplicate of the base image without any objects it contains.

Fill (Ctrl+F)

Opens the Fill dialog box, which allows you to fill an image, selection or object from one of four tabs: Color, Gradient, Texture and Image.

Color Tab

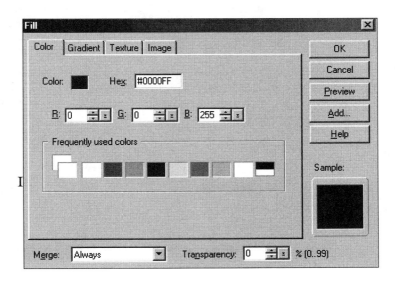

Click in a Color box to open the Ulead Color Picker. Right click in the Color box to select from a greater range of color options, including the Ulead Color Picker, Windows Color Picker, Eyedropper, Color On Screen, Foreground Color, Background Color, the eight most recently used colors, or an array of standard colors. Alternatively, enter the Hex code for a color, custom mix a color using RGB values, or select a color from frequently used colors.

Gradient Tab

Select a fill type, gradient type and colors, merge method and transparency.

> **Fill type** Choose a direction for the gradient fill: top to bottom, left to right, diagonal down, diagonal up, rectangular or radial.
>
> **Fill color** Select a Two color or Multiple colors gradient fill. Click in the Color boxes to choose beginning and ending colors for a Two color gradient fill. Click in the Multiple colors Color box to select a gradient from the Palette Ramp Editor. Click in the Magic Gradient box, from which you can edit the currently selected gradient or open the Palette Ramp Editor.

PhotoImpact 6 Wizardry

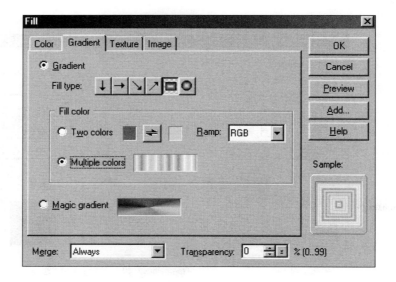

Merge Specify how the color characteristics of the gradient fill will be merged with the colors in the base image.

Ramp Choose how the colors are distributed within the gradient fill: RGB (follows the beginning and ending colors in a straight line around the RGB color cube); HSB Counterclockwise (follows the beginning and ending colors in a continuous arc counterclockwise around the HSB cone); HSB Clockwise (follows the beginning and ending colors in a continuous arc clockwise around the HSB cone).

Transparency Select a transparency level for the gradient fill. Higher values yield more transparent fills.

Texture Tab

Fills with a Natural or Magic Texture.

> **Gallery** Select a Gallery.
>
> **Tab group** Select Natural or Magic Texture from the dropdown list. Magic Textures only can be edited by clicking on the More button.

Chapter 12: The Edit Menu

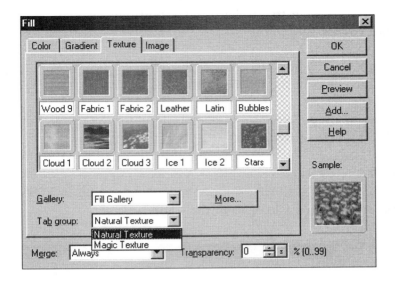

When the secondary Magic Texture dialog box opens, the center thumbnail is selected by default. The other thumbnails represent variations on the selected texture. Click on the thumbnails to edit the texture. Each time you select a thumbnail, it moves to the center and the other thumbnails are redrawn.

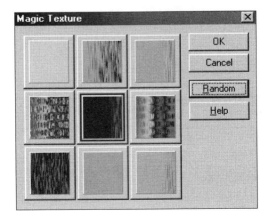

Keep clicking until you get the effect you want. If you get too far away from the desired effect, click Cancel. You can always go back and try again by clicking More. If you like an edited Magic Texture and want to use it again, click on the

289

Add button to open the Add to EasyPalette dialog box. Give the edited texture a name and save it to a Gallery and Tab group. To apply the edited Magic Texture, click OK.

Merge Specify how the color characteristics of the texture fill will be merged with the colors in the base image.

Transparency Select a transparency level for the texture fill. Higher values yield more transparent fills.

Image Tab

Fill with an image from a File or from the Clipboard.

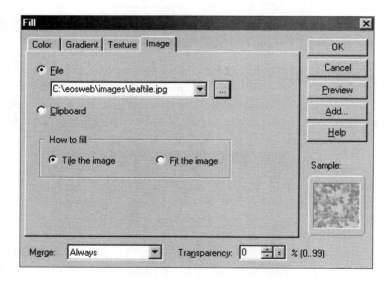

File Browse to the file you wish to use for the fill, or select a recently used file from the dropdown list.

Clipboard Fill with Clipboard contents.

How to fill Choose whether to have the fill automatically resized to completely fill the image, selection or object, or to be tiled within it.

Merge Specify how the color characteristics of the image fill will be merged with the colors in the base image.

Transparency Select a transparency level for the image fill. Higher values yield more transparent fills.

Fadeout (Ctrl+H)

Fadeout makes it easy to blend objects by performing a gradual transparency. For example, use Fadeout to blend numerous objects into one another or a textured background when making a collage.

Fadeout is available for True Color or Grayscale images, selections and objects only. Select attributes from the Fadeout dialog box.

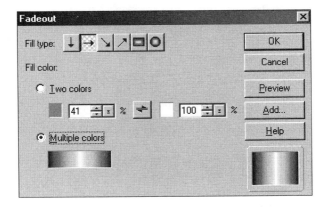

Fadeout results from the application of a grayscale gradient mask. Black completely blocks out underlying pixels, while white is completely transparent. Shades of gray result in varying degrees of transparency, with darker shades more opaque and revealing little of the underlying image, and lighter shades resulting in greater transparency.

Fill type Select a direction for the fadeout gradient fill: top to bottom, left to right, diagonal down, diagonal up, rectangular or radial.

Fill color Choose a Two color or Multiple color gradient fill. For a Two color fadeout, click in the beginning and ending Color boxes to open the Ulead Color Picker. Only black, white and grays will be available. For a Multiple color fadeout, click in the Color box to open the Palette Ramp Editor. Only grayscale gradients will be available. Click on the Preview button to see how the Fadeout effect looks. Click OK to apply.

Expand Canvas

Adds the specified number of pixels around the base image. Expand Canvas is a handy way to add a 1 or 2 pixel contrasting color "frame" around an image.

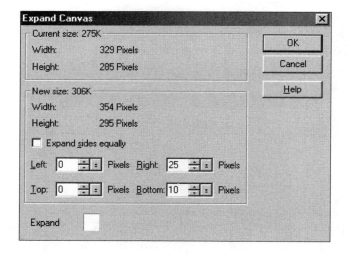

Current Size Shows the current file size and height and width of the image in pixels.

New Size Shows the effect of the added canvas on file size and image height and width in pixels.

Expand sides equally Select to expand canvas the specified number of pixels on all four sides. Deselect to expand selected sides only. Enter the number of pixels to expand for each of the four sides: Left, Right, Top and Bottom.

Expand By default the Expand canvas color is white. Click in the Color box to select a different color.

Rotate & Flip

Presents choices for rotating, flipping or transforming an image, selection or object: Rotate left 90 degrees, Rotate right 90 degrees, Rotate 180 degrees, Flip Horizontally, Flip Vertically or Use Transform Tool.

Stitch

Stitches together two images taken in sequence, a technique often used for creating panoramas, but also useful when you have two pictures of the same subject and want to combine their best features. In the Stitch dialog box, specify an overlap area of transparency, which permits you to see through a layer to position the two images accurately.

Open the images you wish to stitch together. Click on the blue title bar of one of the images to make it active, then choose Edit, Stitch to open the dialog box.

Stitch with Select the other image to be stitched from the dropdown list.

Overlap area transparency Set a transparency level for the overlap. The transparent area makes it easier to line up the top and bottom of the images manually.

Manually Drag the images together yourself, or hold down on the Shift key while establishing reference points for lining them up. Leave Auto fine-tune selected for best results.

Auto stitch Allows PhotoImpact to determine the best Stitch, based on similarity of joined edges. Select an overlap range for the general area where the images will be joined. Enter values for acceptable Vertical and Horizontal tolerance.

Test Click to preview the stitch.

Switch direction Places the images side by side, or click to switch sides.

Deskew Click Horizontal or Vertical to correct misalignment along either axis.

The two images below were stitched together to create a panorama of a large lily pond.

Trace

Traces around the edges of a selection or image to create a path object. This is a great way to turn a selection or 2D image into a 3D path object. If an image contains no active selection, a shape based on the luminosity values of the pixels in the entire image will be traced. Darker pixels are traced, while lighter pixels are excluded from the trace.

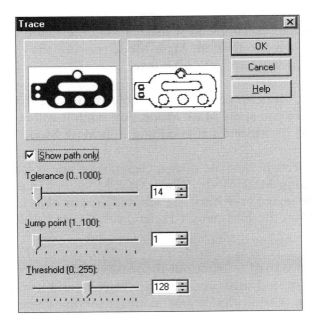

Show path only Shows only the vector path in the right preview window.

Tolerance Lower tolerance values result in a more accurate trace.

Jumppoint Lower values result in smoother curves, but take longer to process.

Threshold Selects pixels based on their luminence. All pixels below the threshold level will be selected for the trace.

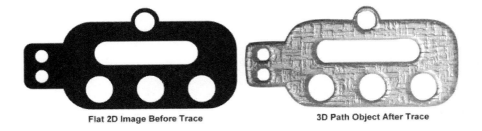

Mask Mode

Use Mask Mode to refine selections. First make a rough selection with the Standard or Lasso Selection tool, then choose Edit, Mask Mode (or click the Mask icon in the Status bar) to tweak the selection down to the last pixel.

You can also use Mask Mode to delete parts of objects. Be sure that you have finished editing an object before you apply Mask Mode. Although it will remain an object, you will not be able to edit its attributes after editing it in Mask Mode.

If there are several objects in the base image, click on the one you wish to edit to make it active prior to selecting Mask Mode. When Mask Mode is selected, a transparent color mask covers the entire image except for the selected area or object. The color of the mask is determined from the File menu's Preferences, General dialog box.

Once a selection or object has been made active and you are in Mask Mode, click on the Paintbrush tool, which is used to paint out the mask or add to it. Paint colors will be restricted to black, white and shades of gray. Use black to add to the mask, and white to subtract from the mask. Use shades of gray to create varying degrees of transparency.

Chapter 13: The Format Menu

Format menu commands access clever fixes for common imaging problems. Use the Format commands to improve the appearance of images by editing color balance or saturation, focus and contrast. These commands will also edit image size, data type, resolution, convert an image to Windows wallpaper, create a Tone Map for your particular scanner, or use the Post-processing Wizard to correct scanned or digital camera images.

The Format commands automate many image correction tasks by offering choices from thumbnail Quick Samples. Often these choices will solve image problems handily. However, associated Options permitting more fine-grained tweaking are available for most dialog boxes, allowing those who prefer to have more control over the image correction process the flexibility to do so. Preview and Reset buttons make it easy to see the effect of edits immediately, and to return to the original appearance if the results are not exactly what you want.

Auto Process

Auto Process makes available six of the most commonly used image correction commands.

Brightness Brightens dark areas and darkens light areas. Brightness edits are generally more helpful for very dark images.

Contrast Increases the contrast between light and dark areas of the image.

Focus Sharpens up blurry parts of the image, while softening areas where edges appear a bit too sharp. Focus is particularly helpful for large images that have been greatly reduced in size.

Straighten Helps align scanned images, which are often crooked, so that the edges of the image line up correctly with the edges of the page.

Crop Automatically removes excess background from the image. Crop works best on images with a solid black or white background. Results can be less successful for large, detailed images. You can also select Ctrl+R or use the Crop tool to crop an image.

PhotoImpact 6 Wizardry

Batch Combines all of the Auto Process options in one handy window. Position the cursor over each option to read a description of its function. Choose a processing option and view the results immediately in the right Preview frame. Click Preview to see the effect applied to the actual image. Click on the Reset button if the results are unsatisfactory.

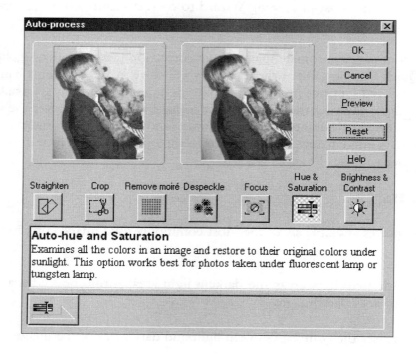

Style

Style filters apply tints of color to images. They can create a surreal mood or look, but they are also helpful for subtle color corrections, such as editing skin tones or adding a cool cyan or blue cast to an image. They are also great for tinting objects. You will have to try them out for yourself to understand their magical effects.

Each tab in the Style box contains effect thumbnails. Select a thumbnail to see its effect applied to the image in the right Preview frame. Remember that you can access Style filters through the EasyPalette's Style Gallery too.

Brightness & Contrast (Ctrl+B)

The easiest way to edit brightness and contrast is to select a Quick Samples thumbnail. Each time a thumbnail is selected, it moves to the center and the others are redrawn.

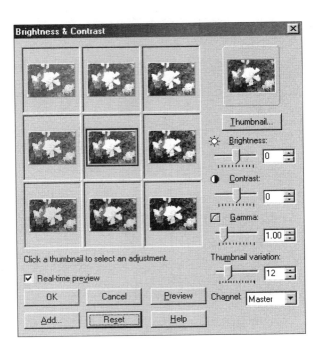

To attain greater control over brightness and contrast than is offered from the thumbnails, edit attributes directly.

Brightness Increases or decreases brightness of an image.

Contrast Higher values emphasize midtones in the image.

Gamma Changes midtones without changing colors at the end of the color spectrum. Higher values strengthen midtones more.

Thumbnail variations Controls the strength of a thumbnail's effect on the image preview. Higher values result in a more powerful difference between the thumbnail options.

Channel Applies edits to all color channels, or to the Red, Green or Blue channel.

Color Balance (Ctrl+L)

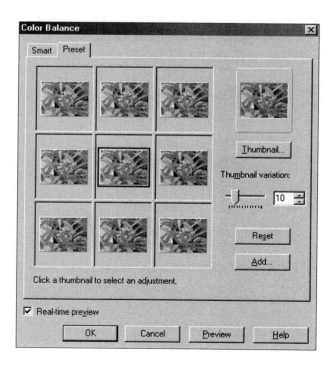

Color balance redistributes all of the colors in an image so that they are more evenly balanced. Edit from either of two tabs: Preset and Smart.

Preset Tab Select a thumbnail from the Preset tab to shift the primary tint of an image. Each time a thumbnail is selected, it moves to the center and the other thumbnails are redrawn.

> **Thumbnail variations** Controls the strength of a thumbnail's effect on the image preview. Higher values result in a more powerful difference between the thumbnail options.
>
> **Reset** Returns to default values so you can start over again.

Smart Tab Achieve greater control over the colors used and their contrast with one another from the Smart tab. Position the cursor over the image in the Preview window and it will change into an Eyedropper. Click on to what should be a "neutral" color such as white or black. This color will appear in the Corrected color box. Click in the Desired color box to replace the Corrected color with a more accurate color.

Hue & Saturation (Ctrl+E)

PhotoImpact 6 features significant improvements for editing hue (color) and saturation (intensity). Two simple slider bars have been replaced with slider bars for Hue, Saturation and Lightness, and the addition of three different editing Methods.

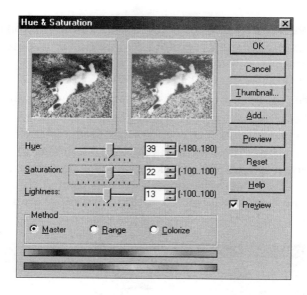

Hue Drag the slider control (or enter values directly into the Hue box) to edit image color.

Saturation Drag the slider control (or enter values directly into the Saturation box) to control the richness of colors. Low saturation results in a muted or grayscale effect, while high values increase the richness or intensity of color.

Lightness Adds a layer of white or black, with positive numbers lightening the image and negative numbers darkening it.

Method Specifies how the colors in the image will be edited.

> **Master** The upper bar displays image colors as they are currently. The lower bar displays the colors used to replace the colors in the upper bar.

Range Use the four sliders in between the bars to adjust color within a targeted range on the upper bar. These color adjustments will be strongest in the dark gray section of the sliders, while effects will be minimal in the lighter gray section of the sliders. When you are satisfied with the colors resulting from the distribution of the sliders, drag on the dark gray section of the sliders to move all four sliders into a particular color range.

Colorize The lower bar displays the color selected via the Hue slider. This color replaces all of the colors in the image.

Focus (Ctrl+Shift+F)

Edits the focus, or sharpness of an image.

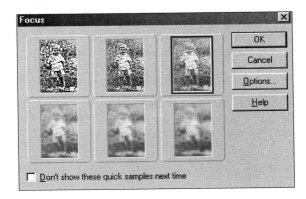

To fine tune focus, click the Options button to open a secondary Focus dialog box.

PhotoImpact 6 Wizardry

From here you may select Auto-adjust, or use the Blur to Sharpness slider and enter Level values for the amount of sharpening. The results of these values will be shown in the right Preview window.

Tone Map (Ctrl+Shift+T)

Tone maps modify the distribution of color in an image to correct color imbalance, increase color range, improve contrast and reduce/enhance shadows and highlights. Tone maps can be invaluable in salvaging old photographs that have lost detail due to faded midtones. Create tone maps from either of two tabs: Highlight Midtone Shadow or Map.

Highlight Midtone Shadow Tab Click this tab to view a histogram of the current color distribution. The histogram will change according to values chosen with the slider controls for the Highlight, Midtone and Shadow colors. Apply these values to the Master, Red, Green or Blue color channel. Click on the Auto button to automatically adjust colors. Click the Save button to save a custom tone map.

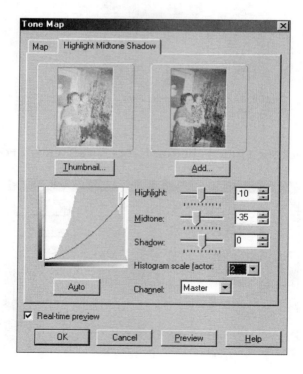

Map Tab Click the Map tab to tweak from presets accessed via the Enhancements button. You may reset the histogram in the Preview window by choosing Reset from the Enhancements list. Choose to apply Enhancements to the Master, Red, Green or Blue channel. Click Accumulatively to apply multiple Enhancements.

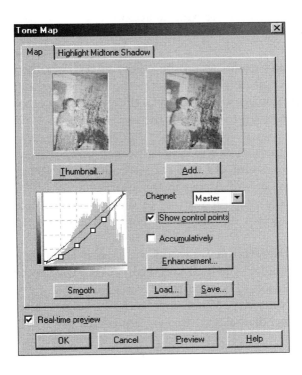

Channel Choose to apply Enhancements to the Master, Red, Green or Blue channel.

Show control points Select to display control points upon which you may drag to redistribute colors.

Accumulatively Select to apply multiple Enhancements in aggregate.

Enhancements Click to apply a preset Enhancement or mapping curve: Darken, Highlight, Lighten, Midtone, Darken Midtone, Lighten Midtone, Shadow & Highlight, Shadow, Use Complete Range, and Reset Curve.

Smooth Smooths the mapping curve, which may create a more natural look.

Load Opens the Load Tone Map dialog box, from which you may open a previously saved tone map.

Save Opens the Save Tone Map dialog box. Tone maps are saved with the .MAP file extension.

Tone maps are particularly useful when the colors in your scanned or digital camera images often do not look quite right. If that is the case, you should consider creating and saving a custom tone map so that editing these images will go faster and easier. Save and access a custom tone map in either of these two ways.

After creating the tone map, click the Add button to open the Add to EasyPalette dialog box. Give the tone map a name and save it to a Gallery and Tab group. Click OK and a thumbnail for the tone map will appear in the appropriate EasyPalette Gallery. The next time you acquire an image via your scanner or digital camera, simply drag and drop the thumbnail onto the image (or double click) to apply the tone map.

Alternatively, click on the Save button to open the Save Tone Map dialog box. Browse your hard drive for the folder to which you wish to save the tone map. It will be saved with the .MAP file extension. The next time you acquire a scanned or digital camera image, select Format, Tone Map. When the Tone Map dialog box opens, select Load to open the Load Tone Map dialog box. Browse your hard drive for the desired tone map.

Invert

Applied to an entire image, Invert changes all of the color pixels to their complimentary (opposite in the color wheel) colors. So greens become purples, pinks and reds appear green, and so on. You can create artistic and startling color effects with this command. When the Invert command is applied to an image with an active selection, the selection area is inverted.

Level

Modifies the number of divisions in an image's color channels, which reduces the number of colors used.

Original Image / After Level Applied

Level results in a loss of detail and a "posterized" appearance. Select a thumbnail from the Quick Samples in the dialog box or click Options to tweak the settings by color Channel.

Histogram

The Histogram presents a graph showing the distribution of colors in an image or selection area.

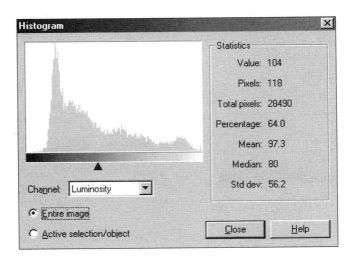

Although you cannot redistribute colors directly from the Histogram, the graphical display of this information can be helpful in making informed edits via other Format commands, such as Hue & Saturation, Color Balance or Tone Map. Drag the small triangular handle along the bottom of the histogram to view Statistics for that particular point in the graph. These data can be obtained for the Luminosity, Red, Green or Blue channels.

Equalize

Automatically adjusts images that are too light or too dark. There are no thumbnail options associated with this command.

Calculation

Calculation permits you to create a new, composite image by blending two images together. By varying the color channel and Operation (Merge method) for the composite image, dramatic effects can be achieved.

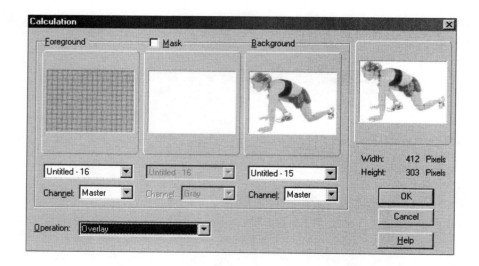

Calculation requires that both images be exactly the same size. If they are not the same size, you will not be able to apply this command.

Foreground Choose a Foreground image from the dropdown list. The Foreground image will be blended on top of the Background image. If you cannot get the effect you want by varying the Operation, try switching the Foreground and Background images.

Mask Selecting Mask applies a grayscale mask to the Foreground image. Try the Calculation command with and without a mask. Selecting Mask can enhance the strength of the effect, and often will, but the ultimate value of adding a mask will vary by the colors in the combined images and the Operation option selected.

Background Choose a Background image from the dropdown list. The Background image will serve as the base image.

Channel Select which Channel (Master, Red, Green, Blue) you wish to merge with the other image. Quite different results can be achieved by varying channels.

Operation Select an Operation to determine how the color characteristics of the Foreground image will be applied to the Background (base) image. The Operation options are essentially the same as Merge method used elsewhere in PhotoImpact. The results of the Calculation on the previous page are shown below. Note how the woven basket texture was applied to the woman.

Post-processing Wizard (F9)

The Post-processing Wizard is a time-saver, an all-in-one feature for correcting common image problems. It is especially useful for processing acquired images. The dialog box sequentially offers the opportunity to Straighten, Crop, Focus, adjust Brightness, adjust Color Balance, Remove Red Eye or add a Frame & Shadow. To perform one of these functions, click on its button. To skip it, click Next. When finished processing the image, click Finish.

Dimensions (Ctrl+G)

From the Dimensions dialog box, resize a base image and/or its objects.

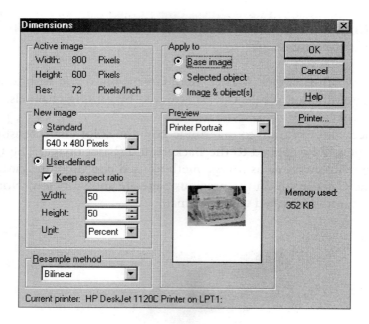

Active image Displays image width, height and resolution.

New image Creates a new image at the designated height and width.

User defined Resize to a specific width and height in pixels, centimeters, inches or percent. Select "Keep aspect ratio" to maintain height to width proportions. This is an easy way to make "thumbnails." For example, to have all thumbnails 100 pixels tall, edit image height to 100 pixels and select "Keep aspect ratio." The width will adjust automatically.

Resample method Choose from Bicubic, Bilinear or Nearest Neighbor (good for small icons and lines/outlines).

Current Printer Displays the default printer.

Apply to Choose from Base image, Selected object(s) or Image and object(s).

Preview Shows how the image will appear on a printed page or on a monitor at the selected resolution.

Resolution

Resolution changes the physical size of an image, but not its file size. Lower resolution creates larger printed images by increasing the space between pixels, and higher resolution creates smaller printed images by packing pixels closer together. Resolution can be tricky to understand because when resolution is changed, the image still looks exactly the same on your monitor. Monitors display all images at 72 dpi, regardless of their actual resolution. You will only see the results of editing resolution in Print Preview or when the image is actually printed.

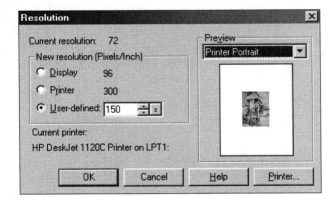

Current resolution Displays the current image resolution.

New resolution Select from default Display, your Printer's default or a User-defined resolution.

Current printer Displays your default printer.

Preview Shows how the image will appear on a printed page or on a monitor at the selected resolution.

Frame & Shadow (Shift+F)

Add a Frame & Shadow from the Format menu commands, or by clicking on the Frame & Shadow button in the Standard Toolbar. The Frame & Shadow dialog box has two tabs, Frame and Shadow.

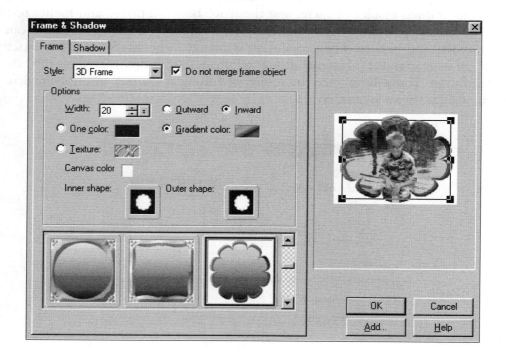

Frame Tab

Style Select a Frame style (2D, 3D, Edge, Magic or Classic) from the dropdown list.

2D and 3D The shapes for both frame styles are the same, but 3D frames have beveled edges. Choose a width for the inner and outer parts of the frame, and click in the One color, Texture or Gradient color boxes to edit frame color. Click in the Inner shape and Outer shape boxes to edit frame shape.

Edge Creates a torn or photo edge. Click in the One color, Texture or Gradient color boxes to edit frame color, or deselect "Photo edge" to make a raggedy edge with no color.

Magic Magic frames offer the most flexibility in editing frames. The Effects dropdown list allows you to select from a number of variations on a particular style.

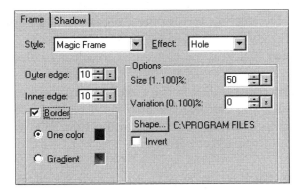

Click in the One color or Gradient color boxes to edit frame color. Options allow you to set values for the size of the frame's inner and outer edges and create variations on the frame.

Classic These beautiful and whimsical frames are editable in PhotoImpact 6.

Do not merge frame object A welcome innovation in PhotoImpact 6 is the ability to edit frames. For 2D, 3D and Classic frames only, "Do not merge frame object" is selected. Leave this option selected if you wish to edit the objects making up the frame. To edit, after applying Frame & Shadow right click and Ungroup grouped frame objects. Choose the Path Drawing Tool and click on a frame object to make it active. Now you can edit the object via the Attributes toolbar, Material dialog box or EasyPalette, just as you would any other object.

Options Editable options vary by frame type. Options are listed below, but not all frame styles include all of these options. If an option is grayed out it is unavailable for a particular frame style.

> **Width** Enter a value in pixels for frame width. Many frames allow you to specify a width for the Inner (extends into the image) and Outer frame edges, or Both.
>
> **Border** Leave Border selected to apply selected colors associated with the frame style. Deselecting removes the colors, leaving only the frame shape around image edges.

Photo edge Leave Photo edge selected to apply the selected color, gradient or texture. Deselecting leaves only a raggedy edge frame around the image.

One color Click in the Color box to select a color.

Gradient color Click in the Color box to open the Gradient Fill dialog box, from which you can select a Two-color or Multiple-color gradient fill. Choose "Use Ramp Control" and click on the Edit Palette button to open the Palette Ramp Editor to select a gradient.

Texture Click in the Texture box to select a Magic or Natural Texture from the Texture Library.

Inner/Outer Shape Click in the shape box to select shapes from the Custom Shape dialog box.

Effect Magic frames only have an Effect dropdown list from which you can edit frames. Included are Tear, Hole, Stroke, Ripple, Fire, Glossy, Stamp, Emboss, Texture, Neon, Seal, Sobel, Bristle and Charcoal. The Options available vary by the selected Effect.

Variation Magic frames only permit this option, which creates an irregular edge.

Shape Magic frames permit you to apply a different mask shape.

Invert Magic frames only allow you to reverse the shape of the frame pattern.

Shadow Tab

Select or deselect a shadow for the framed image.

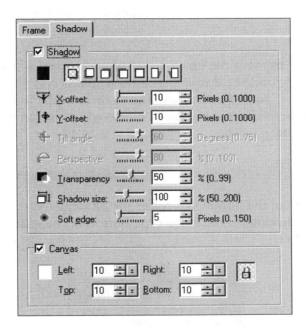

Color Click in the shadow color box to select a color. The default is black.

Direction Select a direction in which the shadow will fall, including new perspective shadows.

X and Y Offset Enter values in pixels.

Transparency Edit transparency, with higher values resulting in lighter shadows and lower values resulting in darker shadows.

Tilt angle Available for perspective shadows only, edits the angle of the shadow.

Perspective Available for perspective shadows only, edits the perspective of the shadow to convey an impression of depth or distance.

Shadow size Indicates the size of the shadow relative to the size of the image. The default is 100%.

Soft edge Selected by default, facilitates blending between the shadow and the base image.

Canvas Automatically expands the image to accommodate an added shadow. Enter a value in pixels for the expanded canvas. The canvas expansion is "locked" to an equal amount on all four sides. To add canvas selectively, click on the lock to unlock it, then enter the desired values. Click in the canvas Color box to edit canvas expansion color from the default of white.

Data Type

Edit Data Type to change the number of colors, or bit depth, of an image. You can also change Data Type by clicking on the Data Type button in the status bar. Data Type options are shown below.

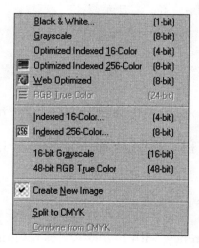

The Data Types listed vary by the type of image currently active. In the list above, for example, RGB True Color is grayed out because the active image is already in RGB True Color. Similarly, no CMYK images are open in the work space, so the Combine from

CMYK option is unavailable.

If you are new to image editing, you may wonder why it might be necessary to change data type. A primary reason for doing so is to reduce the file size of a web image. Lower bit depth means fewer colors and smaller file sizes, speeding download of an image for visitors to your web page. Changing the data type of an RGB True Color image to Optimized Indexed 256 Colors can reduce file size significantly. By the same token, at times it is necessary to increase the bit depth of an Optimized Indexed 256 Color image to RBG True Color to take advantage of PhotoImpact's Creative and Magic effects, to add 3D text to an image, to add a Frame & Shadow or to use the Button Designer.

It is a good idea to leave the default of "Create A New Image" selected, insuring that a copy of the image with the new data type opens on top of the original image. This helps to avoid accidentally saving changes to the original image.

Color Table

The Color Table displays all of the colors used in an Indexed color image. You may delete duplicate or unused colors, load or save color tables, and sort or replace colors. Position the cursor over any cell to read its number in the color table, or its Hue, Saturation & Brightness value, RGB value and Hex value.

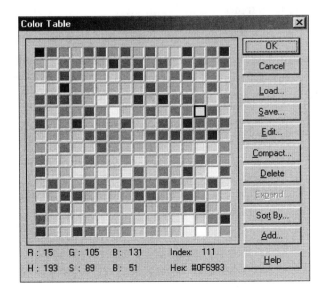

Load Loads a previously saved color table, which will *replace* the current color table. Use caution with Load, since results can be unpredictable. The first color in the newly loaded color table will replace the first color in the current color table, and so on.

Save Save an edited color table for future use.

Add Saves a color table with the .PAL file extension.

Edit Click in a cell, then click Edit to replace the selected color with a different color.

Compact Eliminates duplicate or unused colors from the color table.

Expand Adds cells representing unused colors to the end of the color table.

Sort Sort colors by Red, Green or Blue channel, or by Hue, Saturation and Brightness.

Add Click to open the Add to EasyPalette dialog box. Give the palette a name and its thumbnail will be added to My Gallery in the EasyPalette.

Windows Wallpaper

Creates a Windows wallpaper from the active image. Specify whether the image should be centered or tiled. The wallpaper is applied to the Windows desktop immediately.

If you do not like the wallpaper on your desktop, you must right click on the desktop and choose Active Desktop, Customize My Desktop. When the Display Properties dialog box opens, click on the Background tab and select another pattern for the desktop.

Chapter 14: The Effect Menu

Effect menu commands are the among the brightest stars in PhotoImpact's constellation of image editing features. They allow you to rapidly and easily edit images in spectacular or more workmanlike ways. Tighten up focus and restore detail, soften a harsh image, redistribute colors, tweak acquired images, or create unique tiles. Alternatively, go for fun effects, like adding lightning bolts to an image, creating animated GIF's in the wonderful new Animation Studio or Lighting Gallery, or turning ordinary photos into lovely watercolors and oil paintings.

Each of the Effect menu commands opens a dialog box. Select an Effect variation from the thumbnails in the dialog box, or click Options (available for most Effect commands) to open a secondary dialog box permitting additional editing options. The filters and plug-ins that create these magical effects are built right into PhotoImpact, allowing you to achieve sophisticated results that rival those created by professional photographers and graphics artists. Save custom-edited Effects to the EasyPalette to use again. Remember that many Effect commands can also be accessed from the EasyPalette's Galleries, and that effects can be applied to selections and objects as well as to entire images.

It is difficult to convey in words alone the beauty and impact created by Magic and Creative effects, or detail the dramatic and artistic effects generated by PhotoImpact's built-in filters and plug-ins. However, the following discussion of these commands and how to use them will likely point you toward many hours of rewarding experimentation.

Blur & Sharpen

Image appearance can be enhanced by sharpening up the focus, or by blurring sharper lines for a softer look.

Average Softens the look of an image by changing all of the pixels closer to the average pixel color. The higher the value, the softer the look.

Blur Creates a fuzzy focus.

Emphasize Edges Enhances contrast by emphasizing the edges in the image.

Find Edges Finds areas in the image where the pixels are different in color from one another. This effect is best used in combination with others because the colors in the image can change in unexpected ways.

Gaussian Blur Lends a lovely, blurred effect for a misty appearance. It results from calculating the values of all of the color pixels and shifting them toward the most commonly used color in the image.

Sharpen Forces the edges in an image to stand out better.

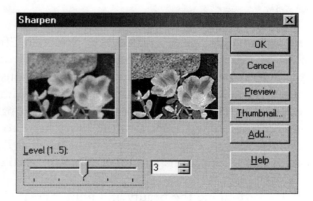

Unsharp Mask Mathemetically determined method of sharpening an image by adjusting by an average pixel color value.

Noise

Noise effects add random speckles or dots to an image, or subtract undesirable speckles.

Add Noise Creates a speckled appearance, distributed either uniformly throughout the image or in a more varied pattern.

Despeckle Cleans an image of randomly distributed speckles or dots.

Remove Moire Removes unattractive speckled or banded patterns in scanned images.

Camera Lens

Camera Lens commands perform quick color adjustments and image distortions.

Cool Adds a cool tint of blue or cyan to an image.

Facet Arranges the image into small tiles, shifted slightly to give the appearance of looking through glass.

Warm Adds a warm tint of red or yellow to an image.

Mosaic Blurs the image into blocks based on the average pixel value within the blocks.

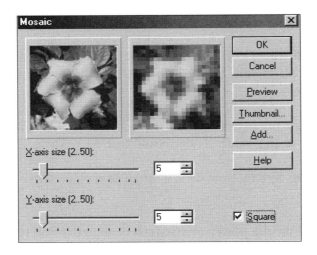

Motion Blur Choose whether to make the image appear as if the subject, light or camera moved, resulting in blurring.

Fat Expands the image in the center, creating a "fat" look.

Thin Squeezes the image in at the center, resulting in a "thin" look.

Remove red eye Eliminates red eye in photographs. This also works well for correcting "glowing green" eyes that often result from flash photography of animals.

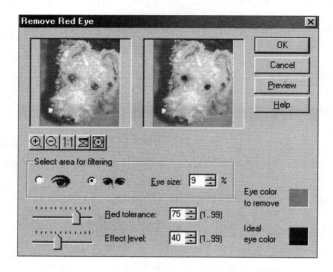

Select area for filtering Drag the circle in the image over to the part of the eye that you wish to edit. Select Two eyes if both eyes are showing and need correcting.

Eye size Adjust the eye size, in percent. The circles will enlarge or reduce in size according to this value. They should just cover the red (or other color) eye.

Red tolerance Specify how wide a range of red (or other color) will be affected.

Effect level Edit the power or strength of the effect on red or other color.

Eye color to remove Click in the Color box to open the Eyedropper dialog box. Move the Eyedropper into the Preview window and click on the color to be removed.

Ideal eye color Click in the Color box to select the color that will replace the red or other color.

2D

Ripple Creates a look like ripples on the surface of water.

Whirlpool Results in a swirling effect, like water going down the drain.

3D

Pinch Squeezes the middle of an image so it looks like it is being pushed into the center of a ball.

Punch Bulges out the middle of the image so that it looks like it is stretched over a ball.

Sphere Distorts the image's appearance with a wide angle camera lens look.

Natural Painting

The Natural Painting commands can create terrific, painterly effects. Choose from a thumbnail in the initial dialog box, or click Options to tweak from the secondary dialog box.

Watercolor Enriches color and softens edges in the image.

Charcoal Vary the opacity, stroke length and coverage to create the appearance of an image drawn in charcoal.

Colored Pen Softens the colors and edges in an image, like drawing with colored pen.

Oil Paint Edit stroke length and opacity to create an effect similar to an oil painting.

Special

Emboss Creates a one color imprint on a solid surface. Click on the Options button to change the color coating (default is gray), depth in pixels and direction of light source from the secondary dialog box. Emboss is a nice way to incorporate a company name or logo into a tiling web page background.

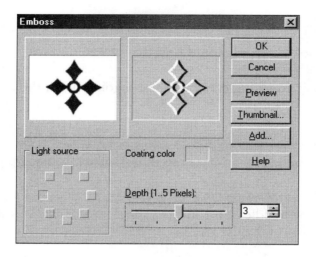

Puzzle This fun effect boxes the image into squares, similar to a sliding puzzle. Click on the Options button to control background color and square size (4 to 50 pixels).

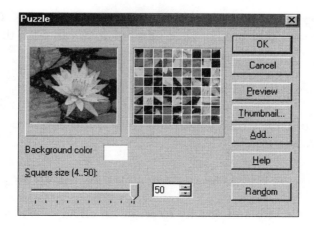

Tile Breaks an image up into irregular, blocky shapes and shifts them around. Click the Options button to set a background color, square size (5 to 50 pixels) and Shift value (randomness of tile distribution).

Wind Click the Options button to choose a direction (left or right), and Moving Offset (strength of 2 to 60) for the wind.

Blast Similar to wind, but a much stronger effect. Click the Options button to select a direction (left or right), and Moving Offset (strength of 2 to 60).

Stagger Creates a wobbling effect on an image. Stagger to the left or right.

Two-Color New to PhotoImpact 6, Two-Color lets you create duotone images.

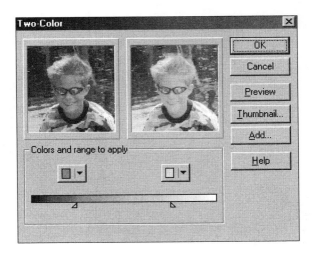

Click the down arrows to open a rainbow-type of color picker. Click the Eyedropper on any color to select it. Alternatively, click in Color box next to the down arrow to select a color.

Monochrome Also new to PhotoImpact 6, Monochrome turns an RGB True Color image into grayscale, but the image data remains in 24 bit RGB data type. This makes it easy to color parts of the image.

Video

Adjust for NTSC Corrects image color to a range acceptable for the United States.

Adjust for PAL Corrects image color to a range acceptable for Europe.

Warping

Drag control points on a fine, medium or large grid to distort parts of an image.

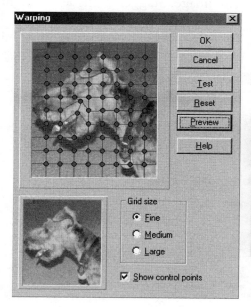

Give your dog
a smile with
Warping

Custom Filters

Create and save custom filters based on complex mathematically determined adjustments to color pixels. It is easiest to start by clicking on the Samples button. Select one of the pre-determined filters.

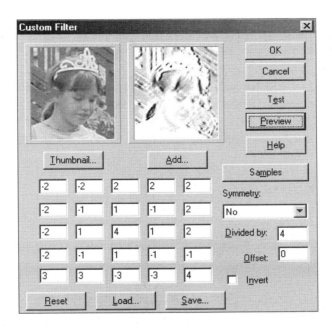

After selecting a Sample filter, fine tune by changing its associated attributes. A 5 X 5 matrix displays values associated with the Custom Filter effect. The left window shows the image in its current state, and the right window shows the results of editing.

Test See the results of your choices in the right Preview window.

Preview View the effect applied to your image in the work space.

Thumbnail Choose whether to have the entire image in the thumbnail, or just a part of the image (useful when you are interested in a filter's effect on a specific portion of the image).

Add Opens the Add to EasyPalette dialog box, from which you can add the custom filter to the EasyPalette.

Samples Choose from the Sample filters: Average, Motion Blur (top to bottom), Blur, Sharpen (light), Find Edges (vertically), Find Edges (horizontally), Emboss (left to right), Paint (dark), Paint (bright), Shake, Scene and Pale.

Symmetry Choose from No, 4-Way, Horizontal and Vertical to view effects quickly.

Divided by Select a value to force all color pixel values to fall between 1-256. The value should be equal to the sum of all of the factors in the matrix.

Offset Enter a value to add to each pixel after the matrix calculation. Positive numbers make the image lighter, while negative numbers make it darker.

Invert Applies complimentary colors to the values chosen by the filter.

Reset Returns default attributes for the selected filter.

Load Opens a previously saved Custom Filter.

Save Saves the Custom Filter with the .CFL file extension (Custom Filter Effect).

Custom Effects

Create custom distortion effects based on the movement of color pixels along a plane. These effects are helpful for emphasizing or de-emphasizing an image feature.

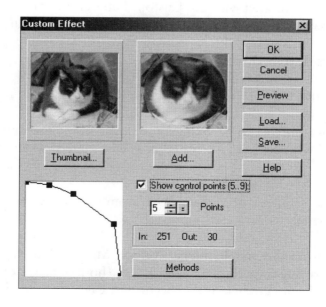

Preview Previews the Custom Effect applied to the image.

Load Opens a previously saved matrix map.

Thumbnail Choose whether to have the entire image in the thumbnail, or just a part of the image (useful when you are interested in a filter's effect on a specific portion of the image).

Add Opens the Add to EasyPalette dialog box, from which you can add the custom effect to the EasyPalette.

Map The Map window shows the curve. If you position your cursor in the window, it turns into a pencil icon. Drag on the graph line to redraw the curve.

Show control points Select to display control points (5-9). You can drag on the control points to facilitate the desired mapping curve.

In/Out When the cursor is in the Map window, reveals the current and remapped pixel coordinates.

Methods Click the Methods button to select a sample reference map. Multiple effects are cumulative. Smooth can smooth out abrupt changes in the curve.

Save Saves the Custom Effect with the .CEF file extension (Custom Effect Files).

Paint on Edges (Shift+P)

Applied to an active selection or object in the base image, Paint on Edges has no associated dialog box. Current Paint or Stamp tool settings will be applied.

Creative

The Creative submenu adds stylish effects and motion to your images. New to PhotoImpact 6 is the Animation Studio, which creates flashy animations similar to those generated by java applets. In keeping with PhotoImpact 6's emphasis on web imaging, most Creative effects can be used to add zip to static images *and* used to create eye-catching animations by working seamlessly with GIF Animator 4, shipped with PhotoImpact 6.

Animation Studio

New to PhotoImpact 6, the Animation Studio applies a variety of special effects to images, including: Ripple, Diffusion, Gaussian Blur, Signature, Wave, Jump, Puzzle, Whirlpool, Droplet, Motion Blur and Turnpage.

Select a thumbnail and click the Play button to view its effect in the Preview window. By default, animation previews only play one time. You can edit effect attributes from the Basic tab. The last two Animation Studio effects only, Motion Blur and Turnpage, have both a Basic tab and an Advanced tab for editing attributes. Click OK to apply an effect to an image, or click Save to save the effects as an animated GIF.

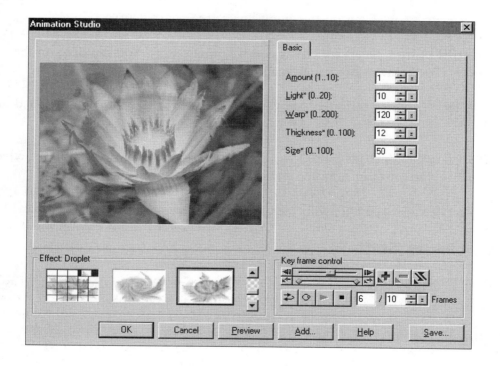

Preview window The upper left portion of the dialog box contains a large preview window.

Effect thumbnails Select an Effect thumbnail.

330

Basic/Advanced Tabs Edit effect attributes from these tabs. Each effect has different attributes. To understand what an attribute does, click the Help button at the bottom of the dialog box to get detailed context-specific help.

Key frame controls The lower right portion of the dialog box contains key frame controls for playing and editing animations.

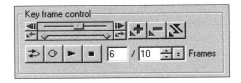

Ping Mode When selected, automatically plays the animation in reverse when it reaches its end.

Loop Mode When selected, plays the animation continuously, over and over again.

Play Plays the animation in the Preview window.

Stop Stops playing the animation.

Current/Total Frames Displays the current frame in the sequence and the total number of frames. All of the preset animations contain 10 frames. This number can be edited by changing the number of total frames, but keep in mind that adding frames can result in much larger file sizes.

Editing key frame animations The Animation Studio's preset animations have only two key frames, represented by small diamonds at the beginning and end of the animation timelines. When a key frame is clicked on to select it, it is blue and the animation jumps to that point in the Preview window. When deselected, a key frame is gray. To edit a key frame animation, click on a key frame to make it active. You can edit the effect's attributes at that point from the Basic or Advanced tab.

Add key frame Click or drag anywhere along the animation timeline slider bar and click the Add key frame button to add an editable key frame to the animation timeline. You will see a diamond added to the timeline.

Delete key frame Click on a key frame and then click the Delete key frame button to remove it from the animation timeline.

Reverse key frame Reverses the sequence of frames in the animation.

When the Animation Studio effect has been fine tuned to your satisfaction, click OK to apply the effect to the image in the work space. This will be a static effect with no animation. To save a key frame animation, click Save to open the Save As dialog box. Save as an animation or a sequence of .BMP files by choosing the appropriate option from the "Save as type" dropdown list.

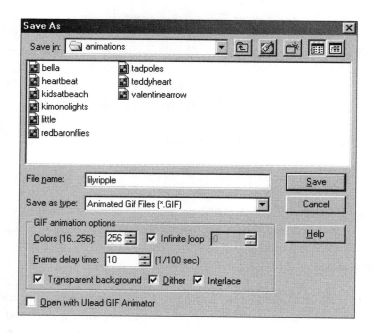

Note the "GIF animation options" at the bottom of the dialog box. By default, the animation will be saved at 256 colors, with infinite looping, frame delay of 1/10 of a second per frame, with a transparent background, dithered and interlaced. If you wish to edit the animation in the GIF Animator, select that option. Since these animations can be quite large, you may want to experiment with selectively removing frames or trimming file size with the GIF Animator's Optimization Wizard. Finally, to add a custom edited effect to the EasyPalette, before saving it click the Add button. You will be offered the choice of saving the effect as a static image effect or as an animation.

Select one of these options and the Add to EasyPalette dialog box opens. Name the effect and save it to a Gallery and Tab group.

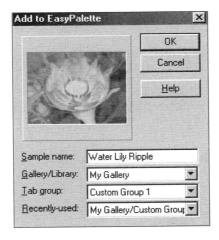

Artist Texture

Artist Texture generates intricate, geometrically determined interlocking tiles. The Storyboard, an Advanced feature, can generate an animation made up of selected tiles. The animation option is integrated seamlessly with GIF Animator.

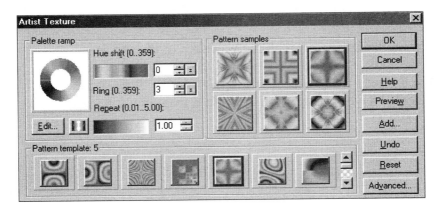

Pattern samples First select a pattern sample. Click the Reset button to begin at the first level. Patterns become more complex as different Pattern templates are selected.

Pattern templates Edit the appearance of pattern samples by clicking on pattern templates. You may edit up to 20 times before you will have to Reset.

Palette Ramp The Palette Ramp window shows the currently selected palette.

Edit Click Edit to open the Palette Ramp Editor and select a different palette.

Hue shift Click or drag anywhere in the Hue shift "rainbow" color box, or enter a value, to shift the gradient to a different hue. The color saturation and brightness will remain constant.

Ring Rotates the order in which colors appear in the ring. Enter a value to rotate the color ring.

Repeat number By default, the pattern is repeated once. Enter a different value (0.01 to 5.00) in the Repeat box to edit.

Preview Preview the selected Artist Texture applied to the image.

Add Click on the Add button to save an Artist Texture to the EasyPalette. When the Add to EasyPalette dialog box opens, give the tile a name and save it to a Gallery and Tab group.

Undo Undoes the last edit.

Reset Resets the Pattern samples all the way back to the first level.

Advanced Click on the Advanced button to open the Storyboard and additional options which enable you to create an animation from multiple Artist Texture tiles.

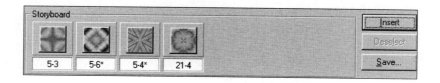

Storyboard The Storyboard holds thumbnails of the Artist Texture tiles you want to use in an animation.

Delete Deletes a selected thumbnail from the Storyboard.

Delete all Deletes all of the thumbnails from the Storyboard.

Normal Returns to the Normal dialog box, without the Storyboard and other Advanced options.

Insert Select an edited Artist Texture, then click Insert to add it to the Storyboard.

Deselect Deselects a selected thumbnail in the Storyboard.

Save Opens the Save As dialog box so you can save the animation to a folder on your hard drive. Save as an animation or a sequence of .BMP files by choosing the appropriate option from the "Save as type" dropdown list.

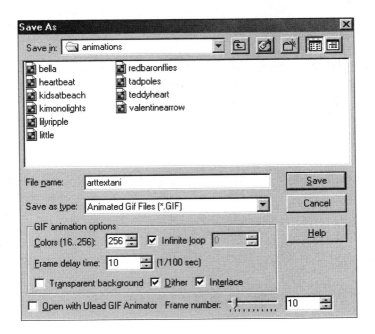

Note the "GIF animation options" at the bottom of the dialog box. By default, the animation will be saved at 256 colors, with infinite looping, frame delay of 1/10 of a second per frame, dithered and interlaced. If you wish to edit the animation in the GIF Animator before saving it, select that option.

Creative Warp

Creative Warp generates original fills or background tiles based on the shapes and colors in an image, selection or object. The colors and shapes are distorted via dividing and mirroring, similar to the constantly shifting patterns viewed in a kaleidoscope.

Like Artist Texture, Creative Warp has a Storyboard as an Advanced option. The Storyboard allows you to create an animation from a sequence of selected patterns. It integrates seamlessly with Ulead's GIF Animator.

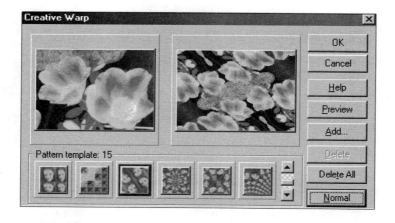

The left window in the dialog box shows the original image, selection or object. The right Preview window shows the effect of the selected Pattern template.

Preview Click the Preview button to view the selected pattern applied to the image.

Add Click Add to open the Add to EasyPalette dialog box. Name the Creative Warp effect and save it to a Gallery and Tab group.

Advanced Click on the Advanced button to open the Storyboard and additional options which enable you to create an animation from selected Creative Warp tiles.

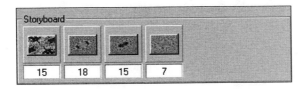

Storyboard The Storyboard holds thumbnails of the Creative Warp tiles you want to use in an animation.

Delete Deletes the selected thumbnail from the Storyboard.

Delete all Deletes all of the thumbnails from the Storyboard.

Normal Returns to the Normal dialog box, without the Storyboard and other Advanced options.

Insert Select an edited Creative Warp tile, then click Insert to add it to the Storyboard.

Deselect Deselects a selected thumbnail in the Storyboard.

Save Opens the Save As dialog box so you can save the animation to a folder on your hard drive. Note the "GIF animation options" at the bottom of the Save As dialog box. Save as an animation or a sequence of .BMP files by choosing the appropriate option from the "Save as type" dropdown list. By default, the animation will be saved at 256 colors, with infinite looping, frame delay of 1/10 of a second per frame, dithered and interlaced. If you wish to edit the animation in the GIF Animator before saving it, select that option.

Lighting

Creative Lighting adds flashlight, lens flare, comet, halos, fireworks, lightning, and other sensational effects to images. Lighting effects are the Effect menu analog of the EasyPalette's Lighting Gallery. Both can create a single image effect, or a key frame animation. The preset key frame animations can be edited.

Select an Effect thumbnail from Lightning, Fireworks, Lens flare, Light bulb, Halo, Spotlight, Flashlight, Meteor, Comet or Laser. Edit effect parameters from the Basic and Advanced tabs.

Basic Tab Basic attributes vary by Lighting effect. For example, the Flashlight's Basic attributes include Brightness, Softness, Spread angle, Distance, Elevation, Skew angle, a Center color and an Outer color. Click the Help button for detailed context-specific information about how each attribute will edit an effect.

Advanced Tab Advanced attributes also vary by Lighting effect. For example, the Spotlight's Advanced parameters include Variance, Lamp size and Project mode (Horizontal floor or Vertical wall). Click the Help button for detailed context-specific information about how each attribute will edit an effect.

Key frame controls

Key frame controls allow you to create animations of Lighting effects such as exploding fireworks, moving spotlights, streaking comets and more. Key frames, represented by small diamonds, can be added to or subtracted from an animation timeline. When deselected, key frame diamonds are gray. Select a key frame by clicking on it to edit. The key frame diamond turns blue, indicating that it is now the active key frame and that the effect's attributes at that point in the animation can be edited. The key frame controls are shown below.

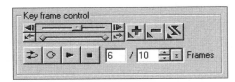

Ping Mode When selected, automatically plays an animation in reverse when it reaches its end.

Loop Mode When selected, plays an animation continuously, over and over again.

Play Plays an animation in the Preview window.

Stop Stops playing the animation.

Current/Total Frames Displays the current frame in the sequence and the total number of frames. The default is 10 frames. Edit the number of frames by changing the number of total frames. You should be aware that adding frames can result in much larger file sizes.

Editing a preset key frame animation The process of editing a key frame animation may seem perplexing at first, but it is actually a straightforward process. Select an effect from the thumbnails, then click on the first key frame diamond to make sure you are starting at the beginning of the animation. If necessary, drag the effect to a different location in the Preview window. If you have difficulty finding where to drag, roll the cursor near the effect in the Preview window until it turns into a double-headed arrow. If you want the animation to be longer or shorter than 10 frames, enter a different value in the Frames box.

To create an animation, drag the animation timeline slider bar to any point on the timeline and click the "Add key frame" button. Alternatively, enter a value in the appropriate box and click on the plus "Add key frame" button. A diamond will appear at that point, indicating that a new key frame has been added. Edit the attributes of the Lighting effect. Drag a little further and click the "Add key frame" button to add another key frame, edit its attributes, and so on. To remove a key frame, click on its diamond then click on the minus "Delete key frame" button to remove it.

The Element section of the dialog box allows you to add another element to a static image effect or to a key frame in the animation. To add an element, in the Element section, click on the plus (+) sign, then click on an Effect thumbnail to add it. Just be sure to click the plus (+) sign *before* adding the Element, otherwise you will lose any key frames you have added, as though you are starting a new animation. Click on the minus (-) sign to delete an Element.

To view an animation in the Preview window, click on the Play button, and to stop the animation click on the Stop button. To preview the Lighting effect applied to a static image, click on the Preview button.

To save a key frame animation, click on the Save button. Doing so opens the Save As dialog box so you can save the animation to a folder on your hard drive. Save as an animation or a sequence of .BMP files by choosing the appropriate option from the "Save as type" dropdown list.

Note the "GIF animation options" at the bottom of the Save As dialog box. By default, the animation will be saved at 256 colors, with infinite looping, frame delay of 1/10 of a second per frame, transparent background, dithered and interlaced. If you wish to edit the animation in the GIF Animator before saving it, select that option. Since these animations can be hefty, you may want to experiment with selectively removing frames or weighing different options in the GIF Animator's Optimization Wizard to trim down file size.

Painting

A stunner among the Creative effects, Painting easily turns the most ho-hum image into a work of art. Painting can also be accessed from the EasyPalette's Painting Gallery. Choose from among dozens of effects mimicking pencil sketches, charcoal, pastels, watercolors, pointillism, and more. Creative Painting also adds textures to images.

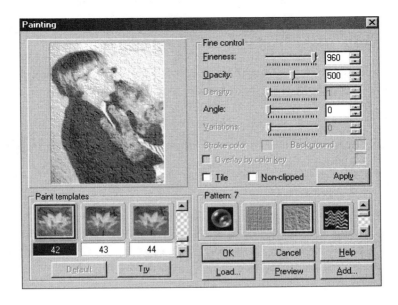

Choose a Paint Template and its default Pattern, or select a different Pattern. Paint templates and patterns can be combined in countless ways, resulting in many different looks for the same image.

Fine control Selectively tweak Painting attributes, including Fineness, Opacity, Density, Angle and Variations. A few Paint Templates permit you to edit Stroke/Background/Overlay by color. If you are not sure what effect a Fine control will have on the image, click on the Help button for detailed, context-specific help.

Tile Creates a seamless tile from the Painting effect.

Non-clipped Excludes strokes beginning outside of the source image's boundaries.

Apply Click on the Apply button to view effects of editing in the Preview window.

Load Click Load to access the Open dialog box. Browse your hard drive to open a previously saved .BMP image that will be added to the Pattern thumbnails for editing Paint templates. Right click on a loaded .BMP pattern to view a list of previously loaded patterns. You may add no more than seven patterns, no larger than 300 X 300 pixels.

Preview Click to minimize the dialog box and view effects applied to the image.

Add Click on the Add button to save the custom Painting effect to the EasyPalette.

Default A default image appears in the thumbnails for every Paint template. Click Default to restore the default thumbnails when you have replaced them with thumbnails of your own image.

Try Click the Try button to substitute your image for the default thumbnails for every Paint template. Click the Default button to return to default thumbnails.

Particle

Creative Particle creates dramatic fantasy effects, including Bubble, Firefly, Rain, Snow, Cloud, Smoke, Fire and Star. The basic attributes of particles can be edited. Many particle effects can be edited individually, which permits a high level of control over the finished image.

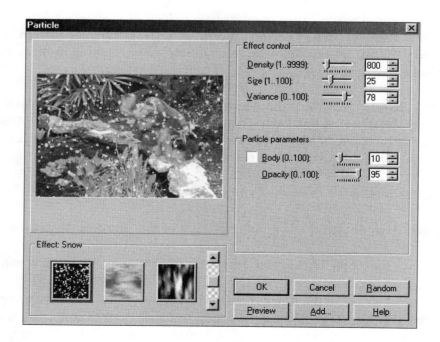

Preview window The Preview window displays the results of currently selected Particle attributes applied to the image.

Effect control Edit Effect control attributes, such as density, size and variance.

Particle parameters Edit Particle parameters such as particle size and color, density, opacity and so on. Click in parameter Color boxes to select replacement colors.

Wireframe Displays a wireframe view of the particles, which saves rendering time.

Select all When selected, edits are applied to all of the particles.

Order Similar to the Pick tool's Order options, this option allows you to change the stacking order of particles by clicking on arrows to bring forward, send back or send to the top or bottom of the stack.

Editing individual particles To select an individual particle for editing, move the cursor into the Preview window until it turns into a double-headed arrow. Click on the particle and it will be surrounded by a bounding box. Drag the particle to another location in the image. This can be a lifesaver when you are happy with the distribution and other attributes, but one or two particles obscure an important part of the image. You can see below that being able to drag particles to different locations can be pretty handy.

Fireflies particle obscure part of face   Particles moved away from face

Random Redistributes the particles randomly. Animated snowglobe makers like to use the Random button to redistribute particles for different frames for their animations.

Preview Click on Preview to view the particle effect applied to the image.

Add Click the Add button to save an edited particle effect. Doing so opens the Add to EasyPalette dialog box. Name the effect and save it to a Gallery and Tab group.

Transform

Like Artist Texture and Warp, Transform generates variations, in this case distortions, of an image which can be applied singly, or assembled in a sequence in the Storyboard to create an animation.

Preview The preview window shows the effect of transformations.

Transformation templates Select a Transformation template from the thumbnails.

Transformation control Edit effects with the Transformation controls, which vary by effect.

> **Range** Enter a desired value to control how much of the area within the image will be affected by the Transformation. Higher values result in a stronger effect.
>
> **Level** Controls intensity of an effect, with higher values yielding a more pronounced effect.
>
> **Space** Enter a value for the amount of space between each brush stroke.
>
> **Effect** Available only for Horizontal and Vertical Transformations, enter a negative number to squeeze the top or left side of an image, or a positive number to squeeze the bottom or right side of an image.

Reset After selecting a Transformation thumbnail, click on Reset to remove its effect.

Insert Select a thumbnail, then click Insert to add it to the Storyboard. Insert a sequence of effects into the Storyboard for an animation.

Delete Deletes a selected thumbnail from the Storyboard.

Delete all Deletes all thumbnails from the Storyboard.

Chapter 14: The Effect Menu

Save To save a Transformation sequence as an animation, click on the Save button. Doing so opens the Save As dialog box so you can save the animation to a folder on your hard drive. Save as an animation or a sequence of .BMP files by choosing the appropriate option from the "Save as type" dropdown list.

Note the "GIF animation options" at the bottom of the Save As dialog box. By default, the animation will be saved at 256 colors, with infinite looping, frame delay of 1/10 of a second per frame, dithered and interlaced. If you wish to edit the animation in the GIF Animator before saving it, select that option.

Creative Type

Now in PhotoImpact 6, not only can you add attention-grabbing type effects to static images, but you can turn these effects into animations. Type Effects are not restricted to Text objects either, which means that you can apply them to 2D and 3D Text, Path and Image objects. Type Effects include Gradient, Hole, Glass, Metal, Emboss, Emboss Outline, Emboss Texture, Concrete, Sand, Lighting, Fire, Snow, Neon, Seal, Imprint, Reverse Emboss, Chisel, Border, Double and Gradient Light. Creative Type effects can also be accessed from the EasyPalette's Type Gallery.

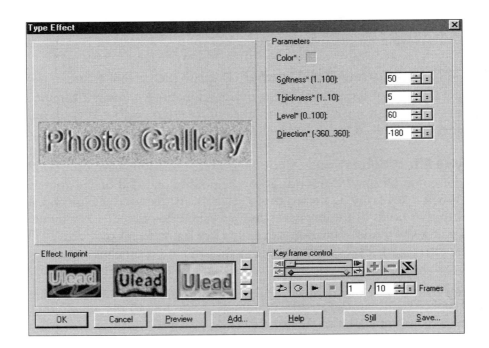

345

Preview Select an Effect thumbnail and view its effect in the Preview window.

Parameters Edit Type Effect attributes in the Parameters section of the dialog box. By editing these Parameters, the look of an effect can be changed markedly.

Key frame controls The lower right portion of the dialog box contains key frame controls for playing and editing Type Effect animations.

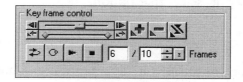

Ping Mode When selected, automatically plays the animation in reverse when it reaches its end.

Loop Mode When selected, plays the animation continuously, over and over again.

Play Plays the animation in the Preview window.

Stop Stops playing the animation.

Current/Total Frames Displays the current frame in the sequence and the total number of frames. All of the preset animations contain 10 frames. This number can be edited by changing the number of total frames, but keep in mind that adding frames can result in much larger file sizes.

Editing Type Effect animations All of the preset animations have only two key frames, represented by small diamonds at the beginning and end of the animation timelines. When a key frame is clicked on to select it, its diamond is blue and the animation jumps to that point in the Preview window. When deselected, a key frame diamond is gray. To edit a key frame animation, click on a key frame to make it active. Then you can edit the effect's attributes at that point in the animation timeline.

Add key frame Click or drag anywhere along the animation timeline slider bar and click the Add key frame button to add an editable key frame to the animation timeline. You will see a diamond added to the timeline.

Delete key frame Click on a key frame and then click the Delete key frame button to remove it from the animation timeline.

Reverse key frame Reverses the sequence of frames in the animation.

Add Click on the Add button to save a custom edited Type Effect. When you click on Add, you will be presented with the choice of adding the effect to the EasyPalette as an Image or an Animation. Choose one of these options to open the Add to EasyPalette dialog box. Give the Type Effect a name and save it to a Gallery and Tab group.

Save Clicking on the Save button opens the Save As dialog box so you can save the animation to a folder on your hard drive. Save as an animation or a sequence of .BMP files by choosing the appropriate option from the "Save as type" dropdown list.

Note the "GIF animation options" at the bottom of the Save As dialog box. By default, the animation will be saved at 256 colors, with infinite looping, frame delay of 1/10 of a second per frame, transparent background, dithered and interlaced. If you wish to edit the animation in the GIF Animator before saving it, select that option.

Magic

Magic effects include a spectacular array of image effects ranging from gradient fills, kaleidoscope patterns, dramatic spotlighting, and slick curled page effects. Magic Gradients are a particularly handy way to fill with sparkling gradients, editable via the Palette Ramp Editor.

Kaleidoscope

If you liked playing with kaleidoscopes as a child, or are simply interested in creating unique background tiles, you will love Kaleidoscope, which generates patterns based on the reflection of an image. Start by opening an image with colors that you really like. Use the entire image or make a selection.

The Kaleidoscope dialog box, shown at the top of the next page, offers three rows of three thumbnails. If you like one, select it and click OK. The Kaleidoscope tile will replace the image or selection area.

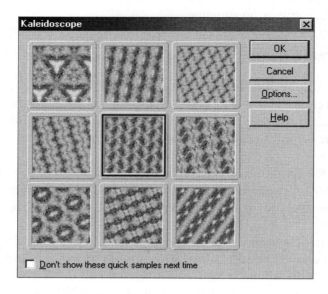

To edit, select a thumbnail and click on Options to open a secondary dialog box.

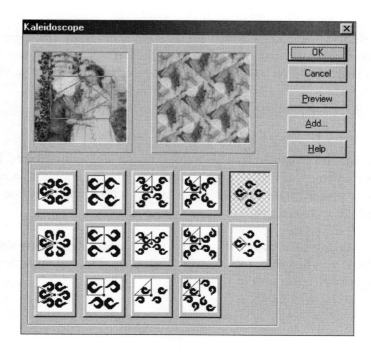

The secondary Kaleidoscope dialog box contains additional thumbnails, each representing a variation of the pattern. Click on thumbnails and observe their effects in the right Preview window. Edit patterns by dragging the control points from the default center of the image in the left window, and by resizing, rotating or moving the area upon which the pattern is based. In other words, if the color or pattern is more pleasing in a specific portion of the image or selection, you can drag the control points to that area.

Preview Click the Preview button to view a Kaleidoscope tile applied to an image or selection.

Add Click Add to save a custom kaleidoscope tile to the EasyPalette. Doing so opens the Add to EasyPalette dialog box. Give the Kaleidoscope tile a name, and save it to a Gallery and Tab group. Then click OK to apply it to the image.

Light

Magic Light is a wonderful way to enhance or change the central focus of an image by adding a colorful spotlight. It is also very useful for salvaging poorly lit photos, such as those taken at indoor sporting or theatrical events.

When the Light dialog box opens, three rows of thumbnails, or Quick Samples, display the effect of light focused on various locations in a clockwise pattern around the image.

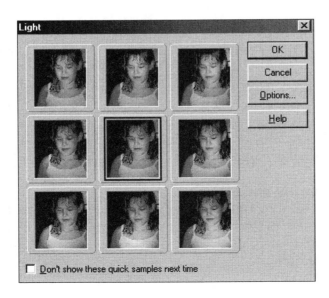

PhotoImpact 6 Wizardry

If you are satisfied with one of these effects, click OK, but remember that you can edit Light effects too. To fine tune the effect, click Options to open a secondary dialog box.

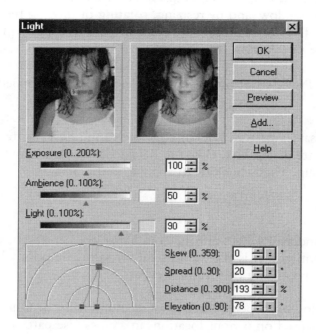

Exposure control bar Shows the current Exposure level. Drag on the red pointer to edit, from 0 to 200%. Higher values result in a more pronounced effect.

Ambience brightness control bar Shows the current Ambience level. Drag on the red pointer to edit Exposure, from 0 to 100%. Higher values result in a stronger effect. The Ambient Brightness color box next to the control bar shows current color. Click in the color box to select a different color using the Ulead Color Picker. Right click in the color box for a wider range of color options.

Light brightness control bar Shows the current Light brightness value. Drag on the red pointer to edit, from 0 to 100%. Higher values result in brighter light. The Light Brightness color box next to the control bar shows current color. Click in the color box to select a different color using the Ulead Color Picker. Right click in the Color box for a wider range of color options.

Light distance, elevation and spread control window A graphical display of light distance and elevation, and light source spread. Drag on the control points to edit, or enter values for Light Skew, Spread, Distance and Elevation.

Click the Preview button to see Light effects applied to the image. Click the Add button to save a custom Light effect to the EasyPalette, or click OK to apply to the image.

Gradient

Magic Gradient applies patterned gradient fills to an image, active selection or object. It is easy to edit gradients from the Magic Gradient dialog box.

Palette ramp The currently selected palette is displayed in the left ring palette window, and its mode is shown in the right Preview window.

Hue shift Click or drag anywhere in the Hue shift "rainbow" color box, or enter a value, to shift the gradient to a different hue. The color saturation and brightness will remain constant.

Ring Rotates the order in which colors appear in the ring. Enter a value to rotate the color ring.

Edit Click the Edit button to select a different palette. Doing so opens the Palette Ramp Editor. When the Palette Ramp Editor opens, select another palette. The palette may be edited by right clicking on control points and choosing to change or delete the color.

Repeat The number of times the ring palette is repeated in the pattern.

Mode Choose a pattern for the gradient from the Mode thumbnails. The appearance of the gradient fill can be changed dramatically by selecting different modes. Below are examples of the same gradient with different Mode patterns applied.

 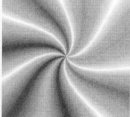 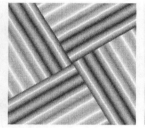 

Slope Click or drag on the red dot to edit the Slope, or direction of the gradient.

Frequency Specify how many times (0.01-20.00) the pattern will be repeated in the gradient.

Amplitude Click or drag on the pointer to edit length and width of the pattern (from -2.00 to 2.00).

Preview Click on the Preview button to see the gradient applied to the image.

Add Click on the Add button to save the edited gradient. Doing so opens the Add to EasyPalette dialog box. Give the gradient a name and save it to a Gallery and Tab group.

Turnpage

Turnpage creates a startlingly realistic effect similar to the curled edge of a photo. You can choose which corner to curl, the shape of the curled edge can be edited, and the appearance of the curl can be shiny, the reverse of the image or semitransparent.

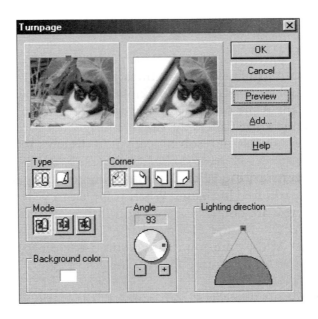

Type Choose a cylindrical or cone type.

Corner Select a corner and direction for the turnpage.

Mode Choose from a shiny Opaque curl, a Reverse image, or Transparent effect.

Background color Click in the color box to select a color from the Ulead Color Picker, or right click to select from a wider range of color options.

Angle Drag on the red control point, or click + and - to change the size of the page curl. Smaller angle sizes result in larger page curl effects.

Lighting direction Drag on the red control point to change the lighting direction and shadow effect.

Click the Preview button to view the effect applied to the image. Click the Add button to save custom Turnpage settings to the EasyPalette. Click OK to apply.

Digimarc

Image misuse and outright theft are not uncommon on the Internet. The addition of Digimarc watermarking capabilities to PhotoImpact 6 will surely be appreciated by both web and traditional graphics artists. Digimarc embeds a "watermark" with identifying information including the name of the artist and copyright date directly into an image's digital data. The watermark itself alters the original image in a barely perceptible manner. Watermarks can be valuable in resolving copyright disputes should they occur.

Registering and Watermarking With Digimarc PhotoImpact 6 users can obtain up to 49 Digimarc watermarks free of charge. When you plan to watermark your first image, make sure that you are online because PhotoImpact will connect you to the Digimarc web site to receive ID and PIN numbers. You cannot watermark your images without these numbers. At the time you register, you may elect to pay for extended service allowing you to watermark more than 49 images.

However, keep in mind that watermarking is only half the battle. For web graphic artists, the Internet is a very big place. Watermarking is of limited utility unless you have a way to find out if people are using your images without your permission. For this reason, you may also elect to pay for a subscription to Digmarc's tracking service. This service will alert you if one of your watermarked images appears on someone else's web page. Tracking is based on information from search engines. Therefore, information from web sites that do not receive a lot of hits (often the ones most likely to misappropriate images) are less likely to show up in tracking.

When you invoke the Effect, Digimarc, Embed Watermark command, the Embed Watermark dialog box opens. If you have not already registered and received an ID number, click the button in the "Personalize" section to open the Personalize Creator ID dialog box.

Chapter 14: The Effect Menu

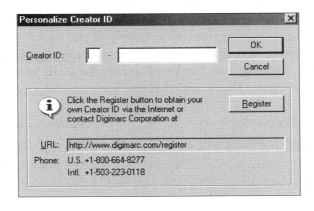

Make sure you are online, then click the Register button to be taken directly to the Digmarc web site. After reading and accepting their user's Agreement, you will be taken to a registration page. This page requests credit card information which you do not have to provide if you are only registering for the free 49 watermarks. If you want to watermark more images, or subscribe to tracking, however, you must pay for these services. Be sure to write down and keep your ID and PIN in a safe place for future reference. After registering with Digimarc, return to the Personalize Creator ID dialog box. Enter your PIN and ID numbers and click OK to close the box. From now on, it will be easy to watermark an image and the PIN and ID numbers will appear in the "Creator ID" section.

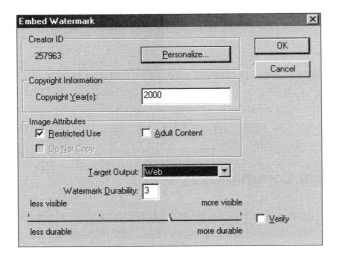

355

In the "Copyright Information" section, enter the "Copyright year(s)." Select Image attributes and specify whether the Target Output is intended for Monitor, Web or Print. You must balance image quality against the strength of the watermark in the "Watermark Durability" portion of the dialog box. Although watermarks are generally unobtrusive, the higher the Visibility and Durability value, the more noticeable the impact will be on your images. Click OK to complete the watermarking process.

Reading a Digimarc Watermark Invoke the Effect, Digimarc, Read Watermark command to view information about a watermarked image currently open in PhotoImpact 6.

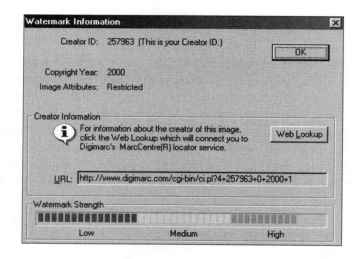

The Creator ID number, Copyright year and any restrictions appear at the top of the Watermark Information dialog box. For more "Creator Information" click the Web Lookup button. Doing so will take you directly to the Digimarc site, where you can find other information about the copyright holder. The watermark's strength is displayed graphically at the bottom of the box.

Other Effect Menu Commands

If you have installed third party plug-ins and filters (a task performed via File, Preferences, Plug-ins), they will appear at the bottom of the Effect menu.

Chapter 14: The Effect Menu

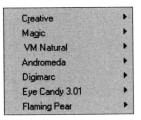

To apply any of these other effects, simply select it to open the appropriate Plug-in's dialog box.

Chapter 15: The Retouch, Paint and Clone Tools

The Retouch, Paint and Clone tools cluster together in the Tool panel. These are familiar and indispensible tools to seasoned PhotoImpact users, with the addition of a fabulous new Retouch Tool, the Colorize Pen.

The Retouch, Paint and Clone tools all function similarly. To access them, you must press and hold down anywhere on the button until a tray of tools slides out. Alternatively, clicking on the tiny blue triangle on the lower right corner of the button causes the tools to slide out.

Click on the tool of your choice. The slide out tray disappears and the icon for the selected tool appears on the button. Remember that you can also display a tool panel with each of the associated tools by selecting View, Toolbars & Panels, Paint Tools, or by clicking on the ⊞ Layout button and selecting the desired Retouch, Paint or Clone Tool Panel.

The "floating" toolbar can be dragged to any area in the work space or docked conveniently. This is a very handy feature when you are switching back and forth from one tool to another.

Although most attributes for the Retouch, Paint and Clone tools can be edited directly in the Attributes Toolbar, the Brush Panel offers even greater control. Choose View, Toolbars & Panels, Brush Panel, hit Ctrl+F3 or click the Layout button, and choose Brush Panel, for advanced Retouch, Paint and Clone tool features. The editable attributes will vary by tool selected.

Constants in the Attributes Toolbar

Depending on the Retouch, Paint or Clone tool selected, one or all of these options will appear in the Attributes toolbar.

Lines Click to choose from Freehand, Straight lines or Connected lines.

Tablet Displays options for pressure-sensitive drawing tablets, only if you have a tablet installed. More advanced tablet controls are accessed via File, Preferences.

> **None** The drawing tablet responds as though you were using a mouse.
>
> **Size** More pressure on the drawing pen results in a thicker line, while less pressure results in a thinner line.
>
> **Transparency** The lighter the pressure on the drawing pen, the greater the transparency.
>
> **Size/Transparency** Combines Size and Transparency options.

Texture Click to select a texture for painting. You can Add or Delete textures from here as well.

Eraser The eraser tool only works if you have painted something on the image first. You cannot erase a base image with this tool. Be sure to toggle out of Eraser mode to continue painting.

Mode When selected, all Retouch, Paint or Clone operations take place on a separate, transparent layer floating over the base image, preserving it from edits. When Mode is deselected, a new Image object is created from the operations performed on this transparent layer. This new object can be edited like any other Image object.

Add After fine-tuning the attributes of a particular Retouch, Paint or Clone tool, you may save them by clicking on Add. Doing so opens the Add to EasyPalette dialog box. Give the custom tool settings a name and save to My Gallery.

Now that you know about the commonalities among the Retouch, Paint and Clone tools, here are the specifics about each set of tools.

Retouch Tools

Retouch tools edit images by adjusting color pixels, modifying their lighting, sharpness, tone, and saturation, or by rearranging or replacing color pixels.

Set the characteristics of each Retouch tool in the Attributes toolbar.

There are 14 Retouch tools:

Dodge

Lightens a selection's colors. It is useful for lightening areas that are too dark, and for creating highlights. Presets: Edge Light, Spot Light and Thin Spot.

Burn

Burn darkens colors and improves contrast. Presets: Wide Burn, Thin Burn and Edge Burn.

Blur

The image look like it is being seen through grease-smeared glass, resulting in a very soft look. Presets: Slight Blur, Water Blur and Heavy Blur.

Sharpen

Makes the edges in an image stand out more sharply. Presets: Slight Sharpen, Edge Sharpen, Heavy Sharpen.

Tonal Adjustment

Darkens, lightens or intensifies colors. Presets: Tone Effect, Highlight and Darken.

Smudge

Literally smears color pixels together like finger paint. Used sparingly, disguises sharp joins in composite images, and blends painted strokes. Presets: Smudge.

Saturation

Modifies color saturation. Presets: Monochrome, Saturate and Age.

Warping

Creates a rippled effect. Presets: Fine Warp and Heavy Warp.

Bristle Smear

Like the Smudge tool, smears color pixels around, adding a bristle texture. Presets: Coarse Smear and Fine Smear.

Remove Red Eye

Removes unwanted red from eyes, a commonly encountered problem in flash photography. In the Attributes toolbar, select from Presets Remove Red Eye 1, Remove Red Eye 2 or Remove Red Eye 3, which render progressively smaller effects, respectively. Click on the red eye in the image to remove it.

Remove Scratch

Remove Scratch works wonders on older scratched or flawed photographs. Presets: Remove Scratch 1, Remove Scratch 2 and Remove Scratch 3.

Remove Noise

Remove Noise is useful for removing noise from scans of pictures from newspapers or magazines. Presets: Remove Noise 1, Remove Noise 2 and Remove Noise 3.

Colorize Pen

Applies a tint of a selected color to the image. This new tool is wonderful for creating an old fashioned "hand tinted" look. Convert any photo to Monochrome, then color with the Colorize Pen. Presets: Colorize Pen 1, Colorize Pen 2, Colorize Pen 3, Colorize Pen 4, Colorize Pen 5.

Paint Tools

Paint tools can be used to edit previously created images, or they can be used to paint new images directly onto an empty canvas. Set the characteristics for each paint tool in the Attributes toolbar.

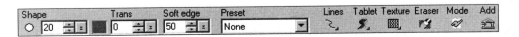

There are 12 Paint tools.

Paintbrush

The most basic of Paint tools, its effects can be changed dramatically by modifying its attributes. Presets: Fine Brush, Fine Point Pen, Horizontal Line, Vertical Line, Fine Round Marker, Wide Square Marker, Fat Marker, Wide Marker, Chinese Calligraphy, Round Stroke 1 & 2, Bricks, Ribbon and Aurora.

Airbrush

Lays down a fine mist of color. The longer you stay in one place the more opaque the effect. Presets: Fat Sroke, Thin Stroke, Flash and Meteor.

Crayon

A gritty look just like you used to get as a kid drawing on lined tablets with chunks of wood pulp in them. Presets: Crayon, Waxy, Pastel, Oil Pastel, Ink Drop and Rubbing.

Charcoal

Results in a texture that looks like charcoal has "skipped" over the surface of the paper. Presets: Charcoal, Soft Charcoal, Gritty Charcoal, Fog and Smoke.

Chalk

Just like chalk drawings on a chalkboard, skips and all. Like Charcoal, but with a lighter and airier look. Presets include Chalk, Soft Chalk, Gritty Chalk and Splatter.

Pencil

Similar to the Paintbrush tool, but slightly narrower. It is good for drawing ruled and fine lines and details. Presets: 2B Pencil, F Pencil, HB Pencil, 6B Pencil, 500 Lbs. and Multicolor Pencil.

Marker

Makes a nice, bold line. Presets: Fine Felt, Round Felt, Square Felt and Soft Felt.

Oil Paint

A painterly effect mimics the look of oils on canvas. Presets: Drop, Thick Stroke, Dry Stroke and Light Stroke.

Particle

Create artistic, highlighting effects with overlapping rounds in soft pastels or bright explosive colors. Presets: Leaf, Particle Brush, Particle Pen, Particle String, Particle Blur, Firefly, Artist, Explode and Dazzle.

Drop Water

Like dipping a brush in water then going over previously applied paint, Drop Water results in a blurry, watercolor effect that softens hard edges. Presets: Solution.

Bristle

Dry brush effects with a scratchy, bristly appearance. Presets: Split 1, Split 2, Split 3, Pepper Dot and Grass.

Color Replacement Pen

Select a color to be replaced and a replacement color by clicking in the Color boxes in the Attributes toolbar. Then scrub the Color Replacement Pen over the image to replace color. Presets: Blue to White and Blue to Pastels.

Clone Tools

You will likely find many uses for the Clone tools. They are invaluable for removing areas that you do not want to include in your final image.

The Clone tools can also copy an image, either in the same image, or in a new image. This makes it possible to not only add copies of a feature of interest to an image, but it also allows you to clone a photograph and then render a unique Chalk portrait in a separate image.

Original Image   Clone Crayon Version

Like the Paint tools, basic characteristics are specified in the Attributes toolbar, including a number of presets, with advanced attributes assigned in the Brush Panel.

There are 9 Clone tools.

Clone-Paintbrush

The basic clone tool is useful for editing out unwanted portions of an image. Presets: Paint Brush, Fade-In, Apparition, Fine Brush, Medium Brush, Thick Brush.

Clone-Airbrush

Lays down a muted version of the cloned area. The longer you stay in one place, the more opaque the result. Presets: Air Brush, Heavy Merge, Apparition and Soft Merge.

Clone-Crayon

Recreates the cloned area as if it was drawn in crayon, little shredded edges along the lines and all. Presets: Crayon, Oil Pastel, Pastel, Soft Linear Fade-in and Fog.

Clone-Charcoal

Textured charcoal appears to skip over the background. Presets: Soft Charcoal, Charcoal, Gritty Charcoal, Soft Texture Merge, Mist and Linear Wipe.

Clone-Chalk

Looks like the cloned area has been drawn over a rough background with chalk. Presets: Chalk, Gritty Chalk, Soft Chalk and Linear Fade-in.

Clone-Pencil

Very similar to the paint brush clone, with somewhat narrower strokes. Presets: Pencil.

Clone-Marker

Appears to have been drawn in felt marker. Presets: Round Marker, Square Marker, Angle Fade-in, Reflection 1 and Reflection 2.

Clone-Oil Paint

Varying textures mimic oil painting brushstrokes. Presets: Oil Paint, Gritty Fade-in and Vapor.

Clone-Bristle

A dry brush look showing a great deal of brush texture. Presets: Bristle.

Brush Panel

While the basic features of the Retouch, Paint and Clone tools can be set from the Attributes toolbar, the Brush Panel offers a higher level of control over a tool's editing properties. Use the Brush Panel to specify a brush angle, stroke spacing, or an Apply method.

Users of drawing tablets can choose options for transparency and pressure from the Advanced tab. Click on the Texture tab to Paint and Clone with textures. To access the Brush Panel, select View, Toolbars & Panels, Brush Panel, click the Layout button and choose Brush Panel or simply hit Ctrl+F3.

The Retouch tools' Brush Panel has three tabs: Shape, Options and Advanced. Options available from each tab vary, depending on the selected tool and data type.

The Brush Panel for the Dodge Retouch tool is shown below.

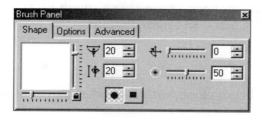

With two exceptions (the Particle and Drop Water Paint tools) the Paint tools' Brush Panel has five tabs: Shape, Options, Color, Texture and Advanced. The options available from each tab vary, depending on the selected tool and image data type. The Brush Panel for the Paintbrush tool is shown below.

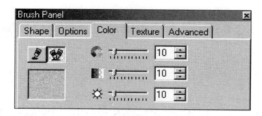

The Clone Tools' Brush Panel has four tabs: Shape, Options, Texture and Advanced. Again, the options available from each tab vary, depending on the selected tool and image data type. The Brush Panel for the Clone Crayon tool is shown below.

As noted previously, tab options vary by selected tool. If you are not sure what a particular option does, position the cursor over its button without pressing the mouse button, until a popup box describing the function pops up. Alternatively, click on the question mark in the upper right corner of the menu bar and click on the option in question. Doing so will open a helpful description of its function.

Painting With Textures

Painting with textures adds interesting surface texture to 2D images. Access this feature when a Paint or Clone tool is selected by clicking on Textures in the Attributes toolbar, or by clicking the Texture tab in the Brush Panel. An improvement in PhotoImpact 6 is the ability to select a texture from thumbnails, rather than a text list.

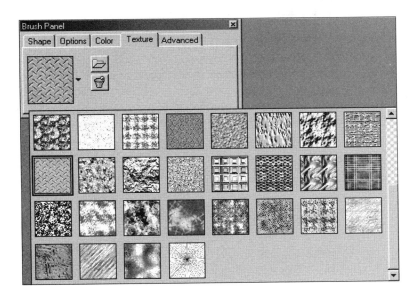

Click on a thumbnail to select a texture. Use your own custom texture by clicking on the Add Texture icon (open folder). Browse your hard drive to select a texture image. A thumbnail for the new texture will be added to the presets. To delete a texture, click on the Delete Texture icon (trash can). You can only delete textures that you have added yourself.

In the example shown at the top of the next page, a custom fine line texture was accessed from a folder on the hard drive to add texture to wavy painted line.

PhotoImpact 6 Wizardry

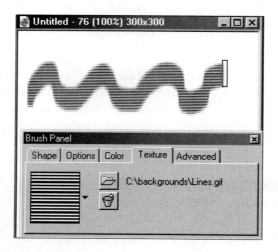

Image Editing: Active Learning Exercises

Pasting and Editing Clipboard Contents

1. The purpose of this exercise is to experiment with different ways to load and paste Clipboard contents into a selection area. Then you will learn how to apply a Fadeout to help the newly pasted Clipboard contents blend into the base image.

2. Choose File, Open to access the Open dialog box. Browse to and select lilypond2.jpg. Click Open.

3. Choose the Standard Selection tool. In the Attributes toolbar, select Ellipse from the Shape Dropdown list, with Soft edge=0.

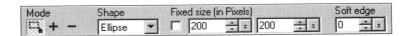

4. Make a rounded, elliptical selection in the dark water in the lower right corner of the image.

5. Choose Edit, Clipboard, Load to access the Open box. Browse to purplelily.jpg and select it. Note that the "File Information" section shows that this is a very large image, 640 X 480 pixels. Click Open.

6. Nothing seems to have happened, but you will soon see that the image has been loaded into the Clipboard without ever having to open it in the work space.

7. Now you will paste and fit this very large image into the small selection area, adding a water lily to the pond. Choose Edit, Paste, Fit Into Selection.

8. The pasted Clipboard contents are an object. Click in the base image to deactivate the object. You will see that it has a hard edge that prevents it from blending into the background. Click back on the purple water lily object to make it active again.

9. To help it blend in better, choose Edit, Fadeout (or hit Ctrl+H). When the Fadeout dialog box opens, select a Radial Fill type. For "Fill colors" select Two Colors. Click in the beginning Color box and select white (transparency=0). The white will preserve the center of the object. For the ending Color, enter a value of 65, for a very pale gray which results in a semi-transparent edge that will blend into the background. Click OK to apply.

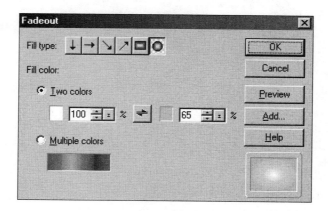

10. The fadeout goes a long way to blending the water lily into the background, but it still needs a little work. To fix that, choose Edit, Fadeout and apply the exact same fadeout to the object again.

11. That should get rid of all but a few obviously light spots around the edges of the purple water lily. To finish up the blending, choose the Object Paint Eraser. In the Attributes toolbar, set the Transparency to 75%. Erasing with a high transparency level and a very soft edge will create a more subtle "fade" at the edges.

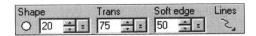

12. Carefully click and drag around the lighter areas that mar the blending. Be careful not to erase part of the purple flower itself.

13. Perform one more step to intensify the color in the purple water lily. Click the Quick Color Control's Contrast (sun) key's plus (+) sign one time.

14. Hit the space bar to deactivate the object. It should blend into the rest of the lily pond. If you did not know better, you might think it was part of the original image.

Stitching and Cloning a Panorama

1. The purpose of this exercise is to stitch two images together to create a panorama effect. The Clone tool will be used also. Cloning is an art that takes a bit of practice. Yours may not turn out exactly like the example, but you should get a good result.

2. Hit Ctrl+O to access the Open dialog box. Select boat1.jpg and click Open. Hit Ctrl+O again to open boat2.jpg.

3. Click on the blue title bar of boat1.jpg to make it active. Choose Edit, Stitch to access the Stitch dialog box.

4. Note that "Stitch with" has selected boat2.jpg automatically. If you select "Auto stitch" and click the Test button, you will not get a very good match. There are too many similar "edges" in this image for Auto-stitch to work well.

5. Instead, select Manually and select "Auto fine-tune." This will allow you to drag the image on the right onto the image on the left to match up the edges yourself. The 50% transparency for the overlap will let you see through and match up reference points. To create reference points, find a "landmark" or reference point that appears on both images (circled in screen shot below).

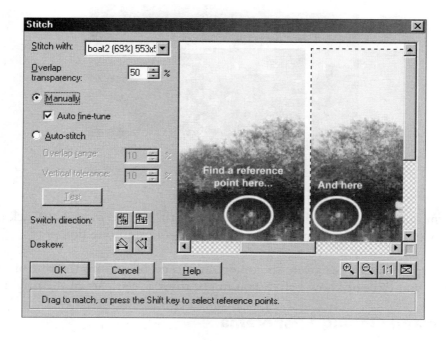

6. Hold down on the Shift key while clicking on the reference point in boat1.jpg, then hold down on the Shift key while clicking on the same reference point in boat2.jpg.

As soon as you click on the reference point in boat2.jpg, they will be lined up automatically. Click OK to close the dialog box. A new image with boat1.jpg and boat2.jpg stitched together appears in the work space.

7. Just for fun, now you will stitch boat1.jpg onto the left side of the new image to make it even wider. Select Edit, Stitch. From the "Stich with" dropdown list, choose boat1.jpg. Select "Manually" and "Auto fine-tune" again. Click the Switch Direction button (arrow) to move boat1.jpg to the left side of the larger image. You will see that the match between the edges is not a very good one.

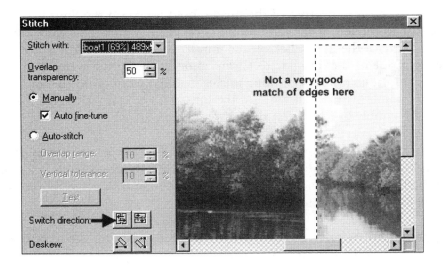

8. Drag the two images together so that they overlap by about ¼ inch, lining up the tops of the images. If you get an alert box telling you that the overlap area is too small, click OK to get rid of it, then click OK to close the Stitch box. The extra image will be added onto the left side of the panorama. Hit Ctrl+0 to view the image at 100% size. It will show obvious hard joins.

9. Select the Clone Paintbrush tool. In the Attributes toolbar, change the brush size to 50 and leave the other values at their defaults.

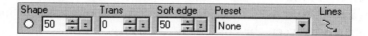

10. Beginning at the very bottom of the image, hold down on the Shift key while clicking just to the left of the hard joining line in the water. This will clone the water on the left side of the line. Click on the join to cover the line with water. Shift+Click on the right side of the join line to Clone some of the lighter water on that side, then click on the join line. Continue in this manner, cloning on the left and right sides of the join line, then clicking on the line to cover it up with water. You will have a soft, wobbly line between the light and dark areas.

11. Drag on the sliders in the image window to move up to the top part of the image, where there is a less obvious join in the sky area. Continue to Shift+Click on each side of the line to clone, then click on the line to hide it. You should be able to get rid of the join line completely.

12. Now that you have cloned out to the treeline, Shift+Click on the trees to the left of the join line to clone that area, then click on the join to hide it. Stay on the left of

the join line, Shift+Clicking to clone, then clicking on the join line to hide it, all the way down to the water line.

13. Change the brush size to 25 in the Attributes toolbar. Shift+Click to clone the tops of the trees on the clump of trees sticking up to the right of the one you have been working on. Return to the join area at the treeline and click on the tops of those trees, adding some variation to the top of them from the cloned area.

14. Change the brush size to 50 in the Attributes toolbar. Shift+Click to clone the reflection of the trees in the water in the clump of trees to the right of the area you are hiding. Return to the join line in the tree's reflection and click on it here and there to add to the reflection and get rid of the join line.

15. To avoid a "cookie cutter" look along the treeline, Shift+Click to clone various treeline areas, then click to place the cloned area over the treeline in a different spot, varying it just slightly. Try not to overdo it, adding just enough variety to create a random look.

16. Now the sky, treeline, and reflection in the water should all look pretty good. Obvious joins in these areas should have disappeared, and there should be some nice variety in the treeline. The main problem left to fix is the obvious division between dark (on the left) and light (on the right) water at the bottom of the image. Of course you could just crop this part out, but here is a different way to fix the problem.

17. Choose the Standard Selection tool with the Shape set to Rectangle in the Attributes toolbar. In the lower left side of the image, make a selection like this one. Right click and Convert to Object.

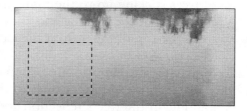

18. Drag the object over to cover the join line. Hit Ctrl+H to access the Fadeout dialog box. Choose the arrow going left to right Fill type. Select Multiple Colors and click in the Color box to open the Palette Ramp Editor. Select Palette 2 and click OK to close the Palette Ramp Editor.

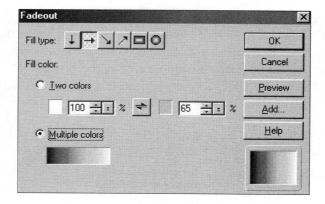

19. Click OK to apply the Fadeout effect. The semi-transparent object will blur the join line quite a bit now. Right click and Merge.

20. Return to the Clone Paintbrush tool. In the Attributes toolbar, change the brush size to 100. Shift+Click to the right of the join line, which should be very faint now. Then click over the line to cover it. Repeat as needed on the left side of the join line.

21. Choose the Burn Retouch tool. In the Attributes toolbar, select Wide Burn

from the Preset dropdown list. Change the brush size to 100.

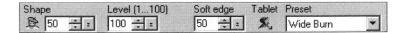

22. Lightly click (do not drag) along the area that you just cloned, creating a random pattern of darks and lights that blend into the dappled water surface. Also darken any areas in the trees that look too light because they were cloned from a sunnier area.

23. Take a good hard look at the panorama now. If you see elements that have been repeated, get rid of them by cloning over them, varying the brush size as needed. This can involve a good bit of trial and error.

    Here is the finished panorama, stitched together and doctored with the Clone and Burn tools. Remember that you can right click and choose Undo if you make a mistake, then try again.

Editing a Photo With a Tone Map and Custom Framing

1. The purpose of this exercise is to learn how to edit a digital photo so that it looks significantly better. First the photo will be resized. A tone map will be applied to redistribute the colors in the image, and the brightness and contrast edited. Finally, you will add a customized frame and shadow.

2. Hit Ctrl+O to access the Open dialog box. Select "Open as Read-only." Select caterpillar.bmp and click Open.

3. This photo of a caterpillar is relatively sharp, but it is dark and mottled, which obscures important detail. At 1600 X 1200 pixels, it is also too large to fit on the screen at actual size, and much too large to post to a web page.

4. To edit the image to a more manageable size, choose Format, Dimensions. In the "New image" section, choose User-defined. Make sure "Keep aspect ratio" is selected, so the width to height proportions are preserved. From the Unit dropdown list, choose Percent. Edit the size to 33 percent. Click OK.

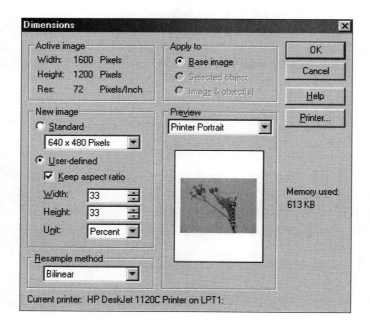

5. Now that the image fits into the work space at actual size, you will edit the distribution of colors within it. Although there are many dark tones, there are not enough light tones for a well balanced image.

6. Choose Format, Tone Map. When the Tone Map dialog box opens, click the Map tab. Leave the Channel at the default of Master. Click the Enhancements button and you will see a number of preset mapping curves which could be selected to redistrib-

ute the lights and darks in the image. However, note that "Use Complete Range" is available, which means that the full range of colors available in this image has not been used effectively. Select the "Use Complete Range" Enhancement.

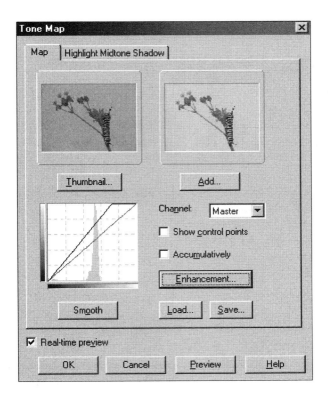

7. Immediately the image will seem brighter and sharper in the right Preview window. Click the Preview button to see the effect of the tone map on the actual image. Click the Undo button to reverse the effect. You will notice that the image looks muddy and blurry again without the tone map. Click Redo to reapply the tone map. Click OK to apply it.

8. Now to sharpen up the focus a bit. Although it is possible to sharpen detail with the Focus command, there is a great deal more flexibility if you use Unsharp Mask instead. Choose Format, Blur & Sharpen, Unsharp Mask. When the Unsharp Mask dialog box opens, do not select a thumbnail. Instead, click Options to open a secondary dialog box.

9. The default values are far too powerful for this image, and indeed for most images. Generally speaking, you will ususally get the best results with a low Sharpen factor value, and an even lower Aperture radius value. If these values are too high, the image will look glaring and detail will actually be lost. Edit the Sharpen factor to 10, and the Aperture radius to 1.

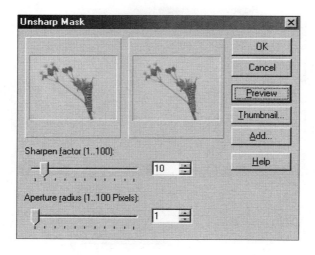

10. Click the Preview button to view the Unsharp Mask settings applied to the full size image. Click Undo and Redo a few times to see the changes that Unsharp Mask creates in the image. When Redo has been clicked, you should see a noticeable brightening of the light areas, creating better contrast and detail. Make sure Redo has been selected, then click OK to apply.

11. To give the image just a little more sharpness, choose Format, Brightness & Contrast (or hit Ctrl+B). When the Brightness & Contrast dialog box opens, the middle thumbnail will be selected by default. Look at the Thumbnail variation default value, which is 12. This value, which affects the amount of change from one thumbnail to the next, is a bit high for an image with a large, flat, light-colored background like this one. Edit the Thumbnail variation value to 6, halving the power of the effect. Now click on the thumbnail to the right of the center, selected thumbnail, as shown at the top of the next page.

Image Editing: Active Learning Exercises

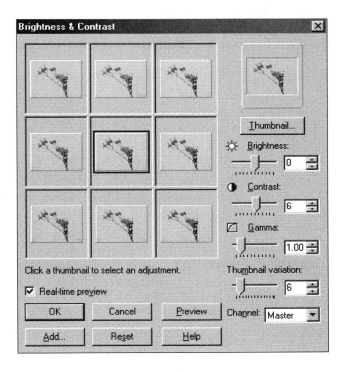

12. Click the Preview button. You should see a noticeable lightening of the background which brings the caterpillar and flower into sharper contrast. Click OK to apply.

13. Hit Shift+F to access Frame & Shadow. From the Style dropdown list, choose Classic Frame. Select "Do not merge frame object," so the frame can be edited after it is applied. Select the first frame on the left in the top row (arrow).

383

14. Click OK to apply. Note that the canvas expands to accommodate the frame. There are 3 objects making up the frame: A large outer frame, a very narrow middle frame, and a wider inner frame. The objects will be Grouped. Right click and choose Ungroup. Hit the space bar to deactivate the objects and select the base image.

15. Select the Path Drawing tool. Click on the outer frame to make it active. In the Attributes toolbar, click on the Options button and choose Galleries, Material, to open the EasyPalette's Material Gallery. Select 3D Collection and double click on Black. The outer frame will change to a textured black.

16. Click on the middle part of the frame to make it active. In the Attributes toolbar, right click in the Color box and choose Eyedropper. When the Eyedropper dialog box opens, click on one of the bright yellow flowers to select that color. Click OK to close the dialog box. The narrow middle frame will turn a bright marigold color.

17. Click on the inner frame, right next to the image, to make it active. In the Attributes toolbar, right click in the Color box and choose Eyedropper. When the Eyedropper dialog box opens, click on a green flower stem to select that color. Click OK to close the dialog box. The inner frame is now green.

18. Right click and Select All Objects. Right click and choose Merge As Single Object.

19. Choose Edit, Expand Canvas. When the Expand Canvas dialog box opens, Expand all four sides by 20 pixels.

20. Right click and choose Shadow. When the Shadow dialog box opens, add a black shadow with the values shown below. Click OK to apply the shadow.

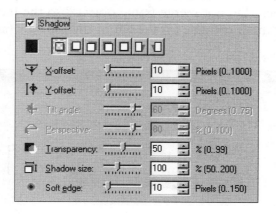

21. Choose Object, Split Shadow. Click the space bar to deactivate all objects and select the base image.

22. Choose the Pick tool. Click on the shadow to make it active. Drag it up and slightly to the right to reposition it. Right click and Merge All.

23. The framed image is too large to show at actual size. Hit Ctrl+0 to view at actual size, then hit Ctrl+U to view Full Screen. Drag the slider bars to view the entire image. When you are done looking at it, hit Escape to return to the work space.

Editing a Photo With a Custom Tone Map

1. Hit Ctrl+O to access the Open dialog box. Select "Open as Read-only." Browse to whitelily.bmp, select it and click Open.

2. This digital photo was taken outside in full Florida sunlight. The contrast between the bright white water lily and the dark water is so great that detail (green lily pads) was lost. The purpose of this exercise is to lighten the midtones in the image in an effort to restore detail and improve color balance.

3. Choose Format, Tone Map, or hit Ctrl+Shift+T, to access the Tone Map dialog box. By default the Highlight Midtone Shadow tab should be selected.

5. Edit the Midtone value to 30. This will increase the midtone range. Edit the Highlight value to 5 to brighten the whites.

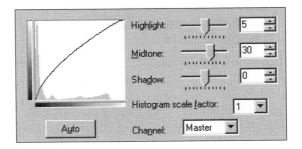

6. Click Preview to view the edits applied to the actual image. Note that you can see the green lily pads now, and that the white flower is brighter, but not bleached out. Click OK to apply.

Editing Photo Color With Style Filters

1. Choose File, Open to access the Open dialog box. Browse to and select fisherman.bmp.

2. The purpose of this exercise is to experiment with Style filters to tint skin tones and backgrounds alike with soft color. Often impressive color corrections, or artistic effects, can be accomplished simply by applying the Style filters.

3. Choose Format, Style to access the Style dialog box. Click the Face tab, then select Blonde. Click the Preview button to view the filter applied to the actual image. Note that the filter produces a subtle effect, making the skin tones appear slightly pinker, while the greenery in the background appears a bit more yellow.

Image Editing: Active Learning Exercises

4. Click Continue to return to the dialog box. From the Face tab, select Lighten and click Preview. This time you will see little change in the background, but the skin tones will appear much lighter with a gray cast. Click Continue to return to the dialog box.

5. Click the Light tab and select Bulb. Click Preview to view the filter applied to the actual image. The entire image will be suffused with a warm, golden-yellow tint. Click Continue to return to the dialog box.

6. Click the Season tab and select Spring. Click Preview to view the filter applied to the actual image, then click Continue to return to the dialog box. Repeat for the remaining three filters in the Season tab. Each of the Season filters will dramatically affect colors in the skin tones and the background. Click Continue to return to the dialog box.

7. Click the Sky tab and select Evening. Click Preview to view the filter applied to the actual image. The entire image will darken with russet tones typical of late afternoon light. Click Continue to return to the dialog box.

8. Click the Filter tab and select Yellow 20%. Click Preview to take a look at the effect applied to the actual image. The entire image takes on a decided yellow cast. Click Continue. When returned to the Style dialog box, leave Yellow 20% selected, but click in the Filter Color box and select the flesh tone from the standard colors (RGB=228, 166, 139). This invaluable little trick lets you selectively add a tint of any color and strength that you desire. Edit the Density value to 30.

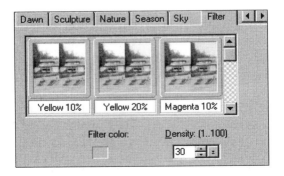

387

9. Click Preview to view the filter applied to the actual image. Notice that the skin tones are much warmer now, and the contrast among lights and darks in the greenery in the background is emphasized. Click Continue to return to the dialog box.

10. Click the Other tab and select Colorful. Click Preview to view the filter applied to the actual image. Notice how the entire image appears to be lit up with sunlight. Click Cancel to close the dialog box.

Color Correcting a Photo With Color Balance

1. Hit Ctrl+O to access the Open dialog box. Browse to hoolahoop.bmp. Select it and click Open.

2. Taken on a cold, overcast day, this photo is too blue. The purpose of this exercise is to restore the pale pink color of the child's shirt, as well as restoring appropriate colors to the entire image.

3. Choose Format, Color Balance to open the Color Balance dialog box. There are two different ways to redistribute the colors in this photo using Color Balance. The quickest and easiest way is to click the Preset tab. By default the center thumbnail is selected. Select the one immediately to the right of the selected thumbnail, adding more red back into the image.

4. Click Preview to apply the color correction applied to the actual image. The colors should appear more evenly distributed, adding pink where it is needed in the child's shirt and making the blacktop on the ground a more appropriate gray color.

5. Click Continue to return to the dialog box, then hit Reset to return to the default settings. This time, click on the Smart tab, from which you may choose a color for correction and a correction color. Generally speaking, it is wise to select an area in the image that should be black or white, but other colors may be selected instead.

6. Position the cursor in the left preview window, until it turns into an Eyedropper. Click in a light area of the child's shirt. The Current Color Color box will show a grayish-lavender color. This color should be pinker, so right click in the Desired Color Color box and select Windows Color Picker. Mix a pale pink-lavender, (RGB=230, 216, 221), then click OK to close the Color Picker.

7. Click Preview to view the color correction applied to the actual image. Again, the

colors will be redistributed, or "balanced," so that pink is slightly more prevalent than before, and the blue cast is toned down. Click Cancel to close the dialog box.

Editing with Hue & Saturation

1. If the EasyPalette is not already open, choose View, Toolbars & Panels, EasyPalette. Click on the Library button. Choose Image Library, Nature. Drag from the Rose 2 thumbnail to an empty area in the work space. A copy of the rose image object will open in its own window.

2. The purpose of this exercise is to edit the colors of the peach colored rose with Hue & Saturation.

3. Choose Format, Hue & Saturation, or hit Ctrl+E, to open the Hue & Saturation dialog box. Make sure Master is selected in the "Method" section. Drag the Hue (color) slider to the left, to –150.

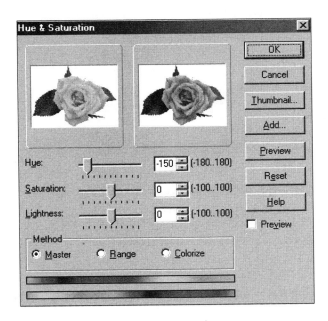

4. Click Preview to view the results of the Hue edit. The rose will appear in shades of blue. Click Continue to return to the dialog box. Drag the Hue slider up to 40 to

create a yellow rose. Drag it up to 145 to turn the rose aqua. Drag it left again to –25 to turn the rose red.

5. Drag the Saturation slider to the left to –45, to "gray" down the red to an "ashes of roses" color.

6. In the "Method" section, select Colorize. The right preview window will show a green rose. Drag the Lightness slider to the right, to 20, to lighten the green.

7. Click the Reset button to get rid of the edits. In the "Method" section, select Range. Drag the right bar under Range all the way to the right. Leave the other 3 bars at their default location. This range limits your options to the colors found between the left and right bars. Drag the Hue slider to the left, to –140. The rose will turn a dark blue-purple. To tone down the color a bit, drag the Lightness slider to the right, to 25.

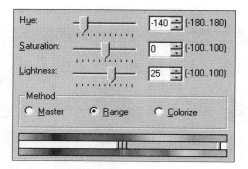

8. Click Preview to view the light purple rose. Click Continue to return to the dialog box. Drag the Saturation slider to the left, to –40.

9. Now click Preview to view the edits. Reducing the color saturation results in a gray-lavender rose. Click Cancel.

Reducing Size and Editing Focus/Sharpness of a Photo

1. Choose File, Open to access the Open dialog box. Select "Open as Read-only." Browse to and select turtle.bmp. Click Open.

2. This is a large (1600 X 1200 pixel) digital photo of a turtle. The purpose of this exercise is to demonstrate how greatly reducing the size of an image can lead to blurring, and how to use the Focus and Unsharp Mask commands to restore detail.

3. Choose Format, Dimensions, or hit Ctrl+G, to access the Dimensions dialog box. In the "New image" section, select User-defined. Make sure "Keep aspect ratio" is selected to preserve height to width proportion. From the Unit dropdown list, choose Percent, and edit the size to 20%. Leave the Resample method set to the default of Bilinear. Click OK to close the box.

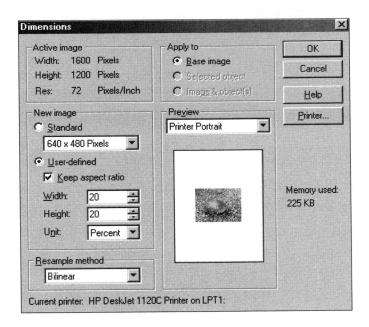

4. Note that at the new, smaller size, there is a loss of detail. The outline of the turtle's shell and the eye look blurry, and the grass no longer looks as well defined. Hit Ctrl+D to produce a duplicate of the reduced size image. This duplicate will serve as a control, so you can compare the before and after results of editing Focus.

5. To restore detail to the duplicated image, choose Format, Focus, or hit Ctrl+Shift+F, to access the Focus dialog box. You could select one of the thumbnails, specifically the one on the right in the top row. However, for this exercise, just click Options to access a secondary dialog box.

6. When the next Focus dialog box opens, note that the Blur to Sharpen level is set to −1 by default. Select Auto-adjust to allow PhotoImpact to select a focus level. Note that the Blur to Sharpen options are grayed out when Auto-adjust is selected.

7. Click Preview to view the Focus edit applied to the actual image. You will not see much improvement. The Auto-adjust edit is not powerful enough for this image. Click Continue to return to the dialog box.

8. Deselect Auto-adjust so that the slider becomes available again. The natural inclination is to sharpen the detail too much. Accordingly, edit this value to 2 and click Preview. This time the image is too sharp and bleached out. Click Continue to return to the dialog box. This time, edit the Blur to Sharpen level to 1.

9. Click Preview to view the results of this edit. Although there is some lightening of the image, this Sharpen level restores a great deal of detail. It is the best choice for this particular image. Keep in mind that you will always have to balance sharpness against image quality when editing Focus. Click OK to apply the edit.

10. Compare the two images to one another. You should see a significantly sharper image as the result of editing the Focus.

11. Now you will compare an alternative method of sharpening the image. Click on the original, blurry image's blue title bar to make it active.

12. Choose Effect, Blur & Sharpen, Unsharp Mask to access the Unsharp Mask dialog box. Ignore the thumbnails and click the Options button to open a secondary dialog box. From here you can fine tune sharpening with greater flexibility than is available with the Focus command.

13. To avoid lightening or bleaching the image out too much, edit the Aperture radius down to 1, the lowest possible level. You should see the image in the preview window darken appreciably once the default value is changed. Edit the Sharpen factor value to 20.

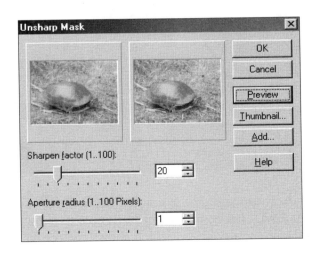

14. Click Preview to view the results of editing applied to the actual image. Click Undo and Redo a few times, noting the subtle but effective sharpening effect of the Unsharp Mask edits. Click Redo and then click OK to close the box.

15. Compare this image to the one sharpened with Focus previously. Note that you have restored good detail, with less bleaching, using the Unsharp Mask command. For this particular image, the Unsharp Mask method yields the best result.

Removing Red Eye from a Digital Photo

1. Choose File, Visual Open. Browse to redeye.bmp, select it and click Open.

2. Like many digital photos taken indoors with a flash, this photo suffers from red eye. The purpose of this exercise is to learn how to remove the red eye from the photo.

3. Choose Effect, Camera Lens, Remove Red Eye. When the dialog box opens, in the "Select area for filtering" section, choose the two eye option (arrow). In the left preview window, drag the two circles over so that they are centered on the eyes.

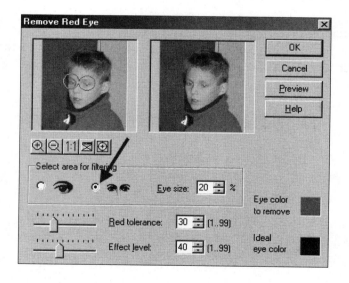

4. Click on the 1:1 button to magnify the image to actual size. Use the scroll bars in the left preview window, if necessary, to get both eyes to show at the same time. If you look in the right preview window, which shows the results of editing, the eyes still look red with the default values.

5. It is important when removing red eye from photos that you do not end up with a dull black eye without highlights. Some experimentation in editing is almost always

needed to get the best result. Accordingly, edit the eye size to 15%. Edit the Red tolerance value to 55, which affects a wider range of red pixels. Edit the Effect level to 75, making the effect more powerful. This child has dark brown eyes, so click in the "Ideal eye color" Color box and select a very dark brown (RGB=49, 32, 26).

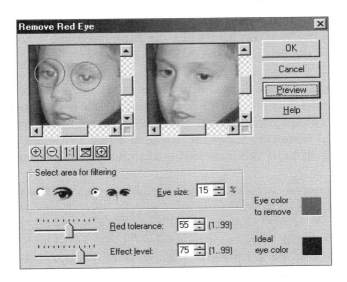

6. Click Preview to view these edits applied to the actual image. The red eye should be replaced with the dark brown, while retaining a little white sparkle in the eye on the right hand side. If the brown extends onto the skin around the eye, click Continue to return to the dialog box. Drag the circle as needed so that the effect is applied to the right area. When you are satisfied, click OK to apply.

Before Remove Red Eye

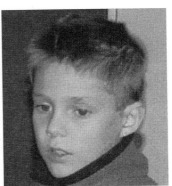

After Remove Red Eye

Removing Green Eye from a Digital Photo

1. Hit Ctrl+O to access the Open dialog box. Browse to greeneyes.bmp. Select its thumbnail and click Open.

2. Glowing green eyes are the pet analog to red eyes in photos of people. The purpose of this exercise is to show you how to fix the problem using the same tools used to remove red eye in the previous exercise.

3. Select Effect, Camera Lens, Remove Red Eye. When the Remove Red Eye dialog box opens, in the "Select area for filtering" section, choose the two eye option. In the left preview window, drag the two circles over so that they are centered on the eyes. Click the 1:1 button to show the image at actual size, then click the minus (-) button once, so that both eyes can be displayed in the left preview window.

4. If you did the previous exercise, you will see "black eyes" in the right preview window. The settings used previously are too powerful for this photo. To edit, change the Eye size to 10%. Edit the Red tolerance value to 65. Edit the Effect level to 50. Right click in the "Eye color to remove" Color box and select Eyedropper. Position the cursor in the left preview window until it turns into an eyedropper. Click in the darker green in the eye on the left hand side to remove the green. Click in the "Ideal eye color" Color box and select black.

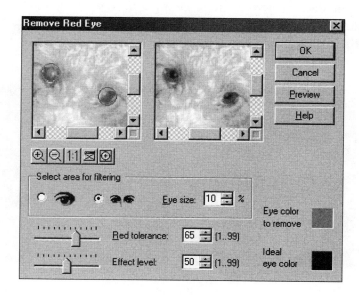

5. Click Preview to view the edits applied to the actual image. You should see shiny black eyes without green. If it does not look right to you, click Continue to return to the dialog box. Drag the circles in the left preview window, if necessary, to center the color correction effectively. When you are satisfied, click OK to apply.

Glowing Green Pet Eyes Before...   And After Remove Red Eye

Making a Snowglobe With Creative Particle

1. Hit Ctrl+O to access the Open dialog box. Select snowglobe.ufo and click Open.

2. There are three objects making up the snowglobe: the blue globe with the moose ballerina, the transparent glass overlay and the gold base. The purpose of this exercise is to apply the Snow particle to the objects to create an animated snowglobe.

3. With the Pick tool, click in the base image to deactivate the objects. Hit Ctrl+D two times to create two copies of the base image and all objects. You will have three identical images open. Be very careful not to move any of the objects.

4. Open the EasyPalette's Layer Manager. You will see thumbnails for the Globe, Glass Overlay and Base. Click on the thumbnail for the blue globe with the moose ballerina to select it.

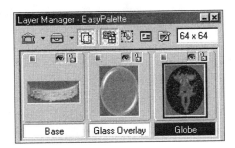

5. Choose Effect, Creative, Particle. When the Particle dialog box opens, select Snow from the Effects. You will see that the blue globe is overwhelmed by snow. In the "Effect control" section, edit the values as follows: Density=1200, Size=10 and Variance=8. This reduces the density and size of the snow particles and makes them more uniform. In the "Particle parameters" section, leave the default color of white, but edit the Body value to 0, and the Opacity value to 85. Now the snow is less transparent and blends in well with the globe background.

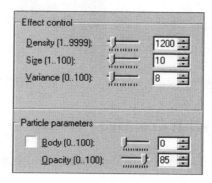

6. Before you apply the snow to the globe, save this custom effect so that you can use it on the other two frames for the animation. Click the Add button to access the Add to EasyPalette dialog box. Give the effect a name and save it to My Gallery.

7. Look at My Gallery in the EasyPalette. You should see a thumbnail for Snow for Snowglobe.

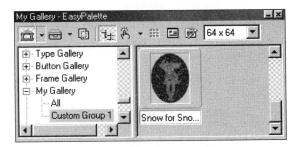

8. When you are returned to the Particle dialog box, click OK to apply the snow effect to the globe.

9. Right click on the image and select Merge All. Choose File, Save As. Save as frame1.bmp to your Desktop or another location where it will be easy to find and delete later.

10. Click on the blue title bar of the second image to make it active. In the EasyPalette's Layer Manager, click on the Globe thumbnail to make it active.

11. Right click on the Snow for Snowglobe thumbnail in My Gallery in your EasyPalette. Choose Modify Properties and Apply to re-open the Particle dialog box. Click the Random button once to generate a different distribution of the Snow particle. Click OK to apply and close the box.

12. Right click on the image and choose Merge All. Choose File, Save As and save it as frame2.bmp (save to the same folder to which you saved frame1.bmp).

13. Click on the blue title bar of the third image to make it active. In the EasyPalette's Layer Manager, click on the Globe thumbnail to make it active.

14. Right click on the Snow for Snowglobe thumbnail in My Gallery in your EasyPalette. Choose Modify Properties and Apply to re-open the Particle dialog box. Click the Random button twice to generate another distribution of the Snow particle. If you do not like the distribution, keep clicking Random until you get one that you like. Click OK to apply and close the box.

PhotoImpact 6 Wizardry

15. Right click on the image and choose Merge All. Choose File, Save As and save it as frame3.bmp (save to the same folder to which you saved frame1.bmp and frame2.bmp).

16. Now that you have made three copies of the image with different distributions of the Snow particle, it is time to put them together in GIF Animator. Click Switch in the upper right corner of your screen and select Ulead GIF Animator 4.0 from the dropdown list.

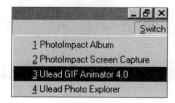

17. When GIF Animator opens, you will get the Startup Wizard. Select Animation Wizard.

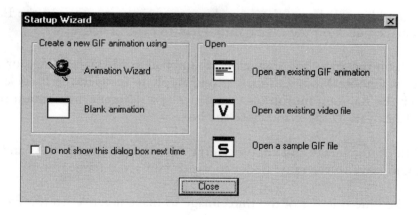

18. When the Animation Wizard – Select Files box opens, click Add Image. Doing so accesses the Open dialog box. Select frame3.bmp, then hold down on the Shift key while selecting frame1.bmp. Doing so selects all three frames at the same time, in numerical order.

Image Editing: Active Learning Exercises

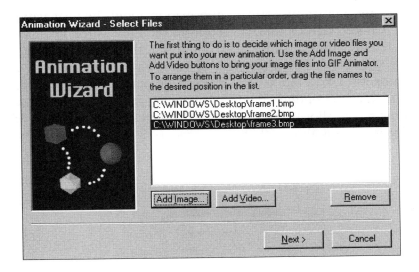

19. Click the Next button to open the Source Type box. Select "Photo oriented (Dither)" and click Next.

20. When the Frame Duration dialog box opens, leave the default values and click Next.

21. Now you are at the Done box. Click Finish to complete the attributes for the snowglobe animation.

22. When the GIF Animator opens, you will see the first frame of the animation, frame1.bmp, selected (highlighted) on the left side of the work space. In the center of the work space you will see four tabs: Compose, Optimize, Edit and Preview. Click the Preview tab to view the animation right in the GIF Animator work space. Use the scroll bars to view the entire animated image. You should see a nicely varied pattern of animated snow which appears only on the blue globe part of the snowglobe.

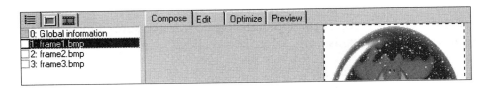

23. To reduce the file size prior to saving the animation, click the Optimize tab. You will no longer see the animation. Instead, information about the image appears in the work space. Choose GIF Optimized 256 from the Preset dropdown list, then click the Optimize Now button. Leave other settings at their default values.

24. GIF Animator will take a moment to process the optimization, then information about the original and optimized animation will appear in the work space. As you can see in the screen shot below, the original animation was just over 55 kb, and the optimized animation is about 40 kb, a savings of 15 kb in file size.

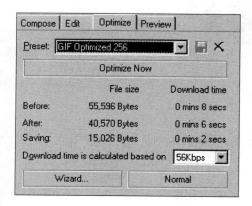

25. View the optimized animation by clicking on one of the browser buttons at the top of the screen. Doing so will open a browser window displaying the animation. When you are finished looking at it, close the browser window to return to GIF Animator.

26. To save the animation, choose File, Save As. When the Save As dialog box opens, give the animation a name and save it to a folder on your hard drive. If you would like to view the animated snowglobe, it is included among this book's files as anisnowglobe.gif.

Natural Painting Applied to a Photo

1. Choose File, Open to access the Open dialog box. Make sure "Open as Read-only" is selected. Browse to 2kids.bmp, select it and click Open.

2. The purpose of this exercise is to gain experience with the lovely effects that Natural

Painting can have on ordinary photos, like this one of two children holding kittens on a front porch.

3. Choose Effect, Natural Painting, Watercolor to access the Watercolor dialog box. You could choose a thumbnail, but for this exercise, click the Options button instead. Doing so will open a secondary Watercolor dialog box. In the "Stroke size" section, choose Small. Drag the Moisture level slider to the left, all the way down to 20.

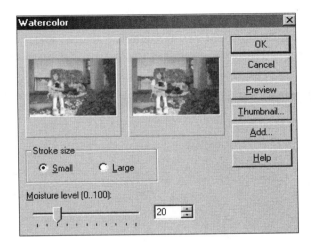

4. Click the Preview button to view the Watercolor effect applied to the actual image. It should look loose and fluid, just like a watercolor painting. Click Cancel.

5. Choose Effect, Natural Painting, Colored Pen. When the dialog box opens, edit the Level to 30. Click Preview to view the effect applied to the actual image. Note that the colors are lighter and more delicate, with a patterning effect mimicking pen strokes. Click Cancel.

Creative Painting Applied to a Photo

1. Hit Ctrl+O to access the Open dialog box. Make sure "Open as Read-only" is selected. Browse to purplelily.jpg, select it and click Open.

2. The purpose of this exercise is to learn how to edit the magical, painterly effect that Creative Painting can have on everyday photos, as well as how to use these commands to add surface texture to images.

3. Choose Effect, Creative, Painting to open the Painting dialog box. Select Paint template 15, which has the default of Pattern 23. Select "Non-clipped" to eliminate brush strokes which begin outside the boundaries of the image. Click Preview to view the effect applied to the actual image. It may take a minute for the image to render, but when it appears it will look like a painting. Click Continue to return to the dialog box.

4. Select Paint template 20. Instead of the default Pattern, select Pattern 28. In the "Fine controls" section, edit the Fineness to 25 to make smaller brush strokes.

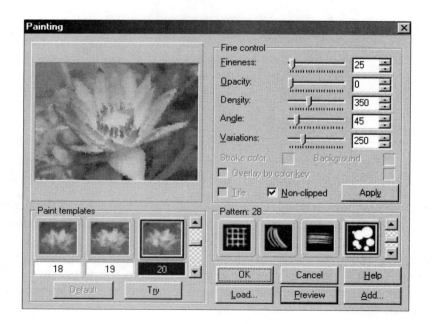

5. Click Preview to take a look at the effect on the actual image. It will look spotty, like many wet dots of paint. Click Continue to return to the Painting dialog box.

6. Select Paint template 30 and leave the default Pattern selected. In the "Fine control" section, edit the Fineness to 125. Click Preview to see the effect applied to the

actual image. It may take a minute or two for the image to render, but it is worth the wait. Little curly "ribbons" appear over the softened image. Click Continue to return to the dialog box.

7. Select Paint template 40 and leave the default Pattern selected. Click the Preview button. When the image is rendered, it will look very much like a needlework version of the photo. Click Continue to return to the dialog box.

8. Select Paint template 45 and leave the default Pattern selected. In the "Fine control" section, change the Angle value to 45. Right click in the Stroke color Color box and select Eyedropper. Move the cursor into the Preview window and click on a dark purple to select it. Click the Apply button to see the results of these edits in the Preview window.

9. Click Preview to view the edits applied to the entire image. It will look as though a fine, diagonal mesh texture has been applied to it.

10. Click Continue to return to the dialog box. Click in the Stroke color Color box again and choose white for the color. Edit the Angle value to 90. Click Apply to see the results of editing in the Preview window.

11. Click Preview to view edits applied to the actual image. Now it should look like it is being viewed through thin, white gauze.

12. Click Continue to return to the dialog box. Select Paint template 45 and leave the default Pattern selected. In the "Fine control" section edit the Angle to 90, causing the "pleated" effect to become vertical. Edit the Fineness value to 100. Click Apply to view these edits applied in the Preview window.

13. Click Preview to view the pleated effect applied to the actual image. It will look as though little pintucks have been applied to its surface. Click Cancel.

Painting and Retouching Image Objects

1. Choose File, Open to access the Open dialog box. Make sure "Open as Read-only" is selected. Browse to paintgirl.ufo, select it and click Open.

2. The purpose of this exercise is to learn how to experiment with editing objects with various Paint and Retouch tools. The nice thing about coloring objects is that the

applied effect "sticks" to the selected object only, so you cannot go "out of the lines." You will select separate objects, then recolor and contour them using Paint.

3. Select the Pick tool. If any of the objects are active, click in the base image to deactivate. Click on the purple dress to make it active. Right click and choose Duplicate to make a copy of it. Drag this duplicate into an empty area in the work space, where it will open in its own window. The reason for this duplicate will soon become clear.

4. Select the Colorize Pen from the Retouch Tool Panel.

5. The Colorize Pen effect is modified by the color over which it is applied.

6. To illustrate this principle, click in the Attributes toolbar's Color box and select the bright lime green color (RGB=169, 233, 105) at the bottom of the Color box.

7. While the purple dress is active, scrub back and forth over the entire object, changing its color completely. The polka dots will remain darker, as will the line of stitching around the bottom of the skirt. Note that the color is not the bright lime green color you selected in the Attributes toolbar. It is more like a deep forest green, because of the underlying purple. The interaction of this color with the underlying purple modifies the application of the bright lime green and darkens it.

8. Select the Pick tool, then click on the blue title bar of the original image to make it active. Click on the purple dress to make it active. Using the Quick Color Controls' Sun (Brightness) key, click the plus (+) sign three times. This should lighten the purple in the dress significantly.

9. Select the Colorize Pen with the same attributes selected previously. Scrub over the lightened dress object. Note that this time, the lime green color appears much

lighter applied over the object after it was lightened.

10. With the Pick tool, select one of the hair bows. Click on the Quick Color Controls' Sun (Brightness) key's plus (+) sign three times to lighten it. Choose the Colorize Pen and scrub over the bow to recolor it. Repeat these steps for the other bow.

11. Choose the Pick tool. Click on the left side hair to make it active. Choose the Colorize Pen. In the Attributes toolbar, right click in the Color box and select Ulead Color Picker. When the Color Picker opens, select a dark auburn red color (RGB=185, 75, 58).

12. Scrub over the selected hair object. You will probably be surprised to see that the hair is not auburn. Instead, it is a very pale orange. The underlying yellow has modified the application of this color. The Colorize Pen will not work here. Instead, select the Paintbrush tool.

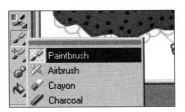

13. In the Attributes toolbar, select Fat Marker from the Preset dropdown list. Click in the Color box and select the dark auburn red color again (RGB=185, 75, 58). Note that when you change the attributes of the Preset, the Preset says "None," but the preset, modified, is still in effect.

14. Scrub the Paintbrush over the hair object to color it auburn. Use the Pick tool to select the bangs then switch to the Paintbrush tool again to color the object auburn. Repeat these steps to select and color the right side hair object.

15. You will see that when objects are colored with the Paintbrush, the black outline around them disappears. To restore this line with Paint on Edges, while the right side hair object is active, select Fine Brush from the Preset dropdown list. Edit the brush Size to 1, and the Soft edge to 1. Again, the Preset will show None, but the effect is still there.

16. Select the Pick tool. Hit Shift+P to apply the Paint on Edges effect. A fine black line will appear around the object. Use the Pick tool to select the bangs, then hit Shift+P to Paint on Edges. Repeat for the left side hair object. If you want to emphasize the other objects, you can select each one and hit Shift+P to add a line around each of them, as well.

17. With the Pick tool, click on the green dress to make it active.

18. Now you will add some shading and contouring. But first, it is a good idea to have your cursor show the exact shape of the selected Paint or Retouch tool. If you have not done so already, choose File, Preferences, General. Click Tools and in the "Painting cursor" section, select Precise Shape. Click OK to close the dialog box.

19. Select the Burn Retouch tool. In the Attributes toolbar, select Wide Burn from the Preset dropdown list. Move the cursor into the image and you will see a large round cursor shape. The idea is to keep this round brush mostly outside the confines of the object, just barely "burning" or darkening it as you go around the edges. Darken the areas in which shadows might be expected to fall, for example, the sides, hem and neckline. Go easy with this, being careful not to overdo it.

20. Use the Pick tool to select a hair bow. Select the Burn Retouch tool and click lightly once or twice to darken the bow. Repeat these steps for the other hair box.

21. Choose the Pick tool. Select the left side hair object. Choose the Burn Retouch tool. While the object is active, burn the bottom edges of the hair only, where you

would expect hair to be darker, underneath. Repeat these steps for the right side hair object. Use the Pick to select the bangs object. Switch to the Burn Retouch tool and burn only the very top edges. The hair should have some natural-looking shading now.

22. Select the Pick tool. Click on the green dress to make it active. Choose the Dodge Retouch tool. In the Attributes toolbar, select Spot Light from the Preset dropdown list. Lightly click three or four times in the center of the dress to add highlights. Do not drag the brush, however, or the dress will turn almost white in those areas.

23. Finally, add some cheek color to the face. Choose the Pick tool, then click on the face to select and make it active.

24. Select the Airbrush Paint tool. In the Attributes toolbar, select Fat Stroke from the Preset dropdown list. Edit the brush Size to 50, and edit the Transparency to 75. Click in the Color box and select a coral-peach color from the color box (RGB=255, 127, 124).

25. Click three or four times on each cheek to add some color. You will have to position the cursor half off the object so that only the sides of the face are touched with color.

26. Select the Pick tool and click on the arm object to make it active. Choose the Airbrush tool again. Click on the hands and drag lightly along the undersides of the arms to add a little bit of color. Now all of the recoloring is done. The little girl looks quite different.

27. Right click and Merge All to finish your work.

Artistic Cloning Effects

1. Hit Ctrl+O to access the Open dialog box. Select "Open as Read-only." Select clonepic.bmp and click Open.

2. The purpose of this exercise is to experiment with a variety of Clone tools and presets in order to produce artistic effects.

3. After the image of a yellow water lily opens, hit Ctrl+N. When the New dialog box opens, in the "Image size" section select Active Image. Make sure the canvas color is

white, then click OK. Doing so will open a new blank canvas the same size as the water lily image.

4. Click on the water lily image's blue title bar to make it active. Select the Clone-Crayon tool.

5. In the Attributes toolbar, select Pastel from the Preset dropdown list. Hold down on the Shift key while clicking in the lower left corner of the image. Shift+Clicking clones this area.

6. Click on the blank image's blue title bar to make it active. Starting in the lower left corner, begin stroking in, lightly, diagonal brush strokes. You will see that the texture leaves a slightly ragged edge around the edges of each stroke. Be careful not to overwork the strokes. There should be some white spaces in the image to give it a rough, hand-drawn look.

7. Choose Edit, Clear to get rid of the cloning. Click on the blue title bar for the original image to select it. Choose the Clone-Oil Paint tool. In the Attributes toolbar, select Gritty Fade-In from the Preset dropdown list. Shift+Click in the lower left corner of the image to clone.

8. Click on the blue title bar for the blank image to make it active. Starting in the lower left corner, lightly scrub across the image to lay down the cloned image. The paint will be quite sheer and highly textured, creating an ethereal look. After you lay down the first "coat" of paint, go over the flower in the middle to darken it, which will help the flower to stand out better. When you are satisfied with it, hit Edit,

Clear to get rid of the cloned paint.

9. Click on the blue title bar for the original image to select it. Choose the Clone-Paintbrush tool. In the Attributes toolbar, select Thick Brush from the Preset dropdown list. Click Texture, Select Texture. When the Texture thumbnails open up, select Paper45.jpg. Shift+Click in the lower left corner of the image to begin cloning from that area.

10. Click on the blue title bar for the blank image to make it active. Beginning in the lower left corner, scrub back and forth to paint the cloned area. The texture will leave small white gaps, creating the appearance of a mesh texture.

11. Click on the blue title bar for the original image to select it. Choose the Clone-Paintbrush tool. In the Attributes toolbar, select Thick Brush from the Preset dropdown list. Edit the brush Size to 100, the maximum size. Shift+Click in the very center of the yellow water lily to clone it.

12. Now you will paint the cloned area back into the image, adding a water lily to the image. Begin by clicking in the extreme lower left corner, with half of the cursor out of the picture window. Part of the flower will not appear in the image. Click lightly to add bits of the cloned flower, radiating out from the center.

411

Cloning to Remove Unwanted Objects

1. Choose File, Open to access the Open dialog box. Select "Open as Read-only." Browse to pelican.bmp, select it and click Open.

2. The purpose of this exercise to learn the very practical art of cloning out unwanted details in images. You will get rid of the people and the striped raft.

3. Select the Clone-Paintbrush tool. In the Attributes toolbar, select Thick Brush from the Preset dropdown list. Change the brush size to 50. Start by Shift+Clicking just to the left of the striped raft to clone that area.

4. Click a few times on top of the left side of the raft to begin cloning it out. Shift+Click just below the raft to clone a new area. Click on top of the raft a few times to clone over the middle of it. To avoid a "stepstone" appearance from reapplying the same cloned area, Shift+Click above the raft to clone, then click on the raft. Shift+Click above and below the raft to clone, then click on the raft to cover it up. Try to avoid any obvious patterning in the sand.

5. Next, clone out the sky just above the horizon. Shift+Click in the blue sky just above and to the left of where the person on the left's head is sticking up. Drag in a straight line across the area to be cloned out. Try not to get any cloned sky into the sand.

6. Now to get rid of the people from the sand. Shift+Click some sand just to the left of the people. In the Attributes toolbar, click Lines and choose Straight Lines. This will help you clone in a perfectly straight horizon. Click to start the cloning and then drag to the right. You will see a "trail" behind the cursor which makes it easy to make a straight line. Click to complete the cloning. You may need to repeat this process one more time. If you make a mistake, right click, Undo and try again.

7. Note that the people and the raft have been completely cloned out of the image.

Creating an Animation Studio Animation

1. Hit Ctrl+O to access the Open dialog box. Browse to and select flag.bmp. Click Open.

2. The purpose of this exercise is to create a waving flag animation by editing the default values associated with the Wave effect.

3. Choose Effect, Creative, Animation Studio to open the Animation Studio dialog box. In the Effect section, select Wave. If you do not know which one is Wave, hold your cursor over a thumbnail until a small popup box appears with the name of the effect, then click to select it.

4. First take a look at the animation with the default attributes. In the "Key frame control" section of the dialog box, click on the Loop mode button (arrow) to make the animation play continuously.

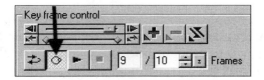

5. Click the Play button to watch the animation in the Preview window. You should see a gently waving flag with relatively little up and down movement. Click the Stop button to stop the animation.

6. To edit the animation for a more pronounced effect, edit the Amplitude value (up and down movement) to 35. To make more waves in the animation, edit the Frequency value to 75. Note that the Level value changes depending upon which frame you were on when you clicked the Stop button, so your Level may not be the same as the one shown in the screen shot below.

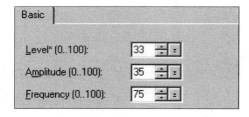

7. Click the Play button again to view the animation in the Preview window. Note that the edited Wave animation shows a much stronger effect now. Click Stop.

8. To create a smoother animation, add frames to the animation. In the "Key frame control" section, change the number of frames to a value of 20.

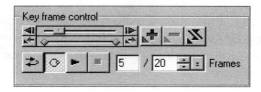

9. Click the Play button again. This time the animation has been slowed down and appears smoother. However, keep in mind that you have doubled the number of frames and that this animation would generate a much larger file size than the default of 10 frames. Change the number of frames back to 10.

10. To save the animation, click the Save button. Doing so opens the Save As dialog box. Browse to the folder to which you wish to save and give the animation a name (e.g., aniflag.gif). If you want to open the animation in GIF Animator for further editing, select "Open with Ulead GIF Animator" in the lower left corner of the dialog box. Note that you can deselect the default "GIF Animation Options" if you wish to do so. To save as is, click Save. If you do not want to save the animation, click Cancel.

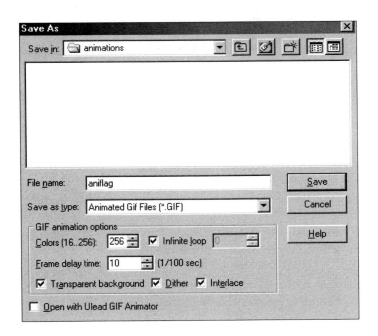

Animating Text With Creative Type

1. Choose File, New to access the New dialog box. Create a new, True Color file 350 pixels wide by 100 pixels high with a white canvas.

2. Select the Text tool. Click in the base image to open the Text Entry Box. Select Arial (Western) from the Font dropdown list. Click in the text Color box and select black. Edit the font Size to 35. Position the cursor in the text box and type PhotoImpact. Click OK to close the box.

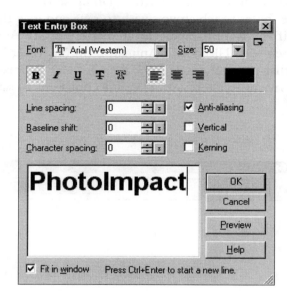

3. Choose Effect, Creative, Type Effect to open the Type Effect dialog box. Select the first effect, Gradient. In the "Key frame controls," click the Play button to run the animation one time with the default values. It is not a very spectacular effect, showing vertical gradient changes from gray to black.

4. In the Parameters section, select Rectangular. Click the Play button to view the animation. This time the gradient fill will move in a rectangular shape.

5. In the Parameters section, select Circular. Click the Play button to view this variation of the animated gradient.

6. Select the vertical (up and down arrow) animation style again. Look in the "Key frame controls" section. You will see two diamonds representing key frames. Advance forward one key frame at a time until you are at key frame 5. Click the "Add

key frame" button, which looks like a plus (+) sign, to add a key frame at that point in the animation. Now there are three key frames.

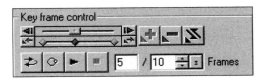

7. Click on the first key frame, at frame 1. In the Parameters section, select "Fill color." Click in the Fill color box and choose a bright lime green color.

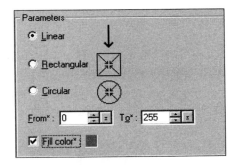

8. In the "Key frame controls" section, click on the second diamond to select it. To edit the color at this point in the animation, click in the Fill color box and choose a bright aqua.

9. Click on the third diamond to select it. Click in the Fill color box and choose purple to edit the color of the animation at the end of the animation.

10. In the "Key frame controls" section, click on "Ping mode" to create an animation that will reverse itself upon completion. Click the Play button. Watch the animation play through a few cycles, then click the Stop button to stop the animation.

11. Note that by adding a key frame and changing the colors, the black text has been turned into a colorful animation displaying subtle shifts of the selected colors.

12. To save the animation, click the Save button. Doing so opens the Save As dialog box. Browse to the folder to which you wish to save and give the animation a name

(e.g., anitext.gif). If you want to open the animation in GIF Animator for further editing, select "Open with Ulead GIF Animator" in the lower left corner of the dialog box. Note that you can deselect the default "GIF Animation Options" if you wish to do so. To save as is, click Save. If you do not want to save the animation, click Cancel.

Creating a Creative Lighting Animation

1. Choose File, Open to access the Open dialog box. Browse to and select clonepic.bmp. Click Open.

2. The purpose of this exercise is to edit a Creative Lighting effect and turn it into an animation.

3. Choose Effect, Creative, Lighting to open the Lighting dialog box. From the Effect section, select the thumbnail for Light bulb. The image will look very dark in the Preview window. A bright starburst effect will appear just to the left of the center of the flower. To lighten the image somewhat, edit the "Ambient light" value to 65.

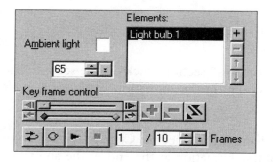

4. In the "Key frame controls" section, you will see two diamonds, representing two key frames in the preset animation. Click on the first diamond to make the first key frame active. Position your cursor in the Preview window over the bright starburst, until the cursor turns into a crossed, double-headed arrow. Drag the starburst into the upper right corner of the image. This is where it will be when the animation starts, in frame 1.

5. In the "Key frame controls," click on the second diamond to make it active. You may have to look hard to find a little bit of the starburst in the extreme upper right

corner of the Preview window. Drag it down to the very center of the flower. This is where it will be at the end of the animation.

6. Click the Play button a few times to view the animation.

7. To save the animation, click the Save button. Doing so opens the Save As dialog box. Browse to the folder to which you wish to save and give the animation a name (e.g., anilight.gif). If you want to open the animation in GIF Animator for further editing, select "Open with Ulead GIF Animator" in the lower left corner of the dialog box. Note that you can deselect the default "GIF Animation Options" if you wish to do so. To save as is, click Save. If you do not want to save the animation, click Cancel.

PhotoImpact 6 Wizardry

Section 5: Adding Sparkle and Color

This section will show you how to add color and surface interest to images, selections and objects. At the most basic level, images, selections and objects can be filled with solid and gradient colors and images. 3D Path and Text objects alone can be filled with sparkling metallic finishes or transparent glass, and further edited with bump maps, reflections and beveled edges to enhance realism. The Fill tools, Material Dialog Box and EasyPalette offer increasingly sophisticated options for adding that little something extra in the way of color and surface texture.

The Fill Tools focuses on the four Fill tools: the Bucket/Solid Fill tool, and the Linear, Rectangular and Elliptical Gradient Fill tools. The Fill tools work similarly, in that color, transparency, merge method and other options are set from the Attributes toolbar. Gradient Fill tools permit you to fill with two colors or multiple colors. You will learn how to use the Palette Ramp Editor to select multiple color gradient fills, including how to custom edit palettes (adding, replacing and deleting colors) and save them for future use.

The Material Dialog Box steps up the dazzle factor in adding color, shine and texture. Find out how to custom edit Path and Text objects from options presented from the Material dialog box's tabs: Color/Texture, Bevel, Border/Depth, Shadow, Light, Shading, Bump, Reflection and Transparency. You can add custom presets with the click of a button.

The EasyPalette is the heart and soul of PhotoImpact. A collection of Galleries and Libraries offer preset image effects, as well as Path and Image objects. Many of its special effects can also be accessed via toolbars and menu commands, but you will learn that the EasyPalette is a quicker, easier and more intuitive way of applying special effects and commands visually, from thumbnails. Find out how to edit directly from a thumbnail, and discover how to manage predetermined Galleries and Libraries, including how to create your own using the Gallery and Library Manager functions.

Active Learning Exercises Using the Fill Tools; Creating an EasyPalette Custom Gallery; Creating Your Own Presets; Exporting and Importing a Gallery; Using a Mask Library Mask; Using a JPG Mask.

PhotoImpact 6 Wizardry

Chapter 16: The Fill Tools and Palette Ramp Editor

The Fill tools let you fill base images, selections or objects with solid or gradient fills. There are four: the Bucket (solid color), and three gradient fill tools (Linear, Rectangular and Elliptical). To access a Fill tool, click on the tiny blue triangle in the corner of the button, causing a tool of trays to slide out. Alternatively, press and hold down anywhere on the button until a tray of tools slides out. You can also click the Layout button and select Fill Tool Panel to display a floating Fill Tool panel.

Bucket/Solid Fill

The Bucket fill tool fills with a solid color. Edit from the Attributes toolbar.

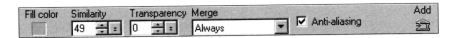

Fill color

Ulead Color Picker Click in the Fill color box to open the Ulead Color Picker.

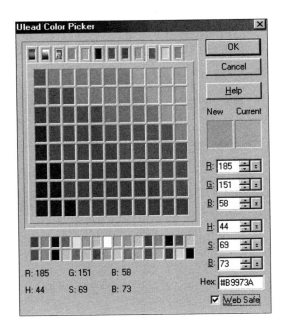

The Ulead Color Picker box has tabs across the top for each of nine basic colors. Click on one of the tabs to display a range of shades for each color. This is a quick and easy way to select tints or shades of the color you need. You may enter RGB or Hex values of your choice to create custom colors, click anywhere in the large "rainbow" box to select a color, or choose from the standard colors arrayed at the bottom of the Color Picker. Note that you can select "Web Safe" to select from only web-safe colors. Click OK to select a color. Alternatively, you can right click in the Attributes toolbar's Fill color box to open a fill box with a wider range of options.

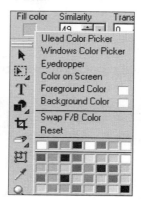

Windows Color Picker Offers standard or custom mixed RGB color choices.

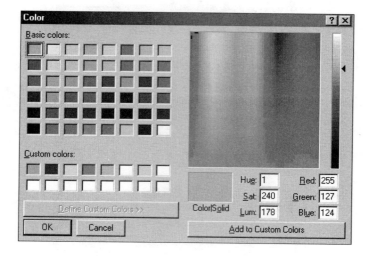

Eyedropper Select the Eyedropper to select a color from an image. Doing so opens the Eyedropper dialog box. Click anywhere in the Preview window to select a color.

Color on Screen This welcome addition to PhotoImpact 6 lets you click on and select any color visible in the work space.

Foreground color Selects the current foreground color.

Background color Selects the current background color.

Swap F/B color Reverses the Foreground and Background colors.

Reset Resets the foreground color to black, and the background color to white.

Recently used colors Select from the 8 most recently used colors.

Standard colors Select from 32 standard colors.

Similarity

Choose a value between 0-255 for the range of colors to be included in the fill. Essentially, Similarity "reads" the pixel you click on with the Bucket fill tool and uses that value to determine a range of color values relative to the indexed pixel. Sometimes when you use the Bucket fill tool on a multicolored or textured selection, the fill is blotchy looking, with some areas resistant to the fill. In that case, select a higher Similarity value to achieve a uniform fill, of use the Edit, Fill command.

Transparency

Choose a Transparency value from 0-99. Higher values result in a greater level of transparency, while lower values result in minimal transparency. For example, for a solid opaque blue fill, select bright blue from the color picker and edit the Transparency to 0. To fill with a pastel blue, select bright blue and edit the Transparency to 80 or higher.

Merge

Choose a Merge method from the dropdown list. The Merge list shown below does not reflect the new Merge methods added by the PhotoImpact 6 patch.

Merge determines which color characteristics of the fill will be applied to the base image. As shown below, different Merge methods can result in dramatically different looks when applied to the same base image.

After selecting a solid color fill's Attributes, position the Bucket fill tool over the image or selection and click to fill with color.

▪ ▫ ◯ Gradient Fill Tools

There are three kinds of gradient fills: Linear Gradient, Rectangular Gradient and Elliptical Gradient. The Gradient fill tools create Two-Color or Multiple-Color gradient fills. The process of making a Two-Color Gradient or a Multiple-Color Gradient fill is the same regardless of which Gradient fill tool is selected. Available options vary according to the type of gradient fill selected.

Two-Color Gradient Fill

Specify characteristics of the Two-Color Gradient fill from the Attributes toolbar.

Fill colors Click in the Fill color squares to select beginning and ending colors for the gradient fill. Click in a color box to open the Ulead Color Picker box, or right click to select from a wider range of color options: the Ulead or Windows Color Pickers, Eyedropper, Color on Screen, Foreground Color, Background Color, Swap F/B Color, Reset, recently used colors and standard colors. You can mix custom colors in the Ulead Color Picker and the Windows Color Picker by entering RGB values.

Color Ramp Specify how a gradient fill will be applied: RGB (a straight line from beginning to end in the color cube), HSB Clockwise (a continuous clockwise arc from start to finish around the HSB color cone) and HSB Counterclockwise (a continuous counterclockwise arc from start to finish around the HSB color cone).

Transparency Edit Transparency from 0-99. Higher values result in a greater level of transparency, while lower values result in less transparency.

Merge Choose a Merge method from the dropdown list. Merge determines how the color characteristics of the fill will be applied to the base image.

PhotoImpact 6 Wizardry

Add Accesses the Add to EasyPalette dialog box. Give the custom Two-Color Gradient fill a name and save to My Gallery.

After selecting Attributes for a Two-Color Gradient fill, position the cursor over the image and it will turn into a Paintbrush. Press and hold down on the mouse button while dragging across the image. You may drag in any direction: top to bottom, bottom to top, side to side, or on a diagonal. Release the mouse button to complete the fill.

If you are not happy with the Two-Color Gradient fill results, choose Edit, Undo, or right click and choose Undo. Adjust the colors or settings in the Attributes toolbar and try again. To reverse the beginning and ending colors, you can click on the "Swap two colors" button between the color boxes.

Multiple-Color Gradient Fill

Specify characteristics of the Multiple-Color Gradient fill from the Attributes toolbar.

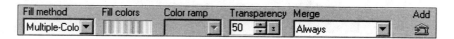

Fill Colors Click in the Fill colors box in the Attributes toolbar to open the Palette Ramp Editor. Scroll through the palette choices to select one. The selected palette will appear in the large Palette Ramp box. Often you will find a palette with the exact look that you want. At other times you may want to edit the palette. You may want to remove a color from a palette, replace one color in the palette with another, or change the starting and ending colors of the gradient. It is easy to custom edit palettes in the Palette Ramp Editor, which is discussed in detail at the end of this chapter.

Transparency Edit the Transparency from 0-99. Higher values result in a greater level of transparency, while lower values result in little to no transparency. For an opaque gradient, set the transparency to 0. To achieve a translucent effect, set the transparency to 80 or higher.

Merge Choose a Merge method from the dropdown list. Merge determines which color characteristics of the fill will be applied to the base image.

Add Accesses the Add to EasyPalette dialog box. Give the custom Multiple-Color Gradient fill a name and save to My Gallery.

After selecting Attributes for a Multiple-Color Gradient fill, position the cursor over the image and it will turn into a Paintbrush. Press and hold down on the mouse button while dragging across the image. You may drag in any direction: top to bottom, bottom to top, side to side, or on a diagonal. Release the mouse button to complete the fill.

If you are not happy with the results, choose Edit, Undo, or right click and choose Undo. Adjust the colors or settings in the Attributes toolbar and try again.

Palette Ramp Editor

The Palette Ramp Editor offers the greatest flexibility in obtaining both subtle and dramatic Multiple-Color Gradient fills. It is one of PhotoImpact's most powerful tools, and as such, merits its own section when discussing the Fill tools.

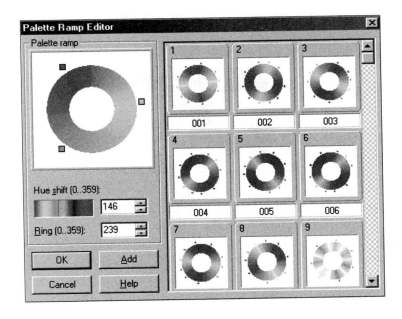

Palette Ramp

The Palette Ramp window shows the selected palette with square order control points along the outside edge. There are several ways to edit a palette from this window.

PhotoImpact 6 Wizardry

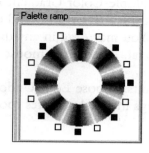

Press and hold down on the mouse button while dragging a control point along the edge of the ring to change its position in the gradient. Press and hold down on the mouse button on a control point to read its position on the ring (0-360 degrees in the circle).

Right click on a control point to change or delete a color.

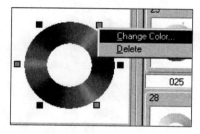

Choose Change color to open the Ulead Color Picker to select a replacement color. Choose Delete to remove the color from the palette.

Hue Shift

Click in the Hue Shift box (it looks like a rainbow) to change the hue of a palette.

The Hue (color) of the palette changes, but the Saturation (richness or intensity) and Brightness of the colors in the palette remain the same.

Ring

Enter a value (1-359, for the degrees in a circle) to rearrange the colors in the palette.

Alternatively, drag control points to change the order in which gradient colors appear.

Add

If you create a palette you like and want to use it again, click on the Add button to save it to the Palette Ramp Editor. After you add a custom gradient, you can apply it by selecting its thumbnail. To delete a custom gradient, right click on its thumbnail and select Delete.

PhotoImpact 6 Wizardry

Chapter 17: The Material Dialog Box

The Material dialog box is where you perform wizardry on Path and Text objects. From the tabs in the Material dialog box you may edit color or texture, add metallic shine, adjust lighting level, or create surface interest by adding reflections and bump maps. Click the Material button in the Attributes toolbar to access the Material dialog box.

Common Elements in the Material Dialog Box

Notice that certain options on the right remain constant regardless of the tab selected.

Preview Pop-up Option

Change the shape of the object in the Preview window by clicking on the Shape box.

PhotoImpact 6 Wizardry

You may also change the background color or switch to a checkerboard, and show/hide the object's highlight from these options.

 **Lights**

The Lights button shows how many lights have been selected to shine on an object. To change the number of lights, or the lighting direction (Direct or Spot), click on the Light tab.

 **Add**

Click the Add button to save custom Material box settings to the EasyPalette. This opens the Add to EasyPalette dialog box. Name the preset and save it to My Gallery.

 **Gallery**

Click the Gallery button to continue editing from the EasyPalette's Material Gallery or any other Gallery.

Color/Texture Tab

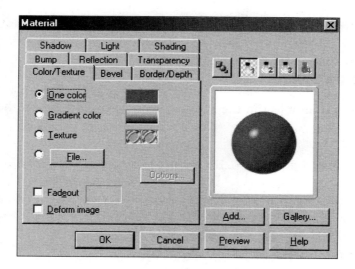

One color Select this option and click in the color box to choose a fill color from the Ulead Color Picker, or right click in the color box to choose from the Ulead Color Picker, Windows Color Picker, Eyedropper, Color on Screen, Foreground or Background color, or a selection or standard colors.

Gradient color Click in the Gradient color box to open the Gradient Fill box. From the Gradient Fill box, make choices for a Two color or Multiple colors gradient fill.

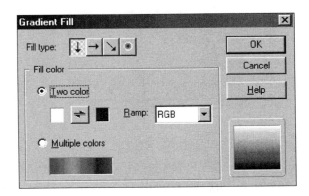

Fill type Select a direction for the fill.

Two color Click in the color boxes to select beginning and ending colors for a Two-Color fill from the Ulead Color Picker. Alternatively, right click in the color boxes to select from a wider range of color choices.

Multiple colors Click in the Multiple colors color box to select a gradient from the Palette Ramp Editor.

Texture Click in the Texture box and choose Magic Texture or Natural Texture fill. Doing so opens the Texture Library, from which you can select a texture for the fill.

File Choose File to fill an object with a previously saved image. Click on the File button to browse your hard drive for the desired image file. After selecting an image file for the fill, the Options button becomes available.

Options Click the Options button to open the Textures Options dialog box, which allows you to edit the way in which the fill is applied to an object.

Fill type

Fit the texture Fits the texture or image to the surface of the object. Choose when you do not want the image to tile, or repeat.

Tile the texture Tiles the texture over the surface of the object. This is a useful option when the image is smaller than the object being filled.

Rotate clockwise

Choose to rotate 0, 90, 180 or 270 degrees clockwise.

Fadeout Applies a mask to the object. When selected, click in the color box to open the Fadeout dialog box, from which you may choose values for a Two color or Multiple color grayscale gradient mask. The Fadeout feature is discussed in detail in the Edit menu chapter.

Deform image When selected, adjusts the fill so that it conforms to the shape of the object.

Bevel tab

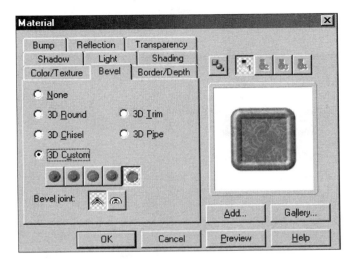

None A flat, 2D appearance.

3D Round A rounded 3D border. It may be necessary to increase or decrease the border from the Border/Depth tab for the best result, depending upon the size of the object. You can also drag on the Border and Depth sliders in the Attributes toolbar.

3D Chisel A sharply defined 3D border. Again, it could be necessary to increase or decrease the border from the Border/Depth tab for the best result, depending upon the size of the object. You can also drag on the Border and Depth sliders in the Attributes toolbar.

3D Custom Select from one of five 3D borders with different types of edges.

3D Trim A more subtle and flatter 3D appearance created by shading colors.

3D Pipe Creates a 3D rounded outline border with a hollow center. Typically this option results in the object taking on a fat, donut shape. Often it is necessary to decrease the 3D Pipe border from the Border/Depth tab, in order to get the look you want. You can also drag on the Border and Depth sliders in the Attributes toolbar.

Bevel joint Choose a mitred or round joint type.

Border/Depth Tab

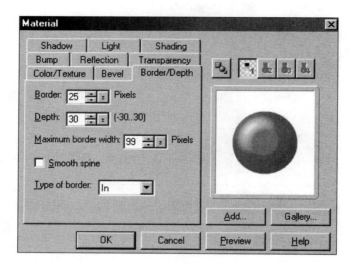

Border Enter a value for border width in pixels. The default maximum border width for the "In" Type of border is 30 pixels.

Depth Enter a value for border depth, with positive numbers resulting in a convex border, and negative numbers resulting in a concave border.

Maximum border width Enter a value for maximum border width in pixels. Adjusting border width is useful for radial gradient fills, as a larger maximum width allows the entire gradient to fit into the object. The maximum border default for an "In" border is 30 pixels. If you decrease the maximum border width while making an object, then make another object, you may find that the border is "stuck" so that the next object that you make looks too flat. To "plump up" the object, click on the Border/Depth tab and increase the maximum border depth.

Smooth spine New to PhotoImpact 6, this option is available only for irregularly shaped objects. When selected, it flattens out surface creases that sometimes appear on irregularly shaped 3D objects.

Type of border From the dropdown list, choose whether to have the border go In, Out or Both.

Bump tab

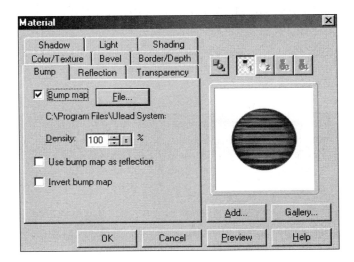

Bump map Select to apply a bump map. Click the File button to access the Open dialog box, and browse for the file you wish to use for the bump map.

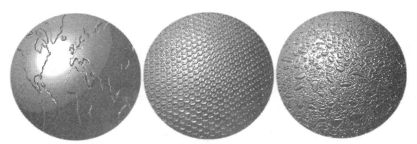

Same 3D Round Object, Different Bump Maps

Density Enter a value for the degree of contrast between the edges of the bump.

Use bump map as reflection When selected, enhances the 3D effect by reflecting the bump map over the surface of the object.

Invert bump map Reverses the bump map.

Reflection Tab

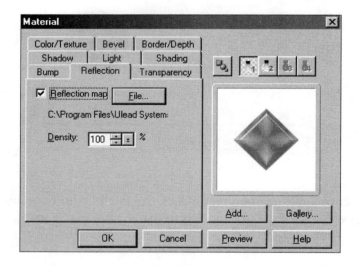

Reflection map Select to reflect a previously created image off the surface of the object. Click the File button to access the Open dialog box. Browse to choose an image for the reflection map. Interesting and enhanced 3D effects can be attained by using the same image as a Bump map and a Reflection.

Density Edit to adjust the transparency of the reflection map. Higher density results in a more pronounced effect, while lower density results in less of an effect.

Transparency Tab

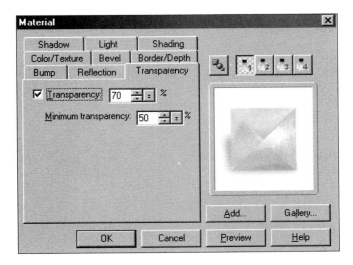

Transparency Enter a value for object transparency. Higher values result in greater transparency, while lower values result in less transparency. Whenever you apply a Glass preset from the EasyPalette, Transparency will be selected and a Minimum transparency set, automatically.

Minimum transparency The transparency of 3D objects must vary in order to create an appearance of depth. Use this option to control just how transparent areas within the object appear. Minimum transparency must be lower than the object's transparency.

Shadow Tab

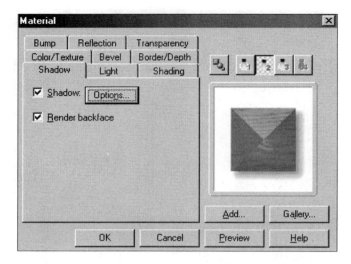

Shadow Select Shadow and click Options. Choose shadow attributes and click OK.

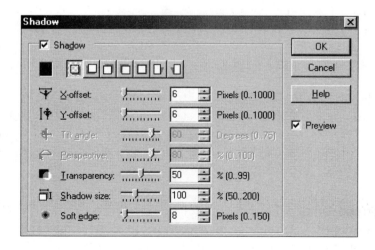

Render backface On a transparent 3D object, reflects the light source from its back face. Match base image background color to page color for the best result.

Light Tab

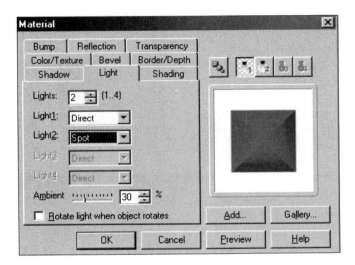

Lights Select from 1-4 lights to be reflected off the object. The default is one Direct light. For each light, choose Direct or Spot from the corresponding dropdown list. Direct light shines brightly on the entire surface, while Spot light creates a darker look with a circumscribed focus on a particular part of the object.

Ambient Ambient light is the backlighting of an object, and presumes that the light hits all areas of the object with the same color and with equal intensity. Edit Ambient light value to increase or decrease the intensity of background illumination. Higher values result in more intense light and brighter objects, while lower values result in less intense light and darker looking objects.

Rotate light when object rotates When selected, light follows the object if it is rotated.

Shading Tab

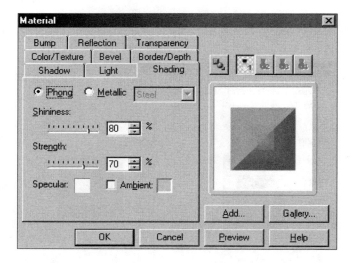

Phong A shiny light is applied, resulting in a glossy, plastic-looking finish. Phong is selected by default when PhotoImpact is first opened.

Metallic A diffuse light is applied, resulting in a matte or flat appearance typical of a metallic finish. Choose a type of Metallic lighting (Copper, Gold, Silver, Steel) from the dropdown list.

When Metallic is selected, the Specular and Ambient light options are grayed out.

Shininess Edits the shininess of an object, with higher values resulting in a smaller surface area showing the reflection.

Strength Edits the shininess of an object by adjusting the brightness or intensity of light directed at the object.

Specular The color of the light reflected back from the surface of the object. The default color is white. Click in the color box to change the color. This option is available only if Phong shading has been selected.

Ambient The color that falls on areas of an object that are in shadow from specular light. The default color is black. Click in the color box to change the color. This option is available only if Phong shading has been selected.

Chapter 18: The EasyPalette

The EasyPalette's Galleries and Libraries are the heart and soul of PhotoImpact. Just double click on a Gallery thumbnail, or drag and drop from the thumbnail onto an image, to apply special effects instantly. Most commands available from the Format and Effect menus are more quickly and intuitively accessed from Gallery thumbnails, which display these stunning effects visually.

The EasyPalette's Libraries include Path and Image objects, masks and web page templates. Just drag from a thumbnail into the work space, and a fresh copy of the object opens immediately. You will never run out! You can add your own Galleries and Libraries to the EasyPalette in order to save special effects and objects that you wish to use again and again.

Accessing the EasyPalette

There are six ways to access the EasyPalette:

1. Click on the EasyPalette button to open the EasyPalette in the work space.

2. Click on the Tile With EasyPalette button to access from graphical tiling options.

3. Click the Layout button and select EasyPalette.

4. Choose Window, Tile With EasyPalette.

5. Choose View, Toolbars & Panels, EasyPalette.

6. Hit Ctrl+F1.

Resizing and Moving the EasyPalette

You may resize the EasyPalette to make room in the work space. Place the cursor over one of its borders until it turns into a double headed arrow, then drag to resize. The EasyPalette can be resized as small as one row and one column, or as large as the entire work space. Click the Minimize button, or double click on the blue title bar, to

PhotoImpact 6 Wizardry

minimize the EasyPalette so that only the blue title bar shows. As shown in the screen shot below, the minimized EasyPalette does not take up much room.

Click the Restore button or double click on the blue title bar to open the EasyPalette back up again. Remember too, that you can drag the EasyPalette to any location in the work space if it gets in your way.

When the default EasyPalette layout is displayed, a branching tree menu of Galleries or Libraries appears in the left pane, and effect thumbnails appear on the right.

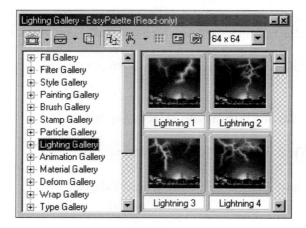

Deselect the "Show Hide List View" thumbnail menu command button to view only Gallery tabs.

At the top of the EasyPalette is a row of buttons which are used to display and manage Galleries and Libraries, access the Layer Manager, hide or show the tree menu, edit thumbnail effects and manage thumbnail properties. If a button is grayed out it is unavailable for the selected Gallery or Library.

Galleries

▣ ▾ Select a Gallery from the dropdown list, including any custom Galleries you have added. Alternatively, select Gallery Manager to access a submenu for managing Galleries.

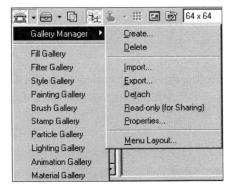

Gallery Manager

The first item in the Galleries dropdown list is the Gallery Manager, which has its own submenu, shown above. Use these options to create or delete your own custom Galleries, to Import or Export Galleries, to rearrange the order of Galleries and add submenus, or to find out about the Properties of a particular Gallery.

Create Opens the Create Gallery dialog box.

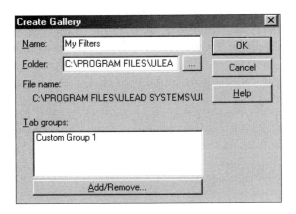

Name Give the new Gallery a name.

Folder Browse to the folder you wish to use for the new Gallery. You do not have to save a Gallery to PhotoImpact's Program Files folder. In fact, there are good reasons to save to a different folder on your hard drive. That way if you have to uninstall and reinstall PhotoImpact for any reason, you will still be able to access custom Galleries.

File name Reflects the path to the selected folder.

Tab groups By default a tab group called Custom Group 1 is created. To add a new Tab group click Add/Remove to open the Group Management dialog box. Click the New button to open the New Group dialog box. Enter a name for the new group and click OK, which returns you to the Group Management dialog box.

To Rename Custom Group 1 (or any other group), select Custom Group 1 (or any other group) and click Add/Remove to open the Group Management dialog box. Click Rename to open the Rename Group dialog box. Give the group a new name and click OK. To Delete a group or change its order within the Gallery, select the group and click Add/Remove. When the Group Management Dialog box opens, choose the appropriate option (Delete, Up, Down). Click OK to apply changes.

Delete Deletes a custom Gallery. You cannot delete PhotoImpact's Galleries, which are "Read-only."

Import Opens the Import Gallery dialog box, which allows you to import a Gallery. Gallery files have the .SMP file extension. By default, "Open as a new gallery" is selected. If you wish to Import a Gallery into PhotoImpact 6 from a previous version, do *not* Import the Gallery directly from PhotoImpact 5.0, 4.2, etc. Instead, either Export the older PhotoImpact .SMP Gallery file to a new folder on your hard drive, or copy the Gallery file you wish to import and paste it into a new folder on your hard drive. Open PhotoImpact 6 and import the desired Gallery from this new folder. If you do not import this way, and you delete your old version of PhotoImpact, you will lose the imported Gallery. The logical corollary of this process is that you should not delete the folder with the .SMP files you have imported.

Export Opens the Export Gallery dialog box, which allows you to Export and save a Gallery to a folder on your hard drive. Gallery files have the .SMP file extension. By default, "All thumbnails of the current group" is selected. Be sure to Export your Galleries regularly as a backup measure.

Detach Be careful with this command, which removes a Gallery from the EasyPalette. Only custom Galleries can be detached. If you accidentally detach a Gallery, use the Import command to bring it back into the EasyPalette.

Read Only If you share custom Galleries with other computers in a network, select "Read-only (For Sharing)" to protect Galleries from unwanted edits.

Properties Opens the Properties box listing the name, number of thumbnails, file size, tab groups, and other information associated with the selected Gallery.

Menu Layout Rearrange the order of Galleries by clicking and dragging on them, or add submenus and separators. You may Rename or Delete custom created Galleries only. Click on the Test button to preview the new arrangement.

Thumbnail Commands for Galleries

Although the first three buttons in the EasyPalette access the Galleries, Libraries and Layer Manager, respectively, when a Gallery has been selected, six remaining buttons access thumbnail commands specific to the EasyPalette's Galleries.

Show/Hide Tree View Toggles in and out of Tree view. When deselected, only tabs for the Galleries appear in the EasyPalette, similar to earlier versions of PhotoImpact.

Use image, selected area or object as thumbnails When selected, replaces default thumbnails with the selected image, selection or object. Click the down arrow to replace the default image on the selected Gallery effect thumbnail, on only visible Gallery effect thumbnails, on all of the thumbnails, or to Reset to the default image.

In the screen shot below, an image open in the work space replaces the default thumbnail image.

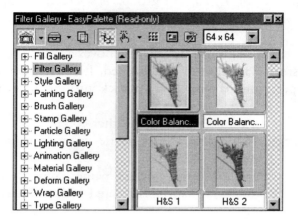

▦ **Variations** Opens a related dialog box for editing the selected effect.

▦ **Thumbnail menu commands** Click for available options: Apply, Modify Properties and Apply, Properties, Description, Cut, Copy, Paste and Delete. The availability of these standard options varies by Gallery. New to PhotoImpact 6 are three thumbnail menu commands. The first of these is the ability to "Add PhotoShop Plug-in thumbnails" so you can add thumbnails for effects created by third party plug-ins and filters.

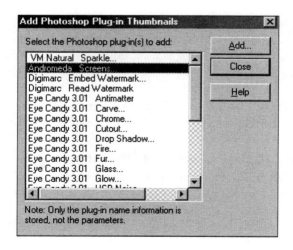

Only the path to the third party filter is stored. You must already have established the path to the plug-in via File, Preferences, General, Plug-ins. For example, if you have PhotoShop, Blade Pro, Andromeda Screens, Eye Candy or other third party filters, you can add thumbnails for them to an EasyPalette Gallery.

The "Add Fill Command" option is great if you often fill with the same image files. When selected, the Open dialog box appears. Select the image you want to use for the fill, then click Open. Doing so opens the Add to EasyPalette dialog box, in which you name and save the fill. A thumbnail representing the fill will be added.

From now on, whenever you want to fill with this image, double click its thumbnail or drag and drop it onto the image or selection.

The "Add Command" option makes short work of frequently applied menu commands. For example, if you often use the Effect, Paint on Edges command, you can add a thumbnail for it.

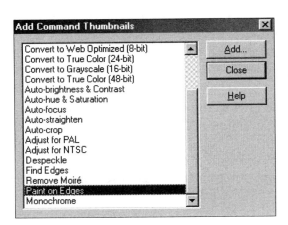

453

View menu commands Click for available options: Find, Find Next, EasyPalette Options, Resize EasyPalette, Resize to One Row, Resize to One Column, or choose from one of four graphical methods of tiling the EasyPalette with an image.

Select Find to locate a particular effect in the selected Gallery. For example, there are numerous Metallic Copper effects in the Material Gallery. When the Find dialog box opens, enter the search term.

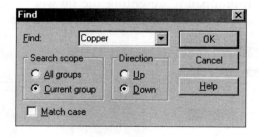

Enter the name of the effect you wish to find, whether to search all groups or the current group only, whether to search up or down from the currently selected thumbnail and whether or not to match case. Choose Find Next (or just hit F3) to jump to the next variation of the effect specified in the Find criteria.

Thumbnail size The default thumbnail size is 64 x 64 pixels. You can choose another size from the dropdown list.

Consistent with PhotoImpact's ease of use, you can right click on a Gallery thumbnail to select from: Apply, Modify Properties and Apply, Variations, Properties, Description, Cut, Copy, Paste and Delete.

EasyPalette Galleries

Click on the down arrow next to the Galleries button to select a Gallery, including the new Animation Gallery. Several new Tab groups have been added to familiar Galleries.

The EasyPalette's Galleries provide a wide range of effects, from the helpful to the spectacular. Right click on a thumbnail and choose "Modify Properties and Apply" to open an effect's dialog box for editing.

It is impossible to describe many of the stunning effects you can achieve via the Galleries with just a few mouse clicks. You will need to try them out yourself to appreciate them fully. The following brief descriptions of the Galleries will surely trigger experimentation or help to point you in the right direction if you are looking for a particular image effect. Remember that many Gallery effects can also be accessed via the Format and Effect Menu commands and the Toolbars.

Fill Gallery Includes: Gradient, Natural Texture, Magic Texture, Background Texture, Textures Mixtures and Artist Texture.

Filter Gallery Includes: Blur & Sharpen, Brightness & Contrast, Color Balance, Hue & Saturation, Two-Color, Noise, Camera Lens, 2D & 3D, Natural Painting, Special, Custom, Kaleidoscope, Light, Turnpage and Creative Warp.

Emphasize Edges · Gaussian Blur · Ripple 1

Style Gallery Includes: Fading, Face, Building, Flower, Leaf, Light, Dawn, Sculpture, Nature, Season, Sky, Filter and Others.

Painting Gallery Includes: Painting Effects.

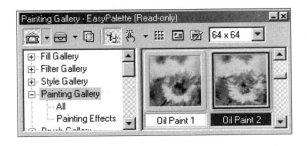

Brush Gallery Includes: Paint Tools, Paint Effect, Retouch Tools and Clone Tools.

455

Stamp Gallery Includes all of the stamps that come with PhotoImpact, but not those you have added yourself.

Particle Gallery Includes: Bubbles, Cloud, Smoke, Rain, Firefly, Snow, Stars and Fire. Snow and Firefly Particle effects are shown below.

Lighting Gallery Includes: Lightning, Fireworks, Light Bulb, Lens Flare, Halo, Spotlight, Flashlight, Meteor, Comet and Laser. Look what lightning can do to add drama to an image.

Animation Gallery New to PhotoImpact 6, these Gallery effects create key frame animations, including: Animation Studio, Animation Lighting and Animation Type.

Material Gallery Includes: Color, Texture, Bump, Reflection, Shading, Plastic, Metallic, Glass, Realistic and 3D Collection.

Deform Gallery Includes: Horizontal Text and Vertical Text.

Wrap Gallery Includes: Bend Text, Text Wrap and Path Wrap.

Type Gallery Includes: Gradient, Hole, Glass, Metal, Emboss, Emboss Ouline, Emboss Texture, Concrete, Sand, Lighting, Fire, Snow, Neon, Seal, Chisel, Imprint, Gradient Light, Reverse Emboss, Double and Border.

Button Gallery Includes: Rectangle Buttons and AnyShape Buttons.

Frame Gallery Includes: 2D & 3D, Edge, Magic and Classic. A Classic frame is shown below.

My Gallery An empty Gallery to which you can save custom effects and tool attributes. Click on the Attributes toolbar's Add button to save a custom effect to the EasyPalette.

🗃 ▾ Libraries

Click on the Libraries button to select a Library from the dropdown list, including any custom-created Libraries you have added. Alternatively, select Library Manager to access a submenu of options for managing Libraries.

Library Manager The first item in the Libraries dropdown list is the Library Manager, which has its own submenu. Use these options to create or delete your own custom Libraries, to Import or Export Libraries, to rearrange the order of Libraries and add submenus, or to find out about the Properties of a particular Library.

> **Create** Opens the Create Object Library dialog box.

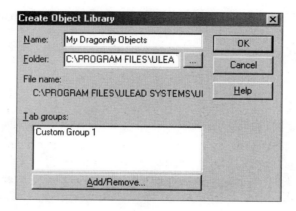

> **Name** Give the new Library a name.
>
> **Folder** Browse to the folder you wish to use for the new Library. You do not have to save a Library to PhotoImpact's Program Files folder. In fact, there are good reasons to save to a different folder on your hard drive. That way if you have to uninstall and reinstall PhotoImpact for any reason, you will still be able to access your Libraries.
>
> **File name** Reflects the path to the selected folder.
>
> **Tab groups** By default a tab group called Custom Group 1 is created.

To add a new Tab group click Add/Remove to open the Group Management dialog box. Click the New button to open the New Group dialog box. Enter a name for the new group and click OK, which returns you to the Group Management dialog box.

To Rename Custom Group 1 (or any other group), select Custom Group 1 (or any other group) and click Add/Remove to open the Group Management dialog box. Click Rename to open the Rename Group dialog box. Give the group a new name and click OK. To Delete a group or change its order within the Library, select the group and click Add/Remove. When the Group Management Dialog box opens, choose the appropriate option (Delete, Up, Down). Click OK to apply changes.

Delete Deletes a custom Library. You cannot delete PhotoImpact's Libraries, which are "Read-Only."

Import Opens the Import Object Library box, which allows you to import a Library. Library files have the .UOL file extension. By default, "Open as a new library" is selected. If you wish to Import a Library into PhotoImpact 6 from a previous version, do *not* Import the Library directly from PhotoImpact 5.0, 4.2 etc. Instead, either Export the older PhotoImpact .UOL Library file you wish to Import to a new folder on your hard drive, or copy the PhotoImpact 4.2 or 5.0 .UFO Library file you wish to Import and paste it into a new folder on your hard drive. Open PhotoImpact 6 and Import the desired Library from this new folder. If you do not Import this way, and you delete PhotoImpact 5.0 or 4.2, you will lose the Imported Library. Obviously, do not delete the folder with the .UOL files you have Imported.

Export Opens the Export Object Library box, which allows you to Export and save a Library to a folder on your hard drive. Library files have the .UOL file extension. By default, "All thumbnails of the current group" is selected.

Detach Be careful with this command, which removes a Library from the EasyPalette. Only custom Libraries can be detached. If you accidentally detach a Library, use the Import command to bring it back into the EasyPalette.

Read-Only If you share Libraries with other computers in a network, select "Read-only (For Sharing)" to protect custom Libraries from unwanted edits.

Properties Opens the Properties box listing the name, number of thumbnails, file size, tab groups, etc. associated with the selected Library.

Menu Layout Rearrange the order of Libraries by clicking and dragging on them, or add submenus and separators. You may Rename or Delete custom created Libraries only. Click on the Test button to preview the new arrangement.

Thumbnail Commands for Libraries

Although the first three buttons in the EasyPalette access the Galleries, Libraries and Layer Manager, respectively, when a Library has been selected, four remaining buttons access thumbnail commands specific to the EasyPalette's Libraries.

Show/Hide Tree View Toggles in and out of Tree view. When deselected, only tabs for the Libraries appear in the EasyPalette, similar to earlier versions of PhotoImpact.

Thumbnail menu commands Click for available options: Copy Object to Image, Copy Object to New Document, Description, Cut, Copy, Paste, Delete, Store Image, Store Image as Selection, Fit Selection, Drag-and-Drop in PhotoImpact Only, Add Image File as Thumbnail and Add Current Document as Thumbnail.

View menu commands Click for available options: Find, Find Next, EasyPalette Options, Resize EasyPalette, Resize to One Row, Resize to One Column, or choose from one of four graphical methods of tiling the EasyPalette with an image.

Select Find to locate a particular object in the selected Library. Doing so opens the Find dialog box. Enter the name of the object you wish to find, whether to search all groups or the current group only, whether to search up or down from the currently selected thumbnail and whether or not to match case. Select Find Next (or hit F3) to find the next object which meets the specifications of the Find criteria. For example, you may save edits to an object in steps (e.g., ,butterflfy1, butterfly2, etc.), so you can go back to recover an earlier stage of editing. Find Next helps you to access the objects you have added to a Library.

Thumbnail size The default thumbnail size is 64 x 64 pixels. You can choose another size from the dropdown list.

Just as for the Galleries, PhotoImpact makes it easy to edit Library objects. You can right click on a Library thumbnail to select from: Copy Object to Image, Copy Object to New Document, Description, Cut, Copy, Paste, Delete, Store Image, Store Selection, Store Image as Selection, Fit Selection, Drag-and-Drop in PhotoImpact Only, Add Image File as Thumbnail and Add Current Document as Thumbnail.

EasyPalette Libraries

Click on the down arrow next to the Libraries button to select a Library, including the new Template Library. Drag from a thumbnail to place a Library object in the base image, or drag into an empty spot in the work space and the object will open in its own window. You can also double click a thumbnail to open a copy in the work space, or right click on a thumbnail and choose Copy Object to Image or Copy Object to New Document.

The Libraries' Path, Image and Template objects can be edited by using the Object menu commands, by right clicking on an active object and selecting from available commands, or by right clicking on its thumbnail in the Layer Manager to access editing options.

Image Library A variety of True Color Image objects for dragging and dropping into images, or into the work space to open in their own windows. Because these are Image objects (not Path objects), Material Gallery effects cannot be applied to them, nor can they be edited from the Material box. Image Library objects can be transformed with the Transform tool. Categories include: Buildings, Celebration, Nature, Special, Stationery and Symbols.

Mask Library An array of preset masks with softened edges. Categories include Soften and Sharpen. These masks can be moved around the base image and resized with the Transform tool. To use a mask from the Mask Library, just drag from the thumbnail onto the image, or double click the mask thumbnail. Now right click on the mask/selection, and Convert to Object. Drag the newly created object into an empty area of the work space, where it will open in its own window. Right click and Merge. This process preserves your original image from edits.

PhotoImpact 6 Wizardry

To use a Grayscale JPG as a mask, as was done above, first click the Mask icon in the lower right side of the status bar, or choose Edit, Mask Mode. A transparent red mask will cover the image. Then copy and paste the Grayscale JPG onto the image, moving and resizing it as necessary. When it is positioned correctly, deselect the Mask icon or choose Edit and deselect Mask Mode. Right click on the mask/selection, and Convert to Object. Drag the object into an empty area of the work space, where it will open in its own window. Right click and Merge.

Shape Library Basic shapes, these Path objects can be dragged and dropped into the work space, or onto another image. Categories include: Frame and Pattern.
When dragged from a thumbnail, the shape is a 2D Object and the Transform tool is automatically selected. Select the Path Drawing tool to switch to a 3D Mode and edit the object from the Attributes toolbar options, the Material dialog box or one of the EasyPalette Galleries.

Create new shapes in graphics programs that can save images in the .AI file type, then Import them into the Shape Library by choosing Object Library Manager, Import. For example, the shapes shown at the top of the next page were created in Expression, saved as .AI files, then imported into PhotoImpact's Shape Library.

Outline Library Outlines of basic shapes, these Path objects can be dragged and dropped into the work space, or onto another image. Outline objects can be combined in many interesting ways. When dragged from a thumbnail, the shape is a 2D Object and the Transform tool is automatically selected. Select the Outline Drawing tool to switch to a 3D Mode to edit the object. Categories include: Basic, Symbol, Border, Pattern, Callout and Realistic.

Path Library Colorful 3D Path objects you can drag and drop into images, or into the work space to open in their own windows. Create fun effects by adding your own objects to the mix (see below).

Path Library categories include: 3D and Call Out. Because Realistic objects are Image objects (not Path objects), Material Gallery effects cannot be applied to them, nor can they be edited from the Material box. Call Outs are Path objects that can be edited by selecting the Path Drawing tool, then editing further from the Attributes toolbar options, the Material dialog box or one of the EasyPalette Galleries.

Template Library The Template Library is new to PhotoImpact 6. It contains predetermined layouts for HTML web pages, business cards, greeting cards, certificates, flyers and labels. Many of the web page templates contain Component Designer objects which can be edited by right clicking on them and choosing Edit Component. Other objects within the templates can be edited as you would normally edit Path or Image objects. If Path objects are Grouped together, you will need to right click and Ungroup them prior to editing them.

Be aware that the HTML editing capabilities in PhotoImpact 6 are not those of a fully functional HTML editor. You cannot build framed pages, for example. It is best to use the web page building features for one time only web page documents that will not be edited later. If you save a web page as a template, the document's page size cannot be modified directly in PhotoImpact 6. So if you create a 640 X 480 pixel web page and edit it to replace the HTML text with considerably more text, part of the HTML text will be cut off in the edited edition.

Ulead offers new free Templates (as well as Component Designer objects) every month from their web site. Be sure to follow the installation instructions carefully. These freebies include seasonally themed bullets, banners, buttons, and web page templates.

My Library An empty Library in which you may store your own objects.

Adding Objects to a Library

There are two ways to save an active object to a Library. You can: (1) Drag the active object to the EasyPalette; or (2) Choose Object, Copy to Object Library. Both methods open the Add to EasyPalette dialog box. Give the object a name and save it to the desired Library and Tab group.

Adding Selections to a Library

You may store selections in the EasyPalette, but you must first convert the selection to an object. Be sure that "Store Selection" has been selected from the EasyPalette's

Thumbnail Menu commands, or simply hold down on the M key while dragging the selection to the EasyPalette and it will not matter if "Store Selection" is selected.

To create a selection from an entire Grayscale image, choose "Store Image as Selection" from the Thumbnail Menu commands. Right click in the image and select All. Then right click and Convert to Object. Now drag the image to the EasyPalette to open the Add to EasyPalette dialog box. Give the selection a name and save it to a Library.

Layer Manager

Objects are PhotoImpact's version of the layers construct used by other imaging programs. If you open a .PSD file in PhotoImpact 6, each layer will appear as an object in the Layer Manager. The more objects there are in an image, the more difficult it can be to keep track of them or to select one for editing. The Layer Manager helps by displaying thumbnails of each object. Clicking on a thumbnail selects its corresponding object in the base image.

This screen shot reveals that there are three objects, or layers, in the base image.

Thumbnail Icons The Layer Manager shows helpful and informative icons on its thumbnails. Using the screen shot above as an example, you can tell that the first object, the sun, is a Path object, that "Birdhouses" is a Text object, and that the little character on the right is an Image object. All of the objects are visible because the "eye" icon is open. The first two objects are not locked within the base image, but you can tell that the character object on the right is locked into position because the lock icon is closed, rather than open.

Object Type The first icon, in the upper left corner of the thumbnail, indicates whether the object is a Text, Image or Path object.

Show/Hide Object On the right side of the thumbnail is an eye icon. If it is open, the object is visible in the base image. Clicking on the open eye replaces it with a closed eye, meaning the object is no longer visible in the base image. Be careful about selecting this option. If you merge and save the image when the eye is closed, the object will not be included in the save.

Lock/Unlock Object The lock icon is on the far right side of the thumbnail. When the lock is deselected, the hasp is open to the left of the lock and the object can be moved freely within the base image. When selected, the hasp is closed and the object cannot be moved.

Selecting Thumbnails for Editing Click on a Layer Manager thumbnail to select its corresponding object for editing.

As you can see below, when the image object is selected in the base image (you can tell by the animated broken line around it), the Layer Manager thumbnail is selected too.

Many of the Object menu commands can be accessed in the Layer Manager as well, by right clicking on the object's thumbnail. In the screen shot below, all three objects have been selected at the same time, and the Merge as Single Object command chosen.

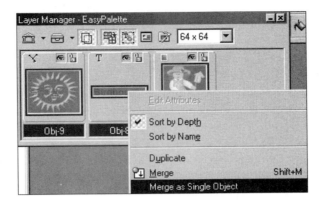

Note that once objects have been merged as a single object, only one thumbnail for the merged objects appears in the Layer Manager.

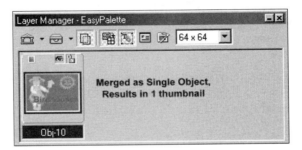

Thumbnail Menu Commands While the first three buttons in the EasyPalette access the Galleries, Libraries and Layer Manager, respectively, when the Layer Manager has been selected, four remaining buttons access thumbnail commands specific to the Layer Manager.

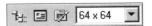

Show/hide list view Toggles in and out of List view, which is shown below.

Hide group members Toggles between showing and hiding Grouped objects. When Hidden is selected, a single thumbnail represents Grouped objects.

Thumbnail menu commands Click for available options: Sort by Depth, Sort by Name, Duplicate, Merge, Merge as Single Object (if more than one thumbnail is selected), Merge All, Delete, Select All Objects, Group or Ungroup (if more than one thumbnail is selected), Align, Arrange, Image Optimizer, Shadow and Properties. Note that these commands can also be accessed by right clicking on a Layer Manager thumbnail and via the Object menu commands.

View menu commands Click for available options: Find, Find Next, EasyPalette Options, Show Detail, Resize EasyPalette, Resize to One Row, Resize to One Column or choose from a graphical menu of tiling commands.

Thumbnail size The default thumbnail size is 64 x 64 pixels. You can choose another size from the dropdown list.

Adding Sparkle and Color: Active Learning Exercises

Using the Fill Tools

1. Hit Ctrl+N to access the New dialog box. Open a new, True Color file, 300 X 300 pixels, with a white canvas.

2. The purpose of this exercise is to fill the new image with the Fill tools.

3. ![bucket] Select the Bucket fill tool.

4. In the Attributes toolbar, click in the Color box and select green. Makes sure that the Transparency value is 0. Click in the image to fill it with the selected color.

5. Right click and Undo to return to the white canvas. In the Attributes toolbar, edit the Transparency value to 75. Click in the image. Note that the fill is a pale green.

6. In the Attributes toolbar, edit the Transparency of the fill to 0 again. From the Merge dropdown list, select Difference.

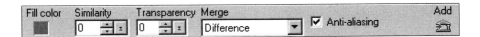

7. Click in the image. Notice that the fill is *purple*. This merge method interacted with the underlying color, filling with purple, which is opposite green in the color wheel.

8. In the Attributes toolbar, select Always from the Merge dropdown list. Click in the image. Now the fill is the same green that you selected in the Attributes toolbar.

9. In the Quick Color Controls on the right side of the work space, click in the background color box and select white.

10. Hit the Delete key. The base image will be filled with the white background color.

11. Select the Linear Gradient Fill tool.

12. In the Attributes toolbar, select Two-Color from the Method dropdown list. Click in the beginning Color box and select red. Click in the ending Color box and choose white. Set the Transparency to 0 and the Merge method to Always.

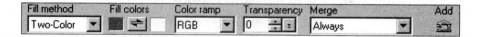

13. Position your cursor on the far left side of the image and drag straight across. You will see a gradient that starts with red and fades to white on the right side.

14. Drag from the far right side of the image to the left side. Now the gradient is red on the right side, fading to white on the left. Since the beginning color is red, and you began dragging on the right, the direction of the gradient was reversed.

15. Hit the Delete key to fill the base image with white.

16. In the Attributes toolbar, select Multiple-Color from the Fill method dropdown list. Click in the Fill colors Color box to open the Palette Ramp Editor.

17. Select Palette 22. Right click on the white control point and select Change Color.

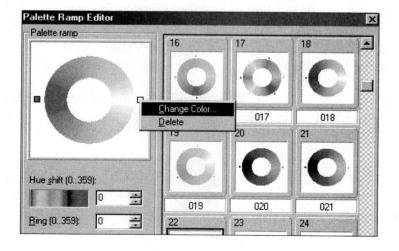

18. Choose a deep aqua (RGB=0, 196, 196) from the Color box. This aqua will replace the white in the gradient. Edit the Ring value to 180, which moves the aqua to the opposite side of the gradient's color distribution.

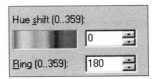

19. Click the Add button to add a thumbnail for the edited palette to the Palette Ramp Editor. Click OK to close the Palette Ramp Editor.

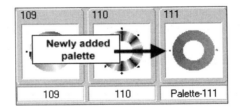

20. Drag across the image in different directions to view the custom palette. No matter which direction you drag the gradient, it will begin and end with aqua, and blue will be positioned in the middle of the gradient.

21. If you do not want to keep this gradient in your Palette Ramp Editor, click the Fill colors Color box in the Attributes toolbar. When the Palette Ramp Editor opens, right click on the thumbnail for the custom palette and select Delete. You will be asked if you are sure you want to remove it. Choose Yes and the palette will be deleted.

22. Click Delete to fill the base image with white.

23. Select the Rectangular Gradient Fill tool.

24. The red and white Two-Color fill attributes should still be active in the Attributes toolbar. Click in the beginning color Color box and select blue. Select Always from the Merge dropdown list.

25. Position your cursor in the middle of the base image and drag upward and outward to fill with the gradient. It will be blue in the middle and white on the outer edges.

26. In the Attributes toolbar, click on the toggle button between the beginning and ending colors to change them. Now white is the beginning color and blue is the ending color. Drag from the center again to get a reverse gradient effect.

27. Hit the Delete key to fill the base image with white.

28. Choose the Standard selection tool. In the Attributes toolbar, select Circle from the Shape dropdown list. Make sure "Fixed size" is deselected. Edit the Soft edge value to 5. Drag a circular selection in the middle of the base image.

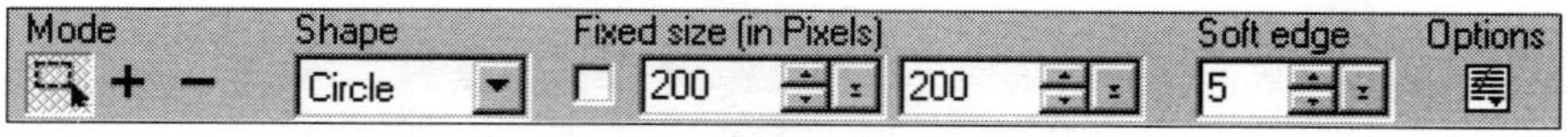

29.  Select the Elliptical Gradient Fill tool.

30. In the Attributes toolbar, select Multiple-Color from the Fill method dropdown list. Click the Fill colors Color box to open the Palette Ramp Editor. Select Palette 26.

31. Starting exactly in the center of the selection, drag a circular shape that conforms to the shape of the round selection.

32. The fill starts with white (the beginning color in the palette), graduating to light and then dark blues. Right click and Undo.

33. In the Attributes toolbar, click in the Fill colors Color box again to open the Palette Ramp Editor. Palette 26 will still be selected. Edit the Ring value to 180, shifting the white beginning color to the other side of the ring.

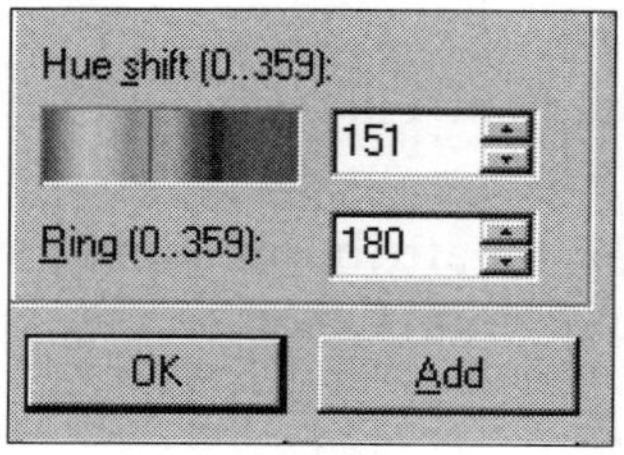

34. Starting in the center of the selection, drag a circular shaped fill. Because the beginning color was shifted, now the middle of the fill looks like a blue ball floating in a light blue gradient background. Right click and Undo.

35. In the Attributes toolbar, click in the Fill colors Color box again to open the Palette Ramp Editor. Palette 26 will still be selected. Edit the Ring value back to 0. Edit the Hue shift value to 350. The entire palette will shift from blues to yellows.

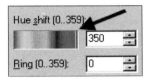

36. Drag from the center of the selection to create a round fill. Once again, the gradient fill will be white in the middle, radiating out to light and then dark shades of yellow.

Creating an EasyPalette Custom Gallery

1. The purpose of this exercise is to create a custom Gallery and Tab groups in the EasyPalette. If the EasyPalette is not open right now, hit Ctrl+F1 to open it.

2. Right click on any existing Gallery and choose Create. Doing so opens the Create Gallery dialog box. Name the new Gallery, e.g., My Presets. Look at the Tab groups box. The default is Custom Group 1. This description is not particularly helpful, so select it and click the Add/Remove Button.

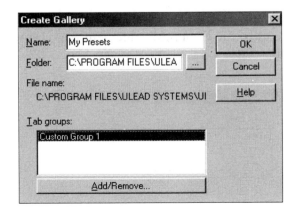

473

3. When the Group Management dialog box opens, Custom Group 1 will be selected.

4. Click Rename to open the Rename Group dialog box. Rename the Group to Reds. Your red presets will be saved to this Tab group. Click OK to close the box.

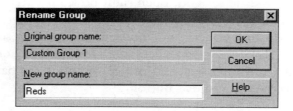

5. When you are returned to the Group Management dialog box, click New. Doing so opens the New Group dialog box. Name the new group Blues and click OK.

6. When returned to the Group Management dialog box, click New again. When the New Group dialog box opens, name the new group Greens and click OK.

7. Now the Group Management dialog box shows three Tab groups, for Reds, Blues and Greens. Click OK to close the box.

8. The Create Gallery dialog box shows that the three Tab groups have been added to the Gallery.

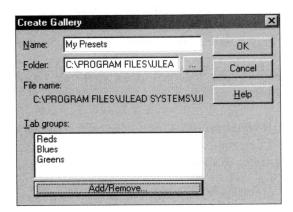

9. Click on the My Presets Gallery and you will see four Tab groups: All, Reds, Greens and Blues. All will always appear as the first Tab group.

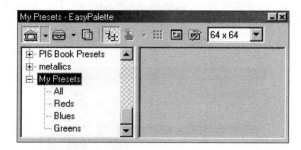

10. Note that there are no thumbnails in the new Gallery. As you add presets to the Gallery in the next exercise, however, a thumbnail will appear for each preset.

Creating Your Own Presets

1. Hit Ctrl+N to access the New dialog box. Create a new True Color image 300 X 300 pixels with a white canvas.

2. The purpose of this exercise is to create several presets in the Material dialog box and add them to the new Gallery created in the previous exercise.

3. Select the Path Drawing tool. In the Attributes toolbar, click Shape and select the Circle shape. From the Mode dropdown list, select 3D Round. Click in the Color box and select light gray. Draw a large round object in the base image.

4. While the object is active, click Material in the Attributes toolbar. Doing so opens the Material dialog box.

5. From the Color/Texture tab, select One Color. Click in the Color box to open the Ulead Color Picker. Click the Red tab and select one of the medium reds from the middle rows (for example, RGB=225, 23, 0). Click OK to close the Color Picker.

6. Click the Bevel tab and select 3D Custom (top of next page).

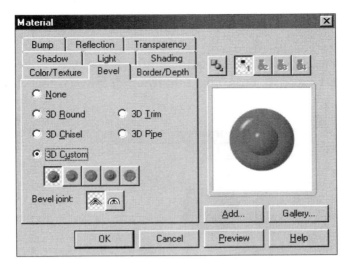

7. Click the Border/Depth tab and edit the Border value to 10, making the double edge a great deal more narrow.

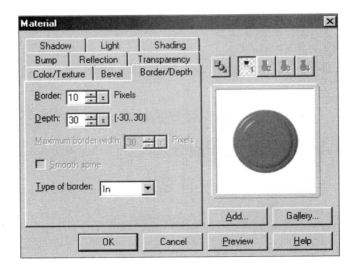

8. To add this preset to your custom Gallery, click the Add button. Doing so opens the

Material Save Options dialog box. Leave the default of "All" selected. Click OK to close the box.

9. When the Add to EasyPalette dialog box opens, give the preset a name, e.g., Red Double Edge. From the Gallery dropdown list, choose My Presets, the Gallery you created in the last exercise. From the Tab group dropdown list, choose Reds.

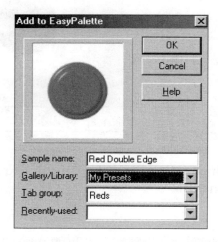

10. Click OK to close the Material dialog box. Take a look at the My Presets Gallery, Reds tab group. You will see a thumbnail for the newly created preset.

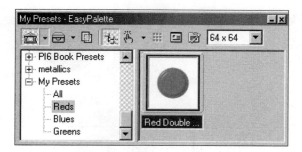

11. While the object is still active, in the Attributes toolbar, select 3D Round from the Mode dropdown list. The custom bevel edge will disappear and be replaced by the 3D Round edge.

12. In the EasyPalette, double click on the custom preset, Red Double Edge. Instantly the border will be replaced with the preset's bevel.

13. Right click on the Red Double Edge thumbnail in My Presets Gallery. Choose "Modify Properties and Apply." Doing so will open the Material dialog box.

14. From the Color/Texture tab, click in the One Color color box and select a bright blue from the Ulead Color Picker. Click OK to close the Color Picker. Note that the Preview window shows the custom bevel edge, but the color has been changed to blue. By modifying the preset's attributes, you have preserved the beveled edge while changing only the color.

15. From the Color/Texture tab, select Texture. Click in the Texture color box and select Natural Texture. Doing so opens the Texture Library dialog box. Select the thumbnail for Grass 4 and click OK. Now the sample in the Preview window shows the object filled with green grass.

16. Click on the Shading tab and select Metallic. From the Metallic dropdown list, choose Gold. Edit the Strength value to 50, which will darken the shine slightly.

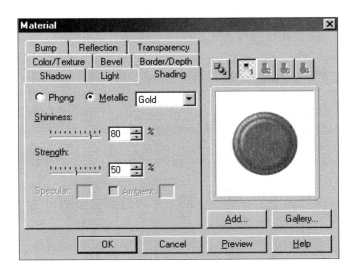

17. Click the Bump tab. Select Bump map, which will open the Open dialog box.

479

Browse to the PhotoImpact 6 Texture folder and select Grass 4. Click OK to return to the Material dialog box. Edit the Density to 85%.

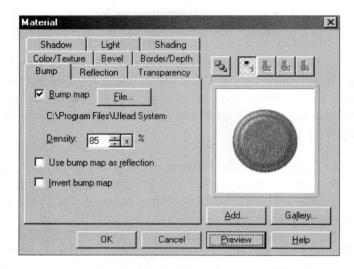

18. Click the Reflection tab. Select Reflection map. Click File to access the Open dialog box. Browse to the PhotoImpact 6 Texture folder and select Grass 4. Click OK to return to the Material dialog box. Edit the Density to 50%.

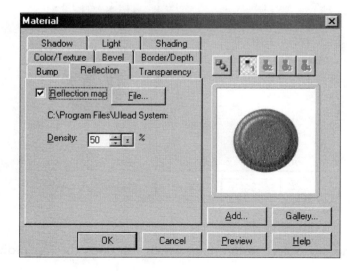

19. Click the Bevel tab. Select 3D Round.

20. Click the Border/Depth tab and edit the Border value to 30.

21. Click the Light tab. Edit the number of lights to 2. For the second light, select Spot from the dropdown list.

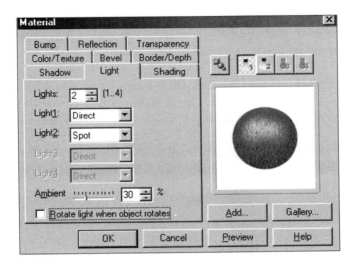

22. This is a very complex preset that you will save to My Presets. Click Add to open the Material Save Options dialog box. Leave the default of "All" selected and click OK.

23. When the Add to EasyPalette dialog box opens, name the preset, e.g., Metallic Grass Texture. From the Gallery dropdown list choose My Presets. Select Greens from the Tab group dropdown list. Click OK.

24. Click OK to close the Material dialog box and apply the preset. Check the Greens Tab group under My Presets. You will see a thumbnail for the Metallic Grass Texture preset.

25. From the EasyPalette, select Material Gallery, Plastic. Double click on Remove Material. The preset will be removed from the object, turning it a pale gray. This is a good way to remove accumulated effects when you want to start over again.

26. Hit the space bar to deactivate the object. Select the Text tool. In the Attributes toolbar, select the Arial font, Size=50. Click in the base image to open the Text Entry box. Type the word PRESET, Bold. Click OK to close the Text Entry Box.

27. In the My Presets, Greens Tab group, double click on the Metallic Grass Texture thumbnail. As you can see, presets can be applied to 3D Path or Text objects.

28. Since the surface area of the font is not very broad, the preset will look very dark. In the Attributes toolbar, edit the Border value to 5, which will shine up the text. Now hit Delete to get rid of the text from the base image.

29. Select the Path Drawing tool and click the object. From the Material box's Color/Texture tab, select File to access the Open dialog box. Browse to and select from the PhotoImpact 6 Textures folder Ice1.jpg. Click OK to close the Open box.

30. Click the Bump tab and select Bump map. Click File to access the Open dialog box. Browse to and select from the PhotoImpact 6 Textures folder Ice1.jpg. Click OK to close the Open box.

31. From the Material dialog box, click the Shading tab. Edit the Shininess and Strength values to 99, to lighten the effect. Select Ambient to edit the color of light falling away from the highlighted area. Click in the Ambient color box and select a bright blue (RGB=107, 82, 254).

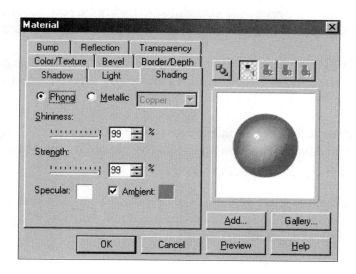

32. Click the Light tab and change the single light to Spot. Edit the Ambient light value to 45, which lightens the effect.

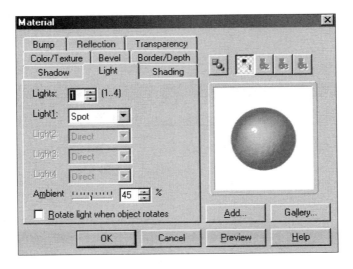

33. Click Add to open the Material Save Options dialog box. Leave the default of "All" selected and click OK.

34. When the Add to EasyPalette dialog box opens, name the preset, e.g., Blue Ice. From the Gallery dropdown list choose My Presets. Select Blues from the Tab group dropdown list. Click OK.

35. Click OK to close the Material dialog box. Look at My Presets in the EasyPalette. Click All and you will see 3 thumbnails for the 3 different presets that you added.

36. Click Reds and you will see only one thumbnail for Red Double Edge. Repeat to see the thumbnails under the Blues and Greens Tab groups.

Exporting and Importing a Gallery

1. The purpose of this exercise is to Export the My Presets Gallery and its thumbnails to a folder on your hard drive.

PhotoImpact 6 Wizardry

2. In the EasyPalette, right click on the My Presets Gallery and select Export. Doing so opens the Export Gallery dialog box. Browse to a folder on your hard drive to which you wish to save the Gallery. Note that the Gallery will be saved as an .SMP file. Leave the default of "All thumbnails of the current group" selected and click Save.

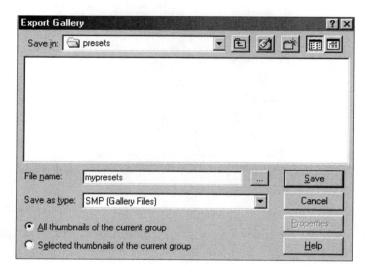

3. Suppose for some reason you had to uninstall and reinstall PhotoImpact? If you had to do so, the My Presets custom Gallery would be lost, and you would have no way to replace your work except to re-create it. This is why it is a very good idea to back up custom Galleries (and Libraries) regularly by Exporting them to a folder on your hard drive.

4. Now for the moment of truth. In the EasyPalette, right click on My Presets and choose Delete. You will see a warning "This command cannot be undone. Are you sure you want to continue?" Click Yes. The My Presets Gallery will be deleted from the EasyPalette.

5. To return the My Presets Gallery to the EasyPalette, click the Galleries button and choose Gallery Manager, Import to access the Import Gallery dialog box. Browse to the folder to which you saved the Exported Gallery. Select mypresets.SMP. Leave the default of "Open as new gallery" selected, and leave "Merge group by group"

selected. Click Open.

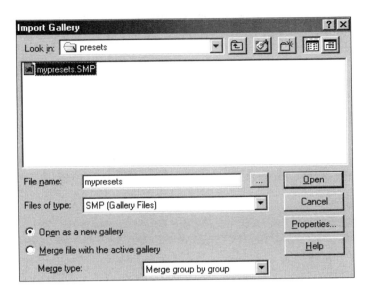

6. Take a look at the EasyPalette Galleries. You will see that the My Presets Gallery has been restored to the EasyPalette Galleries.

7. If you do not want to keep this custom Gallery, feel free to right click on it and choose Delete again. However, you may wish to consider leaving it there to organize custom presets you will surely create as time goes on. You may add other Tab groups to this gallery, for example, you may add a Tab group for Golds, Purples, Glass, etc.

Using a Mask Library Mask

1. Choose File, Open to access the Open dialog box. Browse to and select pilings.bmp. Click Open.

2. The purpose of this exercise is to learn how to use masks from the Mask Library.

3. Open the EasyPalette's Mask Library. Double click on Square05. With the Selection tool, in "Make a new selection" Mode, drag the mask so that it is centered over the

PhotoImpact 6 Wizardry

pelican. If you wish to do so, switch to the Transform tool to resize or distort the selection as desired.

4. Right click on the selection and choose Convert to Object. Drag the newly created object into an empty area of the work space, where it will open in its own window. Right click and Merge All.

5. Leave the pilings.bmp image open for the next exercise.

Using a JPG Mask

1. While the pilings.bmp image is still open, click the Mask icon in the Status Bar, hit Ctrl+K or choose Edit, Mask Mode. The image will be covered with a transparent red mask.

2. Choose File, Place, As Object to access the Open dialog box. Browse to and select mask.jpg, which is a Grayscale JPG image. Click OK.

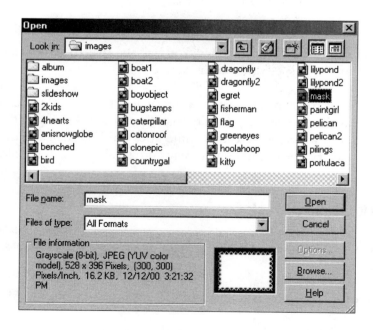

486

3. The white areas of the mask will look transparent over the base image, while the dark areas will show the transparent red mask.

4. Move the mask as needed. You can switch to the Transform tool to resize or distort the selection too. When you are satisfied with its arrangement over the image, click the Mask icon in the Status Bar to get rid of the mask.

5. Right click on the selection and choose Convert to Object. Drag the object into an empty area of the work space, where it will open in its own window. Right click and Merge All.

Section 6: Web Magic

PhotoImpact 6 represents a significant advance in web imaging power. No longer merely an image editor (and a great one at that), it has emerged as an exciting new hybrid combining both an image editor and a simple HTML web document builder. This section targets new capabilities as well as already strong web imaging features like the Component Designer, Button Designer, Background Designer, and the Image Slicer and Image Map, which have been improved and expanded upon. A detailed exploration of the Image Optimizer, also newly enhanced, is essential for web imaging enthusiasts.

Web Menu Commands include a large, diverse group of web imaging tasks. You will learn about each of them in detail, including new commands like Trim object, Rollover and the ability to add HTML text to a web page document. This section walks you, step by step, through editing Component Designer and Rollover buttons, so you will truly understand how to use them. You will also learn how to custom edit 3D buttons, create seamless tiles in a variety of ways and use the Slicer to slice a large image and reassemble it in an HTML web page.

The Image Optimizer is where you save web images in JPG, GIF or PNG file format. Learn how to create transparency in web images, create your own optimization and compression presets, crop, tweak Save settings and more.

Active Learning Exercises Making and Editing Buttons in the Component Designer; Making and Editing a Tile With the Background Designer; Making a Web Page With Rollover Buttons; Making a Rollover Button; Making a "Jewel" With Button Designer, Any Shape; Slicing a Large Image; Making a Transparent Background, Automatically; Making a Transparent Background, Manually; Cropping an Image in the Image Optimizer; Creating an Image Optimizer Preset.

Chapter 19: The Web Menu

PhotoImpact 6 continues to improve upon the program's already-powerful web imaging features. Among Web menu commands new to PhotoImpact 6 are the ability to add HTML text objects and the Trim command, which automatically crops excess space around an object and creates a transparent background. With these tools, not only can you make sophisticated web graphics quickly and easily, but you can also generate code for javascript rollovers, and the HTML code to reassemble sliced images in tables. What is more, you can perform these tasks and preview them right in the work space.

There are some changes in the reorganization of the Web menu. The most significant of these is that the Frame Designer is no longer part of the Web menu. Instead, it can be accessed from the EasyPalette's Frame Gallery, by clicking the Frame & Shadow button or by hitting Shift+F. In addition, the Web Preview function was moved and is now accessed via the File, Preview in Browser command. Veteran users will be pleased to see the return of the PhotoImpact 4.2, Button Designer, Any Shape presets.

Component Designer (F12)

The Component Designer makes it easy to add custom edited web images. It even generates the code for javascript rollover buttons. Select a component and click Next.

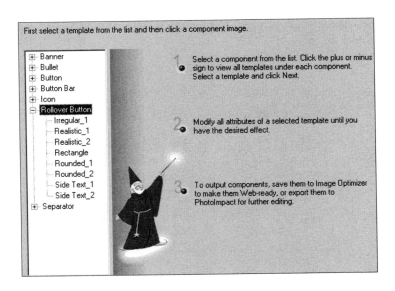

Editing and Exporting Components

Dialog box contents vary by component. Edit background color by clicking in the color box. Walking through the steps for editing a simple button shows how the process works. In the screen shot below, note that the selected button has four parts: Title, Plate, Bend and Screw. Each of these four attributes can be edited.

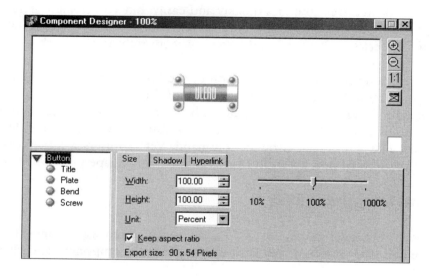

Note also that the button Size can be changed from the Size tab, and a shadow can be added from the Shadow tab.

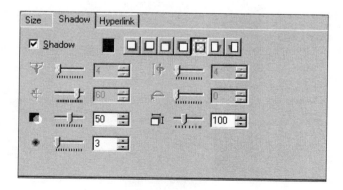

Assign a URL and other web attributes to the button from the Hyperlink tab.

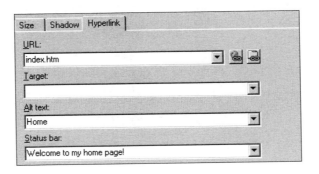

Click on Title. From the Text tab, select the default text and replace. Choose another Font from the dropdown list and select another Style. "Change shape when text changes" enlarges the button to hold more letters. If one button says HOME and another says GALLERY, the second button will be larger. To avoid having different sized buttons, deselect this option.

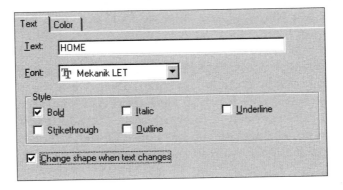

Click on the Color tab to edit text color. To fill with a solid color select the Bucket icon and click in a color square (mix a custom color with RGB values), or select a Gradient or Texture fill by clicking on the appropriate icon and choosing from available options.

PhotoImpact 6 Wizardry

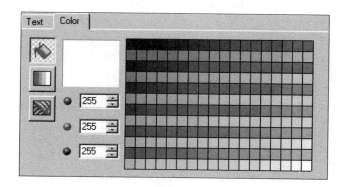

Next click on Plate to edit the color of the main part of the button. Just click on a color square to change colors or enter your own RGB values. Then click on Bend to edit the color of the two bent objects holding the main part of the button. Click on Screw to change the screw color. Only the Color tab is available for Plate, Bend and Screw.

When the button has been edited to your satisfaction, click Export. Choose to Export to the Image Optimizer (to Save and compress), As Individual Objects (in PhotoImpact) or As Component Objects (in PhotoImpact). If you Export to the Image Optimizer, its dialog box will open for you to save and compress the image as a JPG, GIF or PNG image.

If you Export As Individual Objects (to PhotoImpact), the button will open in the work space, where you can continue editing its separate objects, but the previously assigned Web attributes will be lost if you do so. If you Export As Component Objects (to PhotoImpact) the button will open in the work space. To edit it you must right click and choose Edit Component, hit Shift+E or choose Object, Edit Component. Doing so opens the Component Designer again for further editing.

Here are what the buttons look like after editing.

Editing Component Designer Rollover Buttons

Editing Rollover buttons in the Component Designer follows a similar process, except that button attributes can be edited for each of three states: Normal, Mouseover (the mouse rolls over the button on a web page), and Mousedown (the mouse is clicked on the button on a web page). If you like the default colors associated with each state, you may not need to edit anything except button text and web attributes such as URL and Alt Text.

In the sequence that follows, walking through the steps of editing a javascript rollover button illustrates how the process works. First, select a button style.

You will see the three states of the selected button in the Preview window at the top of the dialog box. The basic attributes of the button are edited from the four tabs below the Preview window.

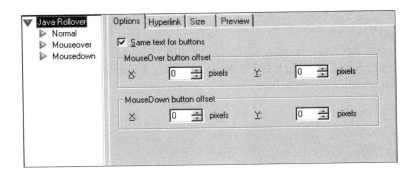

From the Options tab, "Same text for buttons" is selected by default. Deselect if you want the text to be different on different states of the button. From the Options tab you can also elect to have the button "move" on Mouseover and MouseDown by editing its X and Y Offset.

Click the Hyperlink tab to specify the button's web attributes, including URL, target frame, Alt Text and browser Status bar message.

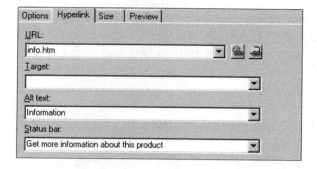

Click the Size tab to edit button size. Click the Preview tab to view the Rollover effect right in the dialog box. Roll your mouse over the button and click on the button to see how it will look on a web page.

Once the basic attributes for the Rollover button have been assigned, you can edit the button's three states by clicking on Normal, Mouseover and Mousedown. Each of these button states present a submenu of editable objects, the number of which vary by the selected button. When the Normal state is selected for this realistic telephone button, there are six objects making up the Normal state of the button: Title, Phone Dial, Phone, Circle, Side Strip and Panel. Clicking on Title displays two tabs, Title and Color, from which those attributes may be edited.

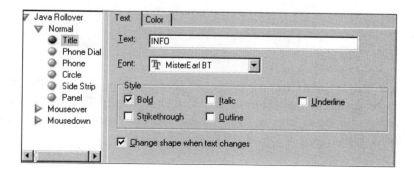

Clicking on the objects comprising the Rollover button displays a Color tab, from which the color of these objects can be edited. This sequence of editing is repeated for the Mouseover and Mousedown states as well.

Exporting Component Designer Objects

When you are satisfied with your Component Designer banner, button, bullet, etc., click Export and choose whether to Export to: Image Optimizer, As Individual Objects (in PhotoImpact), As Component Objects (in PhotoImpact) or (for Rollover buttons *only*) to HTML.

Export to Image Optimizer When selected, this option opens the Image Optimizer. Choose whether to save the component in JPG, GIF or PNG format and save to a folder on your hard drive.

Export as Individual Objects (in PhotoImpact) When selected, the objects making up the component object are exported to a new window in the work space. These objects are separate and may be further edited as desired with the Path Drawing and Text tools. However, the Web attributes assigned to them in the Component Designer will be lost.

Export as Component Object (in PhotoImpact) When selected, the objects making up the component object are exported to a new window in the work space. These objects can be further edited by right clicking and choosing Edit Component, hitting Shift+E, choosing Object, Edit Component or right clicking in the Layer Manager and choosing Edit Component. All of these actions re-open the Component Designer for further editing.

Export to HTML When Export to HTML is selected, the Save As dialog box opens. By default, the Component Designer object(s) will be saved in an HTML file. Browse your hard drive for the folder to which you want to save the HTML code and name the file, e.g., "infobutton.html." Click OK to Save and the Image Optimizer dialog box will open. Choose whether to save the object(s) as JPG, GIF or PNG images, selecting available options from their associated tabs in the Image Optimizer. Click OK to complete saving the Component Designer objects.

Note that you did not have to give the objects a name or navigate to a folder to save them. They were saved automatically to the same folder to which the HTML Page (infobutton.html) was saved. If you have created Component Designer Rollover buttons, they were saved to an "images" subfolder created especially for them. The buttons' names were derived from the HTML file with which they are associated: "infobutton_normal.gif," "infobutton_over.gif" and "infobutton_down.gif."

To make other Rollover buttons with the same attributes as the Information buttons, *do not* close the Component Designer or you will lose your edits. Simply click back on Title again and change the text (e.g., "Order") then Export to HTML again. Save to the same folder to which you saved the Information HTML and buttons, but name this HTML file "order.html." Repeat the process for other Rollover buttons, e.g., an "FAQ" button Exported to HTML as "faq.html."

If you prefer to build your web page with the rollovers in your HTML editor, you will need to do a lot more work than if you placed the buttons onto a web image page in the work space and saved from there. You will also need some experience with inserting code into HTML documents to get the buttons into your web page. From your HTML editor, open the infobutton.html file that you have saved. If you are using a WYSIWYG editor, you will see a blank page with the homebutton_normal.gif image at the top, and this text: "script and //. paste it into your HTML file to compile and //. define your rollover button.————>" Select (highlight) this text and delete it.

In your HTML editor, access the HTML code. You will see the usual code in black, followed by the javascript code for the rollover effect in brown. Leave in all the code after the </HEAD> and above the <BODY> tag. Immediately after the <BODY> tag are two sets of remarks about how to add more buttons by copying and pasting HTML into your web page document. To add the javascript code for the other rollover buttons to your page, you must do some copying and pasting in two different places, as indicated by the remarks. The first of these remarks looks like this:

```
// ———
// . First:
// . You can copy the "AddImageToImageList(...)" script and
// . paste it into your HTML file to compile and
// . define your rollover button.
// . ———

AddImageToImageList("tag_info", "images/info_normal.gif", "images/info_over.gif", "images/info_down.gif");

// ———>
</Script>

<BODY>
```

Copy into the Clipboard this line of code:

```
AddImageToImageList("tag_info", "images/info_normal.gif", "images/info_over.gif", "images/info_down.gif");
```

Below the line of code that you just copied, paste the code back into the HTML document for each rollover button you want to add to the page. For example, the code is already there for the Information button. If you want to add Order and FAQ buttons, paste the code in two more times. You will have three lines of code that are exactly alike.

The last two lines must be edited to reflect the names of the Order and FAQ buttons. For the second line, replace all references to the Information button with Order, and for the third line of code replace all references to the Information button with FAQ.

```
AddImageToImageList("tag_info", "images/info_normal.gif", "images/info_over.gif", "images/info_down.gif");
AddImageToImageList("tag_info", "images/order_normal.gif", "images/order_over.gif", "images/order_down.gif");
AddImageToImageList("tag_info", "images/faq_normal.gif", "images/faq_over.gif", "images/faq_down.gif");
```

Next move down to just below this remark:

```
<BODY>
<! ———
// . Second:
// . You can copy the "<a href=......></a>" script and
// . paste it into your HTML file to compile and
// . define your rollover button.
        ———>
```

Where you will see the following code for the infobutton:

```
<A HREF="info.htm"
   ONMOUSEDOWN="if (bIsSupportOK) ReplaceImage('tag_info', MouseDownState);"
   ONMOUSEUP="if (bIsSupportOK) ReplaceImage('tag_info', MouseOverState);"
   ONMOUSEOUT="if (bIsSupportOK) ReplaceImage('tag_info',DefaultState);
   window.status=window.defaultStatus;return true"
   ONMOUSEOVER="if (bIsSupportOK) ReplaceImage('tag_info', MouseOverState);
   window.status='Get more information about this product';return true;"
   TARGET="">
   <IMG NAME="tag_info" SRC="images/info_normal.gif" ALT="Information"
   WIDTH="92" HEIGHT="46" BORDER="0"></A>
```

Copy all of the Information button code into the Clipboard and paste it back into the document two times for the Order and FAQ buttons. Place the copied code directly below the last line of the Information button code. You will have three blocks of code that are exactly the same. In the second block of code, replace references to the Information button with references to the Order button. In the third block of code, replace references to the Information button with references to the FAQ button. Be sure to replace the Alt Text and Status bar messages with the appropriate information as well.

The three blocks of edited code for the Home, Gallery and Links buttons are shown below:

```
<A HREF="info.htm"
   ONMOUSEDOWN="if (bIsSupportOK) ReplaceImage('tag_info',
MouseDownState);"
   ONMOUSEUP="if (bIsSupportOK) ReplaceImage('tag_info', MouseOverState);"
   ONMOUSEOUT="if (bIsSupportOK) ReplaceImage('tag_info',DefaultState);
   window.status=window.defaultStatus;return true"
   ONMOUSEOVER="if (bIsSupportOK) ReplaceImage('tag_info', MouseOverState);
   window.status='Get more information about this product';return true;"
   TARGET="">
   <IMG NAME="tag_info" SRC="images/info_normal.gif" ALT="Information"
   WIDTH="92" HEIGHT="46" BORDER="0"></A>
<A HREF="order.htm"
   ONMOUSEDOWN="if (bIsSupportOK) ReplaceImage('tag_order',
MouseDownState);"
   ONMOUSEUP="if (bIsSupportOK) ReplaceImage('tag_order', MouseOverState);"
   ONMOUSEOUT="if (bIsSupportOK) ReplaceImage('tag_order',DefaultState);
   window.status=window.defaultStatus;return true"
   ONMOUSEOVER="if (bIsSupportOK) ReplaceImage('tag_order',
MouseOverState);
   window.status='Order this product now';return true;"
   TARGET="">
   <IMG NAME="tag_order" SRC="images/order_normal.gif" ALT="Order"
   WIDTH="92" HEIGHT="46" BORDER="0"></A>
<A HREF="faq.htm"
   ONMOUSEDOWN="if (bIsSupportOK) ReplaceImage('tag_faq', MouseDownState);"
   ONMOUSEUP="if (bIsSupportOK) ReplaceImage('tag_faq', MouseOverState);"
   ONMOUSEOUT="if (bIsSupportOK) ReplaceImage('tag_info',DefaultState);
   window.status=window.defaultStatus;return true"
   ONMOUSEOVER="if (bIsSupportOK) ReplaceImage('tag_faq', MouseOverState);
   window.status='Answers to Frequently Asked Questions';return true;"
   TARGET="">
   <IMG NAME="tag_faq" SRC="images/faq_normal.gif" ALT="FAQ"
   WIDTH="92" HEIGHT="46" BORDER="0"></A>
```

In this example, all three of the buttons are the same size, so their Width and Height are the same. If your buttons are not all the same size, make sure that the Width and Height values are correct for each button.

Save the document and test it in your browser. You should see a different button when you roll your mouse over the normal buttons, and when you click the mouse. If the rollovers do not work as they should, go back to your HTML document and inspect the code. For each button, check to make sure that the appropriate button name has been referenced, that image height and width are correct, and so on, then save and test again.

If you are going to add the Component Designer Rollover buttons to an existing web page, you still have some work to do in your HTML editor. Open your rollover button document, *and* open the document into which you want to add the rollover buttons. Copy all of the code between <HEAD> and </HEAD> from the rollover button document and paste it into the same place in the other document. Then copy all of the rollover code in the <BODY> portion of the rollover button document, and paste it where you want the buttons to appear in the other document. Save the document and test it in your browser.

When everything works OK, you are ready to upload the HTML document and images to your server. It is critical that the directory structure on your server mirrors that of your HTML document. If you do not have a subdirectory called "images" on your server, make one and upload all of the button images to that directory. Alternatively, you can upload the images to any directory you like, and edit the path to all references to the buttons in your document. However, it can be difficult to do this, and it is not recommended unless you are very experienced in editing HTML code.

Again, if you choose to make Rollover buttons in the Component Designer, consider simply dragging them onto a web page sized image in the work space and choosing File, Save for Web, As HTML. Not only is it faster and easier to do it that way, but opportunities to make mistakes are greatly reduced. All of the javascript and HTML code will appear in the correct places, effortlessly.

Background Designer (Shift+B)

The Background Designer generates an almost endless supply of original tiling web page backgrounds. First, choose whether to make a new background tile, or to apply the background to an image, selection or object.

PhotoImpact 6 Wizardry

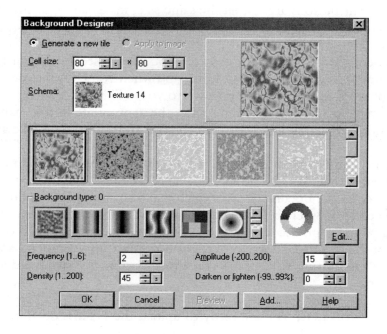

Cell Size Many backgrounds tile well at the default size of 80 pixels by 80 pixels. Change the cell size as desired for larger or smaller background tiles.

Schema From the Schema dropdown menu, choose a texture. Scroll through the larger thumbnails below the chosen schema to select a preset variation.

Background Type Select a thumbnail to edit the chosen Schema with variations of background type. This option is unavailable or "grayed out" for some woven textures. Editing background type can result in remarkably different looking tiles.

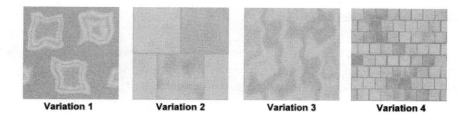

Variation 1   Variation 2   Variation 3   Variation 4

Edit Click on the Edit button to change tile colors with the Palette Ramp Editor.

Frequency Sharpens the pattern edges. This is unavailable for some smoother textures.

Density Pattern repeats, with higher values making a more densely textured tile.

Amplitude Edits contrast, but is grayed out for some smoother textures.

Darken or Lighten Negative numbers darken and positive numbers lighten the tile.

Add Save custom settings to the EasyPalette for future use.

Button Designer (Any Shape)

Turn any irregular shape into a 3D button with the Any Shape Button Designer.

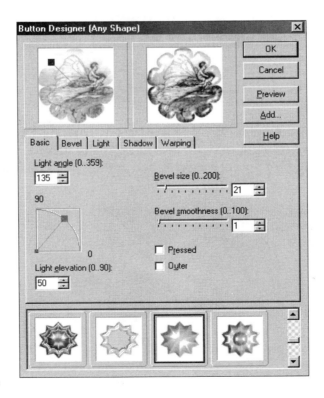

Basic Select options or enter values for basic features: Light angle, Light elevation, Bevel size in pixels, and Bevel smoothness. Choose whether the button will appear to have been pressed in (Pressed), or if the bevel should extend outside of the button area (Outer). Select a preset from the thumbnails at the bottom of the dialog box if desired. Important Note: If you downloaded the patch, these thumbnails will no longer appear.

Bevel Select a Bevel type from the samples. To edit, enter values for Fine control (strength of bevel effect) and Repeat (0-10, for a unique beveled effect). Select Symmetric to duplicate the bevel on the opposite side.

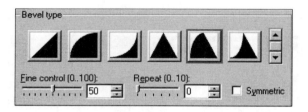

Light Choose from1 to 4 lights. Edit Light effects by entering values for the Highlight, Shadow and Face strength of light, as well as Angle, Elevation, Light value (brightness) and strength of Specular light. Click in the Light color box to edit color.

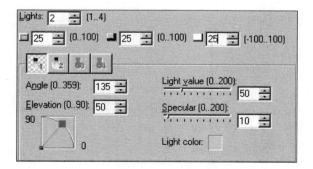

Shadow Select or deselect a shadow, including the "Glow" option at far right. Choose a direction in which the shadow will fall, X and Y offset, Transparency, Glow, Soft edge and Color for the shadow.

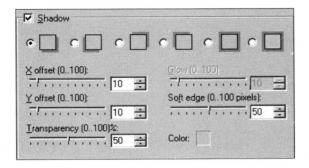

Warping Select or deselect Warping, which distorts the surface of the button. Edit Warping Smoothness or Level (strength).

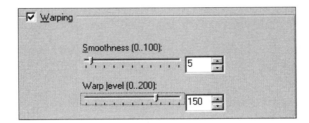

Click on Add to save a custom preset. Doing so opens the Add to EasyPalette dialog box. Name the custom button preset, and save it to a Tab group in the Button Gallery.

Button Designer (Rectangular)

The procedure for making a rectangular 3D button is the same, whether you create a new image or make a button from a selection area in a previously created image. The results of your choices will be reflected in the Preview window. You can also access the Button Designer from the EasyPalette's Button Gallery.

PhotoImpact 6 Wizardry

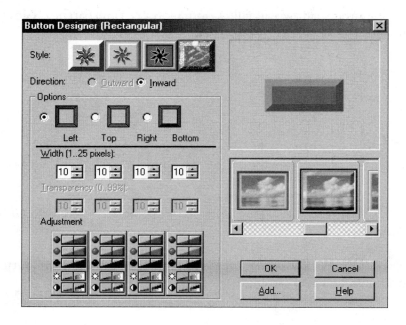

Style Pick a style from the choices available, or select a button thumbnail (scroll horizontally to view all of them) and its corresponding Style will be selected automatically.

Direction Outward expands the area used to make the button, while Inward limits the button to the original size of the image or selection area. Outward is grayed out for the Style on the far right.

Options Select size, color and other attributes for the button's borders.

> **Mirror** Equally adjusts the top and left edges, and the bottom and right edges simultaneously as bevel width is edited.
>
> **Mirror all** Equally adjusts the top, bottom, left and right edges simultaneously as bevel width is edited.
>
> **Individually** Adjust top, bottom, left and right edges individually. This option is only available for the Style on the far right, shown at top of next page.

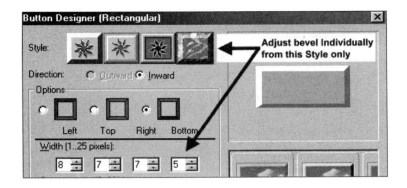

Width Choose a bevel width between 1-25 pixels for the top, bottom, left and right edges of the button.

Transparency Choose a value from 0-99% to adjust how much of the base image shows through the button border.

Colors Click in the color boxes to open the Ulead Color Picker to edit colors used on the button borders. Alternatively, right click in the color boxes to choose from a wider range of color options.

Add Click Add to save custom button settings. Doing so opens the Add to EasyPalette dialog box. Give the custom button setting a name and save it to a Gallery and Tab group.

Add HTML Text Object (Shift+T)

One of the new tools in PhotoImpact 6, Add HTML Text Object allows you to build web pages right in the work space. Have a web page size image open before invoking this command. The text that you add to the web page will be saved with all of the other objects in the file as an HTML page via File, Save for Web, As HTML.

Add HTML Text Object opens the HTML Text Entry Box so you can add text to the web page image. Note that you should *not* select the Text tool to add HTML Text to an image, and that the HTML text attributes can be formatted right from this dialog box.

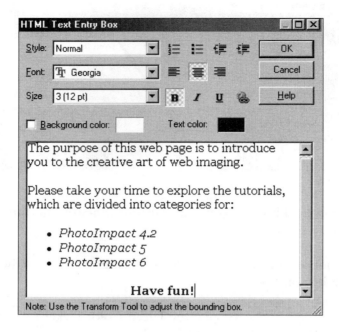

Style Select a formatting style from the dropdown list.

Font Choose a font from the dropdown list. If you know which font you wish to use, click the down arrow and type the first few letters of the font name. Doing so will help you find the desired font quicker.

Size Select a font size.

Numbers/Bullets/Indents Select text and click on the desired formatting option icon.

Alignment Select text and click on the desired alignment option icon.

Style Select text and click on the desired style format: Bold, Italic or Underline.

Hyperlink Select text and click the Hyperlink icon to open the Hyperlink dialog box. Enter the desired URL for the link and click OK.

Chapter 19: The Web Menu

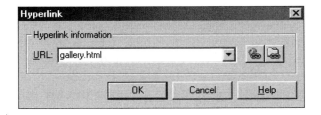

Background color Click in the Color box to select a background color for the text. The default background color is white. Changing the background color can call attention to text by placing it on a different color than the rest of the web page, or to help text stand out better against a busy background tile.

Text color Click in the color box to select text color. The default color is black.

When you click OK to close the HTML Text Entry Box, the text will be added to the image. It will be surrounded by a bounding box with control points and the Transform tool will be selected.

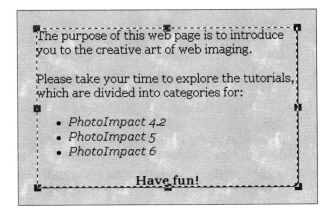

Drag on control points to resize the HTML text box, or drag the box itself to reposition it on the web page. To edit HTML text after adding it to the web page image, right click and choose Edit HTML Text to re-open the HTML Text Entry Box.

509

Grid & Partition

Grid & Partition is a great way to slice an image into separate objects based on a grid of rows and columns. Unlike the Image Slicer, which defaults to saving in a web file format (GIF, JPG or PNG) and Exports to an HTML table page, Grid & Partition allows you to save to any file format, including .UFO. Grid & Partition can only be used with True Color images. You may partition by rows and columns, but the cells in the grid cannot be custom edited.

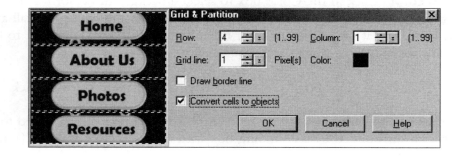

Rows Set a number of grid rows from 1-99.

Columns Set a number of grid columns from 1-99.

Grid Line Set the number of pixels for the grid line width, and click in the color box to pick a color for the line.

Draw Border Line Draws a visible border of the selected color around the edges of the cells. Deselect if you do not want a color border around the cells.

Convert Cells to Objects The grid creates separate objects, all of which are active and locked into position in the base image initially. Hit the space bar to deactivate the cells. Use the Pick or Standard Selection tool to click on a cell to make it active, then right click and choose Properties, or select Object, Properties, to open the Object Properties dialog box. Click on the Position & Size tab, deselect Lock and click OK.

Now you can drag the selected cell out of the base image into the work space, where it will open in its own window. To save as an image, right click and Merge. To save as an object, choose File, Save As and save as a .UFO object. Repeat this process for each cell.

Shift Image

Shift Image helps identify gaps that interfere with a seamless tile. This command moves the left and top edges of an image toward the middle of the image, and moves the middle to the left and top edges. Enter values for the Vertical and Horizontal offsets.

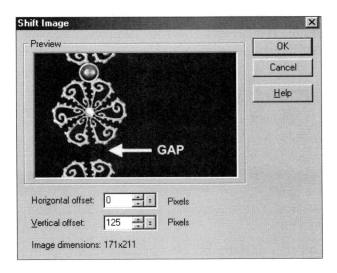

In the example shown above, the border background in the process of being created has a visible gap which will prevent it from tiling seamlessly on a web page. Possible solutions include clicking Cancel to make a different selection and then cropping again, or placing another jewel over the gap to hide it, as shown below.

Create Seamless Tile

This splendid feature lets you make a seamless background tile from a selection in a True Color image. Just make a square or rectangular selection over an interesting detail or array of colors. Try to make a clean selection, one that does not cut an attractive detail in half. Perhaps most important, do not make a selection too close to the edges of the image. The seamless tile maker "borrows" some of the image outside of the selection to get the best result. If it needs to borrow 20 pixels, and your selection area is 5 pixels from the edge of the image, you are unlikely to get a good seamless tile.

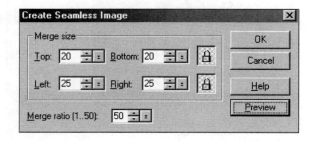

Merge Size PhotoImpact calculates the best overlap, or merge size, automatically. To enter your own values for the overlap on the top and bottom of the tile, or for the left and right overlap, click on the lock to deselect and enter the desired values.

Merge Ratio Also selected automatically, you may override the merge ratio, or level of edge blending, by entering the desired value. Higher levels blend edges more smoothly, but can also result in a blurry look if adjusted too high.

Tiled preview Click Tile preview to see the tile as it would look tiled across a web page. Hit Escape or the space bar to return to normal view.

If you are satisfied with the effect, click OK and the seamless tile will appear in the work space. If you are not satisfied with the default values calculated by PhotoImpact, deselect the locks and enter your own values. Alternatively, click Cancel. Right click and Undo to get rid of the selection area, make another selection, and try again.

HTML Properties (Shift+Enter)

Opens the HTML Properties dialog box, discussed in detail in the File Menu chapter's section on creating web pages in PhotoImpact 6. Edit HTML Properties from each of four tabs: General, Background, File Format and Options.

Image Map (Shift+H)

Image Map lets you create "hot spots" on a web page navigation image and save the code to an HTML page. The image map is saved to an images folder automatically.

First select an area for the hot spot on the image map. Use the Lasso or Standard Selection tool, with Mode set to New, to select an area, then right click on the selection and choose Convert to Object. Select the next hot spot area, then right click, Convert to Object. Continue until all hot spot areas have been selected and converted to objects. Alternatively, place objects for the hot spots onto the base image. Now choose Web, Image Map (or hit Shift+H) to open the Image Map dialog box.

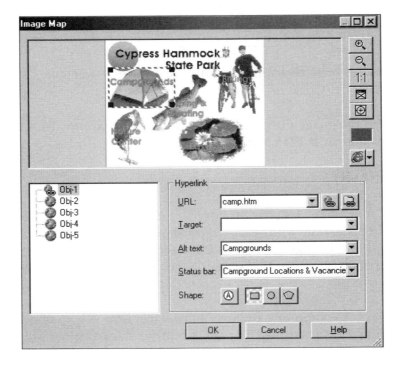

Zoom in Magnifies the image.

Zoom out Displays the image at a smaller size.

1:1 View at actual size.

Fit in window Displays image at the largest size that will still fit in the window.

Center in window Centers image in window.

Hyperlink color Click in the Color box to select a hyperlink color. The default is red.

Preview in Browser Select a browser from the dropdown list.

Object list Displays the objects in the image map. Objects are identified with a globe icon. When a URL has been assigned to the object, a link also appears next to the globe.

Hyperlink In the Preview window, click on each object for which you wish to create a hot spot. Enter a URL for the hot spot, by entering it directly into the box, selecting a URL from the dropdown list or by browsing to a Remote URL or Local URL. Also enter Alt Text, select a Target frame and add Status bar information, as desired.

Shape Defines the shape that will be sensitive to cursor movement. Choose from Auto detect, Rectangle, Circle or Polygon.

Click OK to finish the image map. To save it, choose File, Save for Web, As HTML. The image will be saved as an HTML web page.

Rollover (Shift+R)

Similar to the Component Designer, Rollover creates the javascript code for rollover buttons on a web page, only with Rollover you can use buttons that you have created yourself. New in PhotoImpact 6, you can make three state rollover buttons (Default, Mousedown and Mouseover) or two state rollover buttons (Default and Mouseover *or* Mousedown).

Walking through the creation of a Rollover button can help you to understand the process of making rollover buttons. The three buttons shown below will be used for the

Default, Mouseover and Mousedown button states. Note that the Default text and button background colors change on Mouseover, and that on Mousedown the Default button is highlighted with two "sparkle" stars.

Assigning Attributes to Rollover Buttons

Drag all three of the buttons onto the web page base image. Use the Pick or Standard Selection tool to click on a button, then hold down on the Shift key while clicking the other buttons so that all are selected at the same time. Choose Web, Rollover or hit Shift+R. When the Rollover dialog box opens, you will see the three buttons for the rollover effect. Most likely the buttons will not be assigned to the correct state.

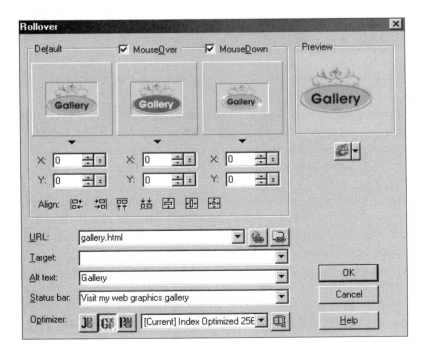

Default/Mouseover/Mousedown In the upper left part of the Rollover dialog box, assign buttons to each of the three states: Default (Normal), Mouseover and Mousedown. Click on the Default down arrow to view thumbnails of all three buttons. Select the button you want to use and its thumbnail will appear under Default. Repeat for Mouseover and Mousedown.

X and Y The X and Y coordinates for each button state can be edited. It you want to shift a button's position by a number of pixels on Mouseover or Mousedown, enter values in the X and Y boxes to shift the button along its horizontal or vertical plane.

Once the buttons have been assigned to the correct state, assign web attributes. Roll your mouse over the button in the Preview window to view the rollover effect right in the work space. Alternatively, click on the Preview in Browser button and preview the rollover in the selected browser.

URL Assign a URL to the button.

Target If you are using frames, select a target frame from the dropdown list.

Alt text Enter text to appear in case visitors to your page have images turned off in their browsers, or that will appear if the images are broken.

Status bar Enter text to appear in the browser's status bar, if desired.

Optimizer Choose whether to save the buttons as JPG, GIF or PNG files in the Image Optimizer. Choose a compression scheme from the dropdown list, or click Image Optimizer to tweak image save settings, then click OK to close the Image Optimizer dialog box. Click OK again to close the Rollover dialog box.

Do not be alarmed when you only see one button in the base image. The information for the other two states of the button are still there. To edit the Rollover, right click and choose Edit Rollover, hit Shift+E or choose Object, Edit Rollover. To restore the three buttons, right click and choose Split Rollover.

Add other Rollover buttons to the web page image in the work space in the same manner. Add HTML Text and other web images as desired, then choose File, Save for Web, As HTML. Doing so will open the Save As dialog box. Give the web page a name and it will be saved as an HTML web page document.

Remember that the Rollover buttons and any other images on the web page will be saved to an images folder. It is important to upload these images to an images folder on your server, or the rollovers will not work.

Slicer (Shift+S)

The Slicer cuts large images into multiple slices, then generates the HTML code to reassemble the slices in a table on a web page. Assign URL's to the slices, or save different slices in different file formats. You can save the slicing pattern as a .USS file, then use it again to slice a variation of the image for rollover effects.

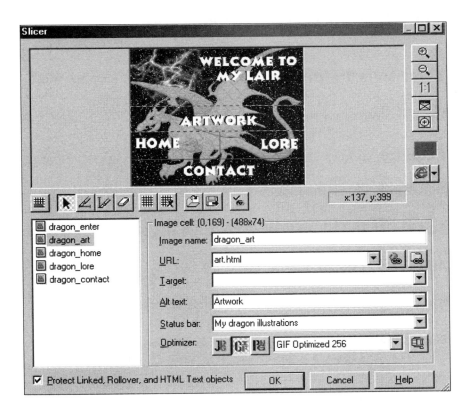

Display Buttons Click on the appropriate icon button to alter display.

⊕ **Zoom in** Magnifies the image.

⊖ **Zoom out** Displays the image at a smaller size.

1:1 View at actual size.

Fit in window Displays image at the largest size that fits in the window.

Center in window Centers image in window.

Slice line color Red by default, click in the color box to select a different color.

Preview in Browser Select a browser from the dropdown list.

Tool Buttons Click on a tool to perform a slicing action.

Autoslice Allows PhotoImpact 6 to automatically slice the image.

Pick mode Click the Pick to select a cell.

Add horizontal sliced line mode Click and drag to slice horizontally.

Add vertical sliced line mode Click and drag to slice vertically.

Erase sliced line mode Click on a sliced line to erase it.

Slice evenly Select to open the Slice Evenly box. Enter values for the number of rows (1-16) and columns (1-16) for the slicing pattern.

Erase all sliced lines Erases all sliced lines, so you can start over.

Import table data Opens the Import sliced table data box, from which you may open a previously saved slicing pattern.

Export table data Opens the Export sliced table data box so that you can save a custom slicing pattern. Slicing patterns are saved with the .USS file extension. If you want to do rollover effects, this is a great way to make sure that both images are sliced exactly the same way.

Optimization preview Preview compressed image as it will appear on a web page.

Image Cell Displays the position, size and properties of a selected cell.

Image Name Displays the name of the cell. The default name can be edited to something more meaningful.

URL Assign a URL to the selected cell from the Remote URL or Local URL button.

Target If you are using frames, assign a target frame to the link.

Alt text Enter text to be viewed in the event that visitors to your web page have images turned off in their browsers, or that will be seen if images fail to load.

Status bar Enter text to be viewed in the browser status bar.

Optimizer Select an image type (JPG, GIF, PNG) for the selected slice, and choose from presets in the dropdown list. Alternatively, click on the Image Optimizer button to open its dialog box to tweak save settings.

Protect Linked, Rollover and HTML Text Objects Selected by default, prevents you from inadvertently slicing a cell containing web attributes. For example, it would not be a good idea to slice a rollover button.

Helper Program (F10)

Specify the program in which you would like to open the active image.

Trim Object

Trims extra space around a selected object and automatically creates transparency around it.

Image Optimizer (F4)

The Image Optimizer is discussed in detail in its own chapter.

Chapter 20: The Image Optimizer

The Image Optimizer saves, compresses and optimizes the palettes of JPG, GIF and PNG image files. These features reduce file size and speed download for visitors to your web pages. In the Image Optimizer you can preview images against a selected background, batch test various levels of compression, compress to a specific file size, save your own optimization presets, resize and crop, and more.

Seasoned users will appreciate the newly streamlined dialog boxes in PhotoImpact 6, as well as the ability to edit color palettes directly from the Image Optimizer's Palette tab. Thanks to new options, creating transparency is an easier, more logical and intuitive process than ever before.

Choose Web, Image Optimizer (or F4) to access the Image Optimizer. Alternatively, you can right click on an active object and choose Image Optimizer. When the Image Optimizer command is invoked and unmerged objects are present in the base image, you will be prompted by an Image to Optimize dialog box.

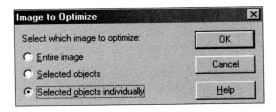

One of the nicest benefits of this dialog box is that choosing "Selected objects" or "Selected objects individually" creates transparent backgrounds for GIF images almost automatically.

Before saving an image in the Image Optimizer, you should choose an appropriate web image file format. Briefly, here are a few facts you should know about web image file types:

> **JPG** format is best for photographs or other images containing many colors. JPG is a so-called "lossy" file format because color information is lost when the image is saved. JPG images do not support true transparency.

GIF format is appropriate for web images like buttons or banners containing broad, flat areas of color or a limited number of colors. The GIF format reduces the number of colors used to 256. GIF images can be made transparent.

PNG is a newer "lossless" file type that supports true transparency, but file sizes can be significantly larger than for JPG images. PNG images can only be viewed in the latest browsers. Unless you are creating web pages for 4.0 or higher browsers only, it might be wiser to stick with GIF or JPG images.

Image Optimizer Similarities

The GIF, JPG and PNG Image Optimizer dialog boxes offer different options from associated tabs, but they all share four primary similarities: (1) They use the same tools for displaying and previewing effects of chosen settings; (2) All offer the ability to Batch test various numbers of colors in order to obtain the best trade-off between compression and quality; (3) They offer the options of saving Image Optimizer presets or deleting them; and (4) They all create transparency similarly from the Mask Options tab.

Similarity #1: Previewing effects of settings

Zoom In

Magnified preview of the image.

Zoom Out

The preview of the image is reduced in size.

Show actual size

Shows the image at its actual size

Fit in window

Useful for larger images, displays the entire image at a size that fits into the Preview frames.

⊕ Center in window

Centers the image in the Preview frames.

☐ Display compressed image

Toggles in and out of showing the compressed image in its preview frame.

Modem speed menu

Calculates approximate download time based on selected modem speed.

Browser preview

Displays the image and its information in the browser selected from the dropdown list.

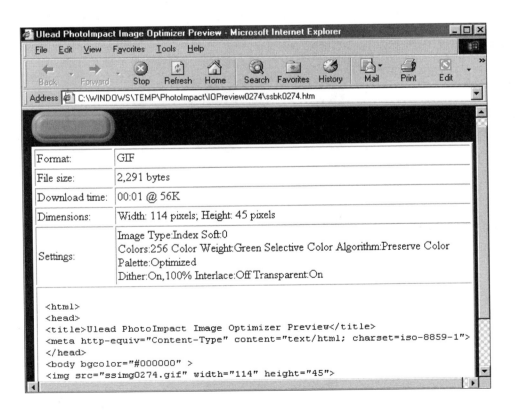

![icon] Resample

Opens the Image Optimizer Resample dialog box for resizing an image.

New Size Choose a new size Width and Height, in Pixels or Percent.

Keep aspect ratio Leave selected to constrain width to height proportion.

Method "Nearest Neighbor" results in the most compact file size, but yields a poorer quality image. "Bicubic" outputs the best quality and the largest file size.

Details Displays the Current and the New (resampled) Width and Height in pixels.

![icon] Crop

Opens the Image Optimizer Crop dialog box. Drag on selection handles to resize the crop box. Zoom in or out, view at actual size, or crop per a selected mask.

Similarity #2: Previewing effects of Batch testing

To test the effects of different numbers of colors on image quality, click Batch.

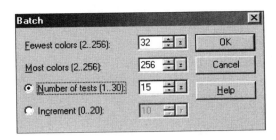

Specify the fewest and most colors, and number of tests/increments, and click OK.

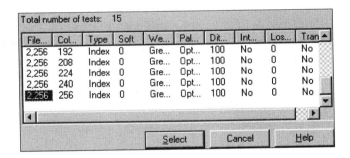

Select a number of colors from the Batch list. The Preview frame displays the effect of this number of colors on the image. This is a wonderful feature that saves you from disappointment after uploading images to your server. This way you will know exactly what the image will look like online at the chosen compression level.

Similarity #3: Saving and Deleting Presets

If you often save images with the same settings in the Image Optimizer, you can create presets to automate the Save process.

525

For example, if you often save PNG Optimized 256 Color images, instead of having to tweak the settings every time, you can save these settings in the Image Optimizer. You could even record a Task in the Quick Command Panel's Task Manager to automatically open the Image Optimizer to your PNG preset.

Add preset

Click to save the JPG/GIF/PNG preset.

Delete preset

Click to delete the selected JPG/GIF/PNG preset.

Similarity #4: Creating Transparency

Transparent images can be created in the Image Optimizer. True transparency can be created for GIF and PNG images only. You should know that because the JPG format does not support true transparency, the Image Optimizer can only mimic transparency in JPG images by applying a specific color or image to the area selected for transparency. The JPG image will not be transparent against any other color or background image. Solid colors or simple, densely grained background textures facilitate the most transparent appearance for "transparent" JPG images.

There are two ways to create transparent backgrounds for web images. Selecting objects in the base image and invoking the Web, Image Optimizer command, makes the process almost automatic. When there are no active objects in the base image, transparency can also be created manually from the Image Optimizer's Mask Options tab.

Automatic Transparency for Selected Object(s)

It is best to select objects such as buttons and other web images which you wish to make transparent, rather than merging them with the base image. If you wish to save more than one object, hold down on the Shift key while clicking on the other object(s) with the Pick or Standard Selection tool, until all desired objects are selected. Then choose Web, Image Optimizer or hit F4. Doing so displays the Image to Optimize dialog box.

Chapter 20: The Image Optimizer

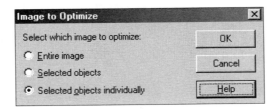

Entire Image Merges selected object(s) with the base image during the save.

Selected objects If multiple objects are selected, they will be merged together as a single object during the save.

Selected objects individually Available only if multiple objects are selected, this option lets you save the objects as separate images.

If you choose to save selected object(s) as one object or individually, transparency will be created automatically in the Image Optimizer. When the Image Optimizer dialog box opens, first choose whether to save as a JPG, GIF or PNG. For GIF or PNG images, select "Transparency" from the GIF Options tab or PNG Options tab (the Transparency option is unavailable for saving a "transparent" JPG). For a GIF or PNG image, choose "None" from the Mask Options tab's Matte dropdown list (for a JPG, select a color or image for the "transparent" background).

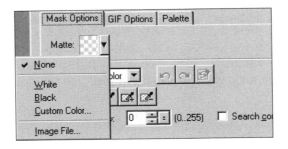

Click the Save As button and save. If you have chosen to save multiple objects individually, after the first object is saved you will be prompted with a Continue Optimizing dialog box.

527

PhotoImpact 6 Wizardry

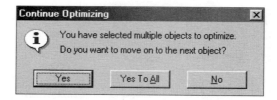

Select the appropriate option and click OK to continue saving other objects.

Creating Transparency Manually

If you elect to merge objects with the base image, you must create transparency manually in the Image Optimizer. Choose Web, Image Optimizer or hit F4. When the Image Optimizer dialog box opens, first choose whether to save as a JPG, GIF or PNG. Next, click on the Mask Options tab. Click the Matte down arrow and choose a web page color or background image.

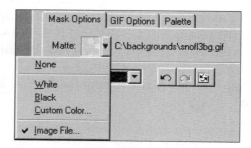

Click the Mask down arrow and select "Pick color" to select a color for transparency, or Import to import a grayscale mask. Either choice will display advanced transparency options. If "Pick color" is selected, the Mask Options tab will look like this.

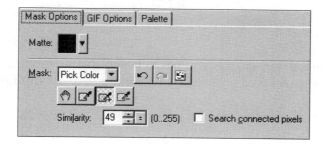

Pick color

1. Select Pick color to select a color for transparency.

2. Select the Eyedropper plus (+) sign "Add to Mask" button to make a color transparent or add to an already selected area. Select the Eyedropper minus (-) sign "Subtract from Mask" button to take away from an already selected area.

3. Select a color Similarity value (0-255), with higher values selecting a greater range of colors. Select "Search connected pixels" if desired.

4. Position the cursor over the uncompressed image in the left Preview frame. The cursor turns into an Eyedropper. Click the Eyedropper in the color you wish to make transparent. Doing so causes the uncompressed image in the left Preview frame to show the gray checkerboard pattern indicating a transparent background. The compressed image in the right Preview frame will show the background color or image chosen from the Matte dropdown list earlier. Click the Save As button to save.

Import Mask

1. Select Import mask to use a grayscale mask. This can help to avoid raggedy-looking edges on merged images.

2. Select "Import" from the Mask dropdown list. Doing so opens the Import Mask dialog box.

3. Click the Browse button to select and apply a grayscale mask to the image.

4. Click the Save As button to save.

Specifics of the JPG, GIF and PNG Image Optimizers

Finally, it is useful to go over, in detail, the specific options accessed from available tabs when saving JPG, GIF and PNG images in the Image Optimizer. You should be aware that the Image Optimizer defaults to the JPG file format. Be sure to select GIF or PNG instead if you do not want to save the image as a JPG.

JPG Image Optimizer

JPG Options Tab

Preset Select from available presets, which will vary by Mode selected. If you have added a custom preset, you may select it from the dropdown list.

Compress By Size... Opens the Compress by Size dialog. Select a compression option.

   Desired file size Enter a value in bytes or kilobytes.

   Compression ratio Select a level of compression.

Mode Select from Progressive (image gradually comes into focus, but some older browsers cannot view progressive images), Standard (larger file size but can be viewed in most browsers), or Standard Optimized (creates the smallest possible file size in non-Progressive mode).

Subsampling Choose YUV411 (smallest possible file size, good for flat images with little detail), YUV422 (good accuracy and compression), or None (generally results in larger file sizes).

Quality Lower compression values result in better quality images, while higher compression values adversely affect image quality. Use the slider or enter a compression value to negotiate a trade-off between image file size and quality. For most images, compression values of 60 to 90 will result in acceptable to high quality.

Soft The amount of blur applied to an image, with higher values creating a smoother look. Softness can offset some of the undesirable effects of dithering. However, higher values can result in excessive blurring.

File type Select True Color or Gray.

JPG Mask Options Tab

Refer to the section on Image Optimizer Similarities, Creating Transparency, at the beginning of this chapter for a detailed explanation of using Mask Options to create transparency.

Matte Select a color or image to fill the the transparent area. Choose from None, White, Black or Image file.

Mask Select "Pick color," or "Import" to import a mask. Adjacent buttons let you Undo, Redo or Reset your choices.

Hand Click the hand tool to drag the image in the Preview window. This is handy when you Zoom In and wish to view every part of the image.

Eyedropper tools Select the Eyedropper and click in the left preview Frame to select an initial color for transparency. Click the Eyedropper plus sign (+) button to add to the transparent area, or click the Eyedropper minus sign (-) button to subtract from the currently selected area for transparency.

Similarity Specify a range of similar colors for transparency. Select "Search connected pixels" to include only colors in the Similarity range that are directly adjacent to the area in which you click. When "Search connected pixels" is deselected, all pixels in the Similarity range within the image are made transparent.

GIF Image Optimizer

GIF Options Tab

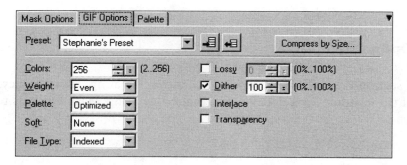

Preset Select from available presets: GIF Optimized 256, GIF Optimized 128, GIF Optimized 64, GIF Grayscale 256, GIF Grayscale 128, GIF Grayscale 64. If you have added a custom preset, you may select it from the dropdown list.

Compress By Size... Opens the Compress by Size dialog. Select a compression option.

Desired file size Enter a value in bytes or kilobytes.

Compression ratio Select a level of compression.

Colors The number of colors can range from 2 to 256. The number of colors reflects the selected preset, but you may edit the number of colors by pressing and holding down on the down arrow to display a slider. Alternatively, enter a number directly into the Colors box.

Weight Select which color to emphasize: Even, Red, Green or Blue. Most of the time you will want to leave the Weight set to Even.

Palette Select from Optimized, Detail, Browser safe or User defined. If you wish to use a previously saved palette, choose User defined. Doing so opens the Load Color Table dialog box, from which you may select a palette to open and apply to the current image.

Soft The amount of blur applied to an image. Higher values create a smoother look and offset some of the effects of dithering, but can result in excessive blurring.

File type Select Indexed or Gray.

Lossy Removes color pixels based on the selected value. Higher values remove more color pixels and reduce file size. However, too high a value can reduce image quality, so try to strike a balance between file size and image quality.

Dither When the number of colors is reduced, subtlety in color changes can be lost, resulting in obvious color banding. When selected, Dither mixes existing colors in patterns in an effort to mimic missing colors. The higher the value, the more dithering in the image.

Interlaced Gradually loads an image online.

Transparency Select to add transparency to the image.

GIF Mask Options Tab

Refer to the section on Image Optimizer Similarities, Creating Transparency, at the beginning of this chapter for a detailed explanation of using Mask Options to create transparency.

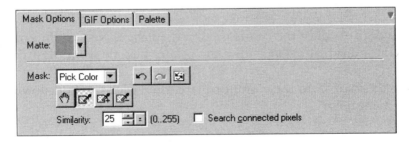

Matte Select a color or image to fill the the transparent area. Choose from None, White, Black or Image file.

Mask Select "Pick color," or "Import" to import a mask. Adjacent buttons let you Undo, Redo or Reset your choices.

533

Hand tool Click the hand tool to drag the image in the Preview window. This is handy when you Zoom In and wish to view every part of the image.

Eyedropper tools Select the Eyedropper and click in the left preview Frame to select an initial color for transparency. Click the Eyedropper plus sign (+) button to add to the transparent area, or click the Eyedropper minus sign (-) button to subtract from the currently selected area for transparency.

Similarity Specify a range of similar colors for transparency. Select "Search connected pixels" to include only colors in the Similarity range that are directly adjacent to the area in which you click. When "Search connected pixels" is deselected, all pixels in the Similarity range within the image are made transparent.

GIF Palette Tab

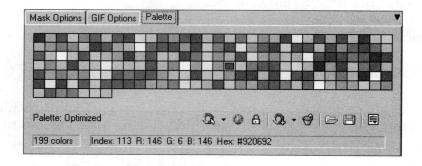

The Palette tab displays all of the colors used in the image. New to PhotoImpact 6 is the ability to edit individual colors within the palette directly from the Palette tab.

Edit First select a color from the current palette, then click the Edit down arrow to select a replacement color.

Web snap Converts the selected color to the nearest web-safe color.

Lock The selected color is locked and remains unaffected by edits to the color palette.

New Click the down arrow to add a new color to the color palette.

Delete Removes the selected color from the color palette.

Load palette Opens the Load Color Table dialog box, from which you may import a previously saved color palette.

Save palette Saves the current palette file as a .PAL file for future use.

PNG Image Optimizer

PNG Options Tab

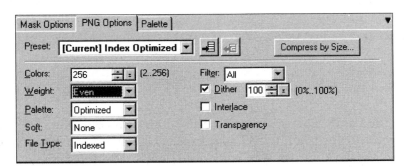

Preset Select from available presets: PNG True Color, PNG Optimized 256, PNG Optimized 128, PNG Optimized 64, PNG Grayscale 256, PNG Grayscale 128 and PNG Grayscale 64. If you have added a custom preset, you may select it from the dropdown list.

Compress By Size... Opens the Compress by Size dialog. Select a compression option.

> **Desired file size** Enter a value in bytes or kilobytes.
>
> **Compression ratio** Select a level of compression.

Colors The number of colors can range from 2 to 256. The number of colors reflects the selected preset, but you may edit the number of colors by pressing and holding down on the down arrow to display a slider. Alternatively, enter a number directly into the Colors box. Colors is grayed out when PNG True Color is selected.

Weight Select which color to emphasize: Even, Red, Green or Blue. Most of the time you will want to leave the Weight set to Even. Weight is grayed out when PNG True

Color is selected.

Palette Select from Optimized, Detail, Browser safe or User defined. If you wish to use a previously saved palette, choose User defined. Doing so opens the Load Color Table dialog box, from which you may select a palette to open and apply to the current image. Palette is grayed out when PNG True Color is selected.

Soft The amount of blur applied to an image. Higher values create a smoother look and offset some of the effects of dithering, but can result in excessive blurring.

File type Select Indexed or Gray.

Filter Built-in algorithyms create filters to help reduce file size. If file size is an issue, select a filter from the dropdown list.

Dither When the number of colors is reduced, subtlety in color changes can be lost, resulting in obvious color banding. When selected, Dither mixes existing colors in patterns in an effort to mimic missing colors. The higher the value, the more dithering in the image.

Interlaced Gradually loads an image online.

Transparency Select to add transparency to the image.

PNG Mask Options Tab

Refer to the section on Image Optimizer Similarities, Creating Transparency, at the beginning of this chapter for a detailed explanation of using Mask Options to create transparency.

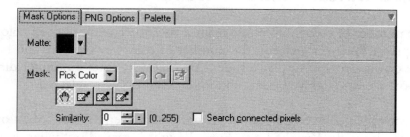

Matte Select a color or image to fill the the transparent area. Choose from None, White, Black or Image file.

Mask Select "Pick color," or "Import" to import a mask. Adjacent buttons let you Undo, Redo or Reset your choices.

Hand tool Click the hand tool to drag the image in the Preview window. This is handy when you Zoom In and wish to view every part of the image.

Eyedropper tools Select the Eyedropper and click in the left preview Frame to select an initial color for transparency. Click the Eyedropper plus sign (+) button to add to the transparent area, or click the Eyedropper minus sign (-) button to subtract from the currently selected area for transparency.

Similarity Specify a range of similar colors for transparency. Select "Search connected pixels" to include only colors in the Similarity range that are directly adjacent to the area in which you click. When "Search connected pixels" is deselected, all pixels in the Similarity range within the image are made transparent.

PNG Palette Tab

The Palette tab displays all of the colors used in the image. PhotoImpact 6 offers a new feature, the ability to edit individual colors within the palette directly from the Palette tab. Palette tab options are available only for PNG Indexed color images.

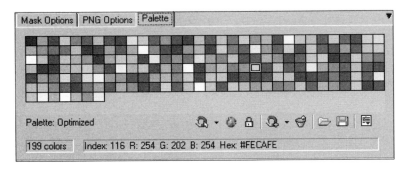

Edit First select a color from the current palette, then click the Edit down arrow to select a replacement color.

Web snap Converts the selected color to the nearest web-safe color.

Lock The selected color is locked and remains unaffected by edits to the color palette.

New Click the down arrow to add a new color to the color palette.

Delete Removes the selected color from the color palette.

Load palette Opens the Load Color Table dialog box, from which you may import a previously saved palette.

Save palette Saves the current palette file as a .PAL file for future use.

Web Magic: Active Learning Exercises

Making and Editing Buttons in the Component Designer

1. Choose Web, Component Designer (or hit F12) to access the Component Designer dialog box. Select Button Bar, Rounded_1. Click on the button bar second from the left in the top row (arrow), then click the Next button.

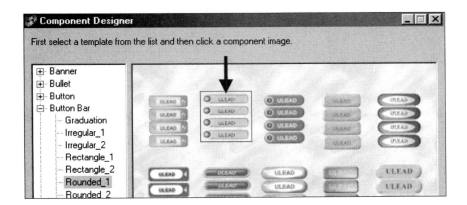

2. Click Next to begin editing the buttons.

3. The Options tab is selected by default. There are 4 lines of default Ulead text for the buttons, with the first one selected (highlighted) in the box above it.

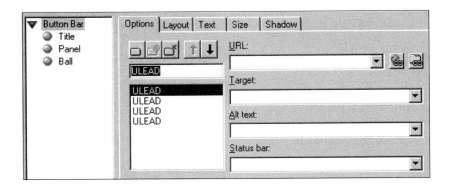

4. Type in HOME to replace the default text and hit Enter. Doing so will edit the first button's text label. You will see the change in the Preview window.

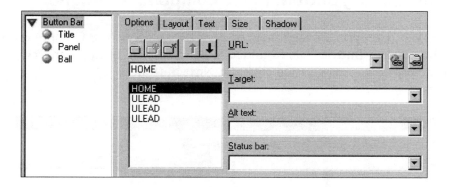

5. Select (highlight) the second line of default text. Type in REVIEWS and hit Enter. Note that the second button's text has been changed.

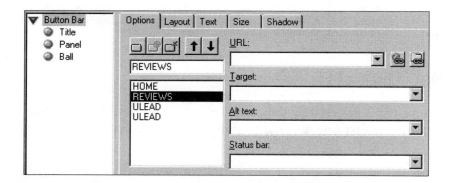

6. Continue selecting default text and replacing it for the last two buttons, replacing default text with PHOTOS and LINKS.

7. Now that you have replaced the text on all four buttons, it is time to add Web Attributes for each button. Select the HOME button and enter a URL (index.html), Alt text (Home) and Status Bar text (Norma's Skating Page Home).

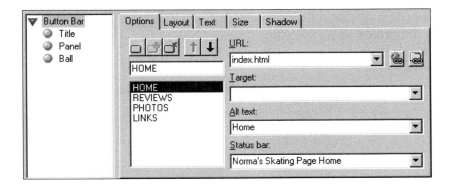

8. Select the Reviews button and enter a URL (reviews.html), Alt text (Reviews) and Status Bar text (Norma's Skating Reviews).

9. Select the Photos button and enter a URL (photos.html), Alt text (Photos) and Status Bar text (Ice Show Photos).

10. Select the Links button and enter a URL (links.html), Alt text (Links) and Status bar text (Norma's Favorite Links). Now you are finished with the Options tab.

11. Click the Layout tab. To edit the layout, select Horizontal bar and the buttons will be realigned in the Preview window.

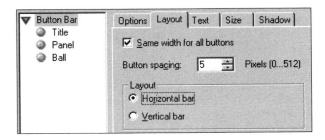

12. Click the Text tab. Select a different font from the Font dropdown list. It does not matter which font you select, just select one you like.

13. Click the Size tab. Leave the defaults as they are, but note that you can edit the buttons' attributes from this tab as well.

541

14. Click the Shadow tab and select Shadow to add one to each button. The default shadow is a bit large for the small button. Edit the attributes of the shadow as shown in the screen shot below.

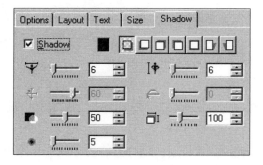

15. In the left panel, click Title. To edit the default black text, position your cursor over the palette, where it will turn into an Eyedropper. Click the navy blue color box to change text color.

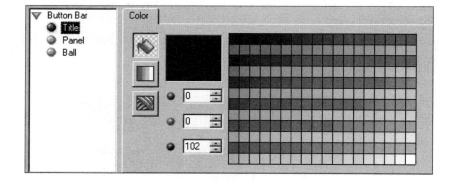

16. Click Panel and note that the button panel color could be edited from here. For this exercise, leave the default blue color.

17. Click Ball. To edit the ball color to a soft shade of green, enter 0, 153, 102 for the RGB values.

18. Click Export and choose As Component Object (in PhotoImpact). The buttons will

appear in their own window in the work space. Close the Component Designer (it will be in your task bar).

19. When you make a component in the Component Designer, you can continue to edit it. Right click on the button bar and choose Edit Component. Doing so opens the Component Designer again.

20. In the left pane, select Panel. Click the Navy color box (RGB=0, 0, 102). You will notice that even though the navy blue is quite dark, the button panel does not darken very much. Because this is a 3D object with bright light focused on it, the effect of the dark color is minimal, compared to the effect it would have on a flat, 2D object.

21. Click OK to apply the edits and close the Component Designer. You will see the button panel color has been changed.

22. Click on any button in the button bar with the Pick tool. Even though you only clicked one button, all four buttons are selected. As they are now, it is not possible to edit the individual objects making up the button bar without using the Component Designer.

23. Right click on the button bar and choose Web Attributes, Split Component. Click the space bar to deactivate all objects. Now click on the blue panel for any button and observe that only that single object is active. Click on text label, the ball accent, and so on.

24. Instead of being a grouped unit of objects, they are now individual objects. Select a button panel. Select the Path Drawing tool and look in the Attributes toolbar. Navy blue appears in the Color box, reflecting the panel's current color. Click in the Color box and choose another color.

25. Once the Component Designer status has been removed by separating them into individual objects, the buttons can no longer be edited in the Component Designer. Right click and choose Properties for any object. When the Object Properties box opens, note that the Web Attributes specified in the Component Designer do not show up in the Hyperlink tab.

26. You must select and merge together the parts of each button, then assign Web Attributes to each button manually.

27. To put a button back together, select the Pick tool. Click on a button panel, then Shift+Click the ball, text and shadow objects so that all four objects making up the button are selected at the same time. Right click and Merge as Single Object.

28. Right click and choose Properties to open the Object Properties dialog box. Click the Hyperlink tab and enter the desired URL, Alt text and Status Bar text. Repeat this process for each button, selecting and merging the objects for each button, then editing the Web Attributes from the Object Properties box.

Making and Editing a Tile With the Background Designer

1. Choose Web, Background Designer (or hit Shift+B). When the Background Designer opens, make sure "Generate a new tile" is selected. Leave the Cell size at the default of 80 X 80 pixels. From the Schema dropdown list, choose Texture 19. From the thumbnails underneath the selected Texture, select the second one from the right (arrow), which is a pastel, multicolored plaid. Note that Background type 12 is the default.

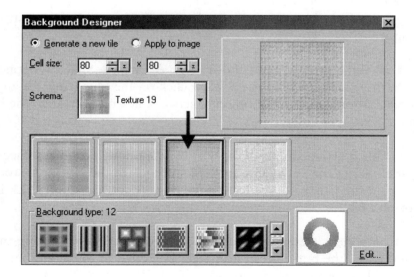

2. The purpose of this exercise is to edit the attributes of this tile. Accordingly, click the Edit button to open the Palette Ramp Editor. Scroll through the palettes and select Palette 38, which contains soft shades of green. Click OK to close the box.

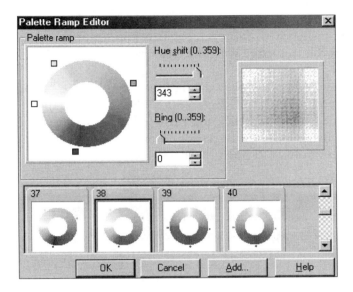

3. To make the tile more dense, edit the Density value to 5. To increase the contrast between the colors, edit the Amplitude value to 50. To darken the tile slightly, edit the Darken or lighten value to -25. Click OK to close the dialog box.

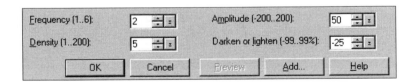

4. A new 80 X 80 pixel tile will open in the work space. To see how it would look tiled in a browser window, choose File, Preview in Browser, As Tiled Background. Close the browser window when you are finished looking at the tile.

Making a Rollover Button

1. The purpose of the next, rather lengthy exercise is to make a web page with rollover buttons for a fictitious book store, The Old Book Shoppe. The entire web page will be built in the PhotoImpact 6 work space. You may wish to save the web page periodically as a .UFO file, in case you have to stop working on it for some reason before you are finished with this exercise. It is important that you do not Merge any of the objects in the web page with the base image.

2. Choose File, New. When the New dialog box opens, in the "Image size" section select Standard and choose Web Page 750 X 550 Pixels. In the "Canvas" section choose Web Background and click the Browse button to open the HTML Properties dialog box. By default, the Background tab will be selected. Select Texture and click the Designer button to open the Background Designer.

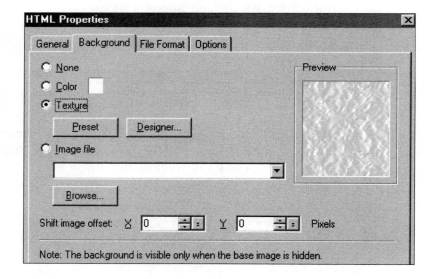

3. When the Background Designer opens, select Texture 4 from the Schema dropdown list. Then click the second thumbnail from the left. Click OK.

Web Magic: Active Learning Exercises

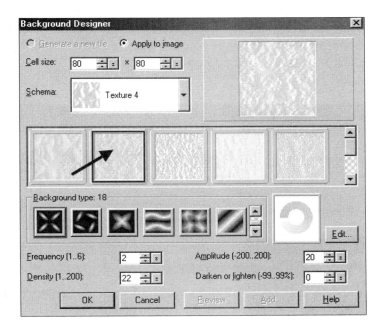

4. To assign Web attributes to the web page, click the General tab. Enter desired information into the appropriate boxes. Leave the default "Image file location" as "images." PhotoImpact 6 will automatically create an images folder for images.

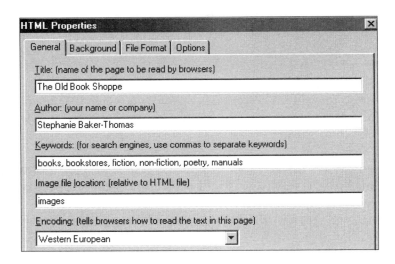

5. Click the File Format tab next. From here, indicate in which web image file format you wish to save the images on the web page. You do not have to accept the defaults. The default for the web page background is 90% Quality JPG Progressive. Select another compression scheme if you like from the dropdown list. Select the GIF Optimized 256 for the other two options.

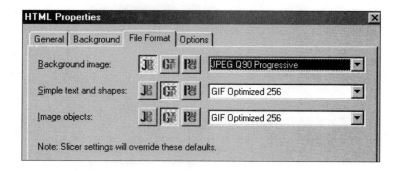

6. Click the Options tab last. Leave all of the defaults selected, unless you are experienced with HTML and you have a specific reason to deselect them.

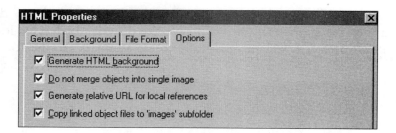

7. Click OK to close the HTML Properties dialog box. Click OK again to close the New box. The new web page image will open in the work space. It will be filled with the selected off white texture.

8. From the EasyPalette's Image Library, Stationery, use the Pick tool to drag from the Books thumbnail to the web page. Right click and choose Properties. When the Object Properties dialog box opens, click the Position and Size tab. In the Size section, choose Percent from the Unit dropdown list and resize to 75%. Make sure "Keep aspect ratio" is selected.

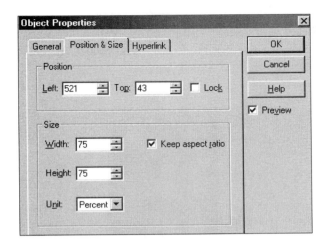

9. Position the book object on the top right of the page to serve as a logo. Select the Text tool. In the Attributes toolbar, select the Arial font, Size=34. Select 3D Round from the Mode dropdown list. Color does not matter. Click in the base image to open the Text Entry Box. Choose the Centered text option and Bold type. Type "The Old" and hit Ctrl+Enter for a new line, then type "Book Shoppe." Click OK.

10. Drag the text onto the book object, centering it on the lower half of the books. While the text is active, from the EasyPalette's Material Gallery, 3D Collection, double click on Bevel 2. The text will take on a yellow to orange radial gradient fill that contrasts nicely with the books. Right click, Select All Objects, then right click, Merge As Single Object.

11. Next, add some Rollover buttons. Choose Web, Component Designer. Select Rollover Button, Side Text 1. Select the first button at left on the top row. It looks like a book opening (arrow).

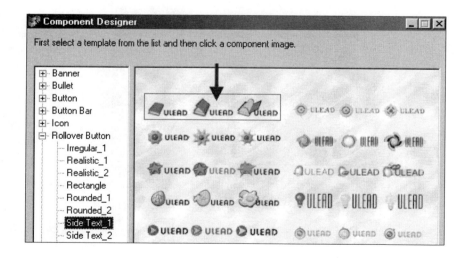

12. Click Next. Note that the Default or Normal state is a closed book, the MouseOver

button shows the book opening slightly with a yellow highlight around it, and the MouseDown button shows the book wide open. Click the Preview tab. Roll your mouse over the button and click on the button to view how it will look on a web page.

13. Click the Hyperlink tab to create the first button, which will be the Home button. Enter index.htm for the URL, Alt text=Home and Status bar=The Old Book Shoppe Home Page.

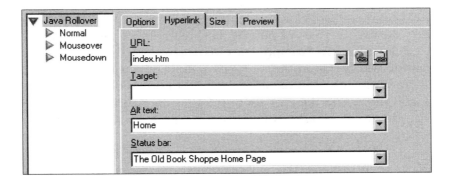

14. In the left pane click Normal, Title to begin work on the Home button. Highlight the default ULEAD text, replace it with HOME and hit Enter. If you want to select another font, select one from the dropdown list.

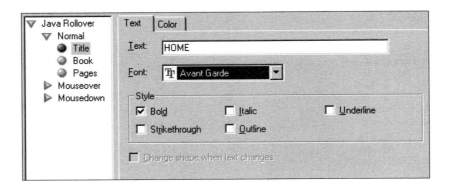

15. Note that under Title there are two other categories, Book and Pages, from which book and pages color may be edited. For this exercise, however, disregard these options and go with the defaults, which harmonize well with the books logo created previously.

16. Click MouseOver, Title. If you changed the font in the Normal state button, change it here as well by selecting the font from the dropdown list.

17. Click MouseDown, Title. If you changed the font in the Normal state button, select the same font from the dropdown list.

18. Here comes the exciting part of putting all three buttons together to make the Rollover. Click Export, As Component Object (In PhotoImpact). In a second or two the button will appear in the work space in its own window. Do not be alarmed because there is only one button showing. The information for the other two buttons is still there. Use the Pick tool to drag it onto the left side of the web page. You will be adding other buttons underneath it to make a vertical column of rollover buttons.

19. If you look at your Task bar, you will see that the Component Designer has been minimized and is still open. This is good! Do not close the Component Designer because you are going to make more buttons using the same basic attributes. Click on the Component Designer icon in the Task bar to open it again.

20. In the left pane, click Java Rollover. Click the Hyperlink tab and enter the following information for the Fiction button: URL=fiction.htm, Alt text=Fiction and Status bar=The Old Book Shoppe's Fiction Selections.

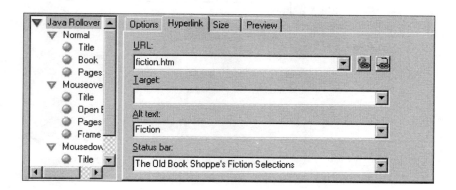

21. Click Normal, Title. Highlight HOME to select it, type FICTION and hit Enter. Since the other attributes for the button were already specified when you made the HOME button, they will "stick." Click Export, As Component Object (In PhotoImpact).

22. Once again, the button opens in the work space in its own window. Drag the Fiction button onto the web page, positioning it just below the HOME button.

23. Click the Component Designer in the Task bar to re-open it. In the left pane click Java Rollover and enter the following information for the Non-Fiction button: URL=nfiction.htm, Alt text=Non-Fiction and Status Bar=The Old Book Shoppe's Non-Fiction Selections.

24. Click Normal, Title. Highlight FICTION to select it, type NON-FICTION and hit Enter. Click Export, As Component Object (in PhotoImpact). Drag the Non-Fiction button under the Fiction button.

25. Click the Component Designer in the Task bar to re-open it. In the left pane click Java Rollover and enter the following information for the What's New button: URL=new.htm, Alt text=What's New and Status Bar=What's New at The Old Book Shoppe.

26. Click Normal, Title. Highlight NON-FICTION to select it, type WHAT'S NEW and hit Enter. Click Export, As Component Object (in PhotoImpact). Drag the What's New button under the Non-Fiction button.

27. Click the Component Designer in the Task bar to re-open it. In the left pane click Java Rollover and enter the following information for the Catalog button: URL=catalog.htm, Alt text=Catalog and Status Bar=Sign Up for The Old Book Shoppe's Print Catalog.

28. Click Normal, Title. Highlight WHAT'S NEW to select it, type CATALOG and hit Enter. Click Export, As Component Object (in PhotoImpact). Drag the Catalog button under the What's New button.

29. Close the Component Designer by clicking it in the Task bar to open it, then click Close.

30. Now there are five rollover buttons in a vertical line on the left side of the web page.

31. With the Pick tool click the top button, then Shift+Click the other four buttons, so all five are selected at the same time. Right click and choose Align, Left. This will line all of the buttons up so that their left edges are in a perfectly straight line.

32. While all five buttons are still selected, right click, Align, Space Evenly. Doing so opens the Space Evenly dialog box. Space the buttons Vertically, Fixed, by 15 pixels. Click OK to close the dialog box.

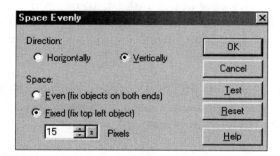

33. While all five buttons are still selected, drag to position them so that their left edges are about ½ inch from the left edge of the web page, and the top button is about even with the text on the book logo.

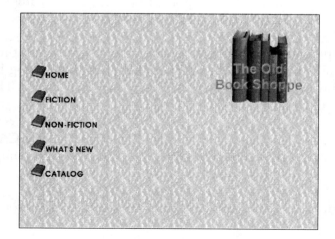

34. Now that the header graphic and rollover buttons have been made, you will add some HTML text to your web page. Note that HTML text is *not* the same as adding text objects with the text tool. Adding HTML text is a completely different process.

35. Choose Web, HTML Text Object to open the HTML Text Entry Box. Choose the following HTML Text attributes: Style-Normal, Size=12 pt, Left justified text, Font color=black. Do not select a Background color.

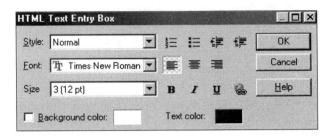

36. Position your cursor in the text box and type the following text. To start a new paragraph, or make a line break, hit Enter. Note that some of the text is left justified and some of it is centered. Choose the appropriate formatting option as you type:

> Welcome to The Old Book Shoppe's web store! We strive to bring you the best of publishing today, and have divided our store into the following sections for your shopping pleasure:
>
> **Fiction**
> **Non-Fiction**
> **What's New**
> **Catalog**
>
> If you cannot find the book you're looking for, please email us. We specialize in tracking down rare and out-of-print books.
>
> Copyright 2001 The Old Book Shoppe. All Rights Reserved.

37. After typing in the HTML text, select the centered list of Fiction, Non-Fiction, What's New and Catalog, then click the bullet formatting option. The extra lines in

between the categories will disappear and a bullet will appear in front of each one.

38. Select the "email us" text and click the Hyperlink button. When the Hyperlink dialog box opens, enter mailto:contact@oldbookshoppe.com. This code creates a hyperlink to open an email message form so that clients can email you with requests for books.

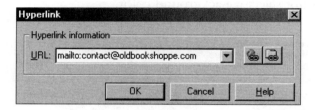

39. Click OK to close the HTML Text Entry Box. The text will appear within a resizeable bounding box on the web page. Drag it so that it does not overlap with any buttons or with the book logo at the top of the page. Drag the control handles to reshape the box so that it is wider and less tall. Make sure all of the text fits on the page and that there is still a little room left at the bottom of the page.

40. Now everything that you need for the web page has been created. However, the white background seems a bit stark and out of character with the warm reds and browns used in the images.

41. To change the background slightly, choose Web, HTML Properties. Doing so opens the HTML Properties dialog box. Click the Background tab and click Designer to open the Background Designer. The Texture 4 Schema will still be selected. From the color thumbnails under the Schema, scroll down to the second row of thumbnails. Select the tan texture that is second from the right. To lighten the tile slightly, edit the Darken or Lighten value to 65.

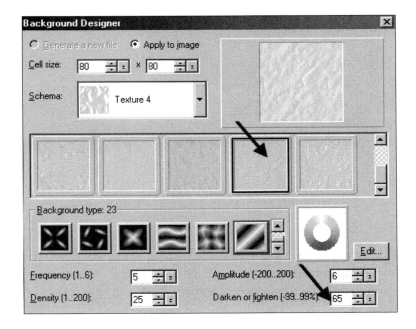

42. Click OK to close the Background Designer, then click OK again to close the HTML Properties dialog box. Now the web page background is a warm, creamy tan color that goes well with the navigation elements.

43. To save the web page, remember that saving an HTML document in PhotoImpact 6 is a completely different process than saving an image. Whatever you do, do *not* Merge the objects on the page with the base image. They must all remain independent objects. Choose File, Save For Web, As HTML (or just hit Ctrl+Alt+S).

44. When the Save As dialog box opens, give the web page a name (e.g., bookshop) and browse to the folder to which you wish to save the web page. It will be saved with the .htm file extension indicating that it is a web page document. Click Save.

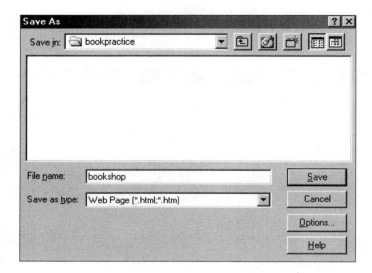

45. PhotoImpact 6 will whirl for a few seconds while it saves the page. If you have overlapped any images or elements on the page, you will get an error message. To correct, reposition any overlapping elements and try the Save again until it goes without a hitch.

46. All of the images on the web page will be saved to an images subfolder, which is created for them automatically. If you go into Windows Explorer and look at the contents of the images folder, you will see that the buttons have been named, sequentially, for the web page, with Normal, MouseOver and MouseDown versions of each button. Note that there is an image called "space." It is very important that you upload this clear spacer GIF to your server when you upload the rest of the images, as it is used to align the elements on the web page.

47. Choose File, Preview in Browser, and select a browser. Now you can see how the web page will look uploaded to your server. Click the email link to make sure that a new email message form opens. Close the browser when you are done admiring your work.

Making a Rollover Button

1. Ordinarily, if you were building a web page with rollover buttons, you would start with a web page size (e.g., 800 X 600 pixels) new image and add several buttons, a banner, an HTML text object, etc. However, for the purposes of this exercise, you will make only one rollover button in a very small file. Hit Ctrl+N to access the New dialog box. Make a new file 300 X 300 pixels with a white canvas.

2. The purpose of this exercise is to make three buttons and turn them into one rollover button by using the Rollover command. You will make an aqua button for the Default or normal state, a green button for the MouseOver state and a purple button for the MouseDown state.

3. Select the Path Drawing tool. In the Attributes toolbar click Shape and select the rounded rectangle. Click in the Color box and select aqua. Select 3D Round from the Mode dropdown list. Draw a rounded rectangle the size of a web button.

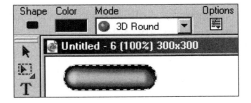

4. Select the Text tool. Use any font, font size and color you wish. Arial, Size=20, black is a good choice for this exercise. Click in the image to open the Text Entry Box, type HOME and click OK to close the box. Center the text on the button.

5. With the Pick tool, right click and Select All Objects. Right click and Group.

6. Right click and Duplicate twice, so you have three blue buttons and text in the image. Position them in a vertical stack, one beneath the other.

7. Right click on the first button and Merge as Single Object.

8. Right click on the second button and Ungroup, to separate the button and text. Repeat for the third button.

9. Select the Path Drawing tool. Click on the second button to make it active. In the Attributes toolbar, click in the Color box and select bright green to edit button color.

10. Click on the third button to make it active. In the Attributes toolbar, click in the Color box and select purple to edit its color. The three buttons are different colors.

11. Select the Pick tool. Click the text on the second button, being careful not to move it. Shift+Click the underlying button so that both the text and the green button are selected. Right click, Merge as Single Object. Repeat for the third button, selecting text and the purple button, then merging them as a single object.

12. Right click and Select All Objects. You should see an animated broken line around all three buttons indicating that they are all selected at the same time.

13. Choose Web, Rollover to open the Rollover box. To assign the aqua button to the Default state, click the down arrow and select the thumbnail for the aqua button.

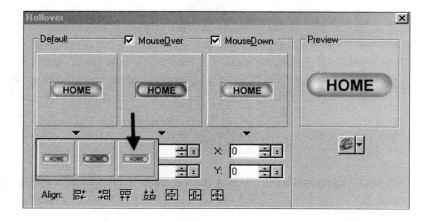

14. Click the down arrow under MouseOver and select the green button. Click the down arrow under MouseDown and select the purple button.

15. Move your cursor into the Preview window in the upper right corner. When you move over the button, the MouseOver green button will show. When you click on the button in the Preview window, the purple MouseDown button will show. If you want to, click on "Preview in browser" to view the rollover in your default browser.

16. Next, assign Web Attributes to the button in the lower half of the dialog box. Enter a URL, Target frame if desired, Alt text and Status Bar message. Choose GIF for saving the button.

17. Click the Image Optimizer button to open the Image Optimizer. Click "Show actual size" (the 1:1 button) to see how the image looks in the right preview window. If it does not look good, consider clicking Cancel to close the box and selecting a different file format for the save. If it looks good in the Preview window at actual size, click OK and you will be returned to the Rollover dialog box.

18. Click OK again to close the Rollover box. Now the only button you will see is the Default aqua button. Do not be alarmed, all three buttons with their Web Attributes are still there.

19. Choose File, Save for Web, As HTML. When the Save As dialog box opens, browse to the folder to which you wish to save the page. Note that this document will be saved as a web page, not as an image file. Give the HTML document a name (e.g., button.htm) and click Save.

20. To view the rollover button, open your default browser and browse to the button.htm file, select it and click Open. The rollover button will appear in your browser.

21. To view your rollover on your web page, you must upload the button.htm file as well as all three rollover buttons (normal, mousedown and mouseover) to your server. The images must be uploaded to an images folder, reflecting the way in which PhotoImpact 6 saves them to an images subfolder.

Making a "Jewel" With Button Designer, Any Shape

1. Choose File, New and make a new True Color image 150 X 150 pixels, canvas=white.

2. Select the Path Drawing tool. In the Attributes toolbar, click Shape and select Circle. From the Mode dropdown list, choose 3D Round. Click in the Color box and select a medium green, RGB=0, 153, 102. Draw a round object about 1 inch in diameter.

3. Choose Web, Button Designer, Any Shape. When the Button Designer (Any Shape) dialog box opens, the default button type is selected. Look at the thumbnails at the bottom of the dialog box. These are preset button settings which can add color, shine and sparkle to any object or selection. Scroll down to the sixth row of thumbnails and select the second thumbnail from the right. It is a bright blue color.

4. Once the thumbnail has been selected, you will see its effect on the round object in the Preview window. This preset turns the green object to a shiny blue. To further

edit its attributes, click the Bevel tab. The default bevel, which yields a distinct bevel, will be selected. To edit the bevel, scroll up to the first row of thumbnails and select the one that is the second from the left. In the Preview window, you will see that the object is now fully rounded.

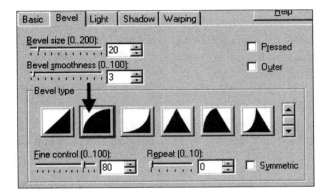

5. Click the Light tab. You will see that there are two lights for this preset. The default for the first light is a bright purple. Click in the Light color box and select the dark green (RGB=0, 136, 0) from the standard colors.

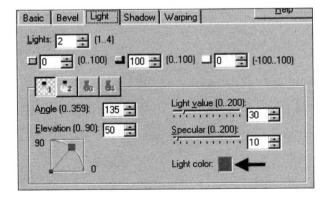

6. Click on Light 2 to select it, then click in the Color box. Select the same dark green used for Light 1. Click OK to close the dialog box.

PhotoImpact 6 Wizardry

7. Your green 3D Round object has turned into a sparkling green, glassy jewel.

Slicing a Large Image

1. From the EasyPalette's Image Library, Nature, drag the Sunflower thumbnail into the work space, where it will open in its own window. Right click, Merge All.

2. The purpose of this exercise is to slice this image so that it can be reassembled in a table on a web page as a navigation graphic. The image will be sliced into 6 pieces, 2 columns across and 3 rows down.

3. Select the Text tool. In the Attributes toolbar, select Arial or a similar font, Size=34. Click in the image to open the Text Entry box. Type "The" (Ctrl+Enter) "Garden Center" for the text. Select the text and center it. Click in the Color box and select Color On Screen. Click on a bright yellow petal to select that color. Click OK. Center the text in the middle of the flower.

4. While the Text tool is still selected, edit the font size to 20. Click in the Color box and select black. Click in the base image to open the Text Entry Box. Type "Vegetables" and click OK to close the box. Repeat these steps to add "Flowers," "Herbs," "Trees," "Tools" and "Books," as shown below. Right click, Merge All.

5. Choose Web, Slicer. When the Slicer dialog box opens, select the "Add horizontal sliced lines" button.

6. Drag across the image twice to slice it into 3 rows, roughly equal in size.

7. If you make a mistake, select the Eraser and click on a sliced line to erase it.

8. Select the "Add vertical slice lines" button.

9. Drag from top to bottom in the middle of the image to slice it into 2 columns, equal in size.

10. Select the Pick mode. In the Preview window, click on the cell on the left in the top row to select it. The corresponding cell will be selected in the left pane. In the "Image name" box, select the default text and type Vegetables. Add the following web attributes: URL=veg.htm, Alt text=Vegetables and Status bar=Vegetable plants for spring. In the "Optimizer" section select JPG and choose a preset from the dropdown list. In this example, a custom preset was selected.

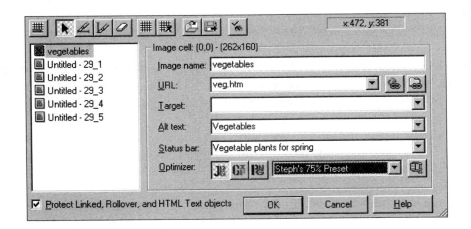

11. In the left pane, click on the second cell from the top to select it. The corresponding cell will be selected in the Preview window. In the "Image name" box, select the default text and type Flowers. Add the following web attributes: URL=flowers.htm, Alt text=Flowers and Status bar=Add color to your garden with flowers. Select JPG and the same preset from the Optimizer dropdown list.

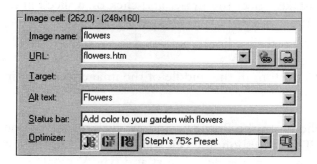

12. Continue selecting cells in the left pane and assigning web attributes.

    For the third cell, in the "Image name" box, select the default text and type herbs. Add the following web attributes: URL=herbs.htm, Alt text=Herbs and Status bar=Add spice to your kitchen with fresh herbs. Select an Optimizer preset.

    For the fourth cell, in the "Image name" box, select the default text and type trees. Add the following web attributes: URL=trees.htm, Alt text=Trees and Status bar=Plant trees for a greener tomorrow. Select an Optimizer preset.

    For the fifth cell, in the "Image name" box, select the default text and type tools. Add the following web attributes: URL=tools.htm, Alt text=Tools and Status bar=The right tools make your job easier. Select an Optimizer preset.

    For the sixth and final cell, in the "Image name" box, select the default text and type books. Add the following web attributes: URL=books.htm, Alt text=Book and Status bar=We recommend our favorite gardening books. Select an Optimizer preset.

13. Now that you have named each cell in the sliced image and assigned web attributes to each cell, click OK to close the dialog box.

14. To check out how it will look on a web page, choose File, Preview in Browser and select your default browser. The sliced image will appear in your browser window as a web page.

15. To save the sliced image, choose File, Save for Web, As HTML. Doing so will open

the Save As dialog box. Browse to the folder to which you will save the HTML document. Give the web page a name and click Save.

16. Remember that if you plan to use a sliced image on your own web site, the file structure on your web site must mirror the file structure on your computer. PhotoImpact 6 places the images into an images folder. Make sure you upload your images to the images folder on your server.

Making a Transparent Background Automatically

1. Choose File, New to access the New dialog box. In the Image size section, select Standard and choose 160 X 120 from the dropdown list. Make the canvas white and click OK.

2. The purpose of this exercise is to learn how to create a transparent background automatically in the Image Optimizer.

3. Select the Path Drawing tool. In the Attributes toolbar, click Shape and select Rounded Rectangle. Choose 3D Round from the Mode dropdown list. Color does not matter. Make sure Anti-aliasing is selected. Draw a pill-shaped navigation button. Do not merge the button with the base image.

4. Hit F4 to access the Image Optimizer. The first thing you will see is an Image to Optimize dialog box. Choose "Selected objects" and click OK.

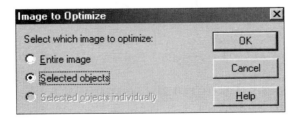

5. When the Image Optimizer opens, choose GIF and select Transparency. The right Preview window will show the checkerboard pattern indicating transparency.

PhotoImpact 6 Wizardry

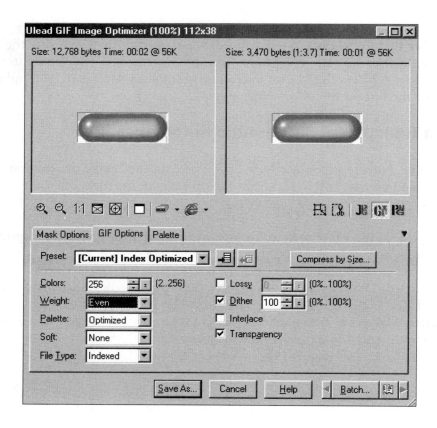

6. Click the Save As button. When the Save As dialog box opens, give the button a name (e.g., button1.gif) and save it to a folder on your hard drive. Remember where you saved it so you can insert it into a web page after completing the next exercise. Click Save to close the Save As dialog box.

7. Leave the button open in the work space for the next exercise.

Making a Transparent Background Manually

1. Return to the button created for the previous exercise. Use the Pick tool to drag it into an empty area in the work space, where it will open in its own window. Right click and Merge.

2. The purpose of this exercise is to create a transparent background manually in the Image Optimizer, using options available from the Mask Options tab. You will note that there are many more steps involved in creating transparency this way, and the results are not as good compared to the automatic transparency method.

3. Choose Web, Image Optimizer or hit F4 to open the Image Optimizer. Select GIF, then select Transparency.

4. Click the Mask Options tab to create the transparent background. From the Matte dropdown list choose None, causing the color box to show the transparent checkerboard pattern.

5. Click the Mask down arrow and choose Pick Color, which results in additional save options directly below. By default the hand icon (Dragging) is selected. Choose the second button to the right of the hand, "Add to Mask." Set the Similarity to 49, which is a good choice for a solid colored background contrasting highly with button color. Select "Search connected pixels" so that colors similar to the transparent color within the button itself will not become transparent.

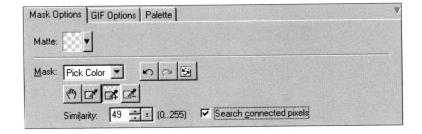

6. In the left Preview window, position your cursor over the white background. It will turn into an Eyedropper. You will notice that there is not much white space around the button, so one click will not select all of it. Click in the white area in the upper right corner, being careful not to click on the button itself. Continue clicking on the white in each corner. Since you are in "Add to Mask" mode, each selection will be added to the previous selections. As you click, the white will be replaced by the checkerboard pattern indicating transparency. You will see the checkerboard in both the left and right preview windows.

7. Click the Save As button. When the Save As dialog box opens, give the button a name (e.g., button2.gif) and save it to the same folder on your hard drive to which

you saved the first button. Click Save to close the dialog box.

8. To compare how the two buttons made in this and the previous exercise fare against different backgrounds, you may wish to open your HTML editor and insert both buttons on a web page document. Test the effects of the two transparency methods by changing the web page background or by using a background image.

Cropping an Image in the Image Optimizer

1. From the EasyPalette's Image Library, Buildings, drag from the Opera House thumbnail to an empty place in the work space. The opera house object will open in its own window. Right click and Merge All.

2. The purpose of this exercise is to crop the image directly in the Image Optimizer. Then you will open it up to see that only the cropped portion was saved.

3. Hit F4 (or choose Web, Image Optimizer) to open the Image Optimizer. Click JPG to save the image as a JPG, then click the Crop button. The Image Optimizer Crop box will open, with a crop box in the upper left corner.

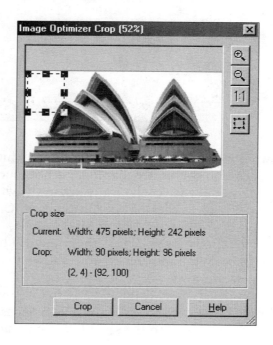

4. Drag on the crop box control points to create a selection including only the left side of the image. Click Crop to return to the Image Optimizer.

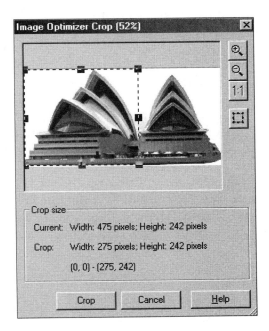

5. In both the left and right Preview windows, you will see that the image now includes only the left side of the opera house image. Click the Save As button to open the Save As dialog box. Give the image a name (e.g., operahouse.jpg) and browse to a folder to which you will save the image. Remember where you saved it.

6. Close out the opera house image in the work space. Choose File, Open to access the Open dialog box. Browse to the folder to which you saved operahouse.jpg and click Open. The cropped image will open in the work space.

Creating an Image Optimizer Save Preset

1. From the EasyPalette, select any object from the Image Library, or use one of your own custom library objects. Drag from the object's thumbnail into an empty area in the work space, where the object will open in its own window. Right click, Merge All.

2. The purpose of this exercise is to create a custom Save preset. Once it has been created, you may select this preset any time you save a web image.

3. Hit F4 to access the Image Optimizer dialog box. Click JPG. From the Mode dropdown list, select Standard Optimized. Edit the Quality value to 85. Leave remaining values at their defaults. These settings will create a Standard Optimized JPG at 85% compression. Click the "Add JPEG Preset" button (arrow).

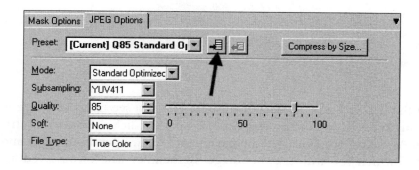

4. When the Add Preset Options dialog box opens, give the preset a name (e.g., My 85% JPG) and click Add.

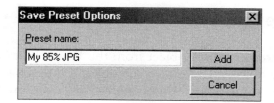

5. The new preset will appear in the Preset list.

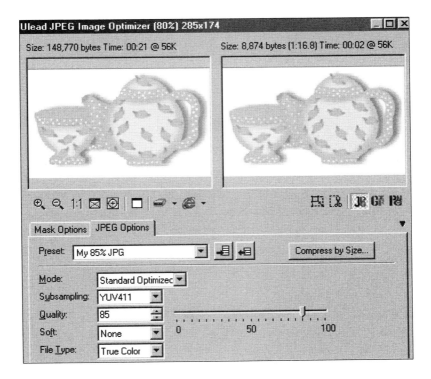

6. Any time you want to use it in the future, you can simply select it from the Preset dropdown list. As an added bonus, this preset will appear in the HTML Properties options for saving images when you build web pages in PhotoImpact 6.

7. If you do not wish to keep this preset, select it first from the Preset dropdown list, then click the "Delete JPEG Preset" button. The preset will be removed from the Preset list.

Glossary

Alt text If a web image is broken, or if someone is surfing your web site with images turned off, Alt text tells them what they are missing. Instead of seeing a red X for a broken image, they will see "Our Wedding Photo," or other text you have provided.

Animated GIF A series of GIF images, each slightly different, are viewed sequentially to create an animation. Make individual frames, then put them together to create an animation in GIF Animator.

Attributes toolbar A constant feature in the work space, the Attributes toolbar lets you edit options associated with a selected tool. These options vary, depending upon which tool you are using.

Base image The base image is the underlying canvas in an image. When objects are added, they remain independent of the base image unless merged with it.

Browser safe palette A palette limited to the 216 colors known to render the same in the Internet Explorer, Netscape and Mosaic browsers.

Bump map Creates surface interest and texture by applying an embossed version of an image to a 3D Path or Text object, thus creating "bumps."

Crop Cropping an image eliminates everything outside of a selection area. It is a good way to zero in on a feature of interest.

CMYK Stands for Cyan, Magenta, Yellow and Black color channels. Often professional printers will ask you to split the image to CMYK. Doing so creates four grayscale versions of your image, each one representing one of the color channels.

Data type Refers to the number of colors in an image. For example, a True Color image can display many more colors than an Optimized Index 256 Color image.

Dingbat A dingbat is a pictorial font showing flowers, hearts, symbols and so on. They are useful for making web page images such as buttons, borders and horizontal lines.

EXE file An executable file that, when opened, runs a program. PhotoImpact 6 creates self-extracting EXE files for web albums and slide shows, so they can be sent as email attachments. The recipient's browser will open automatically to view it.

EasyPalette The EasyPalette's Galleries and Libraries are the central repository for nearly every tool or effect available. Tools and effects are accessed from thumbnails. Custom effects can be saved to the EasyPalette for re-use.

Gallery Within the EasyPalette, Galleries organize similar tools and effects. For example, the Fill Gallery will have "Tab groups" for different types of fills. Use "My Gallery" to store your own custom effects.

Gradient A gradient fill contains more than one color. Choose a two-color gradient or a multiple-color gradient.

Hex code The HTML code used to specify background, text and link colors on a web page. Hex codes start with # and include combinations of 6 letters and/or numbers. For example, the Hex code for navy blue is #000080, while white is #FFFFFF.

HSB Stands for Hue (color), Saturation (richness or intensity) and Brightness of colors. Hold the Eyedropper over any color to display its HSB value in the status bar.

HTML Hypertext Markup Language, the code necessary for building web page documents.

Hyperlink A link to the URL, or internet address, of a particular site. Use hyperlinks so that visitors to your web pages can click these links to jump to other pages.

JavaScript A language that permits interactive effects to take place on a web page. In PhotoImpact, JavaScript is used to create Rollover button effects.

Key frame PhotoImpact uses key frames in its preset animations. Key frames are editable. For example, if you select a key frame, you can edit any attributes associated with the animation at that point in time from the animation's dialog box.

Layer In PhotoImpact, a layer is an independent object that has been added to a base image. A Path, Text or Image object is a layer. Manipulate, position and change the stacking order of layers (objects), in the EasyPalette's Layer Manager.

Library Within the EasyPalette, Libraries organize groups of Path and Image objects.

So the Outline Library will have "Tab groups" for different types of objects. Use "My Library" to store your own custom Path, Text and Image objects.

Mask A mask is a grayscale image or selection which is applied to an underlying color image. Application of a mask affects how a fill or effect will be applied. Black areas within the mask are opaque and will block the fill or effect completely, while white areas within the mask are transparent and will allow the fill or effect to show up on the underlying image. Gray areas within the mask vary in their transparency.

Merge Merge can mean one of two things. Most commonly, Merge means to merge independent object(s) with the underlying base image, or to combine several selected objects into one object. However, Merge also refers to the way in which the colors of a fill or object are applied to the colors of the underlying base image.

Object An object is anything that is added to a base image. Objects are independent, "floating" above the base image. There are three kinds of objects: Path, Text and Image objects. Path and Text objects can be 3D vector objects, and they can be edited endlessly from the Material dialog box and the EasyPalette's Material Gallery, including the application of striking metallic and textured effects. Image objects, on the other hand, cannot be edited in this manner. A frequent complaint of new PhotoImpact users is that they cannot apply gold or glass to a 2D Image object. For example, you could not take a flat photo of a cat, convert it to an object, and apply silver to it.

Plug-in A plug-in is a third party filter used to create artistic image effects. Choose File, Preferences, General, Plug-ins to specify the path to the Plug-in that you wish to use. After doing so, the Plug-in will be available from your Effect menu commands.

Photo edge Among the Frame Gallery's many frames are photo edges, which apply a fancy cutout or torn edge on the outer edges of an image.

Quick Samples Thumbnails showing variations of different options available in a dialog box. The visual representation of the effect makes it easier to choose an option because you can see what it will look like before applying it.

Reflection Like a Bump map, a Reflection creates interest by reflecting a selected image off the surface of a 3D Path or Text object.

Resolution The dots per inch (dpi) used in a particular image. It is one of the most difficult concepts to grasp for people who are just learning about image editing. The difficulty lies in the fact that on your monitor, an image with a Resolution of 300 dpi will look exactly the same as an image with a Resolution of 72 dpi because the default of your monitor is 72 dpi. However, if the same image is printed at 300 dpi, it will be much smaller than if it was printed at 72 dpi. Changing Resolution does not change an image's file size, only its physical size. Lower Resolution spreads out the color pixels further, while a higher Resolution packs the color pixels more closely together.

RGB Stands for Red, Green and Blue, or the amount of these colors making up the colors seen on your monitor. Mix custom colors by specifying the amount of red, green and blue in them. Be aware that the RGB values of colors, as they are seen on your monitor, may not match printed output. Printer inks are based on the CMYK color model. To increase the synchrony between what you see on screen and printed output, take advantage of PhotoImpact's Color Management, accessed through Preferences.

Tablet A drawing tablet or pen that allows you to draw or paint on a plastic tablet, which transports what you have drawn to your monitor. Many people report a higher degree of control and greater accuracy when painting or drawing with a tablet.

Trim PhotoImpact imposes extra pixels of space around objects. After editing or erasing objects completely, choose Trim to rid the object of extra space.

URL Uniform Resource Locator, or the Internet address of a web page or image.

Watermark A way to mark an image with copyright information such as the name of the image creator, etc. PhotoImact 6 includes Digimarc's watermarking capabilities.

Web image An image type used on the Internet. There are three kinds of web image file types: JPG (for photos or other images with up to millions of colors), GIF (for images with few colors and broad areas of flat color, can be made transparent) and PNG (a newer file type that supports millions of colors and transparency). Generally speaking, GIF web images make the smallest files due to having fewer colors. JPG web images tend to have larger file sizes, and lose color information each time the JPG is saved. PNG images generally yield high quality web images as well as the largest file sizes, but they do not lose color information.

Index

Symbols

.AI files 170, 171, 176, 462
.AI files, importing as Custom Shapes 462
.BMP, adding as a Paint template 341
.BMP file sequence 332, 335, 337, 345, 347
.CEF 329
.CFL 328
.EXE 58, 59, 61, 66, 67
.HTM 58, 66, 69
.MAP 53, 56, 306
.PAL 318, 538
.PSD 37, 465
.PSP 37
.RAW 56, 59
.SMP 450, 451
.TSK 30
.TUB picture tube file 203
.UFO 510
.UOL 459
.USS 517, 519
1:1 514, 518
16 Color 38
256 Color 38, 83
256 Indexed Color 40, 176, 181, 192
2D 323
2D and 3D 312
2D Object 172, 176, 181, 191
3D 323
3D Chisel 172, 176, 177, 181, 191, 437
3D Custom 172, 176, 177, 181, 192, 437
3D Pipe 172, 191, 437
3D Round 172, 176, 181, 191, 437
3D Trim 172, 191, 437
4-Way 328

A

Absolute Colorimetric 84, 85
Accumulatively 73, 305
Acquire 53, 55
Acquire dialog box 52, 55
Activation 71
Active Desktop 318
Active Image 41, 310
Active Learning Exercises 93, 145, 239, 371, 469, 539
Active selection object(s) 135
Active window 71
Actual Size 87
Actual Size View 514, 518
Actual View 72, 87
Add 83, 175, 180, 184, 188, 193, 206, 235, 318, 327, 329, 334, 336, 342, 344, 347, 349, 352, 361, 428, 431, 434, 503, 505, 507
Add a control point 185
Add a View 87
Add button 23, 53, 188, 290, 306, 318, 332, 334, 344, 347, 351, 352, 354, 434
Add Command 453
Add Current Document as Thumbnail 460, 461
Add Fill Command 453
Add horizontal sliced line mode 518
Add HTML Text Object 189, 507
Add Image File as Thumbnail 460, 461
Add key frame 331, 340, 346
Add Noise 321
Add PhotoShop Plug-in thumbnails 452
Add point 185
Add preset 526
Add stamp 202
Add Text to Active Path 214
Add Texture 369
Add to an existing selection 124
Add to EasyPalette dialog box 23, 33, 143, 175, 180, 184, 188, 193, 206, 223, 235, 290, 306, 318, 327, 329, 333, 334, 336, 344, 347, 349, 352, 361, 428, 453, 465, 505
Add to Mask 529
Add vertical sliced line mode 518
Adding a custom gradient 431
Adding an edited palette, Palette Ramp Editor 431
Adding Objects to a Library 464
Adding or Removing a Text Object Shadow 197
Adding Selections to a Library 464
Adding your own textures, paint with textures 369
Address 47, 48
Adjust for NTSC 326
Adjust for PAL 326
Advanced 62, 68, 206, 214, 334, 335, 336, 337, 338
Advanced Page Settings dialog box 62
Advanced Tab 330, 338
Airbrush 364
Align 218, 468
Align Bottom 187
Align Center 187
Align center 132
Align Left 132, 187
Align Middle 187
Align Right 132
Align Top 187
Alignment 187, 508
Alignment of paths 187
All 138
All thumbnails of the current group 459
Alt Text 226, 495, 496, 500, 514, 516, 519
Ambience brightness control bar 350
Ambience level 350
Ambient 443, 445
Ambient Brightness Color box 350
Ambient light 444
Amount 213
Amplitude 352, 503
Angle 74, 341, 353
Angle, Light 504
Angular 205
Animation 331, 332, 333, 334, 335, 336, 337, 339, 340, 344, 345, 346, 347
Animation Gallery 457
Animation Lighting 457
Animation Studio 319, 330, 331, 332, 457
Animation timeline 331, 339, 340, 346, 347
Animation Type 457
Annotation on the Pages 62
Annotations 68
Anti-aliasing 126, 127, 129, 174, 179, 183, 195, 237
AnyShape Buttons 457
Apply 341, 452, 454
Apply calibration scheme 53, 55, 56
Apply Enhancement 74
Apply to 311

Arrange 219, 468
Arrange Order options, Pick 219
Arrow 182
Artist Texture 333, 334
As HTML 49
As Individual Object 49
As Single Object 49
Ask when opening 81
Assigning Attributes to Rollover Buttons 515
Associate 82
Associate all available image types with PhotoImpact 82
Attributes toolbar 23, 33, 124, 125, 127, 128, 130, 133, 313, 360
Attributes toolbar, Bucket/Solid fill 423
Attributes toolbar, Clone tools 366
Attributes toolbar, Eraser tool 234
Attributes toolbar, Line and Arrow Tool 180
Attributes toolbar, Multiple-Colors gradient fill 428
Attributes toolbar, Object Magic Eraser 236
Attributes toolbar, Object Paint Eraser 234
Attributes toolbar, Outline Drawing tool 175
Attributes toolbar, Paint tools 363
Attributes toolbar, Path Drawing tool 169
Attributes toolbar, Path Edit tool 184
Attributes toolbar, Pick tool 219
Attributes toolbar, Retouch tools 361
Attributes toolbar, Text tool 189
Attributes toolbar, Transform tool 227
Attributes toolbar, Two-Color gradient fill 427
Auto button 304
Auto detect 226, 514
Auto Process 297, 298
Auto stitch 294
Auto-adjust 304
Automatic transparency 527
Automatic Transparency for Selected Object(s) 526
Automatic transparent backgrounds 521
Automatically 69
Autoslice 518
Available buttons 83
Average 320, 327

B

Background 309
Background color 24, 62, 68, 126, 142, 172, 176, 181, 190, 287, 341, 425, 427, 435
Background color, HTML text 509
Background color of scanner 52
Background color, Turnpage 353
Background Designer 501
Background image 308, 309, 528
Background tab 39
Background Type 502
Base image transparency 87
Baseline shift 195
Basic 504
Basic Color Management 84
Basic Tab 330, 338
Basic/Advanced Tabs 331
Batch 298, 525
Batch Convert 50, 51
Batch list 525
Bend 189, 209, 212, 215
Bending 213
Best quality 74
Bevel 504
Bevel joint 438
Bevel tab 437
Bevel type 504
Bezier Curve selection tool 123, 130
Bezier/Polygon 169, 170, 175, 180, 181, 214
Bicubic 310, 524
Bilinear 310
Black & White 38, 142
Blast 325
Blue title bar 26
Blur 320, 327, 362
Blur & Sharpen 320
Blur to Sharpness slider 304
Bold 508
Border 137, 138, 174, 179, 183, 193, 345, 438
Border, frames 314
Border slider 174, 179, 183, 193, 437
Border width 139
Border/Depth Tab 438
Bottom 218
Bottom up 57
Bounding box 71, 89, 229, 234, 509
Branching tree menu 448
Break Link 211
Brightness 297, 300, 309, 430
Brightness & Contrast 22, 299

Bring Forward 219
Bring to Front 219
Bristle 365
Bristle, frame effect 314
Bristle Smear 363
Browse for Folder dialog box 60
Browser Preview 21, 523
Browser safe palette 532, 536
Brush angle 367
Brush Gallery 455
Brush Panel 31, 32, 33, 206, 235, 360, 366, 367
Brush Panel, Clone tools 368
Brush Panel, Paint tools 368
Brush Panel, Retouch tools 367
Bubble 342
Bucket 493
Bucket fill tool 423
Bucket/Solid Fill 423
Bump map 439, 440
Bump Tab 439
Burn 362
Business cards 464
Button Designer (Any Shape) 503
Button Designer (Rectangular) 505
Button Gallery 457, 505
Button size, Component Designer 492
Buttons, size tags 501
Byte order 57, 60

C

Cache Tab 31
Calculation 308, 309
Calibration 52, 53, 55
Calibration Tab 55, 73
Camera Lens 321
Cancel 289
Canvas 38, 316
Canvas color 292
Canvas, selectively adding for frame & shadow 316
Capture 70
Carriage return, Text Entry Box 196
Cell Size 502
Center Both 218
Center Horizontally 72, 218
Center image horizontally 73
Center image vertically 73
Center in window 514, 518, 523
Center Vertically 72, 218
Certificates 464
Chalk 364
Change 71, 206

Index

Change an existing selection by addition 124, 127, 128
Change an existing selection by subtracting 124, 127, 128
Change Color, Palette Ramp Editor 352
Change shape when text changes 493
Changing data type, reasons to do so 317
Changing the amount of space between text characters 195
Changing the space between lines of text 195
Changing the vertical position of text 195
Channel 73, 300, 305, 309
Channel order 57, 60
Character spacing 195
Charcoal 323, 364
Charcoal, frame effect 314
Check for rendering errors when saving as HTML 79
Check Ulead's web site every (#) days 76
Checkerboard 38, 79, 89, 233, 529
Chisel 345
Circle 124, 131, 169, 175, 226, 514
Classic 313
Clear 135, 285
Clear Undo/Redo History 284
Click thumbnail to select stamp 202
Clipboard 71, 131, 209, 210, 285, 286, 290, 499, 500
Clone Tools 32, 359, 365
Clone-Airbrush 366
Clone-Bristle 367
Clone-Chalk 367
Clone-Charcoal 366
Clone-Crayon 366
Clone-Marker 367
Clone-Oil Paint 367
Clone-Paintbrush 32, 366
Clone-Pencil 367
Close 48, 72
Cloud 342
CMYK 25, 26, 316
Color 176, 181, 198, 206, 220, 315
Color & Line dialog box 178, 182
Color Balance 21, 300, 309
Color box 172, 176, 181, 190, 198, 220, 225, 287, 292, 323, 350, 509
Color channels 304, 305, 306, 308, 309, 318
Color coating 324
Color Management 37, 75, 84

Color Management dialog box 84
Color of box around objects 79
Color On Screen 287
Color Palette 24, 521
Color profiles 84
Color Ramp 427
Color Replacement Pen 365
Color, selecting for transparency 529
Color, Shadow 505
Color Similarity 140
Color Tab 287, 493, 494, 497
Color Table 317, 318
Color type 57, 60
Color/Texture Tab 434
Colored Pen 323
Colorize 303
Colorize Pen 359, 363
Colors 507, 532, 535
Column 510
Combining multiple objects into one object 210
Comet 338
Compact 318
Compare by HSB 129
Compare by RGB 129
Component Designer 39, 209, 210, 464, 491, 494, 497, 498, 501
Component Object 210
Compress 74
Compress bitmap 74
Compress By Size... 530, 532, 535
Compressed image 529
Compression 64, 525
Compression ratio 530, 532, 535
Concave border 174, 183
Concrete 345
Cone, HSB 353
Connected lines 360
Constants in the Attributes Toolbar, Retouch, Clone Tools 360
Context-specific help 331, 338, 341
Continue Draw mode 172, 173
Continue Optimizing dialog box, saving multiple objects 527
Contrast 297, 300
Control handles 71, 133
control points 130, 131, 170, 172, 175, 177, 180, 184, 185, 186, 211, 227, 229, 326, 349, 351, 430, 431, 509
Convert a path object into a selection area 173
Convert Cells to Objects, Grid & Partition 510
Convert file format to 51

Convert Line 186
Convert Object Type 199, 216, 229
Convert Object Type, From Image to Path 216
Convert Object Type, From Path to Image 216
Convert Object Type, From Text to Image 216
Convert Object Type, From Text to Path 216
Convert path to curve segment 186
Convert path to line segment 186
Convert to Object 137, 141, 233, 462, 465, 513
Converting a Selection to an Object for Erasing 233
Convex border 174, 183
Cool 321
Coordinates of an active object 225
Copies 71, 73
Copy 21, 284, 452, 454, 460, 461
Copy button 285
Copy Object to Image 460, 461
Copy Object to New Document 460, 461
Copy Selection to Object Library 143
Copy to Object Library 223
Copyright 200, 354
Copyright Information, Digimarc 356
Corner 353
Corrected color box 301
Count 212
Crayon 364
Create a New Image 25, 317
Create, Gallery 449
Create Gallery dialog box 449
Create, Library 458
Create Object Library dialog box 458
Create Seamless Tile 512
Creating Transparency Manually 528
Creative 329
Creative effects 319
Creative Lighting 337
Creative Type 345
Creative Warp 336
Creator ID 355
Crop 286, 297
Crop box 524
Crop box size 133
Crop button 134
Crop, Image Optimizer 524
Crop tool 133, 135, 286, 297
Cropping a selection 133, 134
Crosshair 78, 285

581

Curled edge 353
Current Palette 24
Current Printer 311
Current resolution 311
Current Size 292
Current/Total Frames 331, 346
Custom Filters 326
Custom colors 424
Custom distortion effects 328
Custom Effect 329
Custom Effects 328
Custom Filter 327
Custom Shape 169, 170, 175
Custom Shape dialog box 169, 314
Custom slicing pattern 519
Custom tone map, saving 304
Customize 82
Customize Buttons dialog box 83, 84
Customize My Desktop 318
Customize Standard Toolbar 75, 83, 169
Cut 21, 284, 452, 454, 460, 461
Cylindrical 353

D

Darken Midtone, Tone Map 305
Darken or Lighten 503
Darken, Tone Map 305
Data Type 25, 38, 71, 89, 283, 316
Data Type and reducing file size 317
Data Type button 316
Deactivating active objects, how to 217
Default 74, 342
Default, rollover button state 514
Default/Mouseover/Mousedown, Rollover button state 516
Define folders for additional memory 82
Deform Gallery 197, 457
Deform image 436
Delay 69, 71
Delete 30, 132, 211, 335, 337, 344, 452, 454, 460, 468, 534, 538
Delete a control point 185
Delete a path 186
Delete all 335, 337, 344
Delete color, Palette Ramp Editor 352
Delete, custom library 459
Delete custom stamp dialog box 203
Delete key frame 332, 340, 347
Delete point 185
Delete preset 526
Delete stamp 203

Delete Texture 369
Deleting a custom gallery 450
Deleting a custom gradient 431
Density 341, 440, 503
Depth 174, 179, 183, 193, 438
Depth slider 174, 179, 183, 193, 437
Description 452, 454, 460, 461
Description Tab 64
Deselect 335, 337
Desired color box 301
Desired file size 530, 532, 535
Deskew 294
Despeckle 321
Destination 51, 52, 55, 56, 71
Destination Tab 54
Detach, gallery 451
Detach, library 459
Details 524
Diamond 169, 175
Diffusion 330
Digimarc 354
Digimarc, Registering and Watermarking 354
Digital Camera 21, 55, 306
Dimensions 56, 310
Dimensions dialog box 310
dingbat font 199, 200
Direction 139, 219, 315, 506
Direction, Shadow 198, 220
Directory structure 501
Disk 26, 90
Display 26, 82, 83, 90, 286
Display a confirmation message when saving 80
Display Buttons, Slicer 518
Display compressed image 523
Display Photo/System Property 25, 26
Display Quick Samples 76
Display reminder to refresh when editing linked object 79
Displaying and hiding Guidelines 91
Displaying control points 184
Distort text to fit path 214
Distorting objects and selections 227
Distorting Text or Path objects 212
Distortions of text objects 189
Distribute Horizontally 132, 187
Distribute Vertically 132, 187
Dither 332, 336, 337, 340, 345, 347, 533, 536
Divided by 328
Do not merge frame object 313
Dodge 362
Double 345

DPI 311
Drag-and-Drop in PhotoImpact Only 460, 461
Draw a New Path 131
Draw Border Line 510
Draw From Center 126
Drawing pen 206
Drawing pen functions 78
Drawing tablet 234, 360, 367
Drop Water 365
Droplet 330
Duotone 325
Duplicate 132, 210, 286, 468
Duplicate a path 186
Duplicate, Base Image Only 286
Duplicate, Base Image With Objects 286
Duplicate, Base Image With Objects Merged 286

E

EasyPalette 22, 26, 33, 137, 173, 178, 183, 188, 189, 190, 197, 209, 210, 211, 215, 217, 223, 235, 299, 313, 318, 319, 327, 329, 332, 334, 337, 340, 342, 345, 347, 349, 351, 354, 434, 447, 448, 451, 453, 454, 460, 464, 491, 503
EasyPalette, accessing 447
EasyPalette Galleries 454
EasyPalette Libraries 461
EasyPalette Options 460, 468
EasyPalette, resizing and moving 447
EasyPalette, tiling with an image 454, 460, 468
Edge 313
Edit 318, 334, 352, 503, 534, 537
Edit Component 464, 494, 497
Edit Existing Path 131
Edit HTML Text 509
Edit menu commands 25, 34, 283
Edit mode 184, 185
Edit, palette 314, 334
Edit Path 211
Edit Point 184, 185
Edit Rollover 516
Edit Task 29, 30
Edit text, five primary ways 189
Edit Wrap Properties 216
Editing 175, 179, 184, 187
Editing a preset key frame animation 339

Index

Editing and Exporting Components, Component Design 492
Editing Component Designer Rollover Buttons 495
Editing frame shape 313
Editing HTML code, cautions 501
Editing individual particles 343
Editing key frame animations 331
Editing Stamps With the Brush Panel 206
Editing Text With the Attributes Toolbar 189
Editing Text With the EasyPalette 197
Editing Text With Material Dialog Box 197
Editing Text With the Object Menu 197
Editing Text With the Object Properties Box 196
Editing Type Effect animations 346
Effect 314, 344
Effect control 343
Effect level 322
Effect Menu commands 77, 319
Effect thumbnails 330
Effects 313
Element 340
Elevation, Light 504
Ellipse 124, 131, 169, 175
Elliptical gradient fill tool 423, 427
Email attachment 57, 58, 67
Embed Watermark dialog box 354
Emboss 324, 327, 345
Emboss, frame effect 314
Emboss Outline 345
Emboss Texture 345
Emphasize Edges 320
Emulated device 85
Emulated Device Profile 85
Enable Color Management 84
Enable slicing 52
Enable undo 75
End height 214
Enhancements 305
Entire Image 49, 135, 527
Entire length 48
Entire page 48
Equalize 308
Erase all sliced lines 518
Erase sliced line mode 518
Eraser 361
Eraser mode 235, 361
Escape 88, 89, 512
Even 219

Even-Odd Fill 131, 173
Excess space around objects, getting rid of 234
Exit 85
Expand 137, 292, 318
Expand Canvas 292
Expand from current selection 140
Expand sides equally 292
Expand/Shrink 139, 140
Export 30, 57, 137
Export As Component Objects (in PhotoImpact) 494, 497
Export As Individual Objects 494
Export As Individual Objects (in PhotoImpact) 497
Export, Component Designer 494
Export, Component Designer objects 497
Export content 222
Export, gallery 451
Export Gallery dialog box 451
Export, library 459
Export Object 222
Export Object Library box 459
Export Selection 142
Export sliced table data box 519
Export table data 519
Export to 222
Export to HTML 498
Export to HTML, how objects are saved in HTML 497
Export to HTML, Rollover buttons 497
Export to Image Optimizer 494, 497
Export Web Album dialog box 60
Exporting 30
Exporting a grayscale mask as a new grayscale image 222
Exporting an object as a selection 222
Exporting Component Designer Objects 497
Exposure 350
Exposure control bar 350
Exposure level 350
Eye color to remove 323
Eye icon, Layer Manager 465, 466
Eye size 322
Eyedropper 23, 24, 172, 176, 181, 190, 287, 301, 323, 325, 425, 427, 435, 529
Eyedropper dialog box 425
Eyedropper tools 531, 534, 537

F

Face strength of light, 504
Facet 321
Fadeout 172, 176, 181, 190, 291, 292, 436
Fadeout dialog box 291, 436
Fat 322
Fax/Mail 54
Fields 65
File 54, 142, 143, 290, 435
File Format tab 39
File formats 82
File Information 56, 59
File Menu 34, 37
File name 42, 46, 450, 458
File Size 41
File type 531, 533, 536
Files of Type 42, 46
Fill 286, 336
Fill color 287, 291, 423, 427, 428
Fill dialog box 286
Fill Gallery 455
Fill Tool panel 423
Fill tools 423
Fill type 287, 291, 435, 436
Filter 453, 536
Filter Gallery 455
Filters, third party 356, 452
Find 454, 460, 468
Find criteria 460
Find dialog box 454
Find Edges 320, 327
Find Next 454, 460, 468
Fine control 341, 504
Fineness 341
Fire 342, 345
Fire, frame effect 314
Firefly 342
Fireworks 338
Fit In Window 88
Fit in window 196, 514, 518, 522
Fit, replacement object 222
Fit Selection 460, 461
Fit text position to path 214
Fit the texture 436
Fit to Page 72
Fit Together 215
Fixed 219
Fixed size 124
Flashlight 338
Flip Horizontally 231, 293
Flip Vertically 231, 293
Flipping 293

583

Floating toolbar 359
Flyers 464
Focus 297, 303
Focus dialog box 303
Folder 450, 458
Font 190, 194, 508
Fonts, and copyright 200
Footer 62, 68
Foreground 308
Foreground Color 24,
　　　172, 176, 181, 190, 28, 425,
　　　427, 435
Foreground image 308, 309
Format 24, 65
Format Menu 35, 54
Format menu commands 297, 312
Forward 45
Frame 64, 66, 332, 346
Frame & Shadow 22, 309, 312, 491
Frame & Shadow button 312
Frame & Shadow dialog box 312
Frame delay
　　　332, 336, 337, 340, 345, 347
Frame Gallery 457, 491
Frame Tab 312
Frames 331
Free edit 131
Free edit mode 185
Free Path 131
Freehand, lines 360
Freehand selection 124
Freely Rotate 231
Freely transform 132, 227
Frequency 74, 352, 503
From Image to Path 229
Full Screen 71, 88
Full screen preview 88

G

Galleries
　　　173, 178, 183, 190, 197, 319, 447, 449
Galleries, backing up 451
Galleries button 454
Gallery 26, 175, 180, 184, 188, 193, 288,
　　　290, 306, 333, 334, 336, 344, 347,
　　　349, 352, 434, 448, 454, 507
Gallery button 434
Gallery Manager 449
Gallery/Library 223
Gamma 300
Gaussian Blur 320, 330
General 75
General Tab 39, 196, 224

Generation quality 76
Get Wrap Path 216
GIF 521, 522, 527, 528, 529
GIF animation options
　　　332, 336, 337, 340, 345, 347
GIF Animator 4, 80, 329,
　　　332, 333, 336, 337, 340, 345, 347
GIF Grayscale 128, 532
GIF Grayscale 256 532
GIF Grayscale 64 532
GIF Image Optimizer 532
GIF Mask Options Tab 533
GIF Optimized 128 532
GIF Optimized 256 532
GIF Optimized 64 532
GIF Options Tab 526, 532
GIF Palette Tab 534
GIF Settings 80
Glass 345
Glossary 575
Glossy, frame effect 314
Glow, shadow option 505
Go to last folder visited 45
Gradient 334, 345, 351
Gradient color 314, 435
Gradient Color box 313
Gradient Fill 172, 176, 181, 190, 351,
　　　352, 423, 435, 493
Gradient Fill Tools 427
Gradient Light 345
Gradient Tab 287
Gradual transparency 291
Graph 329
Gray 531, 533, 536
Grayscale 38, 142, 291
Grayscale, creating a selection from
　　　465
Grayscale gradient mask 291, 436
Grayscale mask 309, 529
Greeting cards 464
Grid 44, 77, 87, 326
Grid & Partition 510
Grid colors 79
Grid Line 77, 510
Grid line color 77
Grid size 79
Group 217, 223, 464, 468
Group Management dialog box
　　　450, 459
Group Path 132
Grouped objects, saving to EasyPalette
　　　223
Grouping 187

Grouping objects, two ways to do it
　　　217
Guidelines 77, 87
Guidelines & Grid 25, 77, 91, 92

H

Halftone tab 74
Halo 338
Hand tool 531, 534, 537
Hard disk 82
Heading 62, 68
Height 41, 48, 89, 134
Height to width ratio 227
Height to width ratio, maintaining 225
Help 22, 331, 338, 341
Help Menu 36
Helper Program 519
Hex code 24, 287
Hex value 317, 324
HiColor dithering 83
Hidden, Layer Manager 468
Hide group members 468
High Color 83
Highlight 304, 504
Highlight inactive objects or selections
　　　76
Highlight Midtone Shadow Tab 304
Highlight, Tone Map 305
Histogram 304, 305, 307
Hole 345
Hole, frame effect 314
Horizontal 328
Horizontal Deform
　　　172, 176, 177, 181, 192
Horizontal offset 511
Horizontal tolerance, Stitch 294
Hot spot 513, 514
Hotkey 71
HSB Clockwise 288, 427
HSB color cone 427
HSB cone 288
HSB Counterclockwise 427
HTML 491, 497, 498, 499, 501, 513, 514,
　　　516, 517
HTML code 66
HTML editing 464
HTML editor 37, 66, 70, 498, 501
HTML Properties 39, 513
HTML Properties dialog box 513
HTML Text attributes 507
HTML Text Entry Box 210, 507, 509
HTML Text, formatting 507
HTML Text Object 219, 210, 491

Index

HTML Text, resizing text box 509
HTML Web Page 58
Hue 302
Hue & Saturation 302
Hue (color) shift, stamps 206
Hue, Saturation & Brightness 24, 317, 318
Hue Shift 334, 430
Hyperlink 508, 514
Hyperlink color 514
Hyperlink dialog box 508
Hyperlink Tab 196, 225, 493, 496

I

Icons 28
ID, Digimarc 354
Ideal eye color 323
Ignore background color 83
Image 46
Image Cell, Slicer 519
Image File 58, 59
Image File Format Options 64, 68
Image Library 210, 461
Image Map 513
Image Map dialog box 513
Image Name 519
Image object 465
Image Object from File 209
Image Object from Library 210
Image Object via Copy 209
Image Object via Cut 209
Image only 222
Image Optimizer
   468, 494, 497, 516, 520, 521
Image Optimizer Crop dialog box 524
Image Optimizer dialog box 516
Image Optimizer Similarities, for JPG, GIF and PNG 522
Image Optimizer, ways to access 521
Image Size 40
Image size 64, 68
Image Slicer 510
Image Tab 64, 290
Image theft 354
Image to Optimize dialog box 526
Image Type 57, 60
Images folder 65, 69
Import
   30, 31, 56, 137, 171, 531, 533, 537
Import from 221
Import, Gallery 450
Import Gallery dialog box 450
Import grayscale mask, Image Optimizer 528
Import, library 459
Import Mask 529
Import Mask dialog box 529
Import Object 221
Import Object Library box 459
Import picture tube 203
Import .RAW File dialog box 56
Import Selection 142
Import sliced table data box 518
Import table data 518
Importing Custom Shapes 170, 176
Imprint 345
In/Out 329
Include all subfolders 51
Include OLE information when copying to the Clipboard 76
Indexed 533, 536
Indexed color 317
Individually 506
infinite looping
   332, 336, 337, 340, 345, 347
Inner frame edge 314
Inner/Outer Shape 313, 314
Input AI File dialog box 171
Insert 335, 337, 344
Interlaced
   332, 336, 337, 340, 345, 347, 533, 536
Interleave 57
Internet Explorer 49, 66, 70
Invert 128, 137, 138, 306, 328
Invert bump map 440
Invert, Magic frames pattern 315
Italic 508

J

Javascript code 514
Javascript code, for rollover effect 498
Javascript rollover button 491, 495
JPG 521, 527, 528, 529
JPG, acceptable compression values 530
JPG Image Optimizer 530
JPG Mask Options Tab 531
JPG, mimicking transparency 526
JPG Options Tab 530
JPG, Progressive 530
JPG, Standard 530
JPG, Standard Optimized 530
Jump 330
Jumppoint 295

K

Kaleidoscope 347, 349
Kaleidoscope dialog box 347
Keep aspect ratio 225, 310, 524
Keep original soft edge 140
Kerning 189, 185
Key frame 331, 337, 339, 340, 347
Key frame animation 337, 340
Key frame controls 331, 339, 346
Keyboard Shortcuts 33, 124

L

Labels 464
Large buttons 91
Laser 338
Lasso Selection tool 123, 126, 296, 513
Layer Manager 197, 211, 217, 224 448, 465, 466, 468, 497
Layers 81, 465
Layout 19, 22, 24
Layout button 359, 367
Layout, EasyPalette 448
Left 133, 218
Lens flare 338
Level 75, 304, 306, 344
Libraries 26, 447, 458, 460, 461
Libraries, backing up 458
Libraries, Delete 460
Libraries, Rename 460
Library 26, 209, 223, 448, 458
Library, adding objects to 464
Library Manager 458
Light 174, 179, 183, 193, 349, 504
Light Brightness Color box 350
Light Brightness control bar 350
Light bulb 338
Light color box 504
Light dialog box 349
Light, Direct 434, 443
Light Distance 351
Light distance, elevation and spread control window 351
Light Elevation 351
Light Skew 351
Light source 324
Light source spread 351
Light, Spot 434, 443
Light Spread 351
Light Tab 443
Light value 504
Lighten Midtone, Tone Map 305

585

Lighten, Tone Map 305
Lighting 337, 345
Lighting direction 354
Lighting Gallery 319, 337, 456
Lightness 302
Lightning 338
Lights 434, 443
Limit hard disk usage to 82
Limit RAM usage to 82
Line and Arrow tool 169, 180
Line break 65
Line spacing 195
Line style 77, 178, 182
Line width 177, 182
Linear gradient fill tool 423, 427
Lines 205, 235, 360
Link Object from File 210
Links between pages 62, 68
List all file formats in the Save As dialog box 80
List view 468
Load 74, 286, 318, 328, 329, 341
Load Color Table dialog box 532, 535, 536, 538
Load palette 535, 538
Load, Tone Map 306
Load Tone Map dialog box 53, 56, 74, 306
Local URL 226, 514, 519
Locate 47
Lock 31, 225, 510, 512, 534, 538
Lock icon 466
Lock/Unlock Object, Layer Manager 466
Locking an object in base image, Layer Manager 465
Look in 42
Loop Mode 331, 339, 346
Lossy 533
Luminence 295
Luminosity 308
Luminosity value 294

M

MAC 57
Macros 26
Magic 313, 347
Magic Effects 319, 347
Magic Gradient 287, 351
Magic Gradient dialog box 351
Magic Light 349
Magic Texture
 172, 176, 181, 288, 314, 435

Magic Texture dialog box 289
Magic Texture Fill 190
Magic Textures, editing 289
Magic Wand Selection tool 123, 128
Magnification 87, 88
Maintain height to width proportions 310
Make a new selection
 124, 127, 128, 132
Manually 294
Map Tab 305
Mapping curve 73, 329
Marker 364
Marquee 87, 89
Mask 25, 309, 436, 462, 528, 529, 531, 533, 537
Mask icon 296, 462
Mask Library 461
Mask Mode 25, 76, 296, 462
Mask Options 536
Mask Options tab 526, 527, 528
Masks, how to use a grayscale JPG 462
Masks, how to use Mask Library 461
Master 302
Material 174, 179, 183
Material button
 172, 174, 183, 189, 193, 197, 433
Material dialog box
 179, 183, 193, 197, 313, 433
Material Dialog Box, common elements 433
Material Gallery 197, 434, 457
Matrix 328, 329
Matte 527, 528, 529, 531, 533, 537
Maximize at Actual View 88
Maximize icon 26
Maximum border width 438
Measurement unit 75
Memory 26, 81, 90
Memory management 82
Menu Bar 24
Menu Commands 20, 29
Menu Layout 451, 460
Merge 196, 210, 224, 288, 290, 291, 309, 426, 427, 428, 468
Merge All 210, 283, 468, 510
Merge as Single Object
 210, 211, 217, 467, 468
Merge as Single Object, two ways to select 210
Merge Ratio 512
Merge Size 512
Merged objects, Layer Manager representation 467

Merging objects with base image 210
Metal 345
Metallic 444
Meteor 338
Method 302, 329, 524
Midtone 304
Midtone, Tone Map 305
Minimize icon 26, 447
Minimum transparency 441
Mirror 506
Mirror all 506
Miscellaneous 36
Mode 124, 127, 128, 172, 176, 181, 191, 192, 352, 353, 530
Mode, Turnpage types 353
Modem speed menu 523
Modify Properties and Apply 452, 454
Monitor gamma 83
Monitor Profile 84, 85
Monochrome 325, 363
More button 288
Mosaic 321
Motion Blur 322, 330
Motion Blur, top to bottom 327
Mousedown, Rollover button state
 495, 496, 514
Mouseover, Rollover button state
 495, 496, 514
Move Down 84
Move Selection Marquee
 125, 126, 127, 129, 132
Move Up 84
Moving and Transforming Selections 132
Moving Offset 325
Multiple Capture 71
Multiple colors 435
Multiple-Color gradient fill 287, 291, 314, 427, 435, 428
My Gallery
 33, 318, 361, 428, 434, 457
My Library 143, 464

N

Name 224
Name, Library 458
Name, Gallery 450
Natural Painting 323
Natural Texture 172, 176, 181, 190, 288, 314, 435
Navigation frame 64
Navigation image 513
Nearest Neighbor 310, 524

Index

Neon 345
Neon, frame effect 314
Netscape 49
New 20, 28, 37, 209, 534, 538
New image 54, 143, 310
New object commands 209
New resolution 311
New Size 292, 524
New Task box 28
Noise 321
Non-clipped 341
Non-free edit mode 185
None 138, 360, 437
Normal 335, 337
Normal dialog box 335, 337
Normal, Rollover button state 495, 496
Number of images 52
Numbers/Bullets/Indents 508

O

Object 205
Object attributes 224
Object center 229
Object Eraser tool 217, 233
Object Library Manager 462
Object list 514
Object Magic Eraser 233, 236
Object Menu 35
Object Menu commands 189, 209, 468
Object Menu commands, available in Layer Manager 466
Object Paint Eraser 236
Object Paint Eraser, combining two or more objects 236
Object Paint Eraser Tool 233, 234
Object Properties dialog box 189, 196, 197, 209, 224, 285, 510
Object, stamps 205
Object Type 465
Objects 26, 38, 87, 465
Objects compared to layers 465
Objects, editing Image vs. Path/Text objects 464
Objects, selecting multiple 526
Odd-Even Fill 173
Offset 328
Oil Paint 323, 365
One color 314, 435
One color color box 313
Opacity 341
Open 20, 42, 48
Open & Save 79
Open as read-only 43, 46

Open dialog box 42, 51, 56, 202, 203, 209, 210, 341, 439, 440, 453
Open each layer as an object 81
Open From Web 46
Open image 142
Open the composited image or first layer only 81
Open to work space 51
Open web page as image 47
Operation 308, 309
Optimization preview 519
Optimization Wizard 340
Optimization Wizard, GIF Animator 332
Optimized Indexed 256 Colors 317
Optimized Screen 74
Optimizer 516, 519
Options 20, 32, 33, 51, 72, 73, 125, 127, 129, 132, 134, 173, 178, 183, 206, 297, 303, 307, 313, 314, 319, 323, 324, 325, 348, 350, 435, 442, 506
Options dialog box 90
Options Tab 40, 495
Order 343
Order, stamps 205
Orientation 71
Original file name 47
Other cursor 78
Other Effect Menu commands 356
Outer frame edge 314
Outer shape 313
Outline Drawing tool 169, 175, 463
Outline Library 463
Output device 85
Output Options 61, 67
Output Tab 61, 67
overlap area 293
Overlap area transparency 294
Overlay color 341

P

Page folder 65
Page Setup Tab 62, 68
Page Title 62, 68
Paint 327
Paint as Object Mode 361
Paint mode 235
Paint on Edges 329
Paint Shop Pro 201
Paint Template 341
Paint Tools 31, 359, 363
Paintbrush 32, 364
Paintbrush tool 23, 296
Painting 340

Painting cursor 78, 234
Painting Gallery 340, 455
Painting With Textures 369
Pale 327
Palette 334, 352, 428, 430, 532, 534, 536, 537, 538
Palette, Browser safe 532, 536
Palette, Detail 532, 536
Palette, editing in the Palette Ramp Editor 428
Palette, Optimized 532, 536
Palette Ramp 334
Palette Ramp Editor 287, 292, 314, 334, 352, 428, 431, 435, 503
Palette Tab 521, 537
Palette, User defined 532, 536
Panorama 293, 294
Paper Size 71
Parameters 346
Partial Load 43
Particle 342
Particle Gallery 456
Particle, Paint tool 365
Particle parameters 343
Paste 21, 285, 452, 454, 460, 461
Paste, As A New Image 285
Paste, As Object 285
Paste, Fit Into Selection 285
Paste, Into Selection 285
Paste, Under Pointer 285
Path Drawing tool 169, 170, 211, 313, 462, 497
Path Edit mode 175, 179, 184
Path Edit tool 169, 179, 184, 209, 211, 216
Path Library 463
Path mode 130, 131
Path object 175, 465
Path tools 169
Pattern 341
Pattern samples 333
Pattern templates 333, 334, 336
Pattern thumbnails, limits on number 341
PC 57
Pencil 364
Perceptual 84, 85
Personalize Creator ID dialog box 354, 355
Perspective 316
Phong 444
Photo edge 313, 314
Photo Properties 89

587

Pick 23, 211, 217, 219, 343, 510, 515, 526
Pick color 528, 529, 531, 533, 537
Pick mode 518
Pick point 185
Pick point mode 186
Picture tubes, used as stamps 201
PIN number, Digimarc 354
Pinch 323
Ping Mode 331, 339, 346
Pixels 140
Place 37, 51, 209
Placement, stamps 205
Play 27, 29, 330, 331, 339, 340, 346
Plug-ins 26, 76, 77, 90, 356, 452, 453
PNG 521, 522, 526, 527, 528, 529
PNG Grayscale 128 535
PNG Grayscale 256 535
PNG Grayscale 64 535
PNG Image Optimizer 535
PNG Indexed color 537
PNG Mask Options Tab 536
PNG Optimized 128 535
PNG Optimized 256 535
PNG Optimized 64 535
PNG Options Tab 527, 534
PNG Palette Tab 537
PNG True Color 535, 536
Pointer 71
Polygon 226, 514
Popup box 19
Position 225
Position & Size Tab 196, 197, 225, 510
Position/Size 213
Post 58
Post to Web 57
Post-processing 52, 55, 56, 71
Post-processing Tab 54
Post-processing Wizard 21, 53, 297, 309
PostScript 74
PostScript printer 73
PostScript Tab 74
Pre-determined filters 326
Precise shape 78, 234
Preferences 37, 38, 42, 75, 85, 92, 235, 283, 296, 347, 356, 360, 453
Preserve Base Image 125, 126, 127, 129, 141, 142
Preset 23, 27, 170, 175, 530, 532, 535
Preset animations 346
Preset Tab 301
Presets, Clone tools 366
Presets, Image Optimizer 525
Presets, Paint tools 364
Presets, Retouch tools 362
Pressure 234
Pressure Sensitivity 78
Pressure-sensitive drawing tablets 360
Preview 42, 43, 69, 292, 297, 311, 312, 327, 329, 334, 336, 340, 342, 344, 346, 349, 352
Preview in Browser 49, 514, 516, 518
Preview Pop-up Option 433
Preview Tab, rollover buttons 496
Preview window 330, 343
Preview window, Rollover dialog box 495
Print 21, 37, 71, 72
Print dialog box 71, 72
Print Preview 21, 71, 311
Print Setup dialog box 71, 75
Printer 54, 73, 75
Printer Profile 84, 85
Progressive 530
Progressive JPG 40
Projection center 229
Proofing 84, 85
Properties 216, 224, 451, 452, 454, 460, 468, 510
Protect Linked, Rollover and HTML Text Objects 519
PSD Open Options 81
PSD Save Options 81
PSD Settings 81
PSP Settings 81
Punch 323
Puzzle 324, 330

Q

Quality 530
Quick Color Controls 24
Quick Command Panel 26, 27, 30, 31, 526
Quick Palette 24
Quick Samples 26, 297, 299, 307, 349

R

Radial Gradient Fill 174, 193
Rain 342
Ramp 288
Random 205, 206, 207, 343
Range 303, 344
RAW Export 59

Read -Only 450, 451, 459
Read-only (For Sharing) 459
Reading a Digimarc Watermark 356
Recent Files 85
Recently used 223
Recently used colors 425
Record 28
Recover 235
Recover button 234
Rectangle 124, 131, 169, 175, 514
Rectangle Buttons 457
Rectangular 226
Rectangular gradient fill tool 423, 427
red eye 322
Red tolerance 322
Redistributing objects, cautions about 200
Redo 21, 284
Reduced-color palette 24
Reference points, Stitch 294
Refining a selection with Object Paint Eraser 236
Reflection 440
Reflection map 440
Reflection Tab 440
Refresh 45
Refresh Link 211
Register, Digimarc 355
Relationship between pressure and transparency, Eraser tool 234
Relative Colorimetric 84, 85
Remapped pixel coordinates 329
Remote URL 226, 514, 519
Remove 30, 84
Remove Menu Bar 88
Remove Moire 321
Remove Noise 363
Remove Red Eye 309, 322, 363
Remove Scratch 363
Remove Wrap 216
Rename a Gallery 450
Rename, Library 459
Render backface 443
Rendering Intent 84, 85
Repeat 212, 284, 352, 504
Repeat number 334
Replace 221
Repositioning focus of light 179, 183
Resample 524
Resample dialog box 524
Resample method 76, 310
Reset 172, 176, 181, 190, 219, 301, 305, 328, 333, 334, 344, 425, 427, 451
Reset center 231

Index

Reset Curve, Tone Map 305
Reset Image Transform 216
Reset Text/Path Object 216
Reset to Default 84
Reshaping an object 184
Resize 71, 227
Resize EasyPalette 454, 460, 468
Resize to One Column, EasyPalette 454, 460, 468
Resize to One Row, EasyPalette 454, 460, 468
Resize when replacing 222
Resizing an image or object(s) 310
Resizing and Moving the EasyPalette 447
Resolution 37, 41, 71, 89, 311
Restore 48
Restore button 88, 448
Retouch Tools 32, 359, 361
Reverse Emboss 345
Reverse key frame 332, 347
Reversing beginning and ending colors 428
RGB 288, 317, 424, 427, 493, 494
RGB True Color 316, 317
RGB values 287
Right 218
Ring 334, 352, 431
Ring, editing value in Palette Ramp Editor 430
Ripple 323, 330
Ripple, frame effect 314
Rollover 514, 515
Rollover buttons 209, 491, 495, 498, 499, 501, 514, 517
Rollover buttons, creating your own 514
Rollover buttons, using with HTML editor 498
Rollover dialog box 210, 515
Rollover Object 210
Rotate 229
Rotate Freely 229
Rotate & Flip 231, 293
Rotate 180 degrees 231, 293
Rotate clockwise 231, 436
Rotate counterclockwise 231, 436
Rotate Left 90 Degrees 231, 293
Rotate light when object rotates 443
Rotate Right 90 degrees 231, 293
Rotating 293
Rounded Rectangle 169, 175
Rows 510
Ruler 25, 72, 87, 91

S

Same text for buttons 495
Sample 327
Sample filter 327
Sample name 33, 223
Samples 326, 327
Sand 345
Saturation 84, 85, 302, 362, 430
Save 21, 37, 48, 74, 286, 318, 328, 329, 335, 337, 345, 347
Save and close 51
Save As 48
Save As dialog box 59, 286, 332, 335, 337, 340, 345, 347, 497
Save as type 332, 335, 337, 340, 345, 347
Save as Web pages 61, 67
Save dialog box 80
Save each object as a layer 81
Save for Web 49
Save for Web, As HTML 501, 507, 514, 516
Save multiple objects as a single thumbnail 223
Save Options dialog box 80
Save pages in a self-extracting EXE file 61, 67
Save palette 535, 538
Save the merged image 81
Save to this folder and close 51
Save, Tone Map 306
Save Tone Map dialog box 74, 306
Scale, stamps 204
Scale to fit the page 73
Scanned images 297
Scanner 21, 51, 53, 306
Scene 327
Schema 502
Schemes 53, 55, 56
Screen shot 70
Scrollbars 87
Seal 345
Seal, frame effect 314
Seamless tile 341
Seamless tiles, making with Shift Image 511
Search connected pixels 129, 237, 529, 531, 534, 537
Security 59, 61, 67
Select all 343
Select All Objects 211, 468
Select area for filtering 322
Select Base Image 137
Select by 237
Select by Line/Area 129
Select From Wrap Gallery 215
Select Image dialog box 60
Select Previous Selection 138
Select Source 51, 55
Select stamp 202
Selected buttons 84
Selected file name 47
Selected objects 521, 527
Selected objects individually 521, 527
Selecting a stamp 202
Selecting multiple paths 187
Selecting Thumbnails for Editing 466
Selection 172, 173, 176, 177, 181, 182, 192, 193, 233, 347
Selection and all objects 134
Selection marquee 133
Selection Menu 35
Selection Menu commands 137
Selection mode 130, 131
Selection only 222
Selection tools 123
Self-extracting 66
Send 37, 58, 59
Send Backward 219
Send EXE file as an email attachment when finished 61, 67
Send to Back 219
Sensitivity 127
Separate objects 205
Sequential 205
Setup 70, 71
Shading Tab 444
Shadow 174, 179, 183, 197, 220, 304, 442, 468, 492, 504, 505
Shadow & Highlight, Tone Map 305
Shadow, how to remove 197
Shadow size 198, 220, 316
Shadow, splitting 199
Shadow Tab 442
Shadow Tab, Frame & Shadow 315
Shadow, Tone Map 305
Shake 327
Shape 74, 124, 131, 139, 140, 169, 175, 180, 206, 226, 234, 314
Shape box 433
Shape, hot spots 514
Shape Library 171, 462
Shape of a selection 124
Sharing Text Objects 199
Sharpen 320, 327, 362
Shift 227, 294, 515, 526

589

Shift Image 511
Shift key 211, 217
Shift value 325
Shininess 445
Show 224
Show actual size 522
Show All Existing Tasks 29
Show Base Image 89
Show Box Around Objects 89
Show control points 73, 305, 329
Show description 65
Show Detail 468
Show /Hide List View 448
Show /Hide Options 194
Show Marquee 89
Show path only 295
Show/Hide Base Image Confirmation 233
Show/Hide list view 468
Show/Hide Object 466
Show/Hide Tree View 451, 460
Showing and hiding the base image 89
Shrink 137
Signature 330
Similar 140
Similarity
    128, 225, 237, 426, 529, 531, 534, 537
Similarity #1: Previewing effects of settings, Image Optimizer 522
Similarity #2: Previewing effects of Batch testing, Image Optimizer 525
Similarity #3: Saving and Deleting Presets, Image Optimizer 525
Similarity #4: Creating Transparency, Image Optimizer 526
Single Color 38
Single object 205
Size 48, 89, 190, 194, 225, 360, 508
Size Tab 496
Size/Transparency 360
Size/Transparency/Soft edge 235
Slant 227
Slice evenly 518
Slice line color 518
Slicer 517
Slicing 52, 55
Slicing pattern, 517
Slide show 37, 66, 67, 70
Slide Tab 68
Slope 352
Smart sending 59
Smart Tab 301
Smoke 342

Smooth 329
Smooth mapping curve, Tone Map 306
Smooth spine 438
Smudge 362
Smudge Retouch tool 32
Snap to Edges 127
Snap to Grid 91
Snap to guidelines 91
Snap tolerance 77
Snow 342, 345
Sobel, frame effect 314
Soft 531, 533, 536
Soft edge
    124, 127, 139, 141, 198, 220, 225, 316
Soft edge, Shadow 505
Soften 137, 141
Soften dialog box 125
Solid fills 423
Sort 45, 318
Sort by Depth 468
Sort by Name 468
Sound file 62, 68
Source 71
Source folder 50
Source image 60, 65, 69
Source Type 50
Space 219, 344
Space Bar 137, 512
Space Evenly 218
Spacing 213
Spacing, stamps 204
Special 324
Specifics of the JPG, GIF and PNG Image Optimizers 529
Specular 445
Specular light 444
Specular light strength 504
Sphere 323
Spline 169, 170, 175, 180, 214
Split Component 212
Split Rollover 212, 516
Split Shadow 174, 179, 183, 199, 221
Splitting a Text Object Shadow 199
Spotlight 338
Square 124, 131, 169, 175
Square size 324
Stacking order, objects 219, 343
Stagger 325
Stamp 205
Stamp, frame effect 314
Stamp Gallery 456
Stamp tool 23, 201
Stamp tool button 201
Stamps, making your own 201

Standard 41, 530
Standard colors 425
Standard Optimized 530
Standard Selection tool 123, 124, 211, 217, 296, 510, 513, 515, 526
Standard Toolbar 20, 37, 83, 312
Star 342
Start From 71
Start height 213
Start position 214
Start/Stop Capture 22
Statistics, Histogram 308
Status bar 24, 91, 124, 226, 316, 462, 496, 500, 514, 516, 519
Step 206
Stitch 293
Stitch dialog box 293
Stitch with 293
Stop 28, 29, 331, 339, 340, 346
Store Image 460, 461

Store Image as Selection 460, 461, 465
Store Selection 461, 464, 465
Storyboard
    333, 334, 335, 336, 337, 344
Straight 180
Straight lines 360
Straighten 297
Strength 445
Stretch to fit 213
Stroke color 341
Stroke, frame effect 314
Stroke Smoothness 78
Stroke spacing 367
Style
    77, 178, 182, 190, 312, 506, 508
Style button 197, 199
Style filters 298
Style Gallery 299, 455
Style/Alignment/Color 195
Subsampling 530
Subtract from an existing selection 124
Subtract from Mask 529
Swap F/B Color 425., 427
Swap Foreground/Background Color 172, 176, 181, 190
Swap two colors, Two-Color gradient fill 428
Switch direction 294
Switch view mode 45
Symmetric 504
Symmetry 328
System 81

Index

System Properties 87, 90
System resources 83

T

Tab group 33, 175, 180, 184, 188, 193, 223, 288, 290, 306, 333, 334, 336, 344, 347, 349, 352, 354, 450, 458, 505, 507
Table 517
Tablet 78, 206, 360
Tags, HTML 498
Target 226, 516, 519
target frame 226, 496, 514, 516, 519
Target Output, Digimarc 356
Task 27, 526
Task bar 296
Task Manager 30
Task Menu 28
Task Report dialog box 51
Tear, frame effect 314
Template Library 464
Templates, free monthly 464
Test 219, 294, 327
Text color 509
Text Entry Box 189, 194, 196, 214
Text object 465
Text Shadow, five ways to add or remove 197
Text tab 493
Text thumbnail layout 65
Text tool 23, 189, 497
Texture 314, 360, 435
Texture fill 493
Texture, frame effect 314
Texture Library 314, 435
Texture, painting with 360
Texture Tab 288
Textures, Paint tool attributes toolbar 369
Thin 322
Threshold 295
Thumbnail 327, 329
Thumbnail Commands for Galleries 451
Thumbnail Commands for Libraries 460
Thumbnail Icons 465
Thumbnail Menu commands 452, 460, 465, 467, 468
Thumbnail options 64
Thumbnail size 454, 461, 468
Thumbnail variations 300, 301

Thumbnails, replacing defaults with your own 451
Thumbnails Tab 63
Thumbs folder 66
Tile 49, 325, 333, 334, 336, 337, 341, 347, 501, 511, 512
Tile EasyPalette with an image 22
Tile the texture 436
Tiled preview 512
Tilt angle 198, 220, 315
Time settings 69
Timeline 331, 340
Title 72, 73
Title bar 447, 448
Title dialog box 72
Toggle 130, 131, 179, 184, 211, 235, 361, 451, 460, 468, 523
Toggle, Bezier curve selection tool 130
Tolerance 53, 295
Tonal Adjustment 362
Tone map 53, 55, 56, 74, 297, 304, 306
Tone map, creating and saving custom 306
Tool Buttons, Slicer 518
Tool Panel 23, 359
Toolbar 24
Toolbar customization 123
Toolbars & Panels 87, 90, 169, 359, 360, 367
Tools 78
Tooltips 91
Top 133, 218
Trace 283, 294
Tracking service, Digimarc 354
Trail 205
Transform 344
Transform tool 132, 227, 462, 463, 509
Transformation control 344
Transformation templates 344
Transparency 78, 198, 204, 220, 224, 234, 237, 288, 290, 291, 296, 315, 360, 426, 427, 428, 505, 521, 526, 527, 528, 529, 533, 536
Transparency, automatic 527
Transparency, manual 528
Transparency, maximum 441
Transparency, minimum 441
Transparency Tab 441
Transparent 38, 526
Transparent background 79, 233, 521, 529

Transparent backgrounds, automatic 521
Transparent color 225
Transparent color mask 296
Tree view 451, 460
Trim 235, 491
Trim Object 234, 520
True Color 24, 38, 40, 83, 83, 172, 181, 189, 291, 325, 510, 512, 531
Try 342
Turnpage 330, 353
Two color 435
Two color gradient fill 287, 291, 435
Two ways to use the Lasso selection tool 126
Two-Color 325
Two-Color gradient fill 427
Two-color gradient fill 314
Type 75, 353
Type dropdown list 60
Type Effects 345, 347
Type Gallery 345, 457
Type of border 439

U

Ulead Color Picker 172, 176, 181, 190, 198, 287, 292, 350, 353, 423, 427, 430, 435, 507
Uncompressed image 529
Underline 508
Undo 20, 21, 283, 334, 512
Undo arrow 283
Ungroup 464, 468
Ungroup Path 132
Ungrouped 217
Ungrouping frame objects 313
Unit button 91
Units 25, 91
Unsharp Mask 320
Up one level 45
Update Image in HTML 49
Uploading and Viewing the Web Album Online 65
Uploading and Viewing the Web Slide Show Online 69
URL 40, 226, 493, 495, 496, 508, 514, 516, 517, 519
Use bump map as reflection 440
Use Complete Range, Tone Map 305
Use image, selected area or object as thumbnails 451
Use PostScript Level 2 features 74
Use Ramp Control 314

591

Use Transform Tool 293
Use Visual Open 79
User defined 41, 310
User-defined preset 40

V

Variation 314
Variations 341, 452, 454
Vertical 195, 214, 328
Vertical Deform
    172, 176, 177, 181, 192, 193
Vertical offset 511
Vertical tolerance, Stitch 294
Video 326
View 72
View Base Image 233
View images with a common palette 83
View Menu 25, 26, 34, 45, 233
View menu commands
    87, 454, 460, 468
View, stamps 204
View, Toolbars & Panels 123
Virtual Trackball 229
Virtual Trackball, limitations 229
Visual Open 44, 45
Visual Open dialog box 79

W

Warm 321
Warping 326, 362, 505
Warping Level 505
Warping Smoothness 505
Watercolor 323
Watermark Durability, Digimarc 356
Watermark Information dialog box 356
Watermarking 354
Wave 330
Web & Internet 79
Web album 37, 60, 61, 66
Web Attributes 211, 494, 493, 496, 497, 516, 519
Web Background 38
Web image files 521
Web Menu commands 491
Web page 39, 47, 49, 57, 58, 59, 67, 464, 507, 513, 517, 528
Web page backgrounds 501
Web Preview, moved to File menu 491
Web Publishing Wizard 58
Web Safe colors 424
Web Slide Show 66

Web snap 534, 538
Weight 532, 535
Whirlpool 323, 330
Width 41, 48, 89, 134, 177, 182, 314, 507
Width to height proportion 524
Wind 325
Window Menu 36
Windows 81, 82
Windows Color Picker
    172, 176, 181, 190, 287, 424, 427, 435
Windows desktop 318
Windows Explorer 82
Windows Wallpaper 318
Wireframe 343
Work space 448
Wrap 189, 197, 209, 212, 215
Wrap dialog box 216
Wrap Gallery 197, 215, 457

X

X and Y Offset 198, 220, 315
X and Y Offset, Rollover buttons 495, 516
X and Y offset, Shadow 505
X,Y coordinates 24, 124, 133

Y

YUV411 530
YUV422 530

Z

Zoom 22, 88
Zoom dropdown list 88
Zoom In 72, 88, 514, 518, 522, 531, 534, 537
Zoom Out 72, 88, 514, 518, 522